# BETWEEN THE THUNDER
# AND THE SUN

# VINCENT SHEEAN

# BETWEEN THE

# THUNDER

# AND THE SUN

RANDOM HOUSE · NEW YORK

THIRD PRINTING

TO THE COMBAT CREWS
OF THE A. A. F.

*Their hearts, contemptuous of death, shall dare*
*His roads between the thunder and the sun.*

George Sterling

# Note

THE materials dealt with, the observations and the analysis in this book are those of a civilian correspondent and have no background of military or official knowledge. Since the termination of the events described in it, the author has entered the armed service of the United States and at the time of its publication is a Major in the Army Air Forces.

# Contents

# BETWEEN THE THUNDER AND THE SUN

# 1. Festival

THE RIVER RAN SWIFTLY through the heart of the little city between narrow banks. Its journey was long, and, except in the craggy high places of its origin, it was forever confined within the civilized ramparts of a thousand cities, towns and farms, the fixed abodes of mankind for ages past. The single molecule experienced great turbulence in these early stages, colliding with an infinity of others in the onrush of waters seeking, at ever lower levels, the relative peace of the broad Danube, the union of all like waters in the henceforth resistless march between banks wider and wider, lower and lower, through the mountains, the hills, the plains, the marshes, out, at the end, to the sea. Thus all the rivers of Bohemia, Moravia, Austria, Slovakia, Hungary, Slavonia, Serbia, Transylvania, Bulgaria, Rumania; thus the Moldau and the Inn, the Sava, the Tisza and the Pruth; thus also our river, the Salzach, bearing at first nothing but the wild impulse of Alpine water, came to pour its strength through the Inn into the powerful common flood, sustaining the barges, the corn, the coal and the iron, the produce of the earth and the work of men's hands, on their way down to the seas of the world.

Here at Salzburg it was still young and not yet useful. The city bridged it with solid bridges, walled it in and watched it. In the summer when much ice had melted and there was a great deal of rain it ran high, so that its surging surface almost reached into the terraces of the river-

3

side cafés. We used to sit and drink beer and look at it, wondering why it did not give one special leap and submerge us all. I proposed marriage in an open taxicab in bright sunlight on a bridge over the Salzach, and wandered along its banks many a time just then, and came back to it quickly from Vienna when the deed had been consecrated; so that the river must carry along with it at every summer's end, in its torrent of remembrance, unless all the fond imaginings of German romanticism are vain, some pulse that belongs to me. What would be left of German poetry and music if we denied to the stream, the tree or the cloud its intimate give-and-take relationship with all the great experiences of life—with what Goethe would shamelessly have called the soul? I, for one, am willing to concede a pulse, a whisper, a drop of blood, into the earth or the rivers or the sea, down the wind and across the sunlight, so as to be able to feel, as I take my turn into the darkness, that of what has seemed so much living, and has perhaps been so little, part may thus abide.

Salzburg—pop. 63,231, the seat of an archbishop—derived its great interest for cultivated members of the middle and upper classes in the early twentieth century from the circumstance that Wolfgang Amadeus Mozart had been born there years before. To tell the truth, the birth of Wolfgang Amadeus Mozart and his subsequent life and works had not much to do with the popularity of the place. Mme Lilli Lehmann and other artists had founded the Mozart Festival there before the last war; it was revived with success in the 1920's, owing a good deal of its renown to the dramatic spectacles directed by Max Reinhardt; and in 1934 it acquired a new reason for existence in the appearances of Arturo Toscanini with the Vienna Philharmonic Orchestra. By the season of 1935, when Dinah and I met there to marry, Toscanini was conducting operas as well as concerts, and the eighteenth-century city was thronged with pilgrims from all parts of Europe and America. The Festival began in July and continued until the end of August. When we went—that first year and afterward—we spent the whole month of August going to the opera and the concerts practically every day, driving out sometimes to the lakes of the Salzkammergut, wandering in the town or by the river.

The combination of picturesque country, a baroque city, very remarkable performances of music and (not least to a good many of the visitors) the attendance of numerous persons celebrated in the worlds of art and society, occurring at a time when other resorts of pleasure had grown stale, captivated the bourgeois imagination and gave Salzburg tremendous popularity for the brief seasons that passed between Toscanini's first performance there and the death of Austria. It was only four seasons in all (1934, 1935, 1936 and 1937), but each was more "brilliant" than the one before, more crowded, more expensive, more difficult to deal with in the matters of hotel rooms, meals and tickets to the theatre. There were still innumerable pensions where prices were a little less than in the hotels, and there were a great many Austrian countesses who had an extra room for properly recommended guests; but the struggle against prices was then, as always, too much for me; I simply forgot about money for the length of my stay, and counted the cost (ruefully) afterward.

The shade of Wolfgang Amadeus Mozart was placated in various performances by the orchestra, the opera company and chamber music groups, and yet the music I remember best—shall remember, indeed, so long as I remember anything—was not by Mozart. Toscanini's *Falstaff*, the first year he conducted it there (1935), was the best performance I have ever heard in opera. His *Fidelio* and a performance he conducted of Brahms' Fourth Symphony were the other high points of a phenomenal contribution to musical life; the young people who heard these things will pass on the conception of them to generations unborn. The most successful young conductor in Nazi Europe today was molded by what he heard Toscanini do; he might deny it hotly, but we were seeing him too much during those seasons not to know. The Toscanini performance which brought them all to a climax was the Verdi *Requiem,* which he conducted in his last season at Salzburg (1937). One left it shivering and sweating at the same time, exalted and unhappy, filled with terror and premonition. It was the end; the shadow of Hitler was already heavy across the mountains, and before the next season came Austria was no more.

## 2

Those who went to Salzburg for the music were probably in the majority. I should not like to think otherwise, since artists of such rare quality worked to produce it. But there was also a very considerable admixture of social, political and economic snobbery in the whole thing, produced by the desire of idle people to share in the excitement of a notable event. Often this desire was lamentably disappointed, since music can be the most formidable of mysteries to those who have not the key; and instead of sharing the excitement, the Philistine was most often supremely bored. Every day produced examples of the kind. At the first *Falstaff* we heard—the best single performance of anything that I have ever experienced—there was present, in the same row of the Festspielhaus with us, a certain peer of the realm. Dinah and I were silent at the intermission; there was nothing to say about such a performance. The peer of the realm touched her on the shoulder, leaned across affably, and said:

"Here's a cushion for you. It makes all the difference, believe me. Just leave it there when it's over. It'll help you to bear the rest."

He had gone to the door and hired a cushion from the usher, thinking, in all amiability, to make Verdi's masterpiece (and Toscanini's) endurable.

Lord X's case was a little special: he had been brought to Salzburg by his sister. But there were others who came of their own accord, spending large sums of money and vast energy upon the enterprise. They sighed or slept through *Falstaff* and the *Meistersinger,* rushing out afterward with reawakened zeal to collect as many people as possible for supper, endlessly making engagements for meals, discussing each other, eyeing the crowd like kingfishers. It was an astonishing display of that social passion which, among those addicted to it, sometimes takes the place of all others, seizing upon any pretext—a music festival, a charitable undertaking, a show of pictures—to gratify the desire for gregarious self-congratulation and pretense. The same curse afflicts all music, particularly the opera, in the bourgeois countries of Western Europe and America, but it was raised to a higher power in Salzburg by the mere fact that it was necessary to come so far and spend so much money upon it.

The thing most difficult to understand was why persons of consequence in the great world should undergo what was obviously an extreme penance for the sake of registering their presence at the feast. Many of them, perhaps most, had the habit of listening to music only on the rarest and most highly certified occasions—once or twice a year, when the concurrence of famous musicians and an audience which had struggled to get in, enhancing the simple performance with the subtle excitements of a thousand overtones, made the event supremely desirable. It was easy to see why simple people from my own part of the world, the Mid-Western states, might wish to visit Salzburg for a day or two, music or no music. There was dramatic heightening of effect in all this concentration —the gaudy characters of the scene, a duchess here, an opera singer there, a film star or a politician posing for photographers in the midst of the breathless throng—but what induced the busy and important people to make offering of themselves? I never knew. They did not have to go to Salzburg to be photographed or to behold each other; they could stay at home and achieve these triumphs. They usually made an appearance for two or three days at most, suffered through one or two Toscanini performances, and then went on to Venice or Cannes with a feeling, I suppose, of having made oblation to the spirit of culture. At any rate, it was abundantly clear that they did not come here for the music. Every remark they made betrayed the fact that they had little or no acquaintance with it and found every masterpiece, of no matter what character or form, "too long." I once heard a certain duchess say that it was a pity Toscanini wasted his talents on "a light comedy" like *Falstaff*. The universal complaint of such people was that they could not get to the performance on time and were not allowed to go in after the music had begun. They also complained of the rain, the difficulty in getting taxi-cabs, the hardness of the seats, the inaccessibility of musical notables to casual acquaintanceship, and other harsh comcomitants of the yearly, mysterious pilgrimage.

At one of the few Toscanini concerts the Maestro began

with a Mozart symphony. I forget which one it was, but its second movement was a vigorous *scherzo*. These concerts took place at eleven o'clock in the morning, and the doors were, of course, closed from the beginning until the intermission. Every seat had been sold for months, and the general atmosphere was one of the most extreme, almost passionate, attention.

Imagine, therefore, the thrill of horror that went over the assembly that morning when, at the end of the first movement of the Mozart symphony, the doors at the side opened to admit a man and a woman. They made their way with quick determination down to the very first row, to seats directly behind the Maestro. The Maestro was wiping his brow with his back to us; we, the audience, and the awestricken musicians on the stage, saw the outrage long before he did. A little subdued hum of amazement swept over the great throng. The late-comers marched on to their seats, causing a prolonged disturbance all down the first row as the customers got up, with some creaking and clatter, to admit them.

Nothing of the sort had ever happened before. The man was dark, elaborately dressed, with a large red carnation in the buttonhole of his morning coat. In due course our eyes, glazed with apprehension, recognized him as the Maharajah of Kapurthala. With him was an elegantly caparisoned lady, who looked French and who seemed, even at a distance, stricken with embarrassment. The Maharajah noticed nothing, plowed on and took his seat. As he did so the Maestro, at last conscious of the disturbance, turned round and looked. He took a good look, incredulity yielding at last to fury in his face. He pulled bitterly at his mustache and frowned. I would not have been in Kapurthala's place for all the treasuries of India; but the Maharajah did not seem to notice. Turning back to the orchestra, Toscanini wagged his head and shoulders from side to side in that movement of extreme exasperation I had known so well in a dozen Italian peasants of the lake district; the audience, which had shown an inclination to laugh at first, fell into a frightened silence. When at last the Maestro attacked the *scherzo* of that symphony he did so with such violence that he almost wrenched the strings from the very instruments before him.

Of this episode I do not suppose that the Maharajah of Kapurthala was more than faintly, remotely conscious. He belonged to a social and economic class which felt itself entitled to do anything. Often, during these years, I encountered examples of this unquestioning self-confidence among those who had never known barriers. Few, indeed, were the ultra-privileged who had any sense of humility before genius. However stupid or valueless their own existence, they regarded a Toscanini, a Duse, a Bernard Shaw, more or less as hired entertainers. As a matter of fact the attitude is by no means peculiar to the late bourgeois decadence; it shadowed the lives of Mozart and Beethoven; it commissioned half the works of the earlier and greater part of German music. The peculiar quality of Richard Wagner that gave him nearly all his triumphs in his own lifetime was an ability—almost unique among composers, artists, scientists or other special workers of great talent—to exact from the rich and great those testimonials of humble gratitude which are usually given only to the dead.

This is not to say, of course, that Toscanini was not surrounded with the adulation of the crowd. He was. There were times when the idolatry that encompassed his whole existence in its present phase grew too much for easy contemplation. Sometimes, when he came into the Oesterreichischer Hof for supper after one of his own performances, everybody in the restaurant stood up, as if for the passage of a king or a flag. This was right; for he was both a king and a flag; but it was also wrong, because the people who yielded this homage did not feel it in their hearts, were not of his kingdom. He was no doubt fiercely aware of this, for the idle and fashionable were kept at a distance from him. And yet, in the resounding and un- precedented success of the Salzburg festival during those short seasons before the eclipse, it was the idle and fash- ionable, the rich and grand, who contributed, by the tribute of their glittering incomprehension, the indispen- sable worldly support. They regarded genius as a hircling; but the true inner bitterness of the matter was that under the present order of things they were right.

Sometimes we had supper with Feodor Chaliapin. He was an example of the other phenomenon, the great artist who has lost interest for the masters of the hour. He had ceased to sing and could not teach; they had no further use for him. His amazing talent quenched, his fame obscured by newer phenomena, he had ceased as a person to engage even the passing notice of the crowd. "Chalia- pin?" they would say blankly. "Oh, yes. I remember."

The enormous peasant with his rumbling voice would reminisce, hold forth, give opinion, employing a sort of mosaic language made up of all the various vocabularies he had learned for the opera and concert stage. French was perhaps the predominant dialect, but there were scraps of Italian, German and Russian throughout, with occasional slanting glints of Spanish over the whole verbal rubbish heap. He was robustly conscious of his departed glory and made much of it—rather pathetically, on the whole, since a Chaliapin should have no use for boasting. He told me, with simple, unashamed pride, how the Tsar and the grand dukes had delighted to honor him. He had an immense, roof-shaking laugh and was completely un-conscious of his surroundings. I think he was rather proud of the way in which the big peasant from the South had conquered the whole world of his day, but at the same time it seemed to him natural that this should be so. He had a good, healthy contempt for all teachers, either of the voice or of anything else, disdained most other artists, and said of Toscanini: "He used to conduct for me often, in Milan." This was the ego of a very simple natural phe-nomenon, unquestioning, lusty and bold. Once, some years later when he was dying, I went to see him at his flat in Paris (he lived around the corner from us) and tried to interest him in an English singer, a farm laborer, whom Dinah and I wanted to send to a teacher in Milan. He burst out, as usual, against all teachers.

"They can teach nothing whatever to an artist," he boomed. "Do you know, I learned more from a weedy little rat of a baritone in the Petersburg opera, a little fellow that sang secondary parts, a colleague of no impor-tance, you understand, than I ever did from any teacher. I had one good teacher once, in Tiflis. He had a little money, which he got from teaching the oafish children of the bourgeoisie, and he used to give me lessons for noth-ing. I had no use for the lessons—they were all nonsense. The fool was even trying to make a tenor out of me—of me! But he was useful, just the same. I made my living by singing occasionally in the houses of the rich. For this it was necessary, in those days, to have stiff white cuffs and a clean collar. I did not possess such things, but the teacher used to lend them to me. That's the only kind of a teacher that is any good—a really useful one."

He was so thoroughly self-centered that most of the minor difficulties of life, the impedimenta, the small acci-

dents and thieves of time, had no existence for him. Such
things as finding a direction, getting a train, obtaining a
ticket, were of no importance; there was always somebody
to struggle with them. I remember once when his exquisite
daughter Marina, lunching with us at the hotel, received
a telephone message from him through the hall porter.
It said, with simple imperative precision: "Meet me at
four o'clock at the inn beyond the church." Poor Marina
gazed at it sadly. What inn? What church? No doubt they
had once been together at some such place, which for him
thereafter had a definite geographical identity, but in a
country studded with inns and churches the direction had
almost no meaning. Marina would, of course, find out,
even if it took her all afternoon, and she had to visit all the
inns and churches of the Salzkammergut; this certainty
was what had sustained his whole life.

At some period in the 1920's, Chaliapin had quarreled
with the Bolsheviks. I no longer remember, if I ever did
know, what this quarrel was about. He had been one of
their darlings (he and Stanislavsky were the first to receive the decoration of "People's Artist"), but at a given
point he became an outcast. I think it may have been his
insistence on roaming the world for vast fees, and the
resultant infrequency of his appearances in Russia. Whatever it was, it had left him with a wonderful, sweeping
finality of opinion about the Soviet Union and its rulers.
"Those Bolsheviks," he would say, "they are all crazy."

I never got any further with his political opinions, if,
indeed, he can be said to have had any.

On the active list at the Festival the most beloved singer
was Lotte Lehmann. The peculiar melancholy expressive-
ness of her voice, the beauty of her style in the theatre, the
general sense that her every performance was a work of

art, lovingly elaborated in the secret places and brought forth with matchless authority before our eyes, made her a delight that never staled. She was like that Chinese empress of the ancient days who commanded the flowers to bloom, except that for Lotte they did. Her Salzburg performances during these years were restricted to *Fidelio* and *Der Rosenkavalier,* and while we were there we never missed one. She did not have the immense voice that *Fidelio* is supposed to demand, but she knew what the words and music meant, and never once did she fail to reveal them to us completely. Toscanini's admiration for her gifts as an artist was unstinted, which made their collaboration on *Fidelio* one of the truly memorable performances of the century. In the *Rosenkavalier* she worked with less masterly conductors, but no conductor—even that wild ass, Knappertsbusch—could impair the exquisite loveliness of her Marschallin. Along with Mary Garden's Mélisande and Chaliapin's Boris, this was that rare summit of perfection in the theatre, arriving by some mysterious concatenation of circumstances when a particular character, style and significance are as if created for the gifts of a single artist. Unlike Garden and Chaliapin, Lehmann was a musician and could also sing songs. Once a year she did a recital with Bruno Walter at the piano, and one of the things I most vividly remember from Salzburg is her rapt and dedicated singing of Schubert's "An die Musik." To this day, although much of the splendor of her voice has departed, I would rather hear her sing than anybody, because she sings not with the voice alone, but with the heart and brain and soul of an artist.

It was a surprise, upon meeting Lehmann, to discover that she had a fund of the simplest gayety, a weakness for bad jokes, and loved to make fun of everybody and every-

thing. The heart-breaking sadness that was her most peculiar quality on the stage seemed to have no part in her
life. Of course this was not true, as I found out afterward
—in the nature of things it could not be. Successive events
in the crumbling of the world affected her profoundly,
made her physically ill in the darkness of an envisioned
future; during the single dreadful year of 1938 she lost
her country, her husband (for whom she had a romantic
adoration), her accumulated fortune and belongings; and
yet when I saw her last she was still laughing.

It is curious to reflect that Mme Lehmann, who seems
to us the essence of Vienna, should have been born in
Hamburg. I think it is curious to her, too; she does not
seem to think of herself as a North German. Her whole
career, after the beginnings, took place in Vienna or in
places to which her Vienna triumphs had sped her. In
Vienna her beloved Otto, then a Guards officer, had fallen
in love with her from the other side of the footlights and
paid his court in spite of a thousand obstacles. Lehmann
had Vienna in her veins; it was mostly for this reason—
since she wasted little time thinking about politics—that
she was anti-Nazi. She stoutly refused to sing for the
Nazis after one or two experiences, and no combination of
threats or bribes would drive her to Berlin. In conversation she lavished upon them some of the choicest epithets
of a first-class Viennese vocabulary. Herself a North German of pure "Nordic" race, she had long worked with Jewish
musicians and fiercely resented the Nazi treatment of
them. All the best string players in the Vienna Philharmonic, violins, violas and 'cellos, were Jewish. There were
only about a dozen of them, at the first desks, but after
1938 when they were no longer there the difference in the
orchestra was immense.

In 1935 we did not worry much about Hitler at Salzburg. Two years later the threat was already heavy upon us, but Mme Lehmann refused to the last to believe that it was real. She was in America when the unfortunate puppet Schuschnigg, betrayed by the Roman gangster in whom he had put his trust, made his pilgrimage to Berchtesgaden. Toscanini, in New York, immediately announced that he would not return to Salzburg. Lehmann, in California, hoping to the end, said she regretted the Maestro's decision but would go to Salzburg just the same. Both she and Bruno Walter took refuge in the time-honored delusion that "art has nothing to do with politics." That was in February; and in March they knew better.

It so happened—since Fate is an extraordinary contriver of these things—that Dinah and I were lunching at Mme Lehmann's apartment in New York on March 11, 1938. Her husband, Otto, was there, as was our friend Marcia Davenport, who used to live at Lehmann's house near Salzburg during the festivals and had introduced us to her. There was a cheerful bustle of coming and going; there was Otto's dark-eyed daughter Manon, newly over from Vienna, and there was the amiable common sense of Margherita de' Vecchi. The Frau Kammersaengerin had her jokes; we all laughed a lot; but every once in a while, in a silence or a movement of the head, Lehmann showed that she felt, and dreaded, the coming of the event. Messages relayed from Toscanini by Margherita de' Vecchi left no doubt of what he thought; he had sailed that day on the *Queen Mary* for what was to be his last look at Europe. Lehmann drove us back to our hotel, where, half an hour or so later, we heard that the German army had invaded Austria. This news reached Mme Lehmann at about the same time; she fainted and was ill for days afterward; for her it was the end of a world.

## 3

One chapter of incident at Salzburg centered about the baroque castle of Kammer. It was a vast and probably haunted structure on the shore of a lake, with a floating population of guests from every country on earth. It belonged to Eleonora von Mendelssohn, I believe, but Alice and Raimund von Hofmannsthal occupied half of it. There were two distinct households, Eleonora's and Alice's, but they usually got themselves so mixed up that nobody but a detective could have determined which guests belonged where. Eleonora had not the habit of counting her guests, but it is recorded that she once inquired, at her own dinner table, for information.

"I can't think who that man is down there," she said, frowning in thought. "He's been here three days now. Does anybody know him?"

The place was unlike any other. Baroque castles were not unusual in the region, but most were smaller than Kammer and in none was there such an extension and co-ordination of the decorative scheme to encompass the whole life. Sometimes Alice and Raimund took their guests out on the lake on a barge, with the liveried attendants holding flares, and villagers in costume playing the guitar and zither for the songs. They played at dinner when we went there, and in the candle-lit room the soft dialect of the region floated over and through the conversation. There was a particular serenade on the lake for Franklin Roosevelt, the President's second son, and his bride; it seemed no trick at all for one of the retainers of the castle to step out into the village and muster an orchestra and chorus. Most of the guests wore *Tracht*, the local costume, leather breeches for the men and bodice and full skirt for the women. The *Tracht* business was indeed one of the leading commercial enterprises of Salzburg, and it was funny and a little sad to see the plump or scrawny figures of Paris, London and New York decked out in peasant finery. Like Marie Antoinette in her milkmaid dress, they seemed all unconscious of their destiny.

One night at Schloss Kammer after dinner a young man walked into the room with a copy of the London *Times* in his hand. It had just arrived.

"The name of the Ritz Hotel in Barcelona," he said, "has been changed to Gastronomic Number One."

The statement embroiled all present in a dispute which went on for about an hour. For some reason which I was unable to fathom, most of the company appeared to resent this change of name as a deadly personal insult. Mr. Cecil Beaton declared in no uncertain terms that the name Ritz meant, to him, everything that was beautiful and romantic in life, and Lady Juliet Duff remarked with relentless logic that it didn't matter in the least what they called the Ritz in Barcelona since nobody was likely to want to go there. Everybody in the room felt called upon to condemn the rash action of the Spanish Republic in terms ranging from disdain to positive vituperation. Afterward, during the Spanish war, I never saw the Ritz in Barcelona without thinking of this absurd conversation. I was there once in a bombing raid when the whole place seemed to shake. I thought of Mr. Beaton's pronouncement, "everything that is beautiful and romantic in life," and laughed helplessly. The oddest thing about the whole debate was that the name of the hotel had, in fact, not been changed to Gastronomic Number One; it boasted the noble name of Ritz through bombs and famine, to the end of the Spanish Republic, and afterward; all that heat at Schloss Kammer had been generated for nothing.

But it was easy to generate heat in a society so complicated and somehow (in spite of its international character and lack of rigid standards) so ingrown. There was always some reason why Fifi was not speaking to Lulu, and this by extension involved all the other persons present in ever-increasing eddies of unnecessary commotion. I remember one afternoon when all the guests at Schloss Kammer were swept up in one frantic movement by Raimund and the others so that nobody should be at home when a certain Frenchman called. The sight of his car in the courtyard had started this scene off: Raimund and his friends ran like lightning through the corridors, warning everybody to escape to an upper floor. Dinah and I did as we were told without knowing in the least what was the matter; at first, as we were whisked along to the staircase, I thought perhaps the house was on fire. It took some time to find out, after we had all been hurled into Raimund's room on the top floor, that we were merely in hiding from an unwanted guest. There were Baba and Jean de Faucigny-Lucinge, I remember, who protested vaguely against this treatment; it seemed that the Frenchman whose arrival so affrighted the house was a friend of theirs. They were immured just the same, lest by going out to greet the stranger they might bring evil upon us all.

Max Reinhardt's castle, Leopoldskron, was a show place with a marble salon and a remarkable library. The one thing it had in common with Schloss Kammer was the benevolent, rotund person of Rudolf Kommer, who seemed to inhabit both. Rudolf Kommer was then, in Salzburg, London and Paris, as he was afterward in New York, an amiable arranger and provider of good things, good occasions and company; I do not know of any other social or economic function he fulfilled, but that was enough. He had come to England and America first, I think, with Reinhardt, for whom he had worked for years. He had arranged for the various amateur madonnas and nuns who played in Reinhardt's production of *The Miracle;* and they were all his friends. The astonishing number of beautiful women who depended upon Kommer for advice, leaned upon his friendship and utilized his gift for social arrangement became a sort of legend of the time, a legend fostered by his habit of lunching a bevy of such beauties at a certain table in a certain restaurant every day. In Salzburg his restaurant was the Mirabell (as it was the Colony in New York and the Ritz in London). I have seen him lunching happily with five beautiful girls and no other men; and what is even more surprising is that the beautiful girls always appeared to be enjoying themselves and would come back, like as not, the next day.

Kommer—known among his friends as "Kätchen"—had a fantastic history. He was born in Czernowitz and has been, with the shifting fate of that singularly ill-placed town, of various nationalities; during most of the time between 1920 and 1940 he was Rumanian by passport. He is heard of in Berlin and Vienna at the close of the last war, and appears to have made his first appearance in England under the unlikely aegis of Philip Snowden and his wife. The width of his acquaintance among people of privileged society both in England and the United States dates from *The Miracle* and was no doubt due originally to Lady Diana Cooper, who played the Madonna in that production. She acquired the habit of regarding "Kätchen" as a sort of wise man—a man who knew everything, could solve all problems—and the same attitude became characteristic of all the beautiful young ladies of wealth and position who have since sat at his table. There was nobody in the whole international society who had quite the same

position as Kommer—nor could anybody define that position. He was a sort of connoisseur, and yet music seemed
often to bore him and his acquaintance with it was limited; he had more natural taste than knowledge, more
curiosity than either; he was fond of *Tracht* and peasant
work and all sorts of arranged and cultivated simplicities,
yet he was himself a creature of the metropolis, subtle and
ingenious beyond the ordinary; nobody could say that he
had discovered or pushed any particular product, artist
or shop, and yet his patronage meant a great deal to those
who lived by luxury and taste. I used to think that the
Lanz brothers, who made a comfortable living out of the
craze for Salzburger *Tracht* in Paris, London and New
York, owed their emergence to Kommer, as did certain
other Austrian invaders of those years before 1938. They
were not always grateful; some even became Nazis when
the hour struck. Kommer himself, being Jewish, had no
choice in the matter and was anti-Nazi from the start, but
I think he would have been anti-Nazi in any case because
the things he seemed to value were those the Nazis destroyed. His life, trailing as it did across the upper Bohemia of half the world, involving him as confidant and
guide in innumerable imbroglios, adviser to the harassed,
the lovesick and the bewildered, had exposed him to a
knowledge of many secrets, some of them vital to more
than one existence; and I have an idea that all were safe.
The appearance of blunt, good-natured indiscretion which
was Kommer's style at, say, one of his lunch parties, was
never accompanied by any genuine malice or betrayal;
he was seldom unkind and gave away nothing essential.
A sort of plump, amiable Jewish Cagliostro, he traversed
his astonishing career without appearing to notice that it
was anything out of the usual run. What he did, in its very
pervasive but undefined activity, would probably have

been impossible at any other period of history save this, in which wealth, rank and fashion were over-complicated, bored and without resistance to new talent of any kind, trembling with indifference upon the brink of the abyss, wanting above all things to distract the last moments with novelty and surprise. Kommer provided the extraordinary novelty of common sense (he could even add columns of figures) and the surprise of guessing at truth better than any soothsayer or psychoanalyst. His existence therefore became indispensable to whole generations of what one is tempted to call his clients—his friends, that is, the ladies at his table.

<h1 style="text-align:center">4</h1>

We had our quarters during the first season with Russians who seemed bent upon proving a whole set of the legendary characteristics of their race. They never knew what the bill was, frequently forgot to order the food, had unfailing charm and extremely funny servants. Nyanya, who had been Olga's nurse years before in Russia, was now one of the mainstays of the household, but could not be depended upon to watch the clock or remember the guests. Once in the midst of a dinner party Olga grew nervous over the long delay in food, went out to the kitchen to see, and found Nyanya day-dreaming in a big armchair, smoking a cigarette with her feet up on the window-sill. She had merely forgotten the party. Another member of the household was Frau Neubach, a plump little blonde Viennese who, when I played waltzes on the piano, used to dance with the broom while she swept.

When we arrived from Vienna, duly married by the majesty of the law, the Stachowitsch household had the

place decked and garnished for us. A large white wedding
cake had been produced by combined effort and in it was a
luck-piece, a fat silver coin of the Archbishop Hierony-
mus in the eighteenth century. Frau Neubach had spent
hours gathering flowers and bestowing them about the
room. We were the favored clients for the whole of that
season, owing to the magic influence of a wedding; even
old Nyanya seemed to treat us with special affection. The
garden and house were a long way from the town, and
sometimes we found it impossible (especially on rainy
nights) to get taxis, so that when we came back again we
stayed at the Oesterreichischer Hof, for convenience's
sake, but with regret.

The Oesterreichischer Hof was in the center of the
town—in a way, *was* the center of the town. It was always
difficult to get rooms there; the management crammed the
clients in wherever they could and charged whatever
seemed feasible. The restaurant and cellars were good, the
terrace lay directly over the Salzach, and the hall porter
was a man remarkable for skill and tact. This Josef was
indeed half the battle against the conditions of life; if you
had him on your side everything was easier. He could
often get tickets when nobody else could; he could get rid
of your tickets at the list price if you were for any reason
unable to go to concert or opera. He had an uncanny influence over the disposal of tables, allotment of rooms and
other details of existence at the Festival. He was a small,
pale, blond Czech with earnest eyes and a gentle, confid-
ing manner, an uncanny memory and unshakable patience.
He remembered from season to season who the guests
were and even who their friends were, so that small miracles of tact were continually being performed by Josef
and taken for granted by the gentry without wondering
how.

The Café Bazar down the way was our favorite resort for beer and *belegtes Brötchen*. There too, we sat over the Salzach under the trees and watched its swift leaping flood. Many of the townspeople used to sit in the Café Bazar for five or six hours in an evening, consuming very little the while but adding to its general air of a comfortable, unmoving throng. The hotel was also crowded, but with the nervous, swift-moving people from Western Europe and America, never for five minutes the same. Here in the Café Bazar, although nearly every seat was taken from noon on, the amount of movement was so slight that you received the impression of an almost static assembly, too contented to stir. The Philharmonic Orchestra players used to frequent the place—so did everybody else, practically speaking—and when we happened to be with Sidney Beer he would collect one or two of them at table to talk about performances. It was quite possible to sit there in perfect contentment for hours; not even in Paris has the sport of café-sitting seemed more indigenous.

The town built round the swift-running river had many churches, convents, palaces, cafés and shops to which we occasionally paid visits. The wood-carving and the *Tracht* were unceasing objects of interest. Kommer gave us, as a wedding present, a wonderfully complicated piece of peasant carving, a painted cabinet with many drawers (one secret) and various tricks of design. The wooden Christ, and Mozart's house, and the Archbishop's palace of Mirabell, the slanting small streets in the rain and the good beer—these are things of Salzburg, to which the mind turns back afterward with nostalgia. The quaintness of the place had as much to do with its success as the music itself, I suppose. And yet, when all is said, it is the music that I shall remember best and longest: first the Toscanini performances of *Falstaff* and *Fidelio*, with

*Meistersinger* and *Zauberflöte* later; Bruno Walter's *Don Giovanni* and Lehmann's Marschallin in *Der Rosenkavalier;* some of the songs Lotte sang; Toscanini with the Fourth Brahms; Toscanini with the Verdi *Requiem.*

Into this wealth of European classical and romantic music there was introduced, during the season of our marriage at Salzburg, a note that was new and strange. A musical hostess, Mrs. Moulton, invited three or four hundred people to an afternoon of songs at the Hotel de l'Europe. The guests included Toscanini, Lehmann, Walter and practically all the other musical powers of Salzburg. The artist was Marian Anderson. I do not think anybody there had heard her before. She had not yet appeared in the Western world; the Soviet Union and Germany had been hearing her, and the reports had drifted along, but she was unknown to this present audience (1935). She sang Bach, Schubert and Schumann, with a final group of Negro spirituals. Her superb voice commanded the closest attention of that audience from the first note. The Archbishop was sitting in the front row, and at his insistence she repeated the Schubert *Ave Maria.* In the last group she sang a spiritual, "They crucified my Lord, and He never said a mumblin' word." Hardly anybody in the audience understood English well enough to follow what she was saying, and yet the immense sorrow—something more than the sorrow of a single person—that weighted her tones and lay over her dusky, angular face was enough. At the end of this spiritual there was no applause at all— a silence instinctive, natural and intense, so that you were afraid to breathe. What Anderson had done was something outside the limits of classical or romantic music: she frightened us with the conception, in musical terms of course, but outside the normal limits, of a mighty suffering. Without the conventional training of an art-singer she would probably never have been able to do this, and yet she did it most of all by a quality of tone and expression which transcended even her rare gift and related her to millions of others; it was most of all a racial quality. To find it in a great singer was something that had not happened before. It made some of the more self-conscious of our Festival manifestations seem pallid and absurd. Anderson's tragic muse, coming from a world outside the formal design and limited aspiration of the baroque town, seemed too much to be contained there, and even at moments when it was most wedded to German romantic music (as in Schubert's "Aufenthalt") invested the whole with a barbaric wildness, a sheer tribal terror, for which our musical experience gave us no clue. She had two recitals in Salzburg, one private and one public, and we went away from both in a kind of thoughtful daze, since the problems posed (all unconsciously, no doubt) by her phenomenal singing were in fact beyond the range of art.

At the end of the summer there was a dispersal of forces to Italy, and France, to Cannes, Biarritz, Venice; it was still not time to go back to London and Paris. The New York contingent usually went straight home from Salzburg at the beginning of September but the others had a little more time. Venice and the Lido claimed a good share of the Salzburg legacy, and with considerable logic: the hot lagoon and the elaborate, melancholy Venetian palaces were akin to Salzburg in their more grandiose way. Toscanini went to his *isolino* in Lago Maggiore; Lehmann, that first year, was going on a motor tour of the Italian lakes; there were some who cruised the Dalmatian coast in white, slim yachts, and others who repaired to the gambling casinos at Le Touquet, Biarritz, or Cannes. The annual sacrifice to culture had been made; in what remained

of the summer there would be nothing to interfere with
the haggard and relentless pursuit of sheer pleasure.

## 5

We set off with Jamie Hamilton for Innsbruck, Milan,
Genoa and Cannes. Jamie was my English publisher, more
decorously known as Hamish Hamilton, and had formerly
been married to Dinah's sister, Jean Forbes-Robertson. He
piloted us across the Alps, only occasionally disturbed by
our desire to pause under the trees beside a stream and
drink beer; he was a good, but purposeful, driver, who always knew in the morning just where he intended to
spend the night. Dinah and I were not averse to lingering
along the way, not only because it was pleasant to dine
in the open air almost among the pinnacles of the Milan
cathedral—or to sit in the Galleria on a late summer evening and watch the crowd—but also because we stood a
little in fear of what might lie before us at Cannes. We
had married legally, with the written consent of the bride's
parents as certified by the Austrian Legation in London,
with due notice given and no secrecy; yet the whole thing
had been somewhat rushed upon them. No doubt more
time and ceremony would have been much preferred by
all concerned, except us. Flying off like that in an airplane
to Vienna, and getting married with a speed never before
recorded (thanks chiefly to George Messersmith, the
American Minister) and then settling down to a season
at Salzburg—was this correct or sensible? It hardly gave
the bride's startled relations time to compose their public
expressions on the matter. As a matter of fact, Sir Johnston
Forbes-Robertson, my father-in-law, spent the next ten

days or so memorizing my name, so little had he been schooled for the event.

But the most difficult relation, because imperious in all things, was Dinah's Aunt Maxine. This was Miss Maxine Elliott, once the most famous of American beauties, who, after a long career on the stage and in society, had built herself a white palace on the water between Cannes and Juan-les-Pins, called it "Château de l'Horizon" and announced her intention of staying there until her death. Except for a week or two at Dr. Dengler's sanatorium in Baden-Baden and a very few weeks in London each year she adhered to this program. In the summer, from May until October, she filled the Château de l'Horizon with guests from London, Paris and New York, most of them rich or celebrated or of high rank or (sometimes) all three. Aside from these general data, and the ruling fact that Dinah and all the other nieces were frightened of her, I knew practically nothing about Maxine before I entered her house. I no longer remember exactly what it was I expected to see, for the power of Maxine's personality was such that she dispelled all preconceived notions: she existed all at once, intact and real, and you never thought of questioning her afterward. She was what Cummings calls an *IS*.

We drove in from the main road across the narrow bridge Maxine had built (with internecine difficulties equivalent to a civil war) across the French State Railway. This was the only access to the Château de l'Horizon, which occupied a tract of land between the railroad and the sea, turning its back firmly upon the former and giving itself, at every possible vantage point, to the air and sunlight and water of the gulf. The driveway sloped down sharply from the narrow bridge to the entrance of the château, where we rang bells in the darkness and hoped nobody was at home. The lights went on in a flood; we were looking through an open door into what seemed a vast marble hall, and across that hall Maxine was coming toward us.

She was white-haired and dressed in white. I think I was too confused just then to notice the commanding beauty of her head. I was noticing above all her firm cordiality, as if the sudden marriage of a favorite niece to a total stranger was something she had long anticipated with pleasure. She took us into the long drawing room, which was all lights and flowers, but empty.

"They've gone down to the Casino," she said. "They're gadabouts, all of them."

This was a reference to her guests, who, in Maxine's eyes, were always "gadabouts" if they showed the slightest inclination to leave her house. I admired the room and she went to turn on some lights over the terraces outside.

"There's no moon tonight," she said rather scoldingly, "and in such cases we simply make our own."

She had actually an artificial moon which hung in some vines on the tower of the garage over the white terrace, the swimming pool and the white chute into the sea. It looked lovely but temporary, like something built for a particular scene and then discarded to crumble and grow old in a store-room. The gulf was at our feet; you had only to slip down the white chute from the swimming pool and you were in the soft swirl of the gulf water around brown rocks.

We retired early—long before the "gadabouts" had returned from their excursion into the town. Dinah and I occupied two very comfortable rooms on the ground floor, overlooking the only bit of grass and flower space near the château. It had to be watered carefully every morning, and there was little of it, for the whole point of the château was that it perched whitely on the brown rock; this small green patch at the side was a minor concession to other ideas. In our rooms and baths there were bells marked "Up" and "Down." In the course of time we discovered that these were answered by different citizens, and we called them "Mr. Up and Mrs. Down." Later on, after we had well broken into their reserve as trained servants, we found that they were called Alexis and Germaine, and once, when Germaine's child had an earache, she allowed us to come and see it.

On the following morning I made acquaintance with the life of the Château de l'Horizon. It began late, seldom before eleven o'clock, often not until noon. The guests all trickled down from their various balconies, from this side or that of the white-terraced house, one by one, dressed as they chose, but at that hour chiefly in bathing dress. The principal notion for bathing costume at the time was to make it as scanty as possible for both sexes, and this fashion was scrupulously observed at the château. Lady C. wore a patch or two of yellow; Lady P. was older and less naked; Lord A. wore practically nothing except a brilliant scarf around his neck. These were the guests, besides ourselves. Mr. Winston Churchill was arriving that morning but we had not yet seen him. Maxine never had large parties; eight or ten guests were her limit; and yet, since every woman brought a maid and every man a valet, and some of them secretaries besides, it was quite enough to fill a house. They stayed a week, two weeks or a month, as they chose, and I never knew Maxine to wish for a guest's departure; even those who did not particularly amuse or please her were encouraged to stay as long as it suited them. She had a kind of natural hospitality of feeling which apparently had nothing to do with her weird, childish snobbishness; she wanted you to stay whether you were of any particular value to the party or not. During those years Dinah and I were seldom in perfect sympathy or harmony, let us say, with any of Maxine's guests, especially after the outbreak of the Spanish war. We were of no worldly consequence, could not play the games the rest delighted in (anyhow, I couldn't), and had nothing really to give or to receive in the conversational exchange. Nevertheless it was difficult indeed to persuade Maxine to let us go away. It turned into a semi-annual visitation, a week in the summer and a week in January; later on these visits coincided with those of Mr. Winston Churchill, which gave them more interest; and after a while Maxine, who knew how to yield with grace upon occasion, ceased asking us with large house parties. Thus, toward the end, our visits to the Château de l'Horizon became something different, something touched with a peculiar historicity, above all our last stay there in January, 1939.

To begin with, we had hit upon the Cannes high season at its highest. I do not know when in the annals of European society the Cannes season changed from winter to summer; I am not familiar enough with such things. I know that in nineteenth-century memoirs and novels the place seems to have been a winter resort. Sometime in the 1920's, I think, the pleasures of sunburn were discovered, and Cannes, like the Lido at Venice, came into its fortune. In my time certainly the late summer season was at once the most crowded, the gayest, the youngest and the most international. In the winter the company tended to be that of elderly rich people in retirement, or of their contemporaries out from London for a week. In August and September there was no such homogeneity. It was a highly colored, half-naked mob, belonging to all races and nations, ruthlessly hounding down its pleasures from one end of the coast to the other.

Owing to Maxine's extraordinary possessiveness, we did not see a great deal of the life of the coast. She really did think it rude of her guests to go outside the Château de l'Horizon. Nobody was ever supposed to have a meal away from the house, and I have heard Maxine roundly ticking off those who infringed the rule. She did not actually refuse permission when it was asked, but she made the petitioner feel that the request was so monstrous that it could not be made again. Dinah and I lunched and dined away from the house only, I believe, when we were Mr. Churchill's guests; once we were allowed to go to tea at Charlotte Boissevain's; but otherwise I cannot remember any time during those years when we were permitted to be absent from meals. The only times of more or less consecrated freedom were the late afternoon, during Maxine's siesta, when we made a hasty visit to Cannes (usually to the terrace of the Carlton), and sometimes after dinner at night, to the Casino. As a rule, if anybody in the party was asked out, we all had to be asked; and since there were so many of us, this somewhat restricted our invitations.

Maxine did not, as a matter of fact, like going out anywhere at all. She loathed the necessity of sitting to the end of a party in somebody else's house. Apparently she enjoyed sitting it out in her own house, and although the fatigue must have been crushing, she did it very often. I have sometimes gone upstairs with her when it seemed she could not possibly climb another step. Her tiny feet (size four) were not strong enough to hold up her heavy body; she tottered sometimes like a Chinese woman with bound feet when she was exhausted. Yet she had the iron of ambition in her soul, mixed with a childish and rather charming kind of snobbishness—the kind of snobbishness that says, "Of course a duke's much nicer than anybody

else; isn't he a duke, and isn't that enough?"—and she
would not give in. So long as cabinet ministers, duchesses,
princes and film stars would come to her table she would
continue to give dinner parties, lunch parties, all kinds of
parties, if she could still walk in or out of a room. In her
seventies, with death coming near, with a blood pressure
that was an incessant menace, she still could derive great
pleasure from distinguished company even when it was
a little too concentrated for the comfort of ordinary mor-
tals. On a night in 1938 when the Duke and Duchess of
Windsor and Mr. Lloyd George came to dinner with nobody else but ourselves and Mr. Churchill, Maxine was, I
think, really happy; such things had the power to bestow
happiness upon her. She said to me after that little dinner:
"It reminded me of the old days at Hartsbourne."

Knowing—as I had come to know—what she thought of
"the old days at Hartsbourne," I could see that the evening had indeed pleased her. For in spite of the lack of
intimacy between us, I was coming to know Maxine as
much by inference and allusion as otherwise. She did not
encourage intimacy and I did not seek it. I never attempted to delve into her memories of a truly extraordinary life; the odyssey of the Maine sea-captain's daughter
who died at the white château over the gulf was one I
shall never write. Sometimes out of sheer historic curiosity
I would ask her about a great figure of the past, and the
reply was always a tantalizing trifle, like the flick of a
scented handkerchief. I once asked her if she had ever
known the German Emperor.

"Mmm, yes, I met him once," she said indifferently, "on
Mr. Morgan's yacht at Kiel. A very rude man. So unpleasant to the gentlemen in his suite."

A good deal of her style of conversation sounded exactly
like that of a conventional, elderly royalty or other grandee

of a vanished age. I had once known such a lady quite well in Rome—a princess of Greece who had married a Russian grand duke—and her whole view of history was like that: "William never had any manners; he was bound to come to a bad end." But the notable thing about Maxine was that she had acquired this way of thinking and speaking relatively late in life; it must have been about 1905 or 1906 before she lived in English country houses, and then or possibly even later before she knew King Edward VII; yet sometimes all the early part of her life seemed not to exist, and she spoke with the overwhelming Edwardian certainty of a dowager duchess addressing the groom of the chambers. You had to remind yourself sharply that she had been born in Rockland, Maine, had worked for many years on the stage, had known to the full how difficult life can be for the young, the poor and obscure; when you re-called all this, you attached a certain special value to the regal performance of her last years, and even so you won-dered how in the world she could do it so well.

Yet she was not always regal. She had a childish love of the films, for example, and out of season, when she did not have large house parties and dinners and lunches, she frequented them indefatigably. On these occasions she wept copious tears, and, if she liked the film, she would sit through it two or three times, weeping and laughing just as much the second or third time as she did the first. One year she came to Paris when a film called *Stage Door* was showing. She took Dinah to it one afternoon and they sat through it twice. During that week Maxine insisted on going to the same film two or three more times, each time sitting through it twice and weeping and laughing just as she had the first time. I found this one of the most incomprehensible things about her—and it was, of course, sheer martyrdom to Dinah or anybody else who was pressed into service as companion. Her passion for the films was such that she positively trembled with delight over any film star who appeared in the neighborhood. I think she derived as much pleasure from the presence of Mr. Douglas Fairbanks or Miss Grace Moore as she did from that of any Royal Highness; the terms of the case admit no stronger comparison.

Toward animals she behaved with the same capricious and (to me) childish *Schwärmerei*. Her monkey Kiki, a lemur brought to her from Africa some years before, was permitted every liberty a monkey's imagination can conceive. Kiki—a male—bit almost every lady who set foot inside the Château de l'Horizon, and sometimes attacked the gentlemen as well. The creature rambled around from balcony to balcony, appearing at the most inopportune moments to the frightened guests, upsetting the breakfast trays, invading the beds, leaving traces of its passing wherever it chose. Everything that Kiki did was droll and touching to Maxine, and those who objected to Kiki were "unreasonable" or "tiresome." One very old friend was practically barred the house because she had been "tiresome about Kiki." I made inquiry and discovered that Kiki had bitten this lady in a particularly tender spot while she was standing on her head beside the swimming pool. It was a nice question whether Kiki or the lady had been more "tiresome," but Maxine always judged such cases in the monkey's favor.

In the years just before I knew her somebody had given Maxine two chicks at Easter. She had accidentally crushed one by sitting on it on her way home from the party. In remorse for this, she elevated the surviving chick into the position of prime favorite. It was a perfectly ordinary chicken, and after its fluffy childhood had gone it looked like any other barnyard pullet, but it was allowed the run

of the house. It apparently used to promenade from one
end of the luncheon table to the other, taking its pick of
the guests' food. I never saw this creature, which in a prolonged and scrawny old age had become one of the leg-
ends of the Riviera; it expired, full of caviar, before I knew
the place; but I have often thought that no barnyard fowl
ever had a more brilliant career in the great world.

The garage was the haunt of abandoned favorites, dogs
and cats who had had their hour of love and were now
relegated to the company of servants. One of these was
my friend, a terrier called Christophe. It was remarkable
how that charming dog was in every respect humiliated
by the caprices of the insufferable monkey. There was rank
injustice in the case; Maxine's whims were imperious and
there was no appeal against them; Christophe finally had
to stay away from the house altogether.

The same woman who behaved like a child about films,
animals and dukes was possessed of a hard, clear intelligence about worldly affairs. She had managed money and
investment with a capacity which drew admiration from
the experts. My brother-in-law, Miles, who looked through
some of her business correspondence after her death—and
who was himself no novice in such matters—told me that
up until the very last years she had controlled every investment herself, giving directions to her far-away brokers
and bankers with complete authority, always knowing
more about these affairs than anybody else did; Miles said
her letters were models of acumen and force. Mr. Thomas
Chadbourne used to say that Maxine would have been a
financial genius if she had been a man. As it was, she
could not actually go into Wall Street and operate, but
she did pretty well from a distance for a good many years,
and until the great depression she had built up a very
large fortune. Even after the depression (if it can be said

to have ended) her fortune was still considerable and still admirably placed and controlled. Her own success with such things gave her a rather intolerant attitude toward people who did not understand them. She was impatient, above all, with opera singers, musicians and actors who made great fortunes in their lifetimes and ended poor. To her this seemed merely silly, since she knew quite well that all of them—Garden, Chaliapin, McCormack and others who came up in talk—need not have lost their money if they had been clever about it. Maxine herself had systematically piled up money over a period of years, going on tour season after season with a play annually tailored to her measure by Clyde Fitch, then returning to New York and making her money work for her by investment and reinvestment. She understood such things through and through, and could have managed a broker's office with both competence and pleasure. For she liked to *talk* about money—this was again a thing almost incomprehensible to me. She did not do it often, because those who surrounded her, for the most part, knew little about it; but when she got somebody like Miles, who understood money, she could talk to him about it for hours with the keenest pleasure, discussing business principles, practice and administration, exchanging ideas and (according to Miles) genuine criticism. From all this side of her mind, which was, I suppose, the most mature and competent, I was shut out by the fact that I did not understand either the desire to make money (aside from what it would buy—just to make it) or the methods by which this could be done.

In purely intellectual matters Maxine was, by the time I knew her, lazy and careless. She cared nothing for music or pictures, read hardly anything but detective stories, treated politics only in the most superficial way for purposes of conversation, had no intellectual curiosity left, and regarded every new movement or tendency as a "Bolshevistic" innovation. She spoke of the whole administration of Franklin Roosevelt with bitter dislike. Once at lunch she said to me: "Do you know what they've got in my theatre in New York now? Bolshevik plays!" With some difficulty I found out (not from her) that the Federal Theatre Project had leased her theatre, but the most "Bolshevik" play they performed in it was Shakespeare's *Coriolanus*.

And yet, out of all the laziness and exhaustion and preference for easy things, sometimes there would come the flash of an able mind. Maxine must have had penetration, taste and judgment to a remarkable degree; she must have possessed a good grasp of at least the bold lines in literature and politics; she must have had an excellent memory and a fine sense of womanly character. Her beauty alone, or even her beauty plus financial acumen, would never have explained her career. Traces of all these other qualities remained, although so lost in the general asepsis of backgammon and mah-jongg that they were hardly distinguishable. Of Lady Russell (the writer "Elizabeth"), who lived on the Riviera, Maxine said: "I don't like anybody who talks proud English." Of Elsa Maxwell she said: "She's the only disinterested adventuress I've ever known." Now and then she made a glancing comment of this sort which showed a sense of the world and a sense of the language; she remembered lines of poetry extraordinarily well, although it must have been many years since she had read any; she was in all such respects of a different breed from most of the people, particularly the younger women, who filled her house. Of these nothing much was demanded save that they be pleasing to the eye, agreeable about playing backgammon, acquainted

with the people and usages of international society, and
not too tiresome about the monkey. Some of the most in-
disputable nitwits in the contemporary world thus dwelt
in Maxine's house, week in and week out, carrying on their
subhuman intrigues and complicated intramural arrangements. She never minded so long as they looked nice,
played games and had some traces of manners. They
understood this perfectly, and conformed. I have seen
Lady C. and others playing backgammon by the hour
when I knew they were longing to get out to other diversions.

On that first morning when I went down to the terrace
by the swimming pool I knew nothing of all this. I knew
that my hostess, my new aunt-in-law, was an extremely
positive character, and from the beginning I determined
to yield to no tyranny. I believe I understood and re-
spected Maxine more than most of the people who were
her willing slaves, but I had a kind of stiff-necked resistance to any attempt to dominate. We fought out our duel
in silence. For the most part I was unconscious of it at
the time; it was instinct and emotion, as I see now in
retrospect. Maxine was no doubt conscious of it from the
first moment, since she was far more cerebral than I. Most
of my arms of offense and defense were unconscious and
quite beyond any possible control of mine. For example,
if there were too many elaborate strangers in the house,
I became violently ill and had to spend the greater part
of my visit in bed, vomiting profusely from morning to
night and attended regularly by Maxine's doctor. This
happened two or three times—it never has happened anywhere else in the world—and I think Maxine understood
that it was some kind of unconscious protest: she stopped
asking me in such company. The last two times I stayed
in the house Mr. Churchill was the principal other guest,

for most of the time the only one, and I had no trouble with illnesses of this sort.

At first the only means I had of resisting Maxine's empire was not to wear bathing trunks in the morning. Everybody else did; it was the rule of the house. I do not know why I did not. Instinct must have informed me that her swimming pool (the finest on the Riviera) was the center of the house in her eyes; that she expected it to be highly valued by everybody who approached it; that the purpose of the human body was to be displayed; that everybody who kept clothed on the brink of her sparkling blue pool was in some way declaring independence of her realm. Whether there was some subconscious reasoning of this sort or not I cannot tell, but I know that this was the effect. Maxine protested at first, only to discover that I had no intention of taking my clothes off. It was about two years before she acknowledged my independence; and yet during my last visits she had yielded and ignored the subject. It probably was indecent for me to remain clothed in the midst of all that nakedness, but clothed I was.

Maxine herself wore bathing suits so constructed that except when she was actually in the water they turned into dresses: a clever arrangement, done by addition and subtraction. For most of the morning she sat over the backgammon board with a long cigarette holder in the corner of her mouth, clacking the dice and carrying on a slow, lazy, inconsequent conversation with whoever appeared on the terrace. Opponents succeeded each other at the board, some of them no doubt because they liked to play, but many because they wished to please Maxine by doing so. Occasionally divine Providence was particularly generous and sent a guest who was willing to play six-pack bézique. Such a one was Johnny Ryan, and I remember one day when he came early for lunch and played a

total of six hours before and after the meal with her. She
thought such guests more precious than rubies.

The whole of the Riviera wandered on to that terrace
at some time or other during the season. Often Maxine
had rather dim ideas of who the people were, but at least
she always knew who had brought them. She could not
be "Bohemian" about such things—she always wished to
know exactly how many were going to sit down to a meal,
although as between thirty and thirty-two or thirty-three
I never could see that it made much difference. As a rule
she knew a great deal about everybody who sat down at
her table, and could tell you their antecedents for a generation or two back; but even her masterful social talent
was unable to cope with the identities of all the guests at
the swimming pool. Some friends along the coast or in the
hills would come and bring their whole party; once
the entire ward-room of the training ship *Arethusa* arrived; a certain number of people had the permanent en-
trée and could bring anybody they liked. The only other
house on the coast occupying a position at all comparable
to Maxine's was the one next door, belonging to Lord
Cholmondeley. He had built it after hers on the one bit of
ledge remaining· between the railway and the sea; but
instead of considering imitation to be the sincerest form
of flattery I think Maxine was always rather annoyed at
this. She consoled herself by thinking that Lord Cholmondeley's house was less successfully contrived than her
own, upon which she had lavished vast amounts of personal attention and hard work. She thought "Rock"—he
was formerly Lord Rocksavage, and they called him
"Rock"—had merely turned over the job to the architects
and let it go at that: which, as any architect who ever attempted to work for Maxine on any of her ten houses
will testify, was not the way she did it.

She had a phrase she used quite often about Lord Cholmondeley's house and the noise of the trains on the State
Railway behind us.

"It's hardly possible to hear the trains here," she would
say, "whereas in Rock's house the moment a train goes
by all conversation ceases."

I heard her say that one evening at dinner just as a
train maliciously hurtled by, and the end of the phrase
was lost; all conversation had ceased.

6

Mr. Churchill first became visible to me in a red bathrobe over bathing trunks; he wore a large, flopping straw
hat, and slippers and a cherubic grin. I think the first
words I heard him say were these:

"My dear Maxine, you have no idea how easy it is to
travel without a servant. I came here all the way from
London alone and it was quite simple."

I remember the tolerant smile of Maxine and the
amused contralto of her deepest voice as she said: "Winston, how brave of you!" True, it had been thirty or forty
years since Maxine herself had stirred anywhere without
a servant in attendance; but she must have been able to
remember a time before that; and in any case she undoubtedly knew that the sentence would sound funny to me.
From the very beginning she had a knack of knowing, in
a general way, what I was thinking about the circumam-
bient world.

Mr. Churchill was painting a great deal that summer
(1935) and used to spend every afternoon up in the hills,
mainly at Saint-Pol. I always thought his painting showed
a definite, although untaught and inexperienced, talent.

Maxine had a number of his pictures in the house, including one of her own swimming pool in which all the figures were brisk dots of white against the green and blue. True, the painting was interesting most of all because it had been done by him, but if it had been the work of a young man I believe it might have been said to show promise. He did it frankly as a hobby; he attached no importance at all to it, and laughed at anybody who pretended to take it seriously. But he did work at it and it gave him great pleasure. In this way it occupied a sort of intermediate place between writing—which he took very seriously, although it was not the prime business of his life—and bricklaying; it engaged his mind, perceptions and sense of form, although not his creative ambition, and had for him the advantages both of work (like writing) and of a simple pastime (like bricklaying). I suppose he probably got more sheer pleasure out of painting than out of any work he did just then except certain passages—the battle pieces, particularly—in his *Life of Marlborough*.

Mr. Churchill survived into Maxine's present life from "the old days at Hartsbourne." I have used this phrase before without explaining it; in Maxine's world it required no explanation. At about the time when she first retired from the stage (1908, probably) Maxine built or restored Hartsbourne Manor in Hertfordshire. Her talent as a hostess was displayed for the first time in England. From all I can make out, Hartsbourne was visited by more or less everybody, but particularly beautiful women and distinguished men. Lord Rosebery ("the great Lord Rosebery"—the one who was Prime Minister), Lord Balfour, Lord Curzon, Lord Birkenhead and Mr. Churchill, among the political men who went there; Lord Ribblesdale and the Duke of Rutland among the non-political; Lady Randolph Churchill ("the most beautiful woman I ever saw in my life," Maxine always said), Lady Ribblesdale (Alice Hofmannsthal's mother), the Duchess of Rutland (Violet, the mother of Lady Diana Cooper), the Duchess of Sutherland (Millicent, mother of the present duke), Lady Alington (Fedora, the mother of Napier), and many others whom I never saw, but whose names became familiar to me through constant repetition, made of Hartsbourne a house which, for its brief career, must have been rather exceptional. Maxine sold it after the last war. It is now a golf club; most of those who made "the old days at Hartsbourne" were dead before I ever knew her; and yet I did get, from the conversation of Maxine and Winston, some vague idea of what that society had been like. It must clearly have been unlike anything existing since 1918, for it was both serious and pleasure-loving in a combination to which succeeding periods seem to have lost the secret.

Maxine and Winston liked to quote the witticisms of "F.E.," Lord Birkenhead, whom they had both inordinately admired. These remarks sounded learned to a high degree and sometimes genuinely funny, but thought out, planned in detail, as no wit since that period has been. I used to listen to these epigrams or turns of phrase (some of them dependent upon Latin or Greek) and contrast them with what passed for wit among my own contemporaries—the remarks attributed by our younger legend to Miss Dorothy Parker, Mr. Noel Coward or Lord Berners. I could see no resemblance at all. The wit of "F.E."—the wit of "the old days at Hartsbourne"—came from a totally different life, in which words and ideas were thought to be funnier than persons, and consequently became both the subject and object of the intellectual exercise.

That Maxine, an American and an actress, should have gathered such a circle as that at Hartsbourne was obviously something well outside the ordinary rules and customs of life in London society before 1914. So far as I could determine, King Edward VII's admiration was what gave Maxine her position, curious, indeed unique, as it was, in London society. It appears that London society in that reign was dominated by the sovereign—a thing that has not happened since, except perhaps in the brief reign of Edward VIII. I have heard (not from Maxine, but from a contemporary) that in one of her first house parties at Hartsbourne the King was a guest with a commanded list of the most recalcitrant members of the aristocracy. Few, in those days, dared to be ill or otherwise prevented from attending when the King commanded. All this was so lost in the mists of the past by the time I went to the Château de l'Horizon that it was impossible to discern exactly the stages by which Maxine was translated into the ranks of a certain very exalted, very grand and much-discussed part of the English aristocracy, but by the time I knew her the thing had long since caught on. She thought and talked, for the greater part of her day, exactly like them; she had a host of memories in common with them, knew all the same people, shared their interests and prejudices, and this had been true for many years; small wonder that she was often hardly to be distinguished from them. She did differ from them profoundly, and most of all in her grasp of affairs; she had a strong, masculine intelligence, was never to be influenced by sentiment in any worldly matter, was relentless when necessary and above all was never to be deflected from any goal. In all these matters she was a different order of being from the aristocratic ladies who were her friends; and yet on the surface she had only their preoccupations (clothes, games, scandal, and in earlier days, no doubt, love) and dwelt intellectually in their zone. She even understood that sense of social responsibility which seems never to be wholly

extinct in an English aristocrat, and in the war of 1914–
1918 Maxine was an indefatigable worker. She equipped
a canteen barge in which she scoured the canals of Belgium, and then (as at times afterward) she put all her
distinguished friends under the obligation to work for
her. She had a strong dislike for demanding money con-
tributions, and consequently paid all the expense of her
war work herself, but she did not mind asking the most
orchidaceous people to work hard and long in a service
she had organized.

Winston—Mr. Churchill to me, but they all called him
"Winston"; so did the greater part of the British Empire
—survived into Maxine's present life from "the old days at
Hartsbourne," and into their conversation continually fell
phrases and ideas that recalled the time that was past, the
men and women who were (so many of them) dead. Most
of Maxine's present friends had known nothing of that
life and were altogether a different breed of creature. The
international society that gathered at Cannes contained
members of the English aristocracy, but it was by no
means aristocratic: it was "fashionable," a very different
thing. The gleaming red fingernails and smooth white
flanks of the lady opposite you might indicate a present
status, but they did not authenticate a past; the slender
brown beauty in the pale blue swimming suit might have
worn wooden shoes ten years ago; the lupanars of Athens
and Alexandria had flowered into that other lady, so de-
mure and quietly elegant, now a princess and the friend
of princesses; the young man in the infinitesimal black
trunks, now displaying a hairy chest and long legs on
the enameled edge of the turquoise pool, came from the
deserts of Australia to make his way by love, love alone;
there was no stability in all this. It came and it went.
Cannes knew next to nothing about even the great men

of "the old days at Hartsbourne"; much less did Cannes know about their families, their more obscure relations, their houses and their private lives. Any saxophone player had more reality for Lady C. than the great Lord Rosebery; and perhaps rightly, for Lord Rosebery was dead. Cannes, like the United States of America, held firmly to the axiom, better a live mouse than a dead lion.

Winston in such a society was slightly out of place—more so even than Maxine—but he never noticed. He went to the South of France for a holiday and he proposed to take it as it happened, accepting whatever company there was, amiably bent upon making the best of everything. Nobody ever had such a lordly way of disregarding what seemed trivial or without significance. He could sit through a whole conversation on some subject that held no interest for him, and not a word of it would penetrate. When he was ready to speak he would speak, but on his own subject. There was one night at dinner on the terrace under the false moon when this quality was more apparent to me than ever before. Maxine, Lady C. and the others had been eagerly discussing a certain scandal, some sort of story that had drawn the attention of the press months before; the heroine (or hero, whichever it was) of this story had just appeared in Cannes. For a long time I thought I was the only person at table who did not know what they were talking about, until, toward the end of the meat dish which he had been conscientiously masticating, Mr. Churchill lifted his head and inquired: "What is it you are all saying? Who are these people?"

Maxine explained, and added: "Now don't pretend you don't know, Winston. It's been all over every paper in the world."

He said: "I never pay any attention to that sort of thing unless I happen to know the people."

In another moment he was off, talking about Ethiopia, Mussolini, German rearmament, the character of Hitler, the nature of the Nazi movement. He took it for granted that the company followed what he was saying, although I am quite certain some of them understood next to nothing and regarded him as a bore. I well remember one day at lunch (a crowded lunch with thirty or forty people, on the terrace above the swimming pool) when Lady C., scratching the inside of her shapely bare legs, inquired in a piercing nasal voice: "Winston, why is it they always seem to go to *Geneva* for their meetings? Seems to me they could pick out a nicer place."

Mr. Churchill paused in his mastication, looked at her benevolently from the shade of his big straw hat, and said, as to a child:

"Because, my dear, Geneva happens to be the seat of the League of Nations. You have heard of it, no doubt?"

Maxine followed his conversation with interest, although she could hardly bear to talk of any serious subject with anybody else. She had a sensible worldly attitude toward anything that was regarded as important enough to occupy much space in the papers; that is, she read it. She could not get it through her head that there were many people who did not read what did not interest them. She had a story she used to tell about Lord Balfour, and how she had once given him a graphic description of the remarkable behavior of the crowds in New York over Rudolph Valentino, the film star. The point of the story was that when she had finished, Lord Balfour said to her: "Well, my dear, who is Rudolph Valentino?" At this point you were supposed to laugh immoderately. I did not think it particularly funny, because, although I knew well enough who Rudolph Valentino was, I was ignorant as a goat about some of his successors, even the most famous of them; and it seemed to me hardly within the bounds of possibility that Lord Balfour should have known. Maxine once told this story to Winston. He smiled his most cherubic smile and said: "Well, I don't want you to think ill of me, Maxine dear, but the fact is that I too must inquire, who *is* Rudolph Valentino?"

"Was, *was*," she said, "he's been dead for years! Oh, *how* is it possible ... ?"

In her seventies, having known busy political personages for more than half her life, she still was constantly being surprised by the fact that they were more interested in politics than in anything else—so much so that they missed knowing half the content of the popular mind. I think Maxine's stage career, which otherwise seemed to have left almost no impress upon her later character, lived on in her interest in films, plays and players. She knew them all so well (whether she had ever actually seen them or not) that she expected everybody else to do the same. She loved going to the theatre as much as she had detested acting in it. She had never been—they say—a really good actress, having relied upon her haughty beauty and languid airs to put her through the endless succession of high society comedies (all alike) in which she appeared. Perhaps for this reason, perhaps for another which I shall come to in due course, she had actively disliked the stage, and, according to all I could gather, survived her long experience upon it chiefly by concentrating upon money (the money to be earned and invested) and the game of bridge. It seems that on her annual tours of the United States she played bridge the whole time when she was not actually on the stage, and the members of her company were chosen for their ability as bridge players rather than for their talent as actors. Even after her retirement she had such a passion for bridge that she used to play it—at Hartsbourne and at her house in St. John's Wood—night after night until dawn. Such was her energy that she could ally with it an equal passion for tennis, and play the one all night and the other most of the day: a really astounding woman.

Mr. Churchill knew how remarkable she was. I doubt if he had ever been among her more ardent admirers; in "the old days at Hartsbourne" apparently a whole generation, perhaps two, had paid court to her, but I think Mr. Churchill was a decade or so younger than most of the others; he had for her the affection of an old friend. Those who knew London before 1914 and have survived into our time tend to a rather condescending pity for us: "I'm always sorry for anybody who never knew London before the war," Maxine used to say, and meant it. Obviously she recalled that era to Mr. Churchill, as he did to her, and when they talked directly to each other it was often of things long since past, incomprehensible to Lady C. and to Cannes.

We lunched, as I have said, in much company, anywhere from twenty to forty people filling the terrace under the awning. Alexis and Michel, the boys, dished out the food from a bar set into the side of the house; we fetched it, buffet style, and it was surprising how well the whole thing was done with only two attendants. Dinner was a much smaller occasion, and except in the case of a party —which was not often—only the guests in the house sat down to it. After Lord Alington and Lady P. went away on that first occasion there were six of us; on subsequent occasions there were only four, Maxine, Winston, Dinah and I. The dinner table was set upon the upper terrace under the balconies to all the guests' rooms, and if there was a real moon over the gulf we dined in its light; if there was not, we turned on the artificial moon. In the summer we never had a meal inside the house, and on my first winter visit there (1937 or 1938) I was surprised to discover that there was a very pretty, although perfectly conventional, dining room at the end of the big salon.

That dining room was the first beyond the kitchen and "usual offices." Next to it came the immense salon, with a great fireplace and massive, conventional furniture, most of it reproductions of old pieces. This room was always filled with flowers and, just before a dinner party, with the faint scent of some kind of incense whisked through the room in a brazier and out again. In the winter time, when the flowers often were lilies, I observed that Maxine never left them in their natural state; they were not precisely gilded, but their inner surfaces were delicately tinted with blue, pink or green stuff sprayed upon them by the attentive Alexis. There were insets of bookshelves in which those books not in collected editions of gold-and-red or gold-and-blue were frankly painted suitable colors. Over the huge plaster fireplace, semi-baroque in style, was a very pretty eighteenth-century portrait in pastel, I think by Perroneau or another painter of his day. On the big piano, which was seldom used, there were flowers and silver-framed photographs of King Edward VII, the Duchess of Sutherland, Lady Portarlington, Lady Patricia Latham and my eldest sister-in-law, Maxine's favorite niece. Beyond this big room was a small library, never used, and an equally small morning room where Maxine used to play six-pack bézique in frowning concentration whenever she could find a victim. All these rooms were in a row over the terraces and the blue gulf. Behind them was the marble hall and our rooms (Dinah's and mine): this was the whole ground floor. On the floor above were the bedrooms, each with its bath and its balcony over the gulf. I never knew exactly how many there were, but they were all comfortable and of pleasant shape and color without being museum chambers. Maxine seldom spent much money on furniture; she wanted it to be agreeable and cared nothing at all about its antiquity. Any pictures and furniture of value were presents; the rest was modern even when it conformed vaguely to the style of a past era. The Van Dyck, the Perroneau, and the Canalettos in her flat in Paris, had all been presents to Maxine. Some of the portraits of herself (one by Boldini, for example, which she did not like and had relegated to the basement storerooms) were also presents. She cared nothing for pictures; I think the only one that appealed to her was a tremendously long and ultra-dramatic portrait of herself at the top of the marble staircase in the Château de l'Horizon. It showed her in riding clothes with a plumed hat on her head and a crop in her hand. Her chin was up, her dark red lips curled in the scornful half-smile which seems to have been always characteristic. The huge dark eyes and the sweep of raven-black hair gave her that look of almost impossible romantic beauty and arrogant lassitude, as of one surfeited with the world's homage, for which she had been famous in those far-off days before 1914. I remember Mr. Lloyd George standing on the marble steps below that portrait and looking up, like a schoolboy at the changing of the guard, saying over and over again: "By Jove! By Jove!"

## 7

In the summer of 1935 the forces of Europe were already beginning to fall into their natural alignment. The farce at Stresa had taken place in the spring, when Mussolini, at the mere suggestion that he might honor France and England by his patronage, had been courted as never before. The agreements reached at Stresa were, of course, *de la poudre aux yeux;* only a fatuous French diplomat who lived on hope could hail them as "the greatest event since the Armistice"; obviously this belated attempt to resume the old entente and exclude Hitler's Germany was bound to come to nothing. When I first went to the Château de l'Horizon it was early September, 1935. Mussolini was openly preparing for his attack on Ethiopia, by which he was to be thrown irrevocably into the German alliance; the German press was encouraging him daily; the French press was in its usual state of alarm and self-contradiction. England had so far not taken the matter very seriously, although Anthony Eden had already given such signs of anti-Fascist principle that his name was anathema in Italy. The tension was considerable throughout Europe, and the whole subsequent series of events (Spain, Austria, Czechoslovakia, the crises that led in the end to general war) could be discerned taking shape nebulously upon the gray and darkening vista of the future.

Mr. Churchill, in spite of the fact that he was on holiday, painting and taking the sun, could not keep his mind off these ominous foreshadows of the day of reckoning. He spoke constantly of the Ethiopian crisis, of the League, of Mussolini, of relations between England and Italy, of Italy's relations with Germany, and of German rearmament. German rearmament afflicted him then sorely, for he had just come upon some incontrovertible evidence of the extent to which it was being pushed forward by the single-minded Nazis. He had already spoken publicly, and was to speak more than once in the coming years, of what this portended for England. His words had been unheard. He had been out of power since 1931—they had preferred Neville Chamberlain to him in making up the new

"National" cabinet—and was to remain in the wilderness
until adversity swept him in again. Most observers thought
him unlikely ever to regain a position of first rank in English politics, for he had, to all intents and purposes, lost
his party. The Tories did not like or trust him; he was not
"safe." They said he was too "brilliant"—what is called "too
clever." He could not return to the Liberals because his
views on imperialism were not theirs, and besides the Liberal party had almost passed out of existence. He was
conspicuous in the House of Commons and in the country,
but as a lone eccentric, too familiar for too long, a character too blazingly and relentlessly famous for any further
use in the humdrum business of government. What England wanted was good, substantial, mediocre men like
Stanley Baldwin and Neville Chamberlain. The pipe of
the earlier sage, like the umbrella of the later one, came to
have symbolic value in English minds: it represented
the solid, uneventful virtue of stupidity, the most popular
quality in public life everywhere during periods when men
feel comfortable and safe.

Winston was "out"—definitely, and, as it seemed, permanently, "out." Even so he could not divorce his interests
from those of the nation. He was deeply concerned over
the developing crisis and read everything he could find on
it in English and French. From the outset he seemed to
see that it was not merely a question of a colonial adventure in Ethiopia, but involved the whole structure of
Europe, with possibilities of realignment carrying the
promise of deadly danger to England. This sense of what
was contained in the germ—a sense of history, to give it its
right name—was what most sharply distinguished Mr.
Churchill's attitude toward these matters from the atti-
tudes of the Baldwin-Chamberlain puddingheads who
were in power through the 1930's. He could see past,

present and future in relation; he knew how to watch, could feel them develop, was quick—even at his age—to develop with them. In the few years since I first heard him talk he has traversed a huge distance in political thought: in 1935 he would not speak to his old colleagues and friends if they had been in favor of even the most modest constitutional reform in India; and in 1942 he was offering India her freedom.

Sitting on the terrace above the swimming pool in his bathrobe and floppy straw hat Mr. Churchill would discourse with unfailing energy, much wit and considerable wisdom, never troubling to notice whether his talk was fully understood or appreciated. On a good many occasions it was not, save by Maxine and me. There were too often people like Lady C., whose whole interest in the matter of a dying world was what she could get out of it in the way of money, jewels or "a good time"; there were also too many people who had never talked politics before in their lives and were afraid to begin. (They made up for lost time in the years that followed.) In the beginning Mr. Churchill hardly noticed me, except occasionally to make a glancing reference to my book *Personal History*, which he was then reading at Maxine's tyrannical behest. ("Very shubvershive," he thought it, smiling amiably as he issued the judgment.) But as time passed I think he grew into the habit of directing some of his political talk toward me because I at least understood it. In visits of the following years at Cannes, Mr. Churchill and I had one definite bond of sympathy and communication: we both felt with overwhelming certainty what was coming, and although our points of view were very different, the certainty did establish a common ground upon which we (and we alone in all that world) could meet. In spite of the immense differences in position, age, experience of life

and scale of values, Mr. Churchill and I were alike cursed
by powerful premonitions, based upon that same sense of
history to which I have earlier referred—a sense which has
no existence, even objectively, for those who do not share
it, as it cannot be dissected or proved—and it sometimes
seemed to me that this brought us very close. It is a sense
much commoner among journalists and writers than
among politicians, and I could name offhand half a dozen
of my own colleagues who have known the course of events
well in advance for years past; aside from Mr. Churchill
and possibly Mr. Eden, I could name no such politicians.

He had a distinction which he tried to bring out in
every talk about Ethiopia just then: it seemed to him very
important. "It's not the *thing* we object to," he would say,
"it's the *kind* of thing." I had not then succumbed as much
to his genial charm as I did later, and I could not quite
accept this. I mentioned the Red Sea, the route to India,
the importance of Aden. Mr. Churchill brushed all that
aside: "We don't need to worry about the Italians," he
said. "It isn't that at all. It isn't the thing. It's the *kind* of
thing."

The distinction was worth making, because hardly anybody in Europe could take England's high-minded ethical
protests seriously just then. Obviously the British Empire
had been created by precisely the kind of thing Mussolini
was now about to attempt in Ethiopia—although, in an age
of slower communication, it had grown up more naturally
and less by deliberate plan. Mr. Churchill was pinned
down firmly one day by an elegant lady, Mme Letellier,
who said that an objection to the *thing* might be practical
and necessary, but that England had no historical right
to object to the *kind* of thing. England had too often
profited by "the kind of thing."

"Ah, but you see, all that belongs to the unregenerate

past, is locked away in the limbo of the old, the wicked days," Mr. Churchill said, smiling benevolently upon her across the luncheon table. "The world progresses. We have endeavored, by means of the League of Nations and the whole fabric of international law, to make it impossible for nations nowadays to infringe upon each other's rights. In trying to upset the empire of Ethiopia, Mussolini is making a most dangerous and foolhardy attack upon the whole established structure, and the results of such an attack are quite incalculable. Who is to say what will come of it in a year, or two, or three? With Germany arming at breakneck speed, England lost in a pacifist dream, France corrupt and torn by dissension, America remote and indifferent—Madame, my dear lady, do you not tremble for your children?"

One day that September Michael Arlen came to lunch and somehow or other got into a discussion of ideal government. He succeeded, by a combination of questions and independent sallies, in irritating Mr. Churchill into a rather ambitious flight, a description of how government ought to be conducted. Economically, it seemed to be a cross between eighteenth-century pre-industrial feudalism and the most "advanced" (in a Bismarckian sense) social legislation and insurance for urban industrial workers. There was a certain haze over the economic structure, but not so the political: here Mr. Churchill's full native flavor came out. He thought parliamentary government and civil administration should be entrusted to a small hereditary class of specialized workers, trained for these purposes from childhood, paid enough to sustain them in honorable and dignified comfort, but without luxury or special emolument; they should not "make money" in any way, should not invest, transmit or inherit money; they should have no economic function in the society, but purely a political one; they ought not to be allied to any particular class in the social organism. It was a sort of ideal governing class, an elevated and purified version of the hereditary aristocracy of the eighteenth century, but somehow cut off from its economic base. Apparently these *samurai* of the government were not to be landowners; they were to have no more to do with the landowning class than with the city bankers or industrialists; they were as highly specialized as the drone or the queen among bees. Thus they differed from the hit-or-miss aristocracy of practical history, in which experience had shown that there were far more drones than queens, far more Dukes of Newcastle and Lord Liverpools (to speak only of prime ministers) than Winston Churchills.

I do not attach undue importance to this flight of Mr. Churchill's fancy. He was only talking, making variations upon a theme, on a summer's day after lunch in the South of France; and yet the improvisation must have corresponded in fact to some deep feeling about forms of rule. I am sure he never has regarded such a born-and-bred governing class as more than the most fanciful optimum, for his experience was too great to permit self-deception in the matter, and yet an optimum it was: he did wish it could be so. In actual practice he was a parliamentarian of parliamentarians, a true House of Commons man, a Liberal in the nineteenth-century sense, a Whig in an earlier sense. The institutions of representative constitutional government meant a great deal to him. They had so entwined themselves about his earliest memories and his lifelong preoccupations that he was sometimes only half conscious of the force with which they influenced his every developed thought. He showed by indirection, allusively and sometimes in the most unthinking assumptions, that he regarded representative democracy as not only the highest form of government, but as the only one under which mankind could evolve in relative freedom. His temperamental dislike for Nazi excesses, for all forms of tyranny, for cruelty, disorder and corrupt or summary courts of law, was the counterpart of this Whiggish insistence upon representative democracy as the only good form of rule. In some ways I should have expected him to be more favorable to the Fascist dictators than the other English political men; he was class-conscious, or had been, and had seemed to dread working-class revolution more than most people in the early 1920's. You might therefore have expected him to succumb to the Fascist argument that Fascism was a bulwark against Communism. I think at the outset he was rather favorable to Mussolini, whom he originally admired, but he was never taken in by the Fascist pretense of historical necessity. He was too intelligent and he knew too much history for that. On the contrary, when Hitler arose to put Mussolini's principles into more serious and dangerous practice, Mr. Churchill saw the trap immediately and reacted with his utmost vigor. His patriotism was rapidly engulfing all other sentiments, emotions and prejudices, so that the awareness of danger to England drove out whatever had originally prepared him for benevolence toward the Fascist principle, and he was willing, in the end, to work with the extreme Left if necessary to defeat the paramount enemy. This evolution I saw. I do not know if Mr. Churchill is aware that I saw it—at first he paid little attention to me—but from 1935 to 1939 were the precise years in which he was traversing this immense ideological area, and it was then (while he was out of office) that his mind was tempered for the supreme crisis. When I first talked to him about Spain he was pro-Franco and greatly concerned over Russian intervention; when I last talked to him (just before the fall of the Spanish Republic) he was saddened and made solemn by the whole thing, perceived the importance of the victory for Hitler and Mussolini, and regarded the fall of the Republic as a blow to England. Again, with respect to Russia, and most of all, with respect to India, these few years produced in him such an extraordinary process of ageing and tempering that he could hardly be recognized, in 1942, as the man who had once thumbed his nose gaily at the whole world outside the British Isles.

That first summer's visit, in all its heat and glitter, ended soon enough. We drove on back to Paris and to England. I made my bow to my parents-in-law, and we flew south to Naples for the rest of that year. On our return to Cannes at Christmas, 1935, Italy had invaded Ethiopia and was completing the conquest in scheduled time in spite of the platonic punishments imposed by Mr. Eden's League of Nations. We stayed for a week or so in Maxine's garage and discovered that Cannes out of season ("out of season" might be defined, for us, as any time when Maxine was not there) could be as charming and quiet as any other place. Then came Egypt, England, Ireland, Switzerland—a long and terrible illness supervened for me, exactly at the outbreak of the Spanish Civil War, July, 1936—and then a house at St. Germain outside of Paris, where I recuperated from my disastrous illness and translated Eve Curie's life of her mother. It was in January, 1938, that we returned to Maxine's for another visit, this time with Mr. Churchill as the only other guest.

He had mellowed exceedingly in two and a half years, chiefly because he had reached the conclusion that his political career was over. He was devoting himself to writing; at the moment he was finishing his long *Life of Marlborough*, and when it was completed he intended to take up his *History of England.* Over at Antibes was Mr. Lloyd George, doing the same kind of thing, except that Lloyd George's sheer word-count was probably higher than that of anybody since Balzac or Walter Scott. Mr. Churchill had of late rediscovered the game of mah-jongg, and during that visit we used to play it all through the afternoon, from the time lunch ended until it was time to dress for dinner, making only the briefest pause for tea without rising from the table. It was a good game, except that—as usual—Maxine was so much better than the rest of us that it must have been a great bore to her. Mr. Churchill was almost as inept at games as I am, but he enjoyed his efforts, and throughout the afternoon he kept up a flow of amiable nonsense which made the game fun for Dinah and me, even though, as mah-jongg, strictly mah-jongg, it probably left everything to be desired.

The abdication of King Edward VIII had taken place in the preceding winter (1937) and the King, under his new name, with the wife for whom he had given up the throne, was living on the hill in the part of Cannes known as Californie. Mr. Churchill had been a champion of King Edward's cause during those brief tempestuous days of the abdication crisis, and the Duke and Duchess of Windsor asked him to dinner one day soon after his arrival. It was his suggestion that they be asked to dine at the Château de l'Horizon with no other guests; later—at, indeed, the last moment—he asked Maxine to invite Mr. Lloyd George as well.

That was a strange, surréaliste evening. As Maxine's nephew-in-law I was appointed to be host—a rôle for which I had little experience. It was my duty to go out with Maxine to the entrance of the château and receive the royal guests. After a brief discussion at luncheon, during which more was implied than said, it was decided that the Duchess of Windsor should be treated as a royalty, with "ma'am" and the curtsy and all the rest of it.

When I came down at nine that night I found Maxine and Mr. Churchill already in the great salon. For him this was very unusual; he liked to work in the evenings and we often did not sit down to dinner until ten o'clock. Fanny, Maxine's indefatigable and indispensable maid— except that she was far more than a maid; she was the house—was whisking a burning incense brazier through the long, flower-laden room. Winston made a little speech which I shall long remember.

"You have a strange party tonight, my dear," he said. "It consists entirely of the *ci-devant*. Ex-kings, ex-prime ministers, ex-politicians. It is like Voltaire."

Alexis came into the room, pale and frightened, to say: "*Madame, ils sont là.*" Maxine and I made our way out into the marble hall and stationed ourselves at the door, which Alexis and Michel opened wide. The Duchess came first out of the darkness, smiling, in black with flowers on her shoulder, accepting Maxine's tentative curtsy and my awkward bow as they were intended, walking with Maxine through the hall into the salon. H.R.H. walked behind them, with me, and since I was well aware of the servants who lined the balconies at the top of the stairs to stare at us, I was self-conscious and aware of my great height. Mr. Lloyd George had already arrived; he and Mr. Churchill came forward from the fireplace to make their bows.

The Prince of Wales in 1935 had lived at Lord Cholmondeley's house next door; the King, Edward VIII, had actually taken this house, the Château de l'Horizon, for August of 1936, and had had a Dalmatian cruise palmed off on him instead by the government of the day; but this was the first time the Duke and Duchess of Windsor had entered the house. I had met the Duchess once, but had never even seen her semi-legendary husband. There was some consciousness of an occasion about this small dinner, perhaps because the exact coincidence of guests was unlikely to occur again, perhaps because the King had so recently been King and the whole drama was still fresh in every mind.

From the beginning the Duke of Windsor dominated the conversation. He sat at the head of the table, like a king, with Maxine at his right, Mr. Lloyd George at her right; the Duchess sat between Mr. Lloyd George and me; Winston and Dinah completed the circle. I cannot truthfully say that the conversation fulminated with shafts of great brilliance, and yet it was lively, well informed and sensible throughout. The Duke had, like most royalties, a fabulous memory, and was able to engage in a reminiscence-match with Mr. Lloyd George (whom he addressed as "L.G."), coming out easily the victor. Apparently Mr. Lloyd George had performed his investiture as Prince of Wales at Carnarvon Castle many years before, when H.R.H. was a child of eleven or twelve. At some point or other there arose a passionate discussion of the welfare of the Welsh coal miners, the conditions of their labor, compulsory work for welfare and hygiene, and the necessity of more comprehensive legislation for their protection. The Duke seemed to have been greatly impressed by the coal mines he had seen in Germany, and by the social legislation of the Nazi régime. (I longed to point out, and did not dare, that most of what they were talking about antedated Hitler by many years. The poor Weimar Republic, so despised and rejected, had at least enacted enough social legislation to furnish forth half a dozen Nazi régimes.)

There was a prolonged conversation between the Duke of Windsor, Mr. Lloyd George and Mr. Churchill, to which the Duchess made an occasional contribution, about compulsory shower baths at the pithead in coal mines. The Duke spoke of his visits to the dreary mining villages of Wales and Northern England, of the terrible dirt there, of the way in which bath-houses existed plentifully or scantily or not at all, in the discretion of the owners. He and the Duchess had been assured by Dr. Ley that every mine in Germany had the most ample, and indeed luxurious, arrangements for bathing at the pithead. They had indeed visited these baths on their tour of the Reich some months before.

Mr. Churchill did not particularly enjoy praise of the Nazi régime, and although he had been remarkably silent throughout the meal (deferring like a schoolboy to the authority of Mr. Lloyd George and the Duke), he now spoke up to say that he had proposed compulsory shower baths at the pithead long ago.

"When I was Home Secretary I introduced the idea," he said. "It must have been about in 1911. As I remember, the proposal was defeated by the miners' representatives themselves."

This produced a flood of reminiscence, explanation and discussion. Nobody could remember quite why the miners' representatives had objected to compulsory baths, but it was agreed that the most likely reason was the fact that the cost was to be distributed between owners and workers; Mr. Lloyd George was of the opinion that the miners had held (and rightly, according to him) that the mining enterprise itself should bear the cost of the innovation. The Duke of Windsor had a reason all his own for the miners' recalcitrance.

"I've always heard," he said, "that the miners' wives

didn't want baths at the pithead because washing their husbands' necks is one of their special prerogatives. They enjoy it, and they expect to do it every evening. They didn't want to be robbed of the privilege."

I sat there musing, taking no part in this conversation. The seriousness of their interest in the question could not be doubted, and yet it was confounded with an incurable frivolity owing to their astronomical remoteness from the conditions of life of which they spoke. The Duke unquestionably knew much more about coal mines than I did; it was not until four years later that I first went down into a pit; and yet in a sense he knew nothing of them, because the people who worked in them were to him another race. He wished to see them clean, healthy and contented, as you might wish your horses or dogs to be; to him they were not men and brothers. I think Mr. Lloyd George probably came nearest my own feeling in such matters, but he had been for such an eternity in the House of Commons that he had acquired the political crust and little of his natural impulses came through. Mr. Churchill seemed to regard it—as he did all social questions—in a purely parliamentary manner, involving the supremely important considerations of who would vote for what, and why, and how a majority could be collected and held. The Duchess, so slim and elegant, so suggestive of innumerable fashionable shops, dressmakers, manicurists and hairdressers, seemed at the uttermost remove from the pithead of a mine, and I tried to imagine what she must have been like when Dr. Ley, all puffed out with the vast consequence of the Deutscher Arbeitsfront plus the snobbery of a German official, showed her the men's baths in the Ruhr. Maxine (who said little throughout this evening) was particularly silent just now; no doubt she was thinking that "in the old days at Hartsbourne" conversation had not dwelt so much upon the crass and unseemly problems of the poor. In the exquisite little room, gleaming with glass and silver, over the flowers and champagne, all so enclosed and private and secure, one who had been King, one who had been dictator, and one who was to be: what did they have to speak of but the dirt on a miner's neck? In the realm of ideas it was like an invention by Salvador Dali, not least because in the grotesque juxtaposition was revealed so much of their inner world of thought and feeling, their sense of the necessity to acknowledge what they could not experience in their hearts because life had set them too high, the agenbite of inwit, the gnaw of an impersonal remorse and a dim perception of the far-off sorrow of others. And yet to all at that table, to all except me, the miner of whom they spoke was alien, forever alien, to be feared or hated or tolerated or even courted, but not loved; water might wash away dirt but not the insuperable differences that kept exploiter and exploited apart to the end of time.

Mr. Churchill was very kind; he reminded me of my duties as host when I forgot them. "The brandy," he would whisper aside, or "I think H.R.H. would like another cigar." This was after the women had left the room and we sat for some time talking, of what I no longer remember. The Duke's small, eager features were attentive to the amiable discourse of Mr. Lloyd George, pink-faced, white-haired and smiling; Winston's round cherubic countenance retired behind clouds of smoke and silence; the room was suspended in a moment of withdrawal from the world. It was like lunch, I thought, in a traffic policeman's tower; if you turned your back and chewed hard on the ham you were unaware of the street. What was the mounting roar, the trembling of the substructure? Organ music only; and the bread, the black bread and the white—roses, my lord, roses.

8

Our last visit to the Château de l'Horizon (there had been others in the meantime) took place in January, 1939. During the preceding year I had been much in Spain and had written of it in the New York *Herald Tribune,* which in its Paris edition printed the only paper that was consistently read by all the Anglo-American inhabitants of the Riviera. Consequently my opinions were perfectly well known to innumerable elderly pro-Franco and pro-Fascist ladies and gentlemen who came into existence for me only at Cannes or occasionally in Paris. (I had met in Paris, in Granville Barker's friendly house, Mme la Comtesse de Chambrun, the American wife of the general commanding the army area on the Spanish frontier; she had referred to Franco's forces as "our army," had said "we shall soon be in Madrid," and had declared quite flatly that if any of Hitler's officers needed help in getting to Spain she would assist them.) I knew to the fullest, and so did Dinah, what kind of sympathy or understanding we could expect from most of our upper-class friends. Dinah had been in Spain and had appealed for money in England for relief of Spanish women and children, particularly for the British hospital in Barcelona; Mr. Churchill and Mr. Lloyd George had actually helped her to get five minutes over the jealously guarded imperial air (the B.B.C.) for this purpose; she had collected two thousand pounds in that five minutes. The money was used to buy dried milk, mostly, although a "non-partisan" committee, with Lady Chamberlain (Austin's widow) and the Infanta Beatriz as rabid defenders of Franco, insisted upon seeing that the proceeds were divided. We had run into the blindness and stupidity of the privileged order everywhere. Some of the

dried milk for which Dinah had collected the money went
to Spain on a British ship that was sunk by the Italians on
the way, and we met an Englishman at dinner in our own
village, a baronet and a member of the Tory party in the
House of Commons, who defended the Italians for sinking it. Dinah argued with him (which I should never have
done, being older and more realistic); in the end he said,
"Well, certainly we don't want the dried milk to get there.
Why should we want to feed Red babies?" It seems incredible, but this was said in all earnestness in the presence of six witnesses.

The past year had been like that everywhere, except in
Spain itself. We had been to America and found the same
thing; we had fallen afoul of it in Paris and London; above
all, we had been to Prague through the heart-breaking
days of September, had lived through the supreme horror
of Munich, when all, or nearly all, was lost without a
struggle; we were watching with dread the advance of
Franco's troops in Catalonia, the beginning of the end in
Spain. The stench of all this was very strong in my nostrils.
I did not want to go to Cannes. I thought even a week
would be too much to bear, since every voice and face
would be hostile, every victory of Hitler, Franco and Mussolini would be the signal for rejoicing around us. But this
time Maxine insisted with far more than her usual force;
we went. I expected the worst. Hoping for an ally of un-
impeachable quality, I even went so far as to ask Arthur
Forbes (Lord Forbes, son of Lord Granard) to come with
us, since he had been in Spain and was pro-Republican
too; as the son and heir of a Catholic peer, and rich besides, he could not have been accused of Bolshevik conspiracy. Arthur was willing, but his employer, Lord
Beaverbrook, forbade it. ("I want that boy to work," he

told me afterward with a fierce growl. "I don't want him coming down here to a place like this to loaf.")

So Dinah and I went without protection, thinking to be flayed alive at every meal. We knew (or thought we knew) exactly what they all felt about the state of the world. Winston was fiercely anti-Munich, but had been unable to do anything about it, and on Spain—the sorest point at that terrible moment—he was as bad as the others. Maxine had been quite simply reactionary on every point. She had been bored and irritated by our activity. She thought it altogether wrong of Dinah to take part in whatever I chose to do, and she had an intolerant incomprehension of what she called "Bolshevik" ideas, by which she meant almost anything that referred to the condition of the generality of mankind. This was what we faced—after Spain and Czechoslovakia, when, in a way, the limit of endurance had already been reached.

There were surprises in store. First of all, Mr. Churchill was extremely cordial. When we came down to lunch on the first day (it was also his first day) he took Dinah's hand and held it firmly. "My dear," he said in an undertone, not heard by Maxine, "I am so glad we're all in the same lobby now. We're all together now." I puzzled afterward over what he meant; I realized the strength of his opposition to Munich, but the rest . . . ? Spain and Russia too? As time went on and we had very long political conversations it became clear that he did mean it. He had completed his long journey from the satisfied Toryism of 1935 and he was ready now to mourn Spain if he could not save it; he wished, sincerely and strongly, for an alliance with Russia. While we were all there at Cannes two articles of his appeared in the *Daily Telegraph*, showing the depth of the change that had taken place in him after

Munich. He deplored the coming victory of Franco in Spain, pointed out the illusions and misconceptions which had made "well-to-do society" so prejudiced in Franco's favor, and saw with foreboding what this might mean for England. Very soon—in a few days—he was to write an eloquent plea, in the same newspaper, for an alliance with the Soviet Union.

It took me some days to get used to Mr. Churchill's new frame of mind and to realize that now, after all, there was more to unite than to divide us. In the main consideration, the desperate danger to all free or freedom-aiming institutions, we were in agreement. This made it possible to talk with him as never before. I think I knew more about Spain than he did, and I could not follow him in his allotment of responsibility to this man or that (Azaña in particular), but even on this question he had moved very far in a few months. I talked to him about Don Juan Negrin, with whom he has always had some points of temperamental resemblance; he seemed well disposed toward the Republican Prime Minister who was then facing the swift, disastrous end of the war. On the whole vista of Germany's plans, preparations and strategical possibilities, Mr. Churchill, as always, saw clearly and spoke in the most downright language. His solemnity broke down into good humor and kindly wit again and again; as always, his emotions were near the surface and he switched from grave to gay with mercurial suddenness. He seemed to have genuine feeling for those friends whom I had constantly in mind, the soldiers in Spain who were fighting for us all. When the news grew worse his sympathy was, I think, sincere, unforced, tinged with a personal regret—perhaps a little with remorse. He had not taken position early enough and he knew it; something might have been done earlier, but now it was far too late. Franco's armies, supported in great strength by the Italian and German air force, were approaching Tarragona.

An even greater surprise than Mr. Churchill was Lord Beaverbrook. He was at the hotel in Cannes, but we saw him often; he came to dinner and he gave a dinner for us. We met him at the Casino; indeed he was to all intents and purposes a member of the party. He, too, showed sympathy toward the Spanish Republic and it seemed sincere. He told me he had always been pro-Republican from the very beginning of the war. About Munich the story was very different: he had supported the agreement and hailed Neville Chamberlain as a great peacemaker (although not quite, as the *Daily Mail* did, in the words "Prince of Peace"). Now he was having the gravest misgivings, was worried and was suspending judgment, although the conviction was obviously growing on him that dark days might be in store for us all. He obstinately refused to believe that war was near, although I think in his heart of hearts he knew better. A strange and complicated character, it seems to me, he had the queer belief which grows, sometimes, in his kind of journalism, that a thing can be made true by saying it. Up to the brink of war he continued to deny that it could take place, and yet he gave me the feeling, very often, that he was essentially vowed to fight it as strongly as Mr. Churchill himself.

An unusual degree of comprehension made constant the relationship between Mr. Churchill and Lord Beaverbrook. Both were highly intelligent, a quality as rare in their world as in any other; they did not need blueprints and diagrams at every turn. Mr. Churchill was, in addition, eminently cultivated and urbane; Max was as crude and rough (deliberately so) as a newcomer from the plains. I thought he stressed this note a little unnecessarily now and then, but I suppose it was only the natural emphasis of a stranger in the life he had adopted. They had been friends for years, and had fought the General Strike (1926) together—a thing which did not endear either of them to me—as well as other battles old and new. Now Mr. Churchill was far in advance and tugging hard. In the years to come he was to pull them all with him, Max included; but just then (January, 1939) he was still "out," and it was within the bounds of reason and sense for Lord Beaverbrook to patronize him a little bit, just to mark the difference between a powerful newspaper owner and an ex-cabinet minister.

This amused me, and I have often thought of it since. Both men would deny it; indeed I doubt if either was conscious of it at the time, although to the observer it was evident enough. Nobody could ever successfully condescend to Mr. Churchill because he was incapable of noticing it, but as near as was possible under the circumstances, Lord Beaverbrook condescended.

On the night when Tarragona fell (January 19, 1939) our party dined at the Windsors' house at Antibes. The fall of Tarragona was an event which made inevitable the final collapse of the Spanish Republic. Up until then it was possible to hope that some last-minute development might strengthen the remnants of the Republic for further resistance. From then on the further steps—the capture of Barcelona and the conquest of all Catalonia—were predetermined. It was clear that France would do nothing. I had been so much in Spain during the preceding year, and there was so much of the war that had entered my consciousness forever—the trenches over the Ebro; the Lincoln Battalion, billeted in stables; the roar of the German planes and the whining of German shells over the desolate river —that even Cannes with all its soft glitter and scent could not drive out the thought of it, even for an hour. I was anxious to get away, to go back to Barcelona, where, indeed, I did go about a week later.

The Windsors' dinner was very grand, and the guests consisted of assorted notables from up and down the coast, mostly English people of high rank who were holidaying in the South. My Lords Rothermere and Beaverbrook had been prevented from attending by colds. (Lord Beaverbrook's cold did not prevent his attendance at the Casino, where we saw him afterward.) When some of the more overpowering guests had departed, after the long and stately meal in the white-and-gold dining room, the Duke of Windsor and Mr. Churchill settled down to a prolonged argument with the rest of the party listening in silence. The Duke had read with amazement Mr. Churchill's recent articles on Spain and his newest one (out that day, I believe) in which he appealed for an alliance with Soviet Russia. "You of all people, Winston," was the gist of his argument, "cannot wish to make friends of these murderers and thieves." At one point Mr. Churchill, who was defending his point of view stubbornly and with undiplomatic vigor, said: "Sir, I would make a friend of the devil himself, if it would save England." It resulted plainly from the statements on the two sides that the self-willed, pleasure-loving little Prince, filled to the fingertips with royal prejudice, had no conception of the deadly danger to England involved in his dalliance with Hitler, while Mr. Churchill, disliking the Bolshevik theory and practice as much as ever, was so thoroughly aware of England's peril that he would seek the alliance of Stalin at once. We sat by the fireplace, Mr. Churchill frowning with intentness at the floor in front of him, mincing no words, reminding H.R.H. of the British constitution on occasion—"when our kings are in conflict with our constitution, we change our kings,"

he said—and declaring flatly that the nation stood in the
gravest danger of its long history. The kilted Duke in his
Stuart tartan sat on the edge of the sofa, eagerly interrupting whenever he could, contesting every point, but
receiving—in terms of the utmost politeness so far as the
words went—an object lesson in political wisdom and public spirit. The rest of us sat fixed in silence; there was
something dramatically final, irrevocable about this dispute. At one point (the subject was Spain) the Duke
turned on me and said point blank: "Perhaps you would
be good enough to give us the Communist point of view."
I do not remember what I replied, but it was something
very brief and so downright that I was not asked to speak
again. The party came to an end late, and Dinah and I
repaired to the Casino with Mr. Churchill. I was very
nervous and distraught over Tarragona, the revulsion
against Cannes, the incredible evening at the Windsors';
when we came into the bar of the Casino we met the
Grand Duke Dmitri of Russia. Anxious to talk about something that had nothing to do with Cannes, I asked him if
he had read his cousin Vladimir's statement on the Ukrainian and other questions. (Vladimir was the "Tsar of all
the Russias" who had just succeeded to the phantom throne
on the death of his father Cyril, and had issued a comprehensive statement in which there was some vague hint of
Ukrainian separatism.) I particularly wanted to know if
the statement was meant to encourage any plans or ideas
of Hitler's. The Grand Duke burst into a patriotic monologue in which it appeared that no power on land or sea,
not Hitler and not God himself, could ever dismember the
holy soil of Mother Russia; Ukrainia was an inseparable
part of Russia, whatever the régime; no possible development in Europe could alter the unity of Russia. Suddenly
becoming aware that the strength of his feeling might

surprise a stranger, he leaned across the table and said with great earnestness:

"But, please note this, I am not a Bolshevik."

The whole thing degenerated into sheer fantasy from then on. I played at the tables and lost consistently; Dinah, having adjourned to the dancing room with a party, got sleepy and went home; when the evening was over I had my hired car (hired for the duration of our visit to Cannes) and a mountain of debt to show for my efforts. Mr. Churchill, displaying great acumen, refused to drive home with me in the hired car. After his taxi had departed I crawled in behind the wheel of my car and set off down the Croisette. When I woke up an hour or so later I was being carried into the Château de l'Horizon, bloody and bruised. Mr. Churchill had waited up for me and was calling all the doctors within reach. It seems that I had gone to sleep over the wheel, and the hired car smashed head-on into a stone wall at the end of the Croisette. The car was demolished. If Mr. Churchill had come along with me he would have been killed.

That was the end of my acquaintance with Cannes, with Maxine and with her world. Two days later we returned to Paris; in a week I was in Spain, sleeping in ditches and on floors again, watching the heart-breaking retreat of the Republic; before long we had said farewell to Europe (we thought quite possibly forever) and were back in America for the duration of the inevitable, the coming war. I knew that I would revisit Europe, but on leaving it that time I felt that I could never live there again. There was finality in all that sequence of events—Munich; the fall of the Spanish Republic; the shameful winter of 1938–1939. These things, as Madame de Sévigné and Marcel Proust would have said, *semblaient me préparer les délices d'un adieu* —seemed to prepare for me the delight of a farewell.

9

The pleasures of privileged-class life during the years immediately preceding the war were, on the whole, uneasily enjoyed. Only by means of subterfuge and social legerdemain was it possible to keep up the pretense of security upon which such societies are based. The thunder was not even far off; it was irrefutably near, and it sometimes required the most obstinate effort to ignore it. An admixture of newcomers from all parts of the world had greatly modified the formula of the privileged and fashionable in Paris, London and Cannes, but along with the newcomers had arrived also an awareness of the outer darkness. After all, in the Victorian and even the Edwardian eras people of the sort I have been describing led relatively sheltered lives; they no longer did in the 1930's. Mr. Winston Churchill's mother records that when she first went to London, and for many years thereafter, no woman she knew dared to dine in a public restaurant. In the 1930's the privileged and fashionable world practically lived in public; private life was, in a manner of speaking, extinct; there were few if any secrets; a ravening vulgarity had engulfed all the old-fashioned reserves, habits, standards and prejudices. The fashionable woman of 1939 was more cultivated, or at least more cosmopolitan, than her grandmother (supposing her to be one of those who had grandmothers). She knew Paris, Venice and Salzburg as well as London, and she was able to keep up a lively conversation about books, music, singers, conductors, travel gossip and superficial movements in politics as well as the customary account of the doings among her acquaintance. In her hands, to a very considerable extent, reposed the fate of any venture in culture—the new men tasted oblivion or quick success in accordance with her whims. The sense of power given by this was, like most of the other phenomena of the time, uneasy, insecure, since the standards of judgment were themselves uneasy. The old certainty was gone, and no amount of varnish on the nails, jewels in the hair or paint upon the lips could take its place.

There is a story often told in nineteenth-century memoirs—it occurs also somewhere in Proust—to the effect that the Empress Eugénie and Queen Victoria, attending the new Grand Opéra together on the occasion of the Queen's state visit to Paris, stood to acknowledge the plaudits of the multitude and then sat down side by side in the imperial box. The exquisite Eugénie, gleaming with her own luscious Spanish beauty and a perfection of Paris jewels and dress, turned to see if the chair was behind her before she sat; the dumpy, stolid but regal Victoria sat down without looking. Something like poor Eugénie's fundamental insecurity had developed with time among the privileged of the 1930's; they were never altogether sure the chair would be there. Rightly (for the time was short) they savored every excellence in their own range, pursued pleasure and tried to diversify experience, but in many of them there was a pervading sense of the transience of these things, a haunting suspicion that one day more might see the downfall of the familiar, the ruinous upsurging riot of the unknown.

For not one orchid produced by the hothouse of Europe either at Salzburg or Cannes was wholly without relation to the rest of life. There were too many ways in which life intruded into the most defended drawing room—by the newspaper, by the radio, by the casual talk of casual comers. Hitler, raging down the winds of the world; a far-off story of cruel disaster in China; some tale of injustice and suffering from Rome, from Vienna; the argument of one serious guest who would not yield; in so many different ways the world-struggle could be, and was, brought into the scented center of the company, to writhe there repulsively until a concerted effort at triviality should hide it again from view. Even the most unrivaled nitwit—even Lady C.—could not be unaware that a momentous opposition of forces was taking shape month by month through those years, engaging the energies of all the best part of humanity, and that the mighty conflict to which all led would determine the shape of our destiny for centuries. The obscure but persistent consciousness of gathering doom showed itself first of all in a determination to get the most out of the moment (*"Après nous le déluge!"*) and afterward in a sort of gnawing uncertainty about the personal future. ("God knows where I'll be this time next year!") It was not supported or dignified by any real knowledge of the situation in Europe or Asia. Even the names of the political leaders (except the most notorious) were unknown to the silken anxieties of Cannes. The main events of the process since 1933 had been but imperfectly registered on the coarse membrane of the fashionable mind, and each new happening occurred without visible ancestry or progeny, a sheer accident, a glaring announcement in headlines, cut off from all its significance for the one day of its life—and forgotten, of course, before the passage of a week. All the great events of the Spanish Civil War had been of this kind, headline dramas uprooted for a day's attention and then forgotten. The vast significance of that struggle, the most decisive of a decade, passed unseen. In the years during which I saw, in many places and at various times, the kind of privileged persons known to me most characteristically at Salzburg and Cannes, the only one I ever knew who seemed fully to understand the accumulating weight and power of Fascism, the inevita-

bility of the war and the disastrous slowness of psychological mobilization on our side was—perhaps inevitably—Mr.
Winston Churchill. No other political figure of importance
in either England or France dared to say, and very few
even wished to say, that the monster of Fascism was un-
appeasable, that it could only be destroyed. The whole
tendency of what passed for thought among the upper
classes was toward deep distrust of the Left, a fear of
revolution so pervasive that it colored all responses and,
objectively speaking, played into the hands of the Fascist
conspiracy with as much effect as if the French and British
oligarchies had actually been its tools. The influence of
society women and drones upon the political climate of
these oligarchies is well known; never was it more keenly
felt than during the Munich period. The women and the
drones, however little they knew of the case, were invari-
ably favorable toward anything that would seem to post-
pone a drastic decision: they were appeasers by nature,
by temperament. As Mr. Churchill himself pointed out in
one of his belated articles on the Spanish Republic, a fear
of Communism had made "well-to-do society" practically
unanimous in its feeling about the Spanish War. If it was
to go wrong, so deeply and tragically wrong, in that most
important opening phase of the struggle, how was it to
right itself quickly enough to meet its fate with some
decorum, some trace of the dignity due to its historical
origins? That was, essentially, the only class question that
still signified much to those among the children of the
oligarchy (a few: a handful) who understood the course
of events.

Mostly, and perhaps, in view of what was coming,
rightly and reasonably, the privileged order was gathering
rosebuds. Whatever your pleasure, you knew or assumed
it to be brief; you savored its brevity and passed on. There

used to be at Salzburg a French lady known to most of us as *la Veuve de Mozart*. She was the most indomitable, passionate and unreasonable of the votaries of Mozart, played his slightest *Albumblatt* at the piano or spinet with incommunicable ecstasy, was an authority on what he had said or written from the age of two, and pursued the great interpreters of the Master from one country to another with unsurpassable zeal. The Widow Mozart was, of course, rich; she could not have affixed such an expensive widow-hood to her mast if she had not been; and she had con-quered a very secure position in the cultivated society of Paris and indeed all Europe by means of this enthusiasm. It was a position not many women would have envied, for she was the subject of great laughter; and yet, as she probably never knew it, that mattered little; she was the *Veuve Mozart*, the only authentic one of the twentieth century, acknowledged as such by everybody from Tos-canini and the King to the least important E-flat clarinet player in the Vienna orchestra. The Widow had, by the era of Munich, so accentuated and stylized her passionate obsession that she was no longer capable of listening to any music not by Mozart, and I have actually sat and watched the magic moment come and go. At a concert conducted by Bruno Walter she sat forward in her box, smiling brilliantly beneath her great picture hat while he led the orchestra through the G-minor symphony. Some-times she nodded slightly when his version particularly pleased her; at other times she made almost imperceptible gestures with her glittering fingers. At the conclusion of this symphony she applauded with immense authority and obviously sincere enthusiasm. Then, as the orchestra began a superb reading of Beethoven's *Eroica*, the Widow Mo-zart sank back into her chair, indifferent, bored, elegantly waiting; it was as clear as if she had announced it through a megaphone that she only endured Beethoven through politeness—*il fallait attendre, vous savez, ma chère, à cause de notre pauvre Walter.* . . .

The Widow's fever, her exclusion of all that did not belong to it, the absurd and baroque self-consciousness of her fixation in plain view of what Paris called "all the world" (which was, in sober fact, such a tiny part of the world) constituted, at the end of the 1930's, an exemplary manifestation we shall not soon forget. For this poor world was soon to vanish forever—where, indeed, is the Widow now?—and the childlike intensity with which it tried to dispel all nightmares by clinging to the one all-absorbing game was like the defenses of those who do not wish to die. Mozart or backgammon, they came to the same thing: in both cases the cold and the dark were excluded for a while, and there was no hint of the toil and sweat of men in field or factory, those who go down in mines or rivet the stout hulls of ships or lay stone firmly upon stone. Work and sorrow, the shame of men and their suffering, their meanness and the sudden unknowing and unknowable glint of golden light upon their tortured dirt, all these, like the weather were shut out of the room. It was an imposing room, with great nodding lilies in it, painted green or blue or pink at their heart's core; kings looked from silver frames; there was a lemur hanging by its tail from the top of the long glass door opening to the terrace and the blue gulf; the piano was out of tune and the marble was false, but the company—ah, the company!—was not bad. There they go on their way, one by one and two by two, through the false marble door into the darkness of the night, trailing behind them the fabrics and scents and colors of a time that will not come again, that would never have come at all if the mind of man had known how to keep pace with his appetites, his capacity for amassing treasure, his selfishness or his fear. Those who tarry are not those who painted the lily, placed silver about the king or esteemed the monkey; these will do new things with the material at hand or will, perhaps, destroy it utterly. The ghosts, the recent ghosts, were never quite sure enough of their dominion in life to wish it extended, and they will not interfere. Eager and forgetting, those who still tarry will make haste to summon fresh faces out of the sea and the land, plant new feet upon untrodden ways, invite, sanctify and approve—if they can; if there is time; if they are not themselves shown firmly, finally, to the door.

# 2. Notre Dame de Paris

THE SPRING CAME ON SOFTLY, with a gentle radiance that seemed to us especially adjusted to the needs of the time, as if—as indeed happens more often than it is comfortable to think—the weather itself formed part of the human drama. Many said it then and have said it since: the spring of 1940 was one of the loveliest Paris has ever known. The chestnut trees bloomed in profusion, the bright days were favorable to the skin and color of youth, and bad news had not dimmed the spirit or quenched the smiles of our friends, even though it was—as we had learned through bitter years of experience to call it—"Hitler's weather," and we could not rise on any morning without a vague dread of the news it might bring forth. There was no possible doubt that a dawn must come, one day or the next, when the gray rivers of the German flood would begin to roll westward over Holland, Belgium and France: it was in fact for this certainty that I had come back from America; and yet, in the way people have, I think we only half believed the inevitable until it had taken place. No matter how certain an event may be in the inescapable future, even if it is defined by a date, it takes on its validity and displacement in our own minds only after it has been hurled there by sorry fact: thus we are protected in spite of ourselves, and there seems no end to the catastrophes we can survive so long as we affront them without too much prescience (or, indeed, too little).

Thus I remember laughing one day when Henri Bernstein was showing us over his beautiful new theatre at the Ambassadeurs in the Champs-Elysées. "You may as well look at it now," he said with a sigh, "before the Germans come along and bomb it into dust. It has not much longer to live." I thought he took an unduly alarmist view of what was coming—this in spite of the fact that I, too, expected invasion and bombings at any moment. Somehow, the specific house, the exact street, the single life, although forever threatened, never seems to be involved in the great general dangers: it is thus that we say, "All must die in the end," and do not really include ourselves.

So it was with Paris. We talked of Norway from morning to night, speculating, apportioning blame for the disaster, wondering what might have happened if Admiral Darlan, the most admired of the French ministers, had directed the operations as he had wished to do. ("Darlan is the greatest military genius of the century," Bill Bullitt, our Ambassador, was in the habit of declaring with his usual enthusiasm.) The general opinion in Paris was that the English were without military talent, that their naval prowess was largely mythological, that they intended to fight the war exclusively by means of Frenchmen, and that, on the whole, Fate had played a shabby trick in wedding France to such a *compagnon de guerre*. In truth the French mobilization had been complete, and most of the able-bodied Frenchmen not required for other war work were inactive, bored and grumbling members of the vast, underpaid army. England had not yet called up the unmarried men of twenty-six, and her war effort in industry and all other fields was kept to modest dimensions by Mr. Neville Chamberlain's desire to retain "business as usual," with the most tender attention to the exchange value of the pound sterling. These things were widely known in France and contributed to the definitely bad moral cli-

mate in which Daladier, Reynaud and a handful of equally
commonplace men attempted to arouse the spirit of combat and sacrifice.

Meanwhile the restaurants and theatres of Paris were
crowded, the dressmakers and jewelers were doing extremely well, and the hats of the epoch reflected a desire
to greet the spring in a manner worthy of the capital.
Dinah visited Mme Reboux on arrival, and as a result was
able to weather the ensuing storms in some very expert
products of the milliner's art; but she had less luck with
the dressmakers, who were indeed so slow with their work,
owing to the rush of orders, that they had not completed
even so much as one dress before the approach of the German army caused them to shut up shop and flee. I went in
to Cartier's to get a watch repaired and was told that the
season had never been better. The well-to-do French, having no faith in their own government, army or currency,
were putting their money into jewels. Meanwhile the
workers were disgruntled, there was a strong pacifist wing
of the Socialists, led by Paul Faure, and the Communists
had gone underground with a defeatist, Brest-Litovsk
propaganda exuded from their inner core of 1917 mono-
mania. Some fifty Communist deputies had been arrested
or proscribed, but Pierre Laval, of course, representing a
far more dangerous anti-national tendency on the other
extreme, was at liberty to roam about Paris at will. The
wives and dependents of conscripts, the conscripts themselves, the workers in war industry and the ordinary bewildered, overtaxed citizen all alike felt imposed upon,
maltreated or ignored; life had become very difficult for
the largest classes of the population; and there was no hint
of fervor, or of anything approaching fervor, about the
war. These things became evident as soon as one arrived
in France—they came out of the press, the daily experi-

ence of the streets, the conversation of friends and strangers. Mountains of distrust surrounded the policies, ideas, personalities and intentions of the government; of all the things sacrificed in the holocaust at Munich in 1938, the most precious was the trust of the democratic peoples. This had been shaken severely before the time of Munich, but after that awful moment people could feel nothing but a sort of weary disgust about the Chamberlain-Daladier-Bonnet régime. Fantastic stories circulated in Paris after Munich and right on up until the arrival of the Germans, having as their chief burden the financial and other benefits which the *Munichois* were said to have obtained by their manipulations. Georges Bonnet was supposed to have made millions; so were many more unlikely people. Any story, however absurd, would be believed by a Frenchman if it was to the discredit of a member of his government. No matter how many people the nervous, foolish, flighty government threw into jail, there were still millions more who resolutely went on telling the most shameful stories about their own leaders, undermining all confidence and destroying the slightest remaining possibility of a successful resistance to the Germans. The government faced this moral and psychological problem with the same thoroughgoing, cowardly incompetence with which it faced the material problem of supplies and organization: that is, by telling lies. It gave false figures on aircraft production, false figures on the Maginot Line, false data on the conditions of labor in war industry, and false information about the actual strength of the air force, artillery and tanks. In December Daladier was telling the people that the Maginot Line had been completed as far as the North Sea; in May he was deploring the fact that it ended at the Belgian frontier. Paul Reynaud clamored for armored divisions in 1936 and purred with delight at the tank situation in 1939. Unlike the French General Staff officer who, in 1909, exclaimed, "Thank God we have no heavy artillery!" the government and staff of 1939–1940 spent its time saying, "Thank God we have plenty of everything we need!" The people were so abundantly aware of the untruth of such statements that it became impossible for the government to command faith. When a government is no longer capable of telling any truth at all it is on the brink of ceasing to be a government. This stage of degeneration had been reached by the French government even before the German invasion of May 10, 1940, and the military disaster only hastened and made public a bankruptcy which was already complete.

We came into this externally lovely and secretly unhappy Paris, the Paris of May, 1940, from Italy and America. Having left Europe in the spring of 1939 forever, I could not resist the urge to return in the spring of 1940. Dinah and I sailed from New York on an Italian ship (the *Vulcania*) April 6th, and when wireless messages about the German invasion of Norway began to pour in two days later I did not, at first, believe them. It was curious indeed to find one's self in an atmosphere in which everybody either wished ardently for a Hitler victory or conceded despondently that such a victory was inevitable. The workers on this Italian ship—stewards, barmen, crew and all—seemed to me to belong to the second class: that is, they hated the Germans and did not want to see Hitler win, but they had been thoroughly indoctrinated with the idea that the Nazis were invincible. Among the passengers, except for two or three Americans, all were Italian, German, Hungarian or other Fascists. The *Regio Commissario*, the Italian naval officer detailed to this ship—there was one on each merchant marine vessel before the war— even wasted some time trying to convert me, and lent me a book which made me laugh a good deal, about Mussolini. It was written in a very terse, ultra-Latin kind of Italian, and its first paragraph said something like this: "Lenin would have been accounted a great revolutionary if he had not had the misfortune to live in the same century as Mussolini; Hitler would have been the greatest of state-builders if he had not also lived in this time; the Caesar of the age overshadows all others." There were books in the ship's library which amplified this thesis, and before we had been at sea three days I felt—from these and other evidences—that Italy had sunk far into the Fascist morass since I left there at the time of the Ethiopian invasion (1935). When I lived in Italy, although Mussolini and Fascism were supreme, there was too much common sense among the people for the extreme forms of Fascist nonsense to be forced upon them. After the alliance with Hitler, and above all after the general war was made inevitable at Munich in 1938, this style of Caesarean false-heroics became the rule, and, as I was to learn in Rome and Florence, the press had been degraded to a level unknown before. At the same time the people, as I learned first on the ship and afterward all through Italy, were more and more apathetic toward these displays of *Romanità*, viewing with sadness and at times with fury the vainglorious posturing of the Duce and his accomplices. Everything that was gentle and urbane in Italian civilization repudiated such buffoonery, and yet, things being as they were, it was all too likely that the sinister buffoon would very soon be leading Italy and the Italian people into the final depths. In New York the preceding winter I had gone down to the New School for Social Research one day to listen to Luis Quintanilla talk about Italian fresco painting. Quintanilla (an old friend of the Spanish war) fired me with the desire to see again those miracles

of grace and beauty that lie strewn across the loveliest of
countries; in a few days I had made the plans for a tourist's spring in Italy, and rather to my astonishment I received the Italian visa. We were going to see pictures in
museums, churches, convents; we were going to lunch in
high places looking down at exquisite valleys; we were
going to listen to the glory of Italian speech in the mouth
of country people and see the sun disappear on the other
side of my blue lake. It seemed to me that these things
might be put out of reach for many years, perhaps forever, by the events that were preparing in Europe. The
meeting of Hitler and Mussolini at the Brenner Pass
(March 19, 1940) bade us make haste; the "phony war"
(Senator Borah's word for it) could not last much longer.

We landed at Genoa and went down to Rome by train
on April 16th. For some reason not apparent, this day and
the one following marked a new high point in warlike tension in Rome. The American ambassador, Mr. William
Phillips, told me there was nothing in the known facts
about troop movements or other dispositions to warrant it,
but that, nevertheless, informed opinion seemed to fear
the immediate entry of Italy into war at Germany's side.
No doubt some remark of Mussolini's, revealing his intentions or the pledges made to Hitler, had been repeated
often and widely enough to produce the psychological
crisis of April 16-17. When it passed without a declaration
of war, the easy optimists who are always in the majority
felt that the crisis was over, that Mussolini was afraid of
the rich and powerful Western empires, that the French
army ("the best army in the world," according to the military experts on our side) had weighed too heavily upon
Italian minds, in short that everything (as usual) was going to be all right. My knowledge of the stupidity and ignorance of our experts warned me that this would be

proved wrong in due course, and the more Italians I talked to the more I realized that they felt themselves condemned fatally, against every desire and instinct, to fight for Hitler against the friendly democratic West.

In the intervals of our sight-seeing we visited a good many Italian acquaintances, most of them technically members of the Fascist party, some really Fascist in mind and spirit. Talk was a little uneasy at first in any circle; afterward, when the ice was broken, I found a unanimity of opinion which I have never met anywhere else in the world at a time of crisis. Every Italian to whom I spoke between April 16th and May 5th believed that Mussolini was bent upon making war at Hitler's side, and every Italian further believed that this would mean ruin for Italy, disaster for the world and a horrible misrepresentation of the Italian spirit. It seemed to make no difference whether the person speaking was an anti-Fascist who had suffered greatly for opposition to the régime, or a Fascist dignitary of high rank, the opinion was identical. The Italians were resolutely opposed to war for Nazi Germany against their traditional friends in Europe. This emerged clearly—as clearly as the other certainty, that war *would* come by Mussolini's will and they could not prevent it.

Once we were lunching with a high military official in whose house no openly anti-Fascist or anti-Mussolini words could be pronounced. Conversation turned upon other things—the audiences given by the new Pope, for example; the novels of Grazia Deledda; the concluding performances of the season at the Royal Opera. As we were leaving the house a Fascist official, a Roman aristocrat who spoke fluent English, asked us if we had seen the gardens of the Villa Celimontana on the Caelian Hill. We had not; he undertook to show them to us. As we walked through the long, shaded walks to the *belvedere* whence could be seen the departed splendor of Caracalla, this moody young man burst forth into passionate speech. He knew that Mussolini was determined upon war and he knew that Italians would never fight it. He felt that they would desert, mutiny and lay down their arms; he abominated the Germans and experienced the strong pull of cultural unity with France and England; he longed for escape from the oppressive conditions of life in Rome. I watched him through this outbreak and mused. He wore the Fascist party badge, of course, as well as a decoration; he was of some position in Rome; his risk in talking thus, if he had been overheard, was considerable. Neither Dinah nor I had ever seen him before. He was not "sounding us out," acting as *agent provocateur*, or otherwise attempting to explore my own opinions, for these had been a matter of public record for years past, and the Italian secret police had only to look the matter up in the files. It must, therefore, be the sincere outpouring of a tortured Italian spirit —the desire of a suffering man to release his pent-up emotion in words that would be understood. I heard of him long afterward by a devious route, after Italy had entered the war, and he was still there: still serving Mussolini and the Fascist war, that is, in a position of some consequence, hating it morning, noon and night.

And indeed, although I had gone to Italy on what was supposed to be a tourist's mission, with churches and museums as my main objectives, it was impossible to escape the daily manifestation of Italian hatred of Mussolini, dread of war and despair over the future. When I had known Italy, between 1922 and 1935, Mussolini had always had wide popularity as a person. Minorities had detested him, but the unthinking masses, seduced by his heroic language and instinct for show, lavished on him the kind of adulation that comes so easily so long as it costs nothing. The popular demonstrations over Mussolini in the early years of Fascism were by no means all staged by the Fascist groups; they involved great non-political layers of the population. The Piazza Venezia in Rome afterward became a sort of theatre in which a chosen throng went through certain well-known rites of leader-worship, but up to the moment when Fascist war became certain (the Munich Agreement, September 29, 1938) even these performances were not wholly without a base among the people. Now all that seemed to have changed. I never heard one good word for Mussolini during those weeks in Italy, and I heard many Fascists say (under their breaths) that they thought the Duce had gone mad. One of the most extraordinary of these incidents took place in the basement bar of the Hotel Excelsior, filled with Fascist spies and German officers in uniform from the various Nazi missions. A celebrated Italian Fascist writer who had fought for Mussolini and Hitler in Spain came into the bar where Dinah and I were sitting with Nancy and Herbert Matthews (Matthews of the *New York Times,* our friend of the Spanish war, now stationed in Rome). He knew Herbert and stopped to speak to us.

"The Duce said today: 'Germany is not only winning, but is over-winning,' " this writer told us.* "He said: 'The historic moment will not pass twice. We must seize our opportunity or forever lose our place in history.' "

The writer's face was gloomy, his voice filled with emotion. If I could use his name it would be recognized as that of a man who had formulated some of the socialist or pseudo-socialist ideals of Fascism: that is, he had always regarded Fascism as a progressive social movement, not as an engine of reaction. His voice and manner now were

---

* In Italian: *non solamente vince, ma stravince.* It is a strong word (*stravince*) which I had not heard before.

those of extreme depression. He obviously felt that Mussolini had determined upon the fatal adventure, and the whole thing made him tense with premonitions of evil. I wondered how he could dare speak like this in a crowded bar. Perhaps sheer unhappiness over the fate of his country had made him reckless. In any case, one thing I know: he was exiled to the islands not more than three weeks later, actually before Italy had been thrust into the war. Sometimes I wondered if his indiscretions in the Excelsior bar were the cause of this—or whether, on the other hand, they were only minor symptoms of the despair caused by some graver, some irreparable crime, such as failure to admire the Duce's prowess as a horseman.

There were many of the American press colleagues in Rome just then—Herbert Matthews, John Whittaker and Don Minifie among them—and we had no lack of company during the intervals of our sight-seeing. Some of these colleagues expected war any moment, and others (notably Minifie) were convinced that it would never come. Anne O'Hare McCormick, the only American journalist who had been on both sides in the conflict, had lately come from Paris and regaled us with stories of the "phony war" as it seemed in the capitals that had given it birth. One day I shall remember for a long time: we drove up to Lago di Nemi and looked at the Roman galleys in the new museum there, stretched in the sun at Rocca di Papa, lunched toothsomely at Castelgandolfo high above the Alban lake, and stopped to walk and look a little at the plain from Frascati on our way home again. Anne and her husband, the Matthews ménage and ourselves constituted the company on this excursion, which, thanks to the weather, was such a farewell to the Roman hill country as we might have dreamed. On another day of matchless Roman sunlight we lunched on the Pincio and talked of war while the honey-colored walls and domes and spires beneath us changed, softened and grew shadowy with the changing light. That view, that justly celebrated view, was never more lovely to me than this spring when it was impregnated with suggestions of a world divided, veiled and half-lost by our mortal struggle. True, the walls of Rome looked permanent enough in the golden light, like all those houses and roofs in the early Corot pictures, but it was impossible not to think of them as menaced by the same fate that hung above us all, and, at the same time, whether menaced, transient or eternal, as being removed by inexorable circumstance from the zones to which I, at any rate, might have access during the coming years. Rome, too, must go the way of Vienna, Salzburg and Munich, Venice and Nürnberg, into the dark realm of the enemy, on the other side of a valley filled with blood: when were we to emerge, and how, and which among us, after time and sorrow?

When our stay in Rome was over we took a car with the Minifies and drove through the Tuscan hills to Florence. Most of the time the spring rain never ceased, and we saw all our churches and museums in a dim religious light. Orvieto, Perugia, Assisi, Arezzo, Siena, San Gimignano—they succeeded each other like a pageant of the Church's splendor and misery, the pinched faces of a cold and hungry people against pink marble temples and golden thrones. The haunted vaults of Assisi made some extra claim to spirituality, but we arrived in Siena on St. Catherine's Day and were instantly involved in Fascist parades, brass bands and glittering prelates. There were so many dignitaries from all over Italy that the hotel was crowded, and the parades were so incessant in the street that it was difficult to move about. It really was an extraordinary sight: the Cardinal Archbishop of Florence was escorted into the

city by a Fascist guard, with blaring trumpets and so
many uniformed high officials that it seemed a thoroughly
secular affair. We were in the Cathedral when the Cardinal Archbishop made his triumphal exit, blessing the pros-
trate throng, and there were times when we were almost
deafened by the cheering. I think Santa Caterina da Siena,
who was at least a good poet, would have found some of
the official celebration both wearisome and in bad taste.
The popular festivities, those which genuinely came from
the heart of the people and sometimes led to excesses,
have been discouraged in recent years in favor of this
Fascist show.

We were in a vein of shows, for when we drove into
Florence it was only to find ourselves again entangled in
police lines and ceremonies: the King of Italy, so called,
was coming to open the Florentine music festival (the
Maggio Fiorentino). This King, one of the most illusory
of modern times, had often been the focus of upper-class
hope for salvation from Fascism and was so again in 1940
as vainly as in other days, for he was worth nothing at all.
Vittorio Emmanuele III had broken his oath to the Constitution in 1922 when he admitted Mussolini to power; that
act supplied the key to all his acts for twenty years. In
successive crises, when Italians of the upper and conservative classes found themselves being pulled headlong into
courses which they regarded as disastrous—or, more simply, when they found themselves personally in disfavor
with the Fascist régime—they tended to pin their hopes
either to Vittorio Emmanuele III or to his absurd and
pompous son, the Prince of Piedmont. During this very
time I had young officers of the aristocratic cavalry regiments tell me they would never go to war save on the
King's orders. "Our King," they said proudly, "can command us. Nobody else can." They seemed by this to indi-

cate a belief that Vittorio Emmanuele III possessed courage or power of will sufficient to defy Mussolini—which was, of course, not the case. The fierce and stupid little King, his strapping big Slav shepherdess wife, the slim, foppish Prince—these were what was left of the pride of Savoy, and it was not enough. As a matter of fact, the circumstance was highly useful to Mussolini: so long as the discontented upper classes (some of whom possessed both energy and intelligence) had no better rallying point than this, no genuine trouble was to be expected from them.

The Maggio Fiorentino, once the King had removed his blight from it, proved to be a carefully prepared musical season of considerable merit, and the galleries and churches by day were no less overwhelming than of old. Such Italian acquaintance as we had in Florence seemed of the same turn of mind as everybody we had met in Rome—fiercely, passionately opposed to the impending war; bitterly antagonistic to the Germans; inclined to think that Mussolini had gone mad. Some were old friends, some new; it seemed to make little difference. Up in the hills—"crowded with culture," Browning rightly said—there were still a number of the English resident families; we visited their villas, looked at their pictures and gardens, drank their tea and wondered why in the name of everything sensible were they still in Italy. In due course it dawned upon me that most of these people—at any rate the older ones—were made blind and deaf by the sheer weight of their possessions. It was not possible to spend twenty or thirty or forty years amassing stuffs, carvings, carpets, sculpture, painting, pots, tapestries, needlepoint, laces, tables, chairs and musical instruments without becoming to some degree oppressed under them, reduced at least to inactivity. The foreigners in the hills above Florence looked at their possessions, remembered their thirty or forty years of peace, sighed and said: "Of course it'll all blow over. The Italians will never fight for Germany."

In Florence, as in Rome, I was sometimes made very anxious over the behavior of people who insisted on showing their opinions. One young friend, whose mother was an American, could scarcely be restrained from insulting Fascist party officials in a restaurant; another spoke loudly against the party one night at the Opera. There were no Germans here to be cold-shouldered as Rome cold-shouldered the Nazi official missions, but there were Italian party chiefs to be stared at and ridiculed. On the whole I think I saw more of this kind of thing during those few weeks in April and early May, 1940, than at any other time I spent in Italy between the Fascist *coup d'état* (1922) and the Ethiopian war (1935).

Our Florentine sight-seeing over, we took the train for Venice and two melancholy days there among the dripping palaces. We were for Paris, and quickly, cutting our Italian spring short because of the news from Norway. I found it impossible to believe that the British had done quite as badly in Norway as the Italian papers said, and although the accounts grew more circumstantial every day, I was anxious to get to Paris and find out what really had happened. I wanted only to spend one last day among my friends, the peasants and fishermen of a village on Lago Maggiore where I had lived and worked for the best part of three years. We stopped at Stresa, crossed the lake in a motorboat on a dazzling day, and spent some hours talking to them all for—perhaps—the last time. They differed little from the aristocrats of Rome and Florence so far as the impending war was concerned. They hated it with all their souls. They had stories, proverbs, sour and bitter as swill, about the Fascists and the Nazis; they were less able to laugh than before, for since I had last seen them there had been campaigns in Ethiopia and Spain, and many of the village boys had gone for ever; but they could still make up a story with a point to it.

"We'll desert, we'll lay down our arms, we'll surrender," they told me in one way or in another. "Nobody can force us to fight for the Germans."

It was the testimony of old friends and new, the unanimous evidence of everybody I met in Italy, that caused me to broadcast to America on the night of Italy's declaration of war (June 10, 1940) some suggestion of what would happen. I said they would lay down their arms in great numbers whenever they got the chance, and that desertion and sabotage would play such a rôle as seldom before in war; for, said I, they were being compelled by their enemies to fight against their friends. This version of the matter, although it drew many sharp protests at the time, was abundantly supported by later events and indeed grew up into a truism within the year—such a truism that it even reached the ears of the military experts.

2

So we came to Paris, anxious about the news of Norway, and found ourselves in the fog of the "phony war." Everything the Italians had said in their press about Norway had been true. It was rather a shock to discover this, because I had systematically discounted a third of everything I read in the Fascist papers (so did the Italians, out of long habit). To find the German High Command so accurate in its communiqués was bad, but to review the situation revealed by those communiqués was still worse. The Norwegian campaign had been light-heartedly undertaken by the British without sufficient preparation and with no remote idea, apparently, of what the enemy could or would do. The Nazi willingness to sacrifice life, ships or any other commodity for the main purpose of gaining an objective was shown for the first time in its true colors in Norway; so also were revealed the new techniques of the Fifth Column, the various ruses and stratagems of a foe without scruple. The Luftwaffe was revealed as a most formidable instrument of war, and the true shortcomings of the R.A.F. were made to seem worse by an unwillingness to sacrifice first-class machines and pilots in numbers. The most startling thing, probably, to all on our side of the struggle, was the speed with which the German victories were accomplished. Only a few days seemed enough for the seizure of the essential points in a plan of campaign: the rest followed swiftly, inevitably, in good order.

Worse still (the worst of all) was that the French betrayed a sort of idiotic satisfaction in England's discomfiture. No sensible Frenchman could fail to see that the campaign had been a disaster and that the future was very dark; and yet even the most sensible Frenchman seemed to take pleasure in saying that France could have managed things better. In the salons, cafés and streets of Paris, in the newspapers and in the revue theatres, you could catch echoes of a sinister cackling, the *Schadenfreude* of a bad ally who compensated for his own inadequacies by dwelling upon those of his friend. This in the midst of the pervading distrust and disquiet on the part of French people with respect to their own government was ominous indeed; it suggested that the hour of attack would find many soft spots here. Herbert Spencer observes in his *Principles of Sociology* that "militant societies must have a patriotism which regards the triumph of their society as the supreme end of action; they must possess the loyalty whence flows obedience to authority—

and, that they may be obedient, they must have abundant faith." By no part of this definition did the French in 1940 qualify as a militant society. Technical proficiency on the part of a general staff or specially trained bodies of different sorts could never take the place of those qualities which, under given conditions of social faith and coherence, pervade the whole national structure and produce the varying phenomena of Shintoist Japan, Nazi Germany and Soviet Russia, all of whom could satisfy Spencer's definition of a militant society in spite of enormous differences in their organization. Britain in the Napoleonic Era was "a militant society" in Spencer's sense, although not a military one; the United States tended to fulfil the conditions in 1861–1865; but there was no denying that democracies, by and large, found it difficult to weld all loyalties and faiths into one. It was in the very essence of democracy to permit a limitless range of belief, and when the crisis of existence arose, this very freedom which was the treasure to be defended made the defense almost impossible. Frenchmen did not regard "the triumph of their society as the supreme end of action"; many of them thought a better society could be evolved out of defeat. This was the point of view of many of the bewildered and floundering Communists, who, after the Nazi-Soviet Pact of August, 1939, fell back upon the example of Brest-Litovsk as one that promised a chance to seize the power. Something not dissimilar drifted through the Catholic and monarchist fantasies of such men as Weygand and (presumably) Pétain, who found "sacrifice and suffering" to be purifying forces, and thought to make an authoritarian, religious and disciplined France out of the catastrophe. At both extremes of the social system there was thought to be more hope in defeat than in victory. (Both would deny it now, but their printed record from the outbreak of war until the defeat gives them the lie.) The point of view of avowed pro-Fascist groups was something else again, and, until the actual German victory, it was not much pressed upon public attention, although it never ceased to exist and to find words in private. As for loyalty and faith, they cannot be said to have flourished on any scale in any French social or political group—and, it must be conceded, with some reason. How could an intelligent man have loyalty to or faith in a government of which Georges Bonnet was an important member? The French have as high a level of general intelligence as any people in existence— a higher, indeed, than most—and they were not to be led along blindly by men and forces they had thoroughly experienced and knew to be bad. A clean sweep was impossible with the parliamentary alignment what it was. There were nineteen parties, and even their own members could not define the differences between them. Léon Blum, head of the largest parliamentary party (the Socialists) remained out of office with the best of his men, but supported the reshuffled and patched-up cabinet of Daladier-Reynaud-Bonnet for the sake of the war effort. Paul Reynaud had emerged as the nearest thing to new blood in the whole business, and at last became Prime Minister (March 21, 1940), but had been obliged to accept Daladier as Minister of War. According to all accounts, he had picked his fellow-ministers purely on the basis of the votes they could bring him for a majority—the normal principle of parliamentary responsibility, it is true, but one which Reynaud had specifically rejected during his years as a rising star out of office. My friends told me he had put X. into the Colonies and Y. into Finance and O. into the Navy without the slightest attention to their aptitudes or abilities. It was a sort of electoral lottery, and Paul Reynaud only disappointed more than others because he had for so long opposed that kind of thing. He had been the man of energy, the man for new solutions, innovations, original ideas; but once in office he did exactly as all the rest did.

The cabinet he had formed six weeks before our arrival in France was the one hundred and seventh in the history of the Third Republic. In not quite seventy years, from Gambetta to Reynaud, the French democracy had run through enough governments to supply a more equable state for several centuries. There had been times when the slightest whim, a quarrel between women, a card game or an unavowable private pique, had been quite enough to overthrow a government. The principle of parliamentary responsibility had been made ridiculous and all but un-workable by the fragmentation of the parties, which, instead of representing broad tendencies or ideas in the social and political struggle, had come to be groups around a single leader. On the Left the parties (Socialist and Communist at the extreme left, Radical Socialist toward the center) had kept their ideological coherence and con-sequently a larger number of votes, but from there on to the extreme Right, where coherency appeared again among the Royalists, there was nothing but a confusion of frac-tions. Even the three great parties of the Left were unable to agree among themselves save for the first min-istry of Léon Blum (June, 1936–June, 1937), a year of conscientious but belated reform which was blamed by the other parties for every misfortune of the French Re-public, including Cécile Sorel's double chins and the rise of Adolf Hitler. Under the two Chautemps ministries (June 23, 1937–January 18, 1938, and January 18, 1938–March 15, 1938) the pace of social reform was slowed down and finally stopped, to make room for the return of Daladier (April 11, 1938–March 21, 1940) and Munich.

The people knew Daladier and did not know Reynaud.

That was a grave disadvantage for the new man and helped make it impossible to disembark Daladier at once, as logic and necessity would have demanded. To keep the co-artisan of Munich in office as Minister of War was a piece of obvious nonsense, and Reynaud only yielded to it, it seems, on the theory that he could still further undermine Daladier in the course of time and get rid of him without endangering the life of the government. This was, in fact, done, and, unless I was misinformed, Reynaud had prepared a new cabinet to present to the Chamber on Monday, May 13th—except that, of course, Hitler forestalled him by invading the West on the preceding Friday.

Daladier, a dirty man with a cigarette stuck to his lower lip, stinking of absinthe, talking with a rough Marseillais accent, pleased the French people in general more than did Reynaud, a man of small stature who dressed a little too neatly and spoke with too much precision. There was, of course, no real loyalty to either of them and no faith in their courses of action. How could there be? Daladier had been untrue to his electoral promises over and over again, had hesitated at all the moments of great crisis, had all but wrecked the state in 1934, had performed the fatal immolation at Munich in 1938; no more unimpressive figure has come forward to perform the mean and sorry deeds of history since the barber of Louis XI. He had a certain southern eloquence, particularly over the air when he could not be seen, and had long since proved his ability to squirm into and out of difficulties in the corridors of the Chamber of Deputies, but beyond these rather low aptitudes he had shown no special ability, no genuine qualification for his high office. Reynaud, by contrast, had given evidence of originality and depth of feeling, had shown very considerable energy in his administrative work, had a real knowledge of the world—having circumnavigated it

three times—and understood something about the historical and military position. As long ago as 1935 he had
submitted a project to the military authorities, calling for
the creation of shock forces or a *corps de manœuvre* based
upon the motorized column and the airplane. His military
adviser, Charles de Gaulle, had imbued him with ideas
which became commonplace after the spring of 1940 but
were nowhere accepted in the Western world before that
time—the ideas which, developed on a very large scale by
the Germans, were to give this war its primary character
on land. De Gaulle's book, *Vers une armée de métier*
(1934), had attacked all notions of war by defense alone,
advocated the creation of entirely mechanized striking
columns to work in conjunction with airplanes, extolled
quality as compared to quantity, and proposed the utili-
zation of all available modern techniques in a professionalized army altogether unlike the vast "citizen army" of
French conscription. De Gaulle's ideas fell on hospitable
ground in Germany and had some influence in Russia, but
they seem to have horrified the French General Staff and
made no impression at all on French politicians with the
exception of Reynaud. In this, as in a number of other
matters, Reynaud showed much more sense of reality than
his associates in the Chamber of Deputies. He was able to
see a few plain facts: the population figures, for example,
the relative strengths of France and Germany in the fundamental matter of inhabitants and birth rate. As he
pointed out in a questionnaire for Robert de Saint-Jean in
1936,* the French bourgeoisie, vacillating and bewildered,
had lost all faith in the parliamentary system by which it
had remained in power for a century, and instead of trying to save the régime by adapting it to present circumstances, did nothing but disparage it; the parties of the

* Robert de Saint-Jean: *France Speaking,* pp. 182–189.

Left believed in collective security but would not vote for
military credits, and the parties of the Right voted for military credits but did not believe in collective security,
whereas both were necessary; France's army, built on the
law of 1927, was an army for defense only and did not
meet the necessities of the situation a decade later; France
needed a mechanized shock corps (the *"armée de métier"*
of De Gaulle) and quantities of modern tanks and guns.

This sort of statement, like a jet of icy water, may have
brought a number of confused Frenchmen to their senses.
It did not constitute a program upon which anybody could
build much political popularity, and as a matter of fact
Reynaud's isolation was his greatest weakness. He had
no party or group of parties behind him, and consequently
had to beg, bargain and cajole in order to amass a majority.
It appears that the parties only trusted him with the
supreme power on the specific promise that he would not
undertake an offensive against Germany—at least that is
a story believed in Paris in the spring of 1940—and M de
Saint-Jean tells us that the idea of attacking Germany was
what the deputies and politicians called *"l'irréparable."*
They were afraid that Reynaud might commit *"l'irréparable,"* and grateful to him when, after a few weeks in
power, he had done nothing decisive. Without doubt there
subsisted enough of the Munich frame of mind to encourage the hope that somehow France might get a peace
without traversing any period of genuine war. This may
seem tragically absurd, but the whole thing had been
muddled in French minds by Russia's war on Finland that
winter, and the Laval-De Monzie point of view, according
to which Hitler's only real enemy was Russia, combined
with the winter's events to suggest that Germany might
perpetuate the Munich arrangements by making peace in
the West and war in the East. So far as most of the French

politicians were concerned, Hitler could have done this at any time he chose up to the moment of the invasion of France.

On March 28th Reynaud had gone to England—Daladier, on the pretext of a sore foot, did not accompany him —and there signed an agreement never to make a separate peace with Germany. This was the agreement from which Reynaud implored Churchill to release him less than two and a half months later; the French armistice with Germany was made by Pétain's emissaries in violation of it. In a sense Reynaud earned the name of being "England's man," and all the anti-British elements in French political life, from extreme Right to extreme Left, had a stick to beat him with. The fixed conviction of the French that England was "using" France's incomparable army and manpower, that "England would fight to the last Frenchman," that England alone would have no choice but surrender, thus became—by what obscure logic I never understood—so many arguments against Reynaud.

These men, Daladier, Reynaud, Bonnet and all the rest, were enveloped in dense clouds of gossip. By some freak of Fate the last days of the French Republic involved all the absurdities of boudoir politics as it had not been practiced since Louis XIV and Louis XV. The mistresses of these men, plus Mme Georges Bonnet—"Madame soutiens-Georges," she used to be called—and a half dozen other persons who had never been elected to any public office, with their friends and their social environment, played a part of which the public was unaware until the worst had already taken place. Three political ladies of importance were Mme Bonnet, Mme la Marquise de Crussol and Mme la Comtesse de Portes. Odette Bonnet and Jeanne de Crussol and Hélène de Portes: that is how the talk of Paris identified them. They disposed of appointments,

assignments, transfers; they negotiated cabinet changes
between themselves; they received the emissaries of Hitler
and the Comité France-Allemagne even before Munich,
danced attendance upon Ribbentrop during the shameful
period just after Munich, and used their power, so far as
can be determined, in a way which was almost uniformly
bad. As compared to Mme de Pompadour, for example,
these ladies were ignorant and dangerous meddlers; they
had neither the culture nor the patriotism of Louis XV's
marquise. Odette Bonnet at her silliest and Mme de Crussol (Daladier's mistress) at her most ambitious were,
however, surpassed by Hélène de Portes, the fantastic
creature who governed Paul Reynaud during the last fatal
months before the catastrophe.

The whole story of Mme de Portes almost defies belief.
We are told that she presided over meetings of the General Staff, invaded the Supreme War Council, broke up
cabinet sessions at will, prepared state papers for Reynaud, dismissed generals and reproved ambassadors in a
way which even Mme de Maintenon or Mme de Pompadour would have found impossible. The evidence in this
matter is overwhelming. If it were not so unanimous and
so voluminous we might be inclined to doubt it, but there
is no doubt possible. I have been told by persons in the
highest positions (cabinet ministers, ambassadors and the
like) that this woman behaved at times like a sovereign,
at times like a fishwife, but at all times as if she had some
vested right, whether constitutional or divine, in the government of the French Republic. Worst of all: I have
it on evidence which I cannot possibly question—and
cannot yet reveal—that the fatal decision to remain in
France in violation of the pledge to Winston Churchill
was taken at this woman's insistence. If she had agreed to
go to Morocco with Paul Reynaud and the government,

the Germans would undoubtedly have occupied all of European France, but French Africa and Asia could have continued the fight and the whole sinister history of Vichy, Pétain and Laval could have been avoided. Mme de Portes said: *"Je ne quitterai jamais le sol de la France,"* and the plan of war—so definitely adopted in Tours only three days before—was abandoned. Paul Reynaud resigned, Pétain whined into the radio and the sorry tale of Vichy unfolded from then on. As Lenin says, no government can fall unless it has first been dropped; but the person who most of all dropped the government of the French Republic, and dropped it hard, was Hélène de Portes.

It may be said, with abundant reason, that the French Republic was doomed anyhow. Corruption, incompetence and confusion had led it into such a pass that there was no hope left for it. All that may be true: and yet (there is certainly so much to be said for the rôle of personality and accident in history, for in this one case I have the proof) at the very end, a legal French government could have been preserved to continue the fight overseas if this one hysterical woman, Hélène de Portes, had been willing to permit it. I have never believed in the "Cleopatra's nose" theory of history, and yet in this case sheer chance did play a part. If Mme de Portes had been a woman of sense, ability or character, if she had not been hysterically anti-British and (at the end) hysterically anti-American as well, she would have permitted her besotted lover Reynaud to keep his word, the French government and fleet would have gone to Africa and a vigorous ally in the struggle against Fascism could have been maintained throughout the world. In Asia alone the possible results (Indo-China, Siam and Malaya) make one's imagination quiver. But Mme de Portes willed otherwise (*"je ne quit-*

*terai jamais le sol de la France"*) and the incalculable consequences have been unrolling ever since.

I knew nothing about Hélène de Portes when I arrived in Paris on May 6, 1940. Her name had never appeared in an American newspaper, to the best of my knowledge, and I had heard none of the Paris tales about her. I was soon to hear so many that I sometimes wondered whether she ran the entire government and army single-handed.

Her name first fell on my ears in a way characteristic of the lady's behavior, at any rate. I had an appointment with our Ambassador, Mr. W. C. Bullitt, at ten o'clock on the morning after our arrival. I had been in his room about two minutes when his secretary came in to say that Mme de Portes was on the telephone. He took the call, and the lady—in what seemed a remarkably brief conversation—summoned him to her apartment on the other side of the river to have chocolate with her. Bill went; I suppose he had no choice; and yet it seemed to me an amazing thing that any republican politician's mistress, even in France, should have the power to summon ambassadors in this way. Bill left me in the care of Douglas MacArthur, one of his secretaries (a nephew of the general) and returned in due course, rosy and cheerful and full of chocolate, to resume the conversation. Apparently this happened quite often, and he was innocently pleased to be on such good terms with the Premier's mistress; it made him feel rather grown-up, I suppose, like a character in a bad novel. Mme de Portes lived with the Prime Minister in a flat in the Place du Palais Bourbon, and a great deal of the business of state was transacted there; she thought nothing of calling the whole General Staff in when she pleased, and although there is ample evidence that her presumption was bitterly resented, nothing seems to have lessened her assurance. Reynaud had come to power (March 21st) at a moment when she was away from Paris, and his friends hoped that he would not recall her; but once his tenure of office seemed moderately secure he brought her back again to live publicly in the bachelor apartment where he transacted more and more of the government's business. The Comte de Portes was with the army; Mme Paul Reynaud was immersed in war work; Paris believed that Mme de Portes, having obtained a war-time decree altering the divorce laws, intended to marry the Prime Minister as soon as the required divorces could be arranged. At any rate Hitler, who had understood Mme de Portes' importance and sent an emissary to her as long ago as the spring of 1939,[*] forestalled all these domestic rearrangements by the invasion of the West on May 10th—an event which, by increasing the nervous tension and general confusion of life, threw Reynaud still more under the influence of his Egeria and made her, for the last two or three weeks of his reign, a figure which, in sheer insolence and lack of shame, has never been surpassed in France or elsewhere.

Pierre Lazareff, the editor of *Paris-Soir*, which by this time had become the largest of Parisian daily newspapers, tells many stories of Mme de Portes,[†] but none odder than one which he dates in April, 1940, presumably a short time after the lady's return to Paris. This is his story: [‡]

"I requested an interview with Paul Reynaud. When I arrived, I found Hélène de Portes sitting at Paul Reynaud's desk. She was presiding over an assorted gathering of generals, high officers, members of the Parliament, and officials. She was talking in a peremptory tone of voice, giving advice and orders right and left. Every once in a

[*] Saint-Jean, *op. cit.*, p. 155.
[†] P. Lazareff: *Deadline*, pp. 210 *et seq.*, 249-251, 263, 264, 268, 273 *et seq.*
[‡] *Op. cit.*, p. 275.

while she would open the door and step into the next
room. One could hear her say: 'How are you, Paul? Now
just relax and take it easy. Don't worry about a thing.
We're working.'

"When she went into Reynaud's room again, the hitherto obsequious yes-men showed their true colors.

" 'Who does this woman think she is?'

"Someone mentioned that the antagonism between Daladier and Paul Reynaud had become even more acute as
the result of a recent week-end they had spent together,
when Hélène de Portes and the Marquise de Crussol had
nearly come to blows.

"All this talk immediately subsided when Hélène de
Portes again took her seat behind the impressive desk."

There would seem to have been at least two important
respects in which the indefatigable Countess had strongly
influenced the course of events even before the last fatal
days at Tours and Bordeaux. One was in the realm of
appointments and personnel in general: here her power
was used badly because she dreaded anybody whose intellectual influence over Reynaud might rival her own.
She succeeded in keeping Charles de Gaulle away until
it was too late for him to do anything; she drove Georges
Palewski, Reynaud's *chef de cabinet*, out of office, and,
when the disaster began to show in its true proportions
(on the evening of May 16th), she profited by Reynaud's
panic to make him dismiss Alexis Léger, the skillful and
experienced secretary-general at the Ministry of Foreign
Affairs. Her pretexts in each case appear to have been
different. Charles de Gaulle was too independent to suit
her; Palewski was definitely an enemy because he had
acquired influence over Reynaud's mind; Léger was
attacked by the lady and some of her friends as being "a

tool of the Russians," personally objectionable to Italy,
and at the same time * "an accomplice of Daladier and
Gamelin." M. Léger was a resolute opponent of the Nazis
and had no patience with their sympathizers in Paris; his
dismissal came as a great shock to numerous Frenchmen
and foreigners who still believed France could resist the
invader.

The second respect in which Mme de Portes' rôle was
nefarious even before the government had left Paris was
in the conduct of relations with Italy. I was informed in
Paris, and have since seen confirmations in whole or in
part in print, that Mme de Portes was anxious to come to
terms with Mussolini. She was a thoroughly unstable
woman, it appears, and could not pursue any policy with
consistency or force, but for the greater part of the time
between her return to Paris (early April) and the flight
to Tours two months later, she dabbled in an intrigue of
which the purpose was an "understanding" with Italy, and
the result merely to expose France's weakness. The evidence is still cloudy and incomplete, but it appears that
she relied upon a motley crew of intermediaries, including
the Comte de Paris (the young hopeful of the Royalists),
M. Pierre Laval, M. Anatole de Monzie, and anybody else
she could press into service. M. de Monzie's pro-Fascist
inclinations were so well recognized that Mme de Portes
kept him in her government as a sort of hostage to Mussolini, in spite of the fact that he and Reynaud hardly
spoke to each other. The governments of Great Britain
and France had done everything possible to appease Mussolini even without the efforts of the Comtesse de Portes:
they had plied him with coal, iron, petroleum, food and
other materials essential to his coming war against them;
they had behaved toward him precisely as the United

* Lazareff, *op. cit.*, p. 280.

States was behaving toward Japan, and it is indeed difficult to see what further steps they could have taken to
please or flatter him. I am not informed as to what the
Countess meant to do—perhaps she had it in mind to give
him Corsica or Nice, or a slice of Africa; in any case her
offerings came too late. Hitler's visit to the Brenner Pass
had been on March 19th, and Reynaud did not come to
power until two days later.

Sometimes, when I muse over the events of the spring of
1940 or read of them—rather as one reads of things that
happened under Caesar Augustus—I try to imagine what
Hélène de Portes thought she was doing all this time. So
busy, shrill and hysterical, lunching and dining in fashionable restaurants so as to be pointed out by the public,
dabbling in the business of all ministries, calling for the
latest news bulletins day and night, preening herself before the other ladies of Paris because her man was the man
of the hour, what was in her mind? Was she playing a
part, and if so, why did she play it so badly? If she thought
of herself as Mme de Pompadour, why did she not copy a
little of the gentility, discretion and grace which characterized that charming woman from the beginning to the
end? Mme de Pompadour would never have made a scene,
raised her voice, called people names or otherwise vul-
garized a quarrel; she spoke and wrote good French; she
made no ostentatious parade of her power. Something in
Hélène de Portes' tragic caricature does recall Pompadour:
the intrigue with foreign diplomats, for example, although
apparently conducted with a total lack of good sense, was
not unlike some of Jeannette's more discreet correspondence. The relations of France with Prussia and Austria
varied a good deal, during some important years in the
mid-eighteenth century, according to the ideas and sus-
ceptibilities of Louis XV's marquise. And Frederick II of

Prussia, who also in some other respects was a precursor of
Hitler, was not above paying his court to Mme de Pompadour at a time when the proud Austrian empress would
not do so. But such resemblances are fleeting, illusory. The
whole social order had changed, and there was hardly
anything in the France of 1940 that would have been
wholly comprehensible to the France of 1740. It is enough
to observe that the France of 1740 was the richest, most
populous and most powerful state in Europe; from that
to the feebleness and hysteria of May, 1940, by way of
vast efforts and profound exhaustion, is a journey which,
inevitably, must end in something like Mme de Portes.

For the strangest thing of all, to me, is that nobody
seems to have found the lady attractive. She has been
described to me as a middle-aged woman, with a shrill voice
and a clamorous, demanding manner, who chattered like
a magpie and lost her temper with ease. She was not
chic, she was not charming and she was not intelligent.
Paul Reynaud was used to her, depended upon her,
needed her: that was all. As a sort of climax of imbecility
for the story, what he chiefly valued in her appears to have
been her "good sense"—the very quality in which she was
most spectacularly lacking. And to make it quite complete,
she seems to have been as cowardly as it is possible for a
human being to be, a real, unrelieved poltroon. Those who
spent much time with her at Tours and Bordeaux have
told me that she lived in chattering fear from the moment
the first German bomb fell, and, after her life had been
threatened, she was afraid to travel except under the protection of the American flag. Her face at Bordeaux, toward
the end, was not recognizable. All the make-up had fallen
off and the natural pale-green skin of the frightened
woman appeared; but she never, even then, stopped talking. While others slept, she talked, talked, talked—and so,

at last, when the catastrophe of France had taken place and she and her *cher Paul* were flitting aimlessly through the Alps, their car turned wrong, just wrong enough to kill her but not Paul, and her political career received the reward which it had been her only fixed policy to escape.

I like to think—and must, on the evidence, consider it likely—that even at the very end she died talking pernicious nonsense.

3

In a few crowded days we renewed acquaintance with the incomparable city. For almost twenty years it had been my *point de repaire*—exactly that: not headquarters, but the place to which I repaired whenever I could. I had lived everywhere in Paris at some time or other, Right Bank or Left, Montmartre or Montparnasse or Avenue du Bois. During the preceding three years we had been living near the church of St. Honoré d'Eylau in a *cité* or closed court called (in defiance of common sense) the "avenue" St. Honoré d'Eylau. Our flat there had been sublet during the past winter to a British diplomat, who was still in possession but was not disposed to object if we moved some of our belongings. Consequently one of our tasks, soon after our arrival in Paris, was to arrange for the shipping of the things we particularly wanted. I had remarked, not once but a hundred times during the preceding year, that we ought to get our books and most valued possessions over to America before the Germans came. It was one of those jokes I often used to make in 1938 and 1939 (like calling the Place de la Concorde the "Adolf Hitler Platz"), which no longer seemed in the slightest degree funny. Now it was bitter earnest: Dinah spent hours with the shippers' men making an inventory of what we intended to ship to New York. Among the books was a beautiful red-and-gold Voltaire, seventy-nine volumes, the edition (1783 as I remember) paid for by the piety of Beaumarchais; there were all the gramophone records; there were Maxine's two Canalettos and a variety of treasured but less valuable objects belonging to our small daughter. What *Gauleiter* or *Herr Oberst* has them now, I wonder?—for of course the Germans came before we had finished the shipping formalities, and we do not greatly regret the things, except for the big white bear that belonged to Linda: since, in point of fact, it would be downright unpleasant to have saved anything of value from Paris. So much was lost there—so much of incalculable consequence—that our sticks and rags may as well go the way of the rest, being regained if the world is regained, if not, not.

We lived at the Hôtel de Crillon, which had in recent years opened a popular bar-restaurant on the Boissy d'Anglas side; that side bar was a meeting place for many people we knew, press colleagues, diplomats and the like. The men from the American Embassy across the street used it as a sort of annex for lunch or dinner, and up until the panic began (May 15th) it was frequented by Parisians of every sort possessing the money to pay its prices. All prices were high, here and at the Ritz, Maxim's, Larue's, all the famous places; but the food was also exceedingly good. After Italy it was a little hard to believe; for Italy, still at peace, had much severer systems of rationing on meat, eggs, vegetables, fruits and alcohol. True, Paris had two meatless days a week (soon to become three), but Italy had five; the same proportion, roughly, seemed to obtain in all other food materials. There never had been a time when food was not better and more plentiful in France than in Italy, but this consideration seemed to have lost its cogency in wartime; to me it seemed more likely that the Fascists were being provident and the Reynaud-Daladier French were not. Some evidence to support this notion appeared after the panic began, when food grew scarce and there seemed neither reason nor remedy for the situation. At any rate, in early May it was possible to dine at Larue's almost as sumptuously as in peace time, and on drinkless days (days when it was forbidden to sell alcohol) everybody quite happily compromised on champagne, which was plentiful and not very expensive. Those who can afford cake have seldom rebelled at being obliged to eat it.

At first I made no attempt to pursue specific inquiries in Paris. It was enough to savor the novelty of the familiar city (the most familiar of cities) at war. During the few days (exactly four) that intervened between my arrival and the German invasion of the West, the war looked and sounded like a "phony war," or, more exactly, like a piece of play-acting paralyzed by the fear of reality. These ladies in uniform, generals lunching at the Ritz, dashing young aviators on leave—they played their parts under the nightmare threat that the piece might become real at any moment. Senator Borah, the originator of the expression "phony war," had undoubtedly meant to suggest that the war in the winter of 1939–1940 still carried many overtones of Munich—that it was not truly meant on the Franco-British side as a battle against Fascist tyranny, and that the Fascist tyrants themselves had not yet decided whether it suited them best to smash at the West or to ignore it. The serious political intention and content of the phrase are clearer now than they were when it was first made; at the time it seemed hardly better than a vulgar gibe by a safe onlooker; and yet one could not go

into a Paris restaurant, café or theatre in the spring of
1940 without thinking of those words. It was necessary
to remember that war, real war, might come at any moment; glittering tables might be fire or ashes, luxurious
diners shattered human wreckage; even so it was difficult
not to wonder what all these people would say if somebody came in and shouted: "Ladies and gentlemen, Hitler
offers you peace on the basis of things as they are." Could
anybody doubt that they would shout back a consent
made raucous with joy? Supposing the messenger called
out, instead: "Hitler offers you peace if you give up Alsace-
Lorraine and your army." What would they have said? I
do not know; I am not sure even yet. Some would have
said no, but more—speaking merely of those people who
could afford the expensive public places of Paris—would
have grasped at the chance to keep their possessions in
peace. They were all like Mr. Joseph Kennedy, the American Ambassador to London, who stopped Jan Masaryk
after the catastrophe of Munich and jovially remarked:
"Now I can spend Christmas at Palm Beach after all." *

On the night of May 9th Dinah and I were asked to
dinner at Bill Bullitt's house. It was a Thursday, and we
gathered that Bill's "Thursdays" had become rather an
institution in Paris since the start of the war. I asked him
if I should wear a black tie and he was shocked. "I haven't
seen a black tie since September 3rd," he told me. As a
matter of fact, for these people to make a parade of not
dressing for dinner was the precise psychological equivalent of spending every evening in fancy dress: it was the
fine flower of "phony war." The women dressed with the
utmost care—so did most of the men, however "busy" they
pretended to be—but they would have regarded it as not

* Virginia Cowles: *Looking for Trouble.* p. 179.

playing up properly if they had slipped into their ordinary clothes for the evening.

The company was large and of mixed nationalities, with French predominating. There were several members of the government, two or three of them ministers; one was Dautry, the Minister of Armaments, regarded as one of the most energetic of the department heads. The British air vice-marshal, Barrett, was there; so was Eve Curie, who had just returned from America; so was Laurence Steinhardt, the American Ambassador to the Soviet Union, who was on his way either to or from Moscow. The evening passed in conversation which tended to fall with monotonous insistence upon the disaster of Norway. It seemed to me that both Frenchmen and Americans took delight in pointing out how stupid the British had been, with the clear inference that in other hands the expedition could have been a success. I pondered, and not for the first or last time, at the composure which people seemed to expect of the British. If you say one single word against the supreme intelligence, courage or skill of the American army, navy and air force to an American he becomes violent with rage; and yet Americans always assume that they can say anything they like about the British to English people and cause no umbrage. Persons of official position were upbraiding the British without the slightest restraint at our Ambassador's house that night, and poor Barrett, the air vice-marshal in command of the R.A.F. in France, had to take it. If he had shown any sign of irritation the Americans and Frenchmen present would have been surprised and perhaps a little amused. Yet if he (or even I) had said one-tenth of these things about an American force or American plan, there would have been an ugly brawl.

At midnight the French ministers and their wives started to go home; after a while Bill himself vanished, leaving Steinhardt, Dorothy Thompson (who had come in after dinner), Barrett, Dinah and me; we adjourned to Dorothy's room at the Hotel Meurice to talk some more. Dorothy had completed her arrangements, at last, to visit the Maginot Line, and was to start the next day. We asked Laurence Steinhardt questions about Russia, which was still the enigma of politics, although apparently more and more bent upon giving co-operation to Germany; we fell back upon Norway at every turn in the talk. And hardly had we broken up for the night when the Germans, striking over classic lines but hardly in a classic way, invaded the West.

Louis Huot telephoned me from Press Wireless at nine in the morning to pass on the news. At the moment he knew nothing except that the invasion of Holland and Belgium had begun at dawn. I crawled into my clothes and made the rounds, confirming the event; my first act was to request credentials as a press correspondent at the Ministry of Information. But I had not yet fathomed the depths of ineptitude into which the French bureaucracy had now sunk. During the next eight or ten days I was to tramp in vain from ministry to ministry, office to office, only to discover every day what had been obvious, although unbelievable, on the very first day—that is, that there was no authority anywhere.

The Ministry of Information was unable to issue press or any other passes from the moment the invasion began. Everything had to go through the Ministry of War. At the Ministry of War everybody was too busy even to consider such applications; the mention of one's business brought astonished laughter. The Ministry of War seemed to assume, from about ten o'clock on the morning of Friday,

May 10, 1940, that the war had already ended in a total German victory. The Ministry of Foreign Affairs caught the panic fairly early and was in complete chaos by May 16th; besides, it had no authority over the Ministry of War and little except a relationship of incessant bickering with the Ministry of Information. The American Embassy could supply me with letters of identification, and could back this up with a personal note requesting aid in pushing my papers through; but that was all. I did everything I was told to do, amassed letters of identification and special recommendations from people of high position, filled out forms in duplicate, triplicate, quadruplicate, showered passport photographs all over every government office in Paris, lost myself several times a day in the dusty labyrinths where all these things were (for a while longer) buried in files; and in the end of all, I got nothing. Not a pass, not the flimsiest bit of stamped paper; by May 20th, when martial law was enforced, I could not have moved from Paris to Versailles.

Pierre Comert had just been named chief of the American section at the Ministry of Information; he did his best for me. So did Robert de Saint-Jean in that ministry; so did a number of helpless officials high and low. Saint-Jean said to me one day, after I had climbed for the eighth or ninth time to his office under the eaves of the Hotel Continental:

"Perhaps by the time this war is over we shall have learned how to run it."

Then it was already late (perhaps May 16th or 17th) and Saint-Jean's fine-drawn face was pale and sad. The paralysis which made it impossible for a simple press pass to be issued by the huge ministry created for that precise purpose—the paralysis which prevented any paper signed in one ministry from reaching its destination in another—

had already shown its symptoms in much more vital details, and it was no longer possible to conceal the dry-rot, the swift crumbling, of the whole system.

Even the most energetic of men stood aghast at the helpless inertia revealed by French officialdom in this crisis. One day I had a long talk with Georges Mandel, then Minister of the Colonies (to be Minister of the Interior after the panic began on May 16th). Mandel, first a protégé and then an associate of Clemenceau's, had been a man of the Right for many years but had never engaged in any traffic with Hitler or the French Hitlerites. His perfectly clean record in foreign politics may have been due, in part, to the fact that he was Jewish and consequently had little choice in the matter, but in any case he was to be held in honor for the enemies he had made. He was a realist, a severe disciplinarian on occasion, an incisive ironist in debate, a man of very considerable quality from any point of view. But for the fact that he happened to be Jewish, he, rather than Paul Reynaud, might have emerged as the "strong man" of the crisis. Under the ministry of Albert Sarraut in 1936 he had been in favor of taking action against the German forces then remilitarizing the Rhineland—the action which, as it now seems, might have greatly delayed the war or altered its balance of forces—and had been battered down by the astonishing contention of General Gamelin that nothing could be done without general mobilization.

Mandel talked to me with considerable freedom and vigor. He knew only too well how badly things were going. He was wondering what practical help might be conjured up out of the strong but platonic expressions of sympathy President Roosevelt had lately given forth. He asked me how much cargo in essential spare parts for airplanes could be carried to Lisbon on the American Boeing seaplanes (the "Clipper"), and how many of such planes we possessed.

I received the impression that, despite his efforts to find a way out, this man, whose vision was clear and steady, whose spirit recoiled at no risk, seeing the corruption and chaos all around him and the mire into which those who struggled became progressively immersed, was approaching the moment when he would say that there was no use trying to do anything further with the Third Republic. By this I do not mean to suggest that Mandel ever despaired, or that he ever willingly acquiesced in the abandonment of the constitution of the Republic—I know in fact that the opposite was true at Bordeaux—yet on that day in Paris I felt that his vision of the coming event held him for the moment aghast, and might rob him of the capacity to react with vigor against the traitors who abounded on all sides. He saw too much, too clearly, too well: and such qualities to be truly effective must come into play while there is still time for them to influence action.

On one of these days I went to the Quai de Bourbon on the Ile St. Louis to see "the other Jew" (as the French Fascists called him), M. Léon Blum. I had no great admiration for M. Blum: I admired his language, his ability to write and speak good French, his cultivated mind and his generally good intentions, but it seemed to me that his record in office had not been good. His mind, so far as foreign policy was concerned, was blighted by pacifism. No man can have a foreign policy at all if he does not accept the fact that war is one of its expressions. Clausewitz, in a much-quoted passage * says, "War is simply the continuation of politics by other means." In another place

* Karl von Clausewitz: *Vom Kriege,* vol. 1, p. 28.

he amplifies the famous formula as follows: * "Everybody knows that wars are called forth only by the political relations of governments and peoples; but ordinarily one pictures the situation as if, with the beginning of the war, these relations cease and a new situation is created subject to its own laws. We assert, on the contrary, that war is nothing but a continuation of political relations with the intervention of other means."

This brutal but irrefutable common sense was alien to M. Blum. He was a moderately wealthy man who had never had to struggle much for anything; the leadership of the French Socialist party, the largest in the state, fell to him as much because of his command of language as for any other reason; he had seen relatively little of the seamy side of life. He and his wife (who apparently had great

* Clausewitz, *op. cit.*, vol. 3, pp. 139-140.

We say mixed with other means in order thereby to maintain at the same time that this political intercourse does not cease by the War itself, is not changed into something quite different, but that, in its essence, it continues to exist, whatever may be the form of the means which it uses, and that the chief lines on which the events of the War progress, and to which they are attached, are only the general features of policy which run all through the War until peace takes place. And how can we conceive it to be otherwise? Does the cessation of diplomatic notes stop the political relations between different Nations and Governments? Is not War merely another kind of writing and language for political thoughts? It has certainly a grammar of its own, but its logic is not peculiar to itself.

Accordingly, War can never be separated from political intercourse, and if, in the consideration of the matter, this is done in any way, all the threads of the different relations are, to a certain extent, broken, and we have before us a senseless thing without an object.

This kind of idea would be indispensable even if War was perfect War, the perfectly unbridled element of hostility, for all the circumstances on which it rests, and which determine its leading features, viz.: our own power, the enemy's power, Allies on both sides, the characteristics of the people and their Governments respectively, etc., as enumerated in the first chapter of the first book—are they not of a political nature, and are they not so ultimately connected with the whole political intercourse that it is impossible to separate them? . . .

If War belongs to policy it will naturally take its character from thence. If policy is grand and powerful, so also will be the War, and this may be carried to the point at which War attains to its absolute form.

influence over him—he was desolate at her death in 1938) were fond of literature, music and beautiful objects, and their attitude toward war was naturally one of detestation. This civilized dislike for the ugly and ruinous extreme statement of political conflict showed itself in M. Blum by a sort of shrinking from fact. Thus his decision to impose an embargo on shipments of arms to Spain (1936), to which so much of the subsequent fatal development was due, was apparently taken through sheer fidelity to the principles of pacifism. It was indeed lucky for Hitler, Mussolini and Franco that such an elegant and high-minded literary man should have been Prime Minister of France during that crucial year. A more resolute, realistic mind than Blum's would have seen immediately that France's life depended upon checking the Fascist advance, and that to present Spain to the enemy, as the embargo policy did, was equivalent to turning over part of France. Blum never saw this until it was too late, and when he recanted, with tears and much contrition, at the Socialist Congress of 1939, the Spanish Republic had already fallen—preceding the French Republic by little more than a year, as we had always thought it would. Given the historic conditions under which the Spanish struggle took place, nothing but resolute action on the part of the French government would have enabled the Spanish government to face the sinister conspiracy of its powerful, well-equipped enemies. Russia was too far away to give effective aid on any scale; England was divided, confused and in part ill-disposed; France alone could have helped the Spanish government in time. Of all the might-have-beens of the years 1935–1938, probably the bitterest is this: that it would have cost France little to defeat Fascism in Spain in 1936 and 1937. If Spain had remained among the democratic powers the general war might have been postponed, or, if fought at all, fought under much better strategic conditions. To the sickening alternatives offered at Bordeaux in June, 1940—war in exile, or peace at Vichy—there would have been a third added, and one which would have given the forces of freedom the thing they were to need most, a foothold in Europe, a front to fight on: Republican Spain. As it was, the resistance of the Spanish Republic had given the blind French and British time—time which they had mostly wasted, but otherwise would not have had at all. In all this ebb and flow of forces fully conscious on one side (the Fascist) and only about half-conscious on the other, one fact stood out with glaring certainty: if M. Blum, the so-called man of the Left, had not decided to place an embargo on arms for Spain in 1936, our enemies would have found the going much more difficult.

M. Blum lived in a comfortable apartment with windows over the Seine. Much had been written in the French conservative and Fascist press about his "luxurious" quarters and extravagant tastes; I thought his flat pleasant but not at all out of the ordinary. It was full (a little too full) of old furniture and books; we talked in a small study which was all books and papers. M. Blum was dressed in gray flannel pyjamas, a sort of *veston d'intérieur,* of considerable elegance: perhaps this style of clothing, which he much affected, had given him the reputation of being extravagant. He received me well, as I had been sent by Bill Bullitt, with whom his relations were always friendly. His language and gestures betrayed the practiced talker, the politician who lives in words as a fish lives in water. His phrase-making talent was of a particular kind; it was not especially vigorous, did not flash out in invective or irony or memorable, strong statement, but in compensation it had a sort of beauty. For example, I spoke to him of Winston Churchill, who had just become Prime Minister in London. I said his point of view about money was entirely different from that of the Chamberlain-Baldwin group of politicians. I told M. Blum that he had once outlined for me what he thought a young man ought to do in politics, and almost the first of his rules was to be careful not to value money too much and not to do anything important for reasons of money. The young man (the hypothetical young man starting out in politics) was to earn what money he needed by writing, but must never allow money to influence his opinions or acts, and must be sure to keep his financial needs low enough to make this possible. M. Blum smiled.

"Yes, it is true," he said, musing. "M. Churchill *n'a pas du tout l'âme capitaliste.*"

Churchill has not the capitalist soul—it was said as an observation of fact, but it implied a whole series of kindred ideas, like the first chords of a meditation. This evocative and almost poetic quality often rose to the surface of M. Blum's language and gave it a pearly iridescence: it was *nacrée,* delicate without being extremely valuable, and was remembered (if at all) by its suggestions of felicity rather than by any strong or sensible truth.

I asked him to talk about the question of the French Communists and their status. They had lost their political rights; many of them had been arrested; their representatives in the Chamber of Deputies had been proscribed, some were in hiding and others had gone to prison. This seemed, from the outside, rather a misfortune; that is, in view of the fact that the French Communists still exercised an influence upon the French working class, it would have seemed, offhand, much better to conciliate than to persecute them, if the main object was the winning of the war. M. Blum rejected this idea with feline vehemence— in another character one might have called it energy.

*"Que voulez-vous?"* he demanded, gesturing with both hands and grimacing at the same time. "The French Communist deputies were members of all the committees at which military and other secrets were discussed—the Military Commission, for example. They could sit through a secret debate, hear figures which cannot be made public, and then go straight to the Soviet Embassy and give a report on the whole thing. From the Soviet Embassy to the German General Staff in Berlin is only a step nowadays, you know. Keeping the French Communist deputies in their places was equivalent to establishing a direct line of communication with the German General Staff. The situation had become intolerable."

I said it seemed to me the French Communist influence among the workers, although no doubt greatly impaired by the Nazi-Soviet Pact, was probably still considerable, and that for this reason I wondered if it was wise to make them any more disaffected and defeatist than necessary.

"Whatever we do or say, they are defeatists," M. Blum declared with some signs of irritation. "We can't deal with those people at all. I know them well—there is nobody who has been more thoroughly *roulé* by them than I have. I would have protected them against arrest and persecution if they had shown the slightest sign of wishing to join in the war effort. But after years of preaching war against Hitler, they suddenly became defeatists when the war arrived. They have fomented strikes, encouraged downright sabotage, made trouble at all public meetings, used their influence to spread rumors, and at all times have been telling the workers not to let themselves be massacred in an imperialist war. This is the war they have been demanding, openly demanding, for the past three years, and now, because their masters in Russia have become friends of the Germans, they oppose it. Fortunately their power among the workers is not what it was. They had to do their about-face much too quickly; it was embarrassing for them, because the French workman is not stupid. Naturally, when his mentors advise one thing on Monday and the opposite thing on Tuesday, he wants to know which advice is really meant."

It was odd to hear M. Blum, in language of which I can only give a rough paraphrase, accusing the Communists of the same crimes which the angry conservatives in France used to put at his own door. I produced for him my favorite hypothesis (which I put into print and said in public meetings many times during 1940–1941), that the inevitable operation of historic force would throw the Russians on the same side as Great Britain and France in this war, sooner or later, and whether they wished it or not. M. Blum disagreed sharply.

"All the evidence is to the contrary," he said. "The collaboration between Russia and Germany grows more effective every month. We have figures on the cotton purchases of Russia which show that the Soviet Union is acting as agent for Germany; we have the figures of transport over the Trans-Siberian Railway. Politically the atmosphere among all those gentlemen is growing more friendly, more serene. Japan was an obstacle, but the difficulties there seem to be removed. It is perfectly possible that we may see a firm alliance between Germany, Russia and Japan before long. We are not so far away from it now. We have masses of evidence on the way in which our French Communists, obeying orders from Russia, have played Germany's game all winter long. I cannot believe there is much chance of what you say—although, certainly, the fault is in part our own. If Great Britain and France had tried hard enough, we might have had the firm alliance of Russia. All that is over now. We must win by our own efforts, with the hope that America may help us sooner or later. Look out there. Do you see any signs of dislocation, of panic, of confusion, among our people?"

He pointed out to the river, where a great convoy of barges was passing slowly along, grim and gray against the spring loveliness of the quais. The German armies were advancing up there, in the north, with apparently irresistible power. The illusion of water-lines, indeed of any lines, seemed to have perished. The German army had crossed the Albert Canal with no difficulty and swept through the precise area which French military experts considered impossible—the forest of the Ardennes: all this in two days, three days. The German army was at Sedan. The British army, with a French army on its right flank, had begun to wheel around in a retreat which was to leave the famous "pocket" (or "bulge," as the London press called it) for rapid German expansion. But during those early days, just the first five days, Paris remained calm, industrious, cheerful, aware of the struggle but not yet alarmed by it, convinced that the initial defeats would be succeeded by victory, and not yet willing to make great alterations in the routine of life. On the night of May 10th Dinah and I went to the theatre. Henri Bernstein had sent us tickets for his *Elvire*, a play about a Viennese refugee, played by Mme Elvire Popesco. There were hardly a score of people in the audience, for the day's news had not been such as to send people to the theatres. Yet during the next few days attendance at all places of amusement improved and the demeanor of the audiences showed hardly any change from the normal.

On that first night, at *Elvire*, the few people who were in the theatre wept a good deal. Mme Popesco, an actress of great power, may have been moved more than usual on this occasion, and her audience was made up of people who had received a terrible shock: the result was harrowing to a high degree. But such emotionalism vanished thereafter. The theatres remained open until May 20th, when they were all closed by decree. At the Opéra and the Opéra-Comique the usual works, including German ones, continued to be performed; I think *Die Zauberflöte* was actually on the bill at the Opéra on the night of May 10th. The last play I saw was on the last night the theatres remained open in free Paris (May 19th). It was by Jean Giraudoux, a fantasy called *Ondine,* and was played by the exquisite Madeleine Ozeraie. I went with Woody Wallner, Douglas MacArthur and some of the other young people from the American embassy, who had resolved to keep up the firm pretense that everything was going to be all right.There was more of a crowd than might have been expected; no doubt the announcement that the theatres were to close brought them out. Giraudoux, who had once led a whole generation in the dream of friendship between France and Germany, had somehow, in the midst of his high government functions, found time to write a dramatic poem of great beauty on the Undine legend—of great beauty and, in its static loveliness, almost totally without meaning. The heroine had the unearthly, starry-eyed imbecility of a Mélisande, and her tragedy passed over her without leaving a trace. Of the theatres of Paris, to which, after all, I was more habituated than to any others, this was my last impression—an audience taut with anxiety, listening in silence and tears to a poem signifying nothing.

After the first two days of the campaign had demonstrated its general character, I persuaded Dinah to take the airplane over to London. If she was to get there in relative security, see her mother and friends, and get home again, it was high time. It seemed to me likely that passenger airplanes might stop running soon—as indeed they did—and that the whole outcome, for us all as for each one, was as hazardous and beclouded with uncertainty as anything had ever been.

For along about then—May 12th, 13th, 14th, just before the panic set in—I began to be haunted by the idea of the fall of the French Republic. The institution from which one of the main currents of the life of man had flowed for a century and a half, sweeping ideas and persons along in its resistless course, was in some way, for some reason, on the verge of annihilation. Internal divisions, corruption and confusion, the nerveless fears of a bourgeoisie unable or unwilling to use its power, lack of faith and lack of incentive had hollowed it out; the great stream of life-giving ideas flowed no more; the whole thing, the Republic, the mother of modern man, was dying; the assaults of the barbarian were effective not only because the barbarian was strong, but because the Republic was weak. Each of those days was like an eternity during which the swift, ruthless advance of the Nazi columns traversed whole centuries of time, crushing the years and the ideas and hopes of men (Descartes and Villon, the lyre and the sword too) into one general rubbishy agglomeration of ruin, the great free world of the West pulverized by an iron wagon and a murderous kite.

For I was not very far off the general (and usually unconscious) French view of the world, by which nothing in the West could be expected to survive if France fell. This was not for lack of appreciation of the pragmatic values of England and America; it was, on the contrary, partly because those countries were strong and set apart from Europe that I doubted them—doubted that they would or could continue a struggle in which their non-European nature must be emphasized by every event that befell the world; in which their natural egoism would find inexhaustible arguments for isolation; in which the relentless foe, exerting himself to make plausible whatever simulacrum of a scheme he had been able to improvise, would woo by reason and convince by fraud; in which England and America, in short, would hesitate, consult the interests of property and security, tap fingers and purse lips, while military and political control passed irretrievably into the hands of the revolutionary anti-libertarian conspiracy of Berlin, Rome and Tokyo. I did not pursue this train to the logical end; indeed, in myself and in others it was not thought out at all. It was the merest haze of suffering, an emotion that came in with the air you breathed, a clutching of horror at the throat. It passed, always passed (you could reason it away); but it was the first and simplest response to the news from the North.

"Do you *realize* what's happening?" my friend Knickerbocker demanded that day when we walked by the river and the Sunday afternoon crowds converged on Notre Dame. "Do you *realize* it?"

"Yes, I know," I said. "It is the end of the world."

The statement seemed neither more nor less than accurate then. Even today I am not sure we were not right. A world regained, half in ruins, is not the same as the one that was lost; the Western mind, in its splendor and misery, depended to an immeasurable extent upon France; what we experienced was "the end of the world" of 1789. I should say the supremely important events of the twentieth century up to then had been two: the Russian Revolution and the Fall of France. What was born in 1917 may perhaps relate to what died in 1940,* but it has turned sharply off the road. *Liberté, Fraternité, Egalité,* they all

* The genealogy of these ideas has been explored by Edmund Wilson in *To the Finland Station.*

three shone forth from the monuments of the Republic of 1789–1940; but Liberty, be it remembered, always came first.

4

The panic began on May 15th and began to turn into a mass migration by the evening of May 16th. Wherever you turned you saw people in flight. At first this was a migration into Paris rather than away from it; at the railroad stations and elsewhere during the first days there was a piling up of the familiar human wreckage, refugees from the North and East, people from Belgium, even from Holland, and from the bombed cities of Lorraine. True stories of suffering, hardship and endurance were plentiful at the railroad stations, but mixed with them were the fantastic inventions that always arise from the popular mind in time of war. Many refugees had seen German soldiers dressed as nuns; the stories of parachutists and fifth columnists were wildly improbable—as improbable as the truth, but with less technical accuracy; many intelligent Frenchmen thought they had actually seen a German parachutist come down at the Etoile, in the heart of Paris. Then the turmoil took on a new character, and after having poured into Paris on every train, the crowds seemed bent upon pouring out again, overloading the traffic and adding greatly to the atmosphere of alarm.

In the streets the first loaded motor cars appeared about May 16th. From then on they became rapidly more familiar, until a few days later it was unusual to see any car that did not carry luggage, bedding or even furniture lashed to its top, back and sides. One of the largest movements of population ever to occur in the Europe of historical times was now taking place. Millions of people from Belgium, Northern France and (to a lesser degree) Holland were in movement; their number must have reached easily eight or nine million at the height of the migration. The French government which capitulated to Hitler estimated that it had seven million refugees in the territory unoccupied by German soldiery; there were certainly other refugees who failed to outdistance the German army; there were always great numbers who broke down by the way. From May 15–16 to the day the Germans entered Paris (June 14th) there were about two million people who moved out of the city with as many of their belongings as they could pack and transport. All this unimaginable uprooting and drifting, through terror and anxiety and despair, toward the doubtful haven of an area where there would be no Germans—that was, most of all, what gave the weeks of the panic their character. A population which stays in its dwelling places may be sorrowful, grim or oppressed, but it could never give rise to the same wild incertitude as that set up in the air of France by this colossal flight. One came to doubt the physical security of the universe, the likelihood that there would be another day, and the possibility of personal survival, not for any exact reason, but because the whole question of life seemed to have lost its bearings in a general downfall of established structures.

My prolonged and unremitting petition to the French authorities for permission to do press work continued, in vain, of course, during these days; for the clearest, sanest discussion of what was taking place I went, not to any Frenchman, but to Don Juan Negrin. The Prime Minister of the vanquished Spanish Republic was living out in Passy, under an unobtrusive police surveillance, I believe, and with instructions from his French "friends" to be as unnoticed as possible, but at any rate in comparative freedom and dignity. Franco and the pro-Fascist French regarded his presence in Paris as an offense to them, and to avoid troublesome debate the French Socialist party—in effect, M. Léon Blum—asked him to abstain from public appearance or activity. As a Socialist he received their protection, although in the life-and-death struggle of the Spanish Republic he had not had their support. I had met him no more than two or three times in Spain, but rather more often afterward in New York; now I saw him practically every day. No other person known to me in Paris had the same plain view of the world's checkerboard. Perhaps he saw it more clearly because he was no longer engaged in the actual moves of power. At any rate I recorded then, and record now, the fact that his mind—as again in June, 1941, when Germany was about to attack Russia—had a prescience and brilliance about actual political developments beyond anything I have ever experienced. Everything he said would come to pass did come to pass punctually; of what he said should be done, much was done by the French, the British and the Americans, but always too late and not well. On the day of the German invasion, I had asked him to have tea at the Crillon with Dorothy Thompson. His first words to her, as I remember, were: "America must adopt conscription as soon as possible. Do you realize this?" The fact was realized and acted upon in Washington some weeks later. From the moment of the invasion, Don Juan told me that what hope existed must depend upon a clean sweep of certain people in the General Staff and the Ministry of War. "Gamelin must go immediately," he said. "The man has no spirit of combat and no sense of how to organize a resistance." I asked him what he would do, if he were in Reynaud's place, since Marshal Pétain was obviously too old and feeble to undertake the job. "I should send for Weygand," he said firmly.

"I know that all our Left friends think he is a Royalist and a Catholic and therefore not to be trusted. Perhaps he is all that. It does not matter. He is the only competent organizer and staff commander for this work. He is a good soldier and a patriotic Frenchman." That was a week before they did send for Weygand, and about nine days before he actually took command. Again, Don Juan Negrin saw very clearly the divisions among the personalities in the French governmental sphere. He would have imprisoned some of those who were most eager to "collaborate" with the Germans a few weeks later, and would have placed reliance where it belonged, on the most energetic men available, Mandel first of all. These were academic opinions, of course, delivered in privacy as between foreigners who were (after all) mere spectators at this terrible tragedy. Negrin would never have expressed such frank opinions to Frenchmen even if he had been in communication with men in the government. He had too much tact and experience; he knew too well how the anguished and reluctant decisions taken at moments of crisis by sleepless, harassed, overworked men are often bound to be irretrievably wrong, and he would not have added to their difficulties by a word of unwanted advice. But I have often thought since then that if he had been able to advise the French government—above all Reynaud, whom he never saw—he could have helped at least in the sense of expedition, at a moment when time meant everything; for in fact the courses he favored were almost all adopted later, and in the case of Reynaud too late.

One night I had asked him to dinner. We talked first in my room at the Crillon, and when it came time to go out, I suggested dining at Larue's. He objected. "That sort of restaurant is always crowded with people, some of them in politics," he said. "My friends here do not like me to show myself in such places. I am in exile here, more or less on sufferance, and the quieter I am the better for all concerned." I assured him there would be nobody in La-rue's. "I was there last night," I said, "and it was empty— only three tables taken." He allowed himself to be per-suaded.

We went round the corner to Larue's, where, by the perversity of Fate, there was a crowd of extremely well-known Parisian figures. I stopped in the doorway. "We can go somewhere else," I said foolishly. "I'm sorry. I seem to have been quite wrong about it."

"It's too late now," Negrin said, imperturbable as ever. The head waiter had approached and offered us a table— the only one free, I believe, on the whole ground floor. Negrin followed him through the room to the *banquette* at the far end, sat down and looked round. He had been recognized by at least half a dozen people and, by another of those small fatalities which make life so improbable, he was sitting on the *banquette* right beside Pierre Laval, their well-covered haunches practically touching. They recognized each other out of the corner of the eye, turned their backs firmly, and we had dinner under these some-what uneasy circumstances.

"Am I imagining things," I said, "or is that who I think it is?"

"You are right," Negrin said impassively, his back firmly turned to Laval. "That is the man who will make the peace with Hitler."

It was less than a month later when these words became fact.

Negrin, of course, recognized from the beginning how difficult it was for a French army inferior in air force and mechanized equipment to resist Germany's full power. His calculations, based upon an experience not dissimilar although on a smaller scale, were all in the direction of resistance for the sake of gaining time which could be used not only by the French themselves, but by the British and Americans. He did not minimize the severity of the ordeal this would mean for the French, but he thought that if they could be rallied and organized for a prolonged, bitter resistance all the way, they themselves as well as the general cause would benefit by the increased chances of final victory. But when it became apparent that the spirit of defeat reigned in all higher quarters, I think Negrin, somewhat reluctantly, came to the conclusion that the French of 1940 were not the Spaniards of 1938, and could not be called upon for such endeavors. Don Juan's spirit was probably the most combative, the least willing to concede defeat, of any I have known, but what was necessary to turn defeat into victory (or into continued resistance) in May, 1940, was something too comprehensive to be accomplished in a day or a week. A series of energetic decisions could have been taken all at once: they were taken piecemeal and too late. But to resolve upon them immediately and to put them into effect would have demanded a whole new set of men in the governing positions in France, and such a clean sweep, at the last moment of the Republic's existence, was clearly not possible.

One thing that revealed the nervous irresolution of the French government as clearly as anything in the military field was the relative treatment of friends and enemies during those days. Pierre Laval did as he pleased, saw whom he pleased, moved at perfect liberty, during a time when "enemy aliens" of all categories were being thrown into concentration camps without distinction.* Among these "enemy aliens" were some of the most determined

* Cf. Leo Lania, *The Darkest Hour*, for an account of the sufferings of the anti-Fascist refugees in France.

opponents of Fascism in Europe, thousands of them, whose services could have been used from the very beginning of the war. In the South of France thousands of Spanish Republican soldiers were prisoners under dreadful conditions; all would have fought Fascism if they had been given the chance. Granted that the experience of Norway and Holland had shown the existence of Nazi agents among the anti-Fascist refugees, it surely was never beyond the capacity of intelligent and politically educated Frenchmen to find out which were which, especially as Hitler's preparations between October and May had given them over six months to do it in. Yet the anti-Fascist refugees, Austrian, Hungarian, Italian, German and Spanish, were treated as enemies, Pierre Laval and his like as friends. Supposing Laval's official position as an important parliamentarian to have put him beyond arrest, supposing his defeatist and pro-Hitler activity to have been mainly in the form of private talk, supposing him to have violated no law—and this is giving him the benefit of every doubt—it still was stupid, in view of his immense potentiality for evil, to allow him perfect liberty to spread his poison and make his plans.

At the time I knew little or nothing of the organized fifth column, of Otto Abetz's career in Paris before the war, of the relations between French society figures (the women particularly) and the Comité France-Allemagne. I did not know that German spies and agents were scattered about the newspaper offices, the homes and resorts of the governing class, the legislature itself; the notable Nazi tools (Marcel Déat, Jean Luchaire and the like) were not so notable, or so frank, before the collapse. The only one I had known was Bertrand de Jouvenel, who had been on the side of Franco and on the side of the Munich Agreement, but without openly declaring a partisanship for Hitler; I had thought of him as misguided, an exception, without ever supposing him to be a true Fascist. But one thing I did know—one thing everybody knew—was that Pierre Laval symbolized a policy of agreement with the Fascist dictatorships at any cost to his own or other countries. To see him thus flourishing like the green bay tree at a moment when the most rudimentary precaution would have put him into confinement was, to say the least, an indication that the French government did not know what war it was fighting.

On the 16th of May the imminence of the disaster became apparent to almost everybody in Paris. No further concealment was possible, in spite of the confident or misleading statements in the press, because too many things were happening in plain view of the ordinary public. At the Ministry of Marine, next to my hotel in the Place de la Concorde, they had been loading up navy lorries with the ministry's files even the night before. This work went on in daylight on the 16th and later. At the Quai d'Orsay, after the news of the German break-through on the night before had been understood, the archives of the Ministry of Foreign Affairs were being burned in the courtyard. Any passerby could see them through the iron grille. In the morning of the 16th plans were being made to move the whole Parliament, as well as the ministries, the files and innumerable employees; in the afternoon the plans were abandoned and Reynaud said he would "never leave" the capital. It was quite impossible to keep the man in the street from knowing what was going on. The news spread through Paris like wildfire: the Germans had come through, they had passed Sedan, they were at Laon, they were by-passing Laon, there was nothing whatever between them and Paris except a broad concrete highway.

It was at the early meeting on this day (May 16th) that

General Gamelin, speaking to the highest officials of the Republic, had said: *"Je ne réponds plus de rien."* ("I am no longer responsible for anything.") The words were repeated in a whisper of panic from one end of Paris to the other. Nobody knows how such secrets get out. No doubt the Comtesse de Portes and (probably) a number of other ladies played their part; at any rate there is no doubt that thousands of people were repeating the news, the words, the plans and all the rest of the secret information before the day was over.

I was trying to help Judith Listowel get off to England that afternoon, since the possibilities of movement were becoming restricted, and while she hastily completed her arrangements I went over to the Quai d'Orsay to ask M. Roland de Margerie to stamp her passport. It was my last visit to the French Foreign Office, at which I made my first professional calls twenty years ago in the time of Poincaré. I think that quarter of an hour gave me the proof that panic had now set in. Nobody seemed to care where I went or what I did; the guards at the gate were perfunctory, the first great rooms empty and slightly disheveled, the *huissiers,* those white-haired old dignitaries in blue uniforms with silver chains, were running thither and yon. My introduction to European politics had been in this place, by the haughty mediation of these same *huissiers* or others exactly like them: now they were too busy to attend to anything. I told one I wanted to see M. de Margerie. "Down that way," he said, pointing rather wildly, and ran on out. I observed that his heavy silver chain, the badge of his service, had fallen askew and was almost off one shoulder. It was an arrow pointing toward disaster; anybody who ever knew those stiff, proud lackeys of the Third Republic would have known by this that the Republic was dying. While I endeavored to catch another

*huissier* to show me the way, the Swedish Minister came
in and stood helplessly. Even for him there was no attention. Presently a less agitated attendant was prevailed
upon to hurry me down the silent, dark old corridors to
Roland de Margerie's office. He was sitting behind his
desk, dressed in uniform, looking pale and a little grim.
He took the passport.

"Tell Lady Listowel," he said in a voice kept under resolute control by an effort, "that if she intends to go she
must go at once. By St. Malo the way is still open. With
this counter-signature she can have no difficulty."

My own passport had an indefinite, semi-diplomatic
visa, of the sort French embassies gave correspondents
without much trouble in the months before May 10th. De
Margerie countersigned it for the Ministry of Foreign
Affairs, in bold red ink. With all this it would, he said, be
possible to go and come at will, as many journeys as might
be necessary. I went away without mentioning the news
or asking what he thought of it; the silver chain on the
*huissier's* shoulder had told me.

After seeing Judith off at the Gare St. Lazare in a scene
of complete confusion I repaired to the American Embassy. There, in the ante-room to the Ambassador's office,
I found Eve Curie and Dorothy Thompson waiting for
Bill. Carmel Offie, the Ambassador's secretary, had provided them with some tea. "You may as well be comfortable," he said, "while you can." Dorothy had decided to
go home that night by way of the train to Genoa, where
she would catch the *Manhattan,* and the wires had been
sizzling with requests for reservations and what we afterward learned to know as "priorities." Eve Curie was looking very pale, very fragile; she had heard all the news and
wanted to make a broadcast to America. I do not know,
now, what we all thought we might accomplish by such

broadcasts, but the same idea had occurred to all of us. Dorothy's had been refused the night before; Eve's was to be refused in an hour or so; mine was refused the same night after I, too, had cabled New York. The American radio companies did not want "un-neutral" accounts of this great disaster or "un-neutral" efforts to disturb the public equanimity. When Bill came in (having been with Reynaud) he said—looking fairly harassed, but in good humor—that the news was a little better. "However, you'll get no military intelligence from me," he added. Dorothy told us what she thought America should do: immediate conscription and an abandonment of the Presidential election of 1940 in favor of some form of national union with both parties in the government. (In part, and with delays, these lines were followed out, although the vast diversion of the Presidential election was allowed to take place as Hitler had known it would.)

I went away from there thinking the same two things about our profession (I have thought them often): first, that it was a petty thing to do in comparison to the effort of those who fought, or the suffering of those who were driven into exile; and second, that it was substantially useless because the forces of public opinion and of official power paid so little attention. Dorothy exercised a remarkable power over great sections of public opinion at home, or so we always thought; and yet even she was unable to obtain fifteen minutes on the radio to discuss the significance of this tremendous event. The theory held by so many newspaper and radio magnates, to the effect that the public needed only the facts in order to make up its own mind, was vitiated by a variety of ways in which these facts were presented, as well as by the proved slowness of the mass to appreciate their significance. The function of comment could not be useful—could scarcely be exercised at all—when it was regulated by some such sterile concept as that of "neutrality." Who is neutral when the house is burning down? Those on the second floor, those on the third, or only those on the roof?

## 5

I had been eating lunch in Knickerbocker's flat on the Quai de Béthune with Woody Wallner of the American Embassy, its tenant. Knick had just arrived from America a day or so before.* He came in as we finished lunch and sat down to look at the view. The room was lined with books all the way up to its fairly high ceiling, and the windows opened on to the smiling river. It was Sunday afternoon, May 19th, an exquisite day, and neither air-raid alarms nor the rapidly growing exodus from Paris could lessen the loveliness of the chestnut trees in bloom, the shimmering beauty of the Bois, the Champs-Elysées, the Seine. This flat on the Ile St. Louis had been Knick's headquarters for years now, and I think he was made gloomy in part by the thought that it would not be so much longer. The "pocket" or "bulge" had opened wide, wider, was extending now in the direction of the English Channel. The French were frantically improvising schemes of defense on water-lines, the Somme today: it might be the Loire in a week. Like me, Knick had been unable to obtain any sort of permission to work as war correspondent at or near the front. He suggested that we might go to the

---

* H. R. Knickerbocker, the celebrated correspondent of the Hearst press, was one of those most honored by Nazi enmity, had been expelled from Germany, attacked repeatedly by Dr. Goebbels' organization, and labeled with such tags as "Jewish war-monger," in defiance of fact—chiefly, I think, because his work had been very widely read in German before it was banned by Hitler.

Embassy and have another talk with Horace Fuller, our military attaché—then a colonel, afterward a general. We walked out along the river, looking for a taxicab, and found one with some difficulty. As we came down the Quai de Montebello I noticed an unusual confluence of people on the bridges and squares opposite, around Notre Dame de Paris. I asked the driver what it meant. "I don't know," he said indifferently. "There must be something going on at Notre Dame." I wanted to stop and see what it was, but Knick would have none of it. "The trouble with you," he said, "is religion. I suppose you want to go and pray." I denied this with vigor and we went on to the Embassy.

Colonel Fuller was not in, neither was the Ambassador. In the offices of the military attachés (there were several) we met some officers we knew gathered around maps. There was a Canadian general there, covered with decorations from the last war. When we asked for Fuller, he said: "He's gone to the Cathedral." Somebody else told us the Ambassador had gone to the Cathedral.

"What have they gone there for?" I asked.

The Canadian general looked at us rather severely.

"To pray," he said.

"Do you mean to say," Knick inquired, "that that's the best we can do?"

The Canadian general's expression of severity did not relax.

"The time may come soon when you will be glad to pray," he said, and returned to his maps.

Another officer told us that the American Ambassador and the British Ambassador and their staffs were attending a ceremony at Notre Dame in which the whole French government, including the President of the Republic as well as the cabinet, were to be present. The service was one of prayer for the salvation of the Republic.

Knick protested for some time, assailing what he called my "incurable religion," but in the end I had my way and we got into another taxicab to go to Notre Dame.

"Partly," I told him, "it's the desire to see what's going on. That's journalism. Partly it's a desire to watch the captains and the kings depart. That's historical irony or maybe sadism. But in any case it's not religion."

"Wait and see," he told me. "When you get there you'll be on your knees. Irish Catholic. I know you."

As we came near the Cathedral the taxicab was obliged to drive more slowly through crowds of people out for their Sunday airing in the sun. I think they were converging on the Cathedral out of the same impulses of curiosity as mine. Certainly they did not look particularly concerned, although their manner and general behavior seemed more subdued than they might have been on such a day in another spring. There were the family groups of every Sunday afternoon, *papa* and *maman* and the children, there were some soldiers with their girls, a lot of small boys scurrying about on their mysterious occasions, any number of working girls in groups or men in groups enjoying their weekly holiday. The cafés in the neighborhood all seemed full. Around Notre Dame itself there was an imposing array of guards—*un service d'ordre*—and I suspect that it would have been impossible to penetrate to the church even if we had tried. Large, shining limousines were lined up around the side streets to take their owners away from the ceremony. As we stood on the corner, looking at the crowd, the dignitaries began to come out and get into these lustrous black cars and be whisked away. There was no cheering that I heard, no demonstration of any kind. There was a kind of blank, polite indifference in the faces turned to them from the crowd. I think no régime ever said its farewell to God or man with less effect. It was pure T. S. Eliot: not with a bang but a whimper.

"Do you want to go in there and pray," Knick asked, "or do you want a drink?"

We had a drink in the café on the north side of the Cathedral and watched the captains and the kings depart. In the crowded café there was an undertone of talk about the war, but every clear or loud remark was about ordinary matters. The ominous certainties were to be felt rather than heard, and the fatalism of the people consisted in ignoring them. These results had been built up over seventy years, they seemed to say, and to take apart the structure of causation would be like removing Notre Dame stone by stone: therefore the only thing to do was to wait, hold your breath, clear your throat, get the mist from your eyes, and—while you wait—speak of other things.

We walked along the quais of the Ile de la Cité and the Ile St. Louis. Once for a long time—six months or so—I had lived in a little hotel pinched between the converging Quai des Orfèvres and Quai de l'Horloge. My room looked down on the statue of Henri IV, *le Vert Galant*, and the busy Pont Neuf, with the big Samaritaine department store on the other side and the Louvre not far off. That was, I always thought, the most characteristic, and one of the most beautiful, points in all Paris, and yet it was occupied by a hotel of tenth or twelfth class—the kind to which the snobbish Baedeker does not even attach the phrase "well spoken of." I was very young and fantastically poor, but the machinery of compensation had worked well, and I doubt if I ever fully realized how poor I was. The *Vert*

*Galant* seemed to confirm, with a twirl of the mustache, the irrelevance of such statistics, although he spoke from the point of view of a king; and to come home late at night and find him still doing guard duty on his prancing horse had always given me a kind of moral sustenance, so to speak, in evil ways. Or were they so evil? Henri IV, at any rate, had meant no harm—"a chicken in every pot" was not a bad policy—and the rest was a question of custom.

Those river banks of the islands in the Seine meant a more enduring Paris than any other, not only because they had been there from the earliest days, but because, as the heart of the city, they received and dispensed its tolerant, even flow; they had inhaled and exhaled so much life in all these centuries that a great many of the ideas, hopes and passions which together constituted the spirit of the French culture clung to their very stones. The French civilization in general was something larger than the specific creative effort of 1789–1940. That was what you could see if you looked long enough at the Ile de la Cité. When the historic unity of 1789–1940 bade farewell, it was here that it came, to the stones worn smooth by the tread of uncounted generations. What was Notre Dame itself but the creative effort of an earlier age in the life of this blithe and fecund people? The Third Republic did not say its farewell at the Palais de Justice, which was, after all, on this same tiny island; nor did it do homage at the Bourbon or Luxembourg palaces, the houses of its shattered and discredited legislature; it came to the stones of Notre Dame. Some pulse of continuity with the entire life of Gaul moved in these men, very few of whom were Catholics, and bade them incline before an earlier France in supplication for the renewal of strength. It was the secular shadow of an ancient rite, the worship of the ancestor, of the family, of the past—like the rites of ancient Greece and Rome, of modern China and Japan—and did not in the least imply that the historical conditions which had once raised Notre Dame on high could be made to exist again, or that any person among the bewildered supplicants thought that this could be so. The Church had been no friend to the Republic. It had frowned upon its first struggling ideas before 1789, had opposed its course for a century and a half and was now, in certain places and times if not in all, fully associated with the enemies of freedom. For centuries it had burned and flayed, where it could, the protagonists of Liberty, Fraternity, Equality. Yet in the time of its grandeur as a world order it had called out the united energies of Frenchmen in monuments like those of Chartres, and it was to such monuments that the stricken heirs must turn when they would assure themselves that the civilization of their race was not the creature of one century alone, but part of a vital thrust that had taken other forms in the far differing past and would assert still others in the unknowable future. The faith to which they turned in the dark hour was not that which now occupied Notre Dame de Paris, but that which had raised it—France itself.

That night the Place de la Concorde was filled with a moonlight which made the blackout useless. In that luminous, empty space, in a city which seemed almost deserted, Geoffrey Coxe and some other colleagues and I walked for a while. Geoffrey told me something I had never known or noticed for twenty years, that the statues along the Tuileries side of the square represented the cathedrals of France. One of them—Strasbourg—had been draped in black between 1870 and 1918, he said. When we turned back to the Crillon the navy lorries at the ministry next door were working harder than ever, loading up their files. All over the city the preparations for flight were going on, while reassuring statements were made on the radio from time to time and the people were supposed to know nothing. I remember that we stood for a long time under the arcade in front of the Crillon looking at the empty, moon-drenched square.

The next day somebody—I never knew who it was—canceled a passage on the plane to London about one hour before the time of departure. The passage (they were extremely difficult to get) was offered to me and I took it, thinking to get Dinah off to America as quickly as possible and then return to Paris for the inevitable retreat. I left my clothes and papers in the Crillon, including a great bundle of documents belonging to somebody else. I kept my room; I was coming back in two or three days. But of course when I got to London the return had already become impossible. All visas were stopped, including my extra-special one countersigned by the Ministry; the French Embassy in London, which I besieged for days, could do nothing for me. My clothes, papers and Chesterfield cigarettes, of which I had many, must have fallen into the hands of some German officer, for the Crillon became German military headquarters not long afterward. The whole sorry tale of the retreat, the confused and contradictory stories of Reynaud, the British, the Comtesse de Portes, Pierre Laval and Pétain—all that I was to follow from London, bit by bit, as friends arrived from France and told those things which are never printed in the papers. The tragedy appears to have been consummated without a touch of dignity in high places. Only among the so-called common people does there appear to have been honor, courage and grief. Perhaps when the day of liberation comes and they are called upon to build upon the ruins they will remember and keep the power in their own hands, if they can, so as to lay stones firmly this time one upon the other in a structure—whatever its name, its social or economic character—that will not collapse upon them in the hour of trial; a structure that can call forth all the energies of the people as the Church once did in ages past, a structure which, in beauty as in duration, deserves the heritage of Notre Dame de Paris.

# 3. Our Village

BETWEEN HASTINGS ON ONE SIDE and Margate on the other, edging a land as fair as any that ever whetted the appetite of conquest, the southern coast of England confronts the continent across seas too narrow and too uncertain for easy passage. Julius Caesar made his landing at Dover; William of Normandy fought his battle at Hastings. All along the Kent and Sussex coasts are the memorials of another threat that was desperate, too, in its day: the Martello towers, round fortified look-out posts, were put there when Napoleon was massing his fleet at Boulogne. At the narrowest part of the straits (Folkestone, Dover and Deal) where peacetime traffic was most incessant, the high chalk cliffs drop off sheer and lovely, like the Norman cliffs on the other side, and railroads, ports and dwelling places all huddle into an occasional low-lying bight between. The downlands of Sussex and Kent, behind this high coast line, are soft, rolling hills on which sheep and cattle have found fat nutriment for centuries, great houses and ancient parks occur at intervals, villages are feudal in tenure as in mood, and, in the absence of great cities or heavy industry, there is little to suggest either the stresses of capitalist society in times of peace or the tension of combined effort in war.

Between Dover and Deal on the high middle of the southern cliffs is the village of St. Margaret's, with a winding walk down to St. Margaret's Bay and its thin crescent of beach. This was "our village"—that is, my wife's family had lived there for years and thought of it as home. After a while I came to think of it as a kind of home, too, although it bore little resemblance to my native Illinois prairie; whenever I could pass a month or two there I did, and nothing was easier on the battered nerves after a time in Spain (say) than the wind along the high cliff over the sea, the sun on the rose garden and the friendly sound of south-of-England voices.

It was not a feudal village. The property thereabouts was all, or nearly all, freehold; retired civil servants and business men had built cottages all along those cliffs; the original feudal lord (I think it was Lord Granville, since the village pub was named after him) must have been getting rid of land for a long time. It was not particularly old or picturesque, although there were houses in the general neighborhood of very respectable age. It came near to being a "seaside resort," and was saved (or condemned) only by virtue of its extreme smallness. There was not room enough on the beach at the foot of the cliff for any great crowd. Even so, during August, and particularly over the August Bank Holiday, it was visited by as many city people as could get into the restricted space. There were some houses along the cliff which showed evidence of wealth and taste, but most of them were modern cottages of which the tenants demanded chiefly that they should be able to see, smell and hear the sea. On clear days the similar cliffs on the French side of the water stood up luminous and lovely, the perpetual reminder that at some time or other there had been no intervening water here, but only high chalky land stretching well into the great plain of France.

When I first saw it the late summer roses were blooming and no more tranquil corner could have been found on the broad earth. We had come from Salzburg and Cannes;

we had just been married; my wife's somewhat surprised
but philosophical family were prepared to welcome us
home. Lady Forbes-Robertson, driving a small car whose
intricacies she never seemed altogether to master—"Oh,
dear," she would say, and stop dead in the road—met us
in the rain at Dover pier. Her gentle beauty was akin to
her sister Maxine's, but softened and subdued by a character as different as night from day. She drove us up from
Dover along the great cliff, expostulating with the car the
while, and asking questions about the gay doings at Salzburg and Cannes. She was averse to criticism of the accomplished fact, and although we realized that she would
have preferred a different sort of wedding, a ceremonial
or unhurried family observance, she never said a word to
suggest it. By coincidence as much as skill she drew the
car up at the cottage gate, and there we were at "Bloms."

It was called Bloms because it had been bought, years
before, chiefly at the wish of the eldest daughter, Blossom
(sometimes called Blommy or Blom). For years the family had referred to it as "Blossom's house" or "Blom's
house," and finally as "Blom's." In the end the name had
become so established that they decided to paint it on the
gate, and Bloms it was. Strangers always thought it a surprising name and took pains to correct us in it, saying
"Blooms" or "Bolms" or other more reasonable variants. It
was a house without deliberate style, rambling a bit—particularly after a large room called "the New Room" had
been added to it at right angles some years earlier—and I
suppose it was not greatly different from many others on
the south coast of England; but years of family life and
careful gardening and fair dealing between people had
created a style for it, the style of love and kindliness. I
think you could tell by looking at it from the garden side,
and from walking through the rooms on the ground floor,

that those who lived here meant well toward each other and toward all others outside the gate. The rooms on the ground floor were a library at one end (very small, preempted for years by Dinah as a workroom with books and papers), a morning room of the same size, turned into a bedroom when there was an overflow of guests, and a drawing room with French windows on the garden. It was a low-ceilinged room with a fireplace and a piano opposite the garden side. Next to this was the dining room, its windows at one end half hidden by clematis and flowering shrubs. The New Room, built onto the house at right angles, was actually a separate structure and you reached it by walking a few steps in the open, beneath an added roof. This room, beautifully proportioned with a big fireplace at the end, was my favorite in the house; I wrote the greater part of two books there at the long refectory table that ran down the middle; and I remember Sir Johnston best as seated or standing by the fireplace there.

Sir Johnston Forbes-Robertson * was the heart and center of the house. I suppose that in his youth he must have had his share of human frailty, possibly even of the seven deadly sins; but of this not a trace remained at the time when I knew him. He was a very beautiful old man with a noble, even a majestic, head, with a voice of surprising power when he chose to use it, and with a manner so gentle and courteous that he charmed everybody who came near the place. Everybody in the house worshipped him

* Born 1853, died 1937; went on the stage in 1874. He acted for years with Ellen Terry, Sir Henry Irving and Modjeska before becoming an actor-manager in 1897. In that year he took the Lyceum Theatre, with Mrs. Patrick Campbell as his leading lady, and made a number of memorable productions, of which his *Hamlet*, repeated for years afterward, was the most celebrated. He married his new leading lady, Gertrude Elliott, in 1900. His most successful parts on the stage were in *Hamlet*, *Othello*, *Romeo and Juliet*, *The Light That Failed* (dramatized for him), *The Passing of the Third Floor Back* and Bernard Shaw's *Caesar and Cleopatra* (written for him). He retired from the stage in 1917.

—and not only those in the house. There was a large reti-
nue of devoted friends of both sexes and all ages who
came and went, sometimes staying in the house for weeks,
sometimes appearing only on special occasions, such as
his birthday (January 16th). These were people he had
known in his London life, or sometimes relatives of relatives, or sometimes people who had played in his company
on tours throughout the world. The idolatry was not of the
obvious or nauseating kind—there was none of the "dear
Master" atmosphere which infests the last years of such
men in Paris, for instance. The attitude was rather that of
mild heckling: "Come on, Dad, don't pretend you don't
know it's time to go to bed." Even so he was worshipped,
and when he died, the house, the family as such, ceased
to exist. He had only to express the slightest wish, and
unless it was forbidden by the doctor it took effect at
once.

His weapon—a mighty one—against boredom or un-
pleasantness was his great age, accompanied by deafness.
When an unwanted visitor stayed too long he simply went
to sleep. Sometimes he was known to wake up suddenly
and ask in a clear stage whisper that could have been
heard in the top balcony of the Metropolitan Opera
House: "What? Has that woman not gone yet?" We could
never fully determine whether he realized the carrying
power of these whispers or not. In the same way he was
totally unable to hear anything he did not wish to hear,
and we never knew whether this was deliberate or not.
At other times he could overhear things said in an undertone. He had been an actor all his life—rather against his
will; he would have preferred to paint—and no doubt the
theatre had left its imprint throughout his consciousness,
so that he could not have been too sure of himself where
reality ended and acting began. When he went out for a

walk in London with his coat and stick and square bowler hat he tottered majestically. Dinah used to aver that he was perfectly able-bodied until he reached the front door, and then began to be fragile, distinguished and ancient the moment he was under public observation. This may be so. I once asked Bernard Shaw whether he thought so and he replied, rather brusquely: "Why, of course. Anybody with a trace of histrionic instinct would do the same." I gathered that in Mr. Shaw's opinion all the world was a stage and all the men and women, indeed, players.

Such was the world of Sir Johnston, at any rate. It had a kind of magic and you found yourself involved in it, playing in it, "playing up." On that first night when we arrived at Bloms they had finished supper long since, but were waiting with another supper for us. Sir Johnston greeted us in his stately way—a mixture of affection and ceremony—in the drawing room and took us into the dining room. There was champagne, and at a given moment he rose to his feet, raised his glass in the air and sang out in a voice of astonishing power and resonance: "Here's to Mr. and Mrs. Vincent Sheean!" For a moment all his fragility had vanished; he was acting (if acting it was) as a man in his thirties. In another moment he had subsided into his armchair and was old again. I afterward heard that he had spent a whole week memorizing my name, repeating it over to himself loud and soft to get it right, since he had a great weakness for mixing up names.

Much of the charm of his conversation came from reminiscence and the repetition of things said (and found good) in years past. This is true of all old people, I suppose, but the peculiarity of Sir Johnston's repertory in that respect was that repetition by no means dulled it. He had such incredible skill in acting (or whatever it was) that he could tell the same story three times in the same eve-

ning and it was still funny, perhaps even funnier the third
time. His daughters knew all his stories by heart and
could give him a word or a cue if he chanced to forget.
If he forgot a name (such as Caruso, or Liszt, or Mrs. Patrick Campbell—he forgot all the most astonishing names)
they supplied it. He had been a friend of Whistler, of
Oscar Wilde, of Samuel Butler, of Coquelin; he had
played with Modjeska and Ellen Terry; as a small child
in London it had been his nightly task to take Swinburne
home and keep him from going inside the stained-glass
doors of the public-house. He could remember his mother's
very pre-Raphaelite parties where Swinburne read his
own poetry; he had studied painting with Rossetti ("my
dear Master") and was, indeed, the model for the figure
of Love in Rossetti's "Dante and Beatrice." His life seemed
to have touched the whole London culture of three-quarters of a century, here and there, and he remembered a
great deal; so that, to anybody with a sense of history, it
was a delight to hear him talk when he was in the mood.
His pre-Raphaelite youth, his painting and poetry in general, had given him rather a different attitude toward the
world from that of most actors, and most of his stories had
nothing to do with the stage. The theatre came in, with
all its witchery, in his way of telling them, but not in the
stories themselves—which is my idea of a good play in
any case. I recall very few stories of his which had to do
specifically with the theatre. One of the best was his account of his first meeting with Ellen Terry. It was the custom in the 1870's for an actor engaged in the company to
call upon the leading lady. Forbes-Robertson did so, with
his tall hat in his hand. In those days they carried the hat
into the drawing room and put it down on the floor under
the chair, upside down with the gloves in it (as in Proust).
The young actor, having fulfilled all these requirements,

was sitting there on the edge of his chair, looking in amazement and some terror at his surroundings, which were weird in the extreme for the year 1874. At a period when Victorian taste was at its height, rooms were crowded with furniture and knickknacks and any departure from the average was regarded as bizarre, Ellen's drawing room was almost bare of furniture and was hung with blue velvet. At one end was a sort of pilaster with the Venus de Milo upon it, before which incense was burning. After a certain delay the bewildered young man saw an exquisite Greek figure come from behind this pilaster and stand looking at him. It was Ellen, dressed not at all in the style of the period, but—indecently, the Victorians would have said—in a Greek robe of white. Forbes-Robertson was too overwhelmed to speak much to her, but I think he was at her feet from then on. There was always a touch of romantic fire in his voice when he spoke of her, even in his latest years, and his portrait of her is the best painting by him that I have seen.*

It took me a year or two to adjust myself to the peculiar magic of Sir Johnston, the way in which he lived mostly in the past, the way in which all times and ages had come to be nearly the same to him. He would speak of "dear" Mary, Queen of Scots and Napoleon as if he had known them; and, considering the remote figures he had actually known, it took a second's thought to decide whether these were among them. His favorite characters in history were Joan of Arc, Mary Stuart and Napoleon, and he had hundreds of books about them which he pored over in the evenings. Whenever a new one came out the family hastened to get it for him. When I first arrived at Bloms, I remember that he was reading the translation of Caulaincourt which had recently been published and Napoleon

---

* I think it has been given to the National Portrait Gallery.

figured largely in all conversation. It was two years later
(the summer of 1937) when I felt myself genuinely and
fully accepted by Sir Johnston into the family. He was
standing by the fireplace in the New Room with a small
glass of port in his hand, sipping it occasionally, with the
family all sitting round. Suddenly, with a firmness which
brought us all to attention, he said:

"You know, my dear Sheean, I have been thinking about
Lincoln and Napoleon. I have decided that Lincoln was a
greater man because he did not wish to kill people. Napoleon—yes, but he killed many people, and wished to do so.
Lincoln was a greater man."

This was clearly a tribute to the American nation and
done in my honor. Nothing more astonishing could have
been said in that room, where for many years everybody
had been accustomed to hearing Sir Johnston expatiate
on the all-round greatness of Napoleon. It was sheer courtesy, a quality Forbes-Robertson had bone-deep in him,
that made him throw over his lifelong hero in honor of an
American. He proved it by re-reading books about Lincoln for weeks afterward and telling his visitors how great
a man was that. In fact he shamed me into reading some
of the same books, and I (who was born in Lincoln's own
country) learned most of what I know about Honest Abe
in that house.

We stayed at Bloms a week that first time, and it was
in other summers (1937 and 1938) that I grew to know it
better. We had it to ourselves for a month or two at a
time, before the family came down from London, and
there was nowhere better for sleep, for work, for tranquil
happiness. At the end of the lawn was a rose garden, and
at the right, screened by high shrubs, the tennis court and
a field of wild poppies. On the left of the lawn was a
planted garden, vegetables and some flowers, lavender

and sweet peas, with a summer house at the top of the hill where the baby and her friends spent their time. From that summer house the coast of France was clear and white on most summer days. When the family came down we moved to a cottage on the North Foreland cliff, further toward Dover (Channel Cottage, it was called, and looked onto a hollow of the downs). I had some prevision, of course, of what was to become of all this; in fact in 1938 I wrote a poem of sorts about that garden, suggesting that it was preserved in its tranquility only by those who were now dying in Spain; but these premonitions were uncertain, flickering things; mostly one was content to be there in the sun.

The house, the village, the family, included of course a number of other houses and villages and families. There were Blossom and Miles—the eldest Forbes-Robertson daughter and her husband—who made airplanes. I met them first at Bloms but afterward used to go to their house near Twyford, in Berkshire, as often as I could. They bridged the immense distance between the world of Sir Johnston, with its timeless remoteness, and the blaring modern struggle in which I mostly lived. They made airplanes; and there was in fact nothing more relentlessly modern than their house and their airdrome, their factory and their office. Their child knew a dozen different types of airplanes before he was seven, and could easily pick them out as they wheeled over the house; by the time he was eight he could build an airplane of his own; and yet nobody could remember lines of Shakespeare, or Forbes-Robertson's vast store of anecdote, or who had played at what theatre in 1880, better than Blossom. The Elliott and Forbes-Robertson strains seemed to have blended most harmoniously in her, so that her eyes suggested the one, her nose and chin the other, in a baffling and exquisite

Mendelian fantasy. Then there was the next sister, Jean, an actress of rare quality, whose Hedda Gabler and Rebecca West (in *Rosmersholm*) almost frightened us out of the theatre one year in London; and there was Chloe, *farouche* and taciturn, who painted with great fury for weeks on end and then abandoned the brushes when the spirit moved her. She lived at Bloms and we had many bellicose engagements over the works of Mozart: she played and I sang and we never really came to treaty terms on the tempo. Nonny—Miss E. M. Biller—had brought the children up for a good part of their lives while their parents were off on tours of America, Australia, South Africa; she was of enormous importance and authority in the family. And there were the friends who were practically relatives—Maud Buchanan, "Uncle Alfred," half a dozen others who had their place in the orderly revolution of the seasons in the house.

Down the lane were George and Flo Arliss, with whom we used to play bridge and talk about things far from the village (Hollywood, for example). Flo's Yorkshire terrier, the flowers and the goldfish, along with the weather and some of George's books, constituted the drama of their garden. In the last war one bomb had fallen in the hollow between George's house and Bloms, beside the lane. The spot was still pointed out: "That was the place where the bomb fell, during the war."

2

The Forbes-Robertson house in London, at 22 Bedford Square, was also an integral part of our village. It was an Adam house from which some enterprising dealer had removed all the best wood-carving many years before, but no merchant could thieve out the proportions of the big front room on the first floor, the drawing room. Such houses have too many stairs for twentieth-century domestics, and the servants were mostly of a good age. Mrs. Happy, who "did" on Wednesday when all the others were out, seemed like something right out of a theatre, with her apple cheeks, her extraordinary deafness and her curtsy. "The boys"—there were two of them—were from the Depressed Areas (I never knew exactly where) and had been trained to domestic service by some philanthropic agency so that they could come up to London and get jobs and not be so Depressed. They seemed merry as grigs throughout the time when I knew the house. Lady Forbes-Robertson's maid, Nellie, had been a theatrical dresser for thirty years or so; she was married to the Second Grave-Digger in *Hamlet,* and took a corporative interest in the Forbes-Robertson productions. When John Barrymore's *Hamlet* was on view in London she went to see it and reported: "We didn't do it that way." Nellie had a slight tendency to tyranny in her own field and would never allow anything to be thrown away. "Oh, you couldn't do without that, m'lady. It'll come in handy some day, you'll see." As a result there was a fabulous collection of ageing haberdashery, millinery and drapery in the house, tucked away in odd corners and stored ceiling-high in the cupboards.

The *cassone* in the hall, on which hats and coats were laid, was from *Romeo and Juliet* (either the one with Modjeska or the one with Mrs. Patrick Campbell, I do not know which). At the end of the hall was a pennon in the royal Danish colors, with one streamer saying "Hamlet, Prince of Denmark" and the other saying "Johnston Forbes-Robertson." It had been given to Sir Johnston after his performance of *Hamlet* at Elsinore. (When the tenor Melchior came to the house to see some costumes and designs for *Othello* he looked at the Danish flag and said: "What a delicate compliment!") There were such symbols and trophies everywhere: the *Hamlet* rug, on which Sir Johnston had leaned, over many years, during the play scene at the feet of his two Ophelias, Mrs. Campbell and Gertrude; the *Hamlet* bell at Bloms, which called us to meals there with its full, mellow tone, had rung up his production of the play all the time he had played it.

Barnardo.   Who's there?
Francisco.   Nay, answer me: stand and unfold yourself.
Bar.   Long live the king!
Fra.   Barnardo?
Bar.   He.
Fra.   You come most carefully upon your hour.
Bar.   'Tis now struck twelve; get thee to bed, Francisco.
Fra.   For this relief much thanks, 'tis bitter cold,
And I am sick at heart.

The 16th of January, Sir Johnston's birthday, was the greatest fixed festival of the year. I was only present once at this feast; it was in 1936, on his eighty-third birthday, when Dinah and I happened to be in London between Egypt and Ireland. The early part of the annual celebration we missed, as we were living in a hotel, but I have no doubt the telegrams started coming at an early hour and continued through the morning. We used to cheat a bit on this, and put our friends up to sending telegrams of congratulation; it helped swell the volume and make an occasion. And indeed I think there is something triumphal about every birthday for all old people: it marks another victory over time, the greatest victory of which man is capable. Sir Johnston was not unaware of this and could even treat it with some lightness. When Dame Madge

Kendal died—a celebrated actress of the previous century, an old friend—he said: "Poor old Madge! Well, she was no chicken."

At lunch time on the birthday the whole family gathered: the immediate family, that is, the four daughters and their husbands. Later in the afternoon there was a sort of open house for all the relatives and friends; cousins came up from the country; dignified old gentlemen never seen at any other time of the year would put in an appearance. The festivity I attended (the eighty-third birthday) was graced by such an arrangement of weather as would have suited a story by Dickens. Snow was falling in great, clean, lazy flakes, lying soft and white on Bedford Square. The dining-room windows looked out upon the square. The table and chairs were Chippendale. There were portraits of the girls on the walls; their grown-up versions sat beneath them with the strangers, Miles and me, who had been thrust into this family by Fate. A Highland piper known as "Peeper Duff" appeared in the snow outside the windows midway through the meal and tramped up and down valiantly in a rusty-looking tartan, blowing away on his weird instrument. This had become part of the ceremony; the same piper had appeared for some years past. I am not sure who was responsible for arranging this part of the festival, but I suspect it was Jamie Hamilton (an incorrigible Scot). Somebody had to go to the door and ask the piper in; he came in, a vast red fellow with bare knees knobbled with the cold, and piped his way around the dining-room table, strutting and swinging his kilt as if he had been on some mountain top in a rising of the clans. It was a strange and almost intolerably moving noise. When he finished Sir Johnston poured him out a whole tumblerful of neat whisky, which the man tossed off in no time at all, prefacing the draught, in a sort of ami-

able bellow, with birthday wishes ("happy retur-r-r-rns")
to Sir Johnston. When this was accomplished he swung
round and made his exit.

We were all, I think, somewhat shaken by the sheer theatre of all this; I saw tears in Jean's eyes and was not far
from them myself. It was Sir Johnston who—characteristically—brought us back to a more sensible estimate.

"Did you see the way that fellah swigged off a whole
glassful of neat whisky?" he inquired, his head expressing
surprise and admiration. "I never saw such a thing."

He had been seventy-five before he discovered that
whisky was not fatal to the system; he had two weak
whiskies every evening, on the doctor's orders, and although he began by protesting, he ended by liking the
potion. Even so his allowance of it was very small, and I
think his esteem for the vast red piper who could drink a
tumblerful of it neat was an unaffected tribute.

At this point the doorbell rang and Maxine walked in.
She always carried with her a breath of the great world,
of dukes and palaces and the latest fashionable intelligence. She was wrapped in a mink coat and wore her
large pearls and diamonds; she had just arrived in London
a day or so before on one of her brief visits. The enclosed,
ingrowing quality of this house—its magic, I have called
it: at any rate its self-sufficiency, its settled and myth-
making life within its own strict limits—was something
that must always have escaped her. Perhaps it did not interest her; probably not. At any rate she looked at us all
in some surprise and said: "Why are you all gathered here?
What's happened?" Then, as realization dawned on her,
she turned on Sir Johnston and said: "Why, Forbie, is it
your birthday? My dear, I never dreamed . . ." This had
been the great day of the year for all the Forbes-Robertsons
for decades, and it is not possible that Maxine did not

realize it; but with her very different preoccupations she had simply forgotten. In spite of her deep, possessive affection for all her sister's family she somehow always remained a stranger to it because she did not see, or did not wish to see, what it most treasured—what gave it, for good or ill, its peculiar quality.

In the afternoon scores of people came and went. Sir Johnston did not always recognize them at first, and his deafness made him unaware of the carrying quality of his own voice. "Good God, who's this coming now?" he would exclaim quite audibly, and then, a moment later: "My dear, how good of you to come and see me. I am delighted, delighted." A little later he stood in a corner and told some of his best and most familiar stories to his sons-in-law and some other younger men; you could see that he was transported for a moment back to his clubs, which he had once frequented daily and could visit no more: he drew the Beefsteak and the Garrick about him. ("I stopped going to the Garrick when Pinero died. I knew so few people there any more.") His stories were purity itself; if even so much as a lady's ankle were mentioned he thought the theme a bit *risqué*; and yet there was a definite club manner that came over him when he had an audience of men. He was still repeating (in 1936) witticisms made in the 1880's at the Beefsteak, and we all knew the names of these forgotten wits of another age. (A favorite was named Pellegrini; and there was one called Judge Chetty.) That afternoon he told, I remember, several Wilde-and-Whistler stories. (I think there was the one about how Whistler— "dear Jimmie"—seeing an unknown young man at a party of Wilde's, went up to him and said: "Pardon me, but are you somebody's brother?") He introduced it by explaining, "It was just before poor Oscar got into that awful trouble."

All this time the snow fell clean and white in Bedford Square. I never saw snow like that in London before or afterward.

It was during this same visit—during the same week I believe—that the Shaws came to lunch. Gertrude, my mother-in-law, had not only an angelic character but a tenacious memory. She had stayed with us for a month that autumn at Cava dei Tirreni, below Naples, and during the course of those long sunlit days Shaw's name came up. (We talked of *Caesar and Cleopatra*, in which Sir Johnston and Gertrude had played.) I betrayed such interest in the subject that she remarked: "You ought to meet him. I'll ask him to lunch." Months later, when we came to London, I discovered that she had remembered and had indeed asked him to lunch on a day in January.

We were all a little afraid of Mr. Shaw—all, that is, except Sir Johnston, who was afraid of nothing. His reputation for rudeness, built up by a thousand stories repeated through this whole century; his overwhelming fame; his terrifying wit and his underlying wisdom were all together enough to create a formidable prelude to any meeting. It seemed to me that even the servants were a little spruce, a little nervous, when they knew that Mr. Shaw was coming to lunch. There was an artful vegetarian lunch for all of us—although I afterward discovered that when you went to Mr. Shaw's house only he ate vegetarian food— and the only wine was a little sherry beforehand. I was actually sipping my thimbleful of sherry when he was announced. I put it down at once, but his eagle eye had seen it. After he had made his greetings all round he came toward me and said: "There you are, tippling again. You made yourself out to be a great drunkard in your book but I thought perhaps it was an exaggeration. I see it's all true."

Mrs. Shaw's great kindness somehow saved me from having to make an answer and we went down to lunch. Through the meal I was struck by the way in which Shaw —and even Mrs. Shaw—seemed to be entirely of the theatre; they talked of plays and players unknown to me, some obviously famous in another day, some no doubt obscure, but all vivid in their memories. They shared with Sir Johnston and Gertrude a purely professional attitude which I had never expected from them. In the vast range of Shaw's interests the theatre must obviously have come first, at least aesthetically, but until I heard him talk I never realized it. In the years when I used to read and re-read his plays I thought of him as a rebel against the theatre, an intellectual on the outside of the business forcing the commercial enterprises to accept him, after many delays, on sheer merit. It was a surprise to find that he could think and talk in terms as exactly professional as if he had been Pinero himself. For example, people of the theatre—at least in London—attach great importance to the actual theatre itself. They will say: "That was at the Court Theatre. No, it wasn't, it was at Drury Lane." Or: "That was during the brief period when X. had the Lyceum." As a member of the general public I had never been particularly conscious of which theatre I happened to be in; I looked at the name on the ticket for the purpose of getting there, and once there I forgot it. The Shaws, like the Forbes-Robertsons, had the professional consciousness in this matter as in many others. I hardly know how to specify the slight turns of phrase, tricks of thinking, shades of significance which make people of the theatre, but by all these nothings, added together, the Shaws were theatre folk too. I think there is even an element of acting in it, since hardly anybody who has to do with a theatre escapes some influence of that kind; and Shaw himself

would certainly say so—"anybody with a trace of histrionic instinct would do the same."

Sir Johnston enjoyed himself immensely in that company. There were not many people who had actually
known his oldest friends—Samuel Butler, for instance, or
Ellen Terry. Butler had long been dead; it was strange to
me to hear living men talk of him as a great friend, re-
count stories, laugh over his vagaries. When we were upstairs again after lunch my mother-in-law maneuvered me
into a place on the sofa between Forbes-Robertson and
Shaw. They engaged in a long conversation about Ellen
Terry, who was also little more than a shadowgraph to
me. Conscious of my awkward and silent presence between
them, I ventured a remark at one point. "The only thing
I've known about Ellen Terry as a person," said I, "was
that she had awful luck with men." On both sides I was
assailed with protests. "Nonsense, nonsense," said Shaw.
"All the most charming men in London were in love with
Ellen." Sir Johnston sputtered: "Ellen conquered everybody who ever saw her. I remember once . . ."

This first meeting with the Shaws was followed by a
number of others. Dinah and I went to see them two or
three times in the country, in Hertfordshire, and on some
occasions in the next few years I lunched with them at
Whitehall Court, in London. It took several years of these
meetings at wide intervals for me to understand and appreciate Mr. Shaw. I began by being intimidated, which
is no basis for any form of understanding; I progressed to
a sort of rebellious semi-hostility ("Why does he tell me
all this? I've heard it before; I've read his plays and his
prefaces. Why the performance?"); and then, in the end,
I came to some sort of reconciliation with his style, his
general line. Of his celebrated rudeness, recorded in so
many books and recounted in so many stories, I never ex-

perienced a single blow. There was one time at tea in Hertfordshire when he went into a long disquisition about T. E. Lawrence and me; he traced some resemblance between my *Personal History* and Lawrence's book; he thought we both had "the sickly conscience," and that it was a peculiarly modern disease, peculiarly of the era to which he was glad he did not belong. He made inordinate fun of Lawrence, so that the comparison was by no means flattering. There was a great deal of this. I was a little uncomfortable, but not downright miserable, and in any case I never thought of it as rudeness; he was launched on a wonderful flight of words, and I recognized even then that this word-spinning and idea-spinning was his style and had been his style for so long that to complain of it would be like complaining of the weather. Apparently Mrs. Shaw (who had been very fond of Lawrence) thought otherwise, for she said, rather decisively: "The subject really must be changed. I think we've had quite enough of this." The subject was immediately changed, although I think Mr. Shaw was genuinely startled at the ultimatum and had never once thought that he might be making anybody unhappy.

My sort of observation (which has so little to do with ideas) was at work during this extraordinary hour at tea, and what I remember best is not Mr. Shaw's thesis about Lawrence and me and our "sickly conscience," but the way in which he crumbled up and ate his cake. It was a cake with several layers of different fruit pastes and a center of heavy, delicious brown stuff. Mr. Shaw had delivered me one of his little lectures about this cake. "Don't eat the middle part," he said. "That's muck. It'll do all sorts of things to your insides. Eat this outer part—it's all good orange and lemon and other fruit in sugar form. That can do you no harm." Then he started on his long, high-winged flight about Lawrence, a sustained monologue of real fluency and brilliance, during which he picked at his cake until he had eaten every single bit of it, including the "muck" I was not supposed to touch. I was only half following his argument. My mind was divided between two things, one the bemused wonder: "Can he be talking about *me?*" and the other a fascinated concentration upon his nervous fingers and the cake.

I have often puzzled about what people meant when they said he was rude. I can only suppose that his extreme directness, his way of talking on a subject and ignoring unrelated considerations, must be regarded as rudeness by conventional people. The only story I happen to remember at the moment is one about Lady Randolph Churchill (Winston's mother), who telegraphed him an invitation to lunch once before the last war and received the reply: "Certainly not. Are you not aware of my habits?" To which she replied: "I know nothing of your habits but your manners are deplorable." I suppose that was rudeness on his part; he should have said politely, I am a vegetarian and I do not go out to lunch much for that reason, please excuse. But it does not seem rudeness to me because it was natural to him and he was only saying what was true, and saying it succinctly.

The strongest and most permanent impression I have of his character, aside from his ideas or style, is one of extreme kindness. I know nothing in that line to equal his performance in the matter of Frank Harris' *Life of Shaw.* His account of it to me was that Harris, ageing and impoverished somewhere on the Riviera, thought he might make some money out of a life of Jesus and wrote his publishers in New York suggesting it. The publishers cabled him, "No market for Jesus, but do you know Shaw?" Harris had a contract in no time at all, proceeded to write the book and then died. His widow sent it in manuscript form to Shaw for correction. Shaw said it abounded in misstatements of fact.

"His opinions and interpretations and all that are a matter of indifference to me," he said. "But I could not allow them to rush into print with a thing which got even the simplest dates and facts wrong. I corrected all that—I put it straight for him. If you ever really want to know anything about me, in the way of dates and facts, read Harris' book."

On this recommendation I read the book, which was as scurrilous a production as was ever put forth about an eminent man during his own lifetime. The dates and facts were no doubt correct, since Shaw put them in himself; but the "opinions and interpretations" were malevolent, offensive balderdash worthy of the smatterer and blowhard that Harris was. And why did Mr. Shaw permit the publication of this tawdry patchwork? Because Harris' widow was destitute.

I have some knowledge of other benefactions of his, but he keeps all that side of his character in the dark whenever possible. He has cultivated throughout his life a sharp, splintery brilliance which does not go with kindness; no doubt he would heartily reject any imputation of the quality. In the same way there is a deliberate buffoonery about his treatment of serious subjects which has concealed, sometimes too successfully, the depth and breadth of his wisdom. Sometimes I have listened with a complex interaction of shock upon shock, as when a machine goes slightly out of gear in all its parts, while he talked of subjects that seemed to me desperately serious; and a year or two later I remembered what he said and thought that underneath all the words, all the jokes, all the fireworks, he had been right.

The accusation of dryness, intellectuality, lack of humanity, is another which, taken upon hearsay and slight acquaintance, could not be supported on better knowledge of him. The case of Lawrence in that conversation in 1936 is one in point. At first it seemed that—since Lawrence had been a familiar of the house, and was so recently dead in so sudden a way—it was inhuman of Shaw to make fun of him. (He ridiculed all those extraordinary phobias and manias which were the result of Lawrence's tortured self-consciousness, made them into something perilously near to childish pretense.) Yet when Mrs. Shaw spoke he immediately abandoned the subject, and I think that in the fascination of developing an idea, a whole series of ideas, he had quite forgotten that anybody might take his improvisation amiss. The fact appears to be that he was remarkably kind to Lawrence in life, and the only reason why he felt free to exercise his wit upon him afterward was that an idea had started its flight and should not be suppressed.

Mr. H. G. Wells once told me part of the truth (of what I think the truth) about Shaw. He said that he was an artist. "Remember that," he said. "Shaw is a man with a remarkable aesthetic gift. He has never thought so; he has always thought he was a thinker. I can't really see how anybody can qualify in that way without a scientific basis, don't you know. I mean without biology and chemistry and genetics and physiology and all that sort of thing. But he had a sense of form, don't you know, and all that sort of thing, and no matter how much he may talk about socialism and that sort of thing, the fact is that he is first and foremost an artist and always has been."

Certainly his consciousness as an artist was always resolutely turned toward the social aspect of individual life. The general and the didactic were always, or nearly al-

ways, more interesting to him; or at any rate the point of
intersection between the individual and the general life
was his preferred point of investigation. This was not
through lack of the creative or poetic gift. It is not possible
to see a good performance of *Candida*, for example, without feeling the warm, lovely glow of a creative gift which
might have expressed itself without the slightest concern
for the general welfare of mankind. But, owing no doubt
to the social and economic conditions of the century, the
flow of intellectual influences, the psychological imperatives whatever they were, he became—in spite of his lack
of scientific training—a socialist, concerned over many
years with questions of social thought and organization; in
the historic balance he may even have contributed as
much to socialist thinking (not in a party sense, at all) as
any scientist.

The didactic bent of his mind brought me, chiefly,
amusement. He had a number of fixed ideas about food
and drink and would hold forth upon them at any time. I
never dreamed of contesting anything he said, but neither
did I alter my preferences in food or drink. Once, I remember, he had been reading or thinking about the theories
of a certain doctor in London who sounded like an arrant
quack, a man who said he could cure almost any ordinary
malady by posture, by making people hold their necks,
heads and shoulders in a certain position. The main part
of this panacea was the posture of the neck, and Mr. Shaw
demonstrated to us how it should be done. I think he even,
for the moment, half believed it. In the same way he
seemed to be fiercely serious when he delivered me little
homilies on my own food and drink, and I doubt if it ever
occurred to him that such proselytizing can scarcely ever
be effective. I could not resent a lecture of this sort from

Mr. Shaw; I was, in fact, flattered that he should think the matter worth an effort.

Those few conversations in the years before 1940 stick in my memory along with the unrelated things of our village, the high cliffs where we used to walk, the Dover Memorial, the New Room at Bloms and the beach at St. Margaret's. Mr. and Mrs. Shaw belonged to our village, whether they had ever seen it or not; they were of the theatre, like the Forbes-Robertsons, of the country too, like them, and somehow in tune with the kind of thinking and feeling that went on in our village. I do not think of them in relation to the great world of which I had glimpses with Maxine, nor in relation to my own professional existence, but as akin to the quiet rooms at Bloms, the efforts of my stronger moments to do good work, the tradition to which I feel most drawn (that of an objective effort to use the human reason for the purpose of social organization) and the calm kindliness of unruffled lives in a time of peace. When I think of England before 1940 they are there, in it and of it, a moving force by no means spent, an autumnal light over the mild green fields and the wooded lanes. There are many things I should never have seen or understood if I had never known them.

### 3

When I flew to London from Paris in late May, 1940, it was with the intention of returning to Paris as soon as I had seen Dinah safely onto a ship for America. I did this by early June but was then unable to get back to Paris. Not only were the airplanes taken for official business, but the French had suddenly decided to refuse all visas, even such impressively red-inked visas as mine. I fumed and fretted and watched the immense catastrophe of France from across the Channel.

During her few days in England Dinah and I went down to see Gertrude (Lady Forbes-Robertson), who was living at Hurstmonceux in Sussex. She had left St. Margaret's because the constant explosions in and across the Channel made it impossible to sleep. Bloms had become a hospital at the outbreak of war and she had spent the intervening months in a friend's house. Now the whole south coast of England was a military area, the threat of invasion had suddenly risen like a dark cloud over the whole island, and the explosions in and across the Channel were more constant than ever. We spent Saturday and Sunday at Hurstmonceux. There were no explosions to be heard there, but the barricading of the roads was going on all through the country, and you did not have to travel far down any one of them to see the sudden, feverish construction of tank traps and airplane obstacles. On Sunday morning, when Dinah and her mother went to church, there was a day of national prayer as ordered by the King; this was the one which was immediately followed by the Belgian surrender. (The next day of national prayer was immediately followed by the French surrender.) Dinah told me that the gentry and the villagers prayed with unaffected fervor, and that there was the sense of a truly solemn moment about the whole ceremony.

On the Monday morning we drove down the coast to Dover and St. Margaret's in a hired car. Strictly speaking, this was against military rule, although we did not know it then; I was an alien and as such had no right even in the district, much less driving along its most forbidden coastal road. However, nobody appeared to bar our way.

The few sentries we did pass at barricades along the road either saluted with smiles or cheerfully gave us directions for going farther. It was a lovely spring day, with a shower now and then to soften its brightness. Dinah had wanted to see her old home once more, since she was going to America at a moment which made return seem a little problematical. As our drive neared its end and we topped the great hill between Folkestone and Dover, coming out onto the immense white cliff for the home stretch, we saw and heard full proof of the war's approach. It was just over there, across the friendly Channel, to be seen in clouds of smoke and clouds of flame, to be heard in the rise and fall of thunder from gun, tank and plane. There was one great flame which remained almost steady that day and night and the next morning: we judged it to be over Calais, and thought it might be oil reserves on fire. There were lightning flashes everywhere along the French coast, and the air quivered from time to time with a greater crash of the man-made thunder. Dover seemed, as we drove through, to have gone into uniform, but its shops were all open and its general look—except for the khaki—familiar enough. We went on to St. Margaret's.

Here we ran into the clearest show of a sense of war. The gentry seemed to have vanished, for the most part, boarding up their houses and moving farther inland. The villagers showed some scorn at this. Our pink-cheeked friend Mrs. Paye, who used to "do" for us before the family came down, stood in the door of her cottage and told us how it was. "The gentry's all gone away," she said, her eyes twinkling with some enjoyable malice. "It was the same in the last war. I never did 'old with going away the minute there's a bit of trouble." We found our friend Edward, who kept the garage at the top of the hill, busy with new duties: he had been appointed ambulance driver for the village and was to organize his unit.

There at the top of the hill, not far from his garage, was Bloms. We went along to visit it, having been forewarned that its condition was not exactly that which we remembered. Inside the house we were greeted by a cool, surprised V. A. D. nurse, a little supercilious, who gave us permission to walk round.

It was a hospital at the time, although only minor cases had been brought there so far. The New Room, where I had worked long and (for me) well, was now a ward with rows of beds in it. All the rooms were bare and clean, without rugs or curtains or furniture.

But the garden was a real surprise. One large dug-out shelter in three sections occupied its whole center. It was, so far as I could see, a perfectly useless shelter, as it had only about a foot and a half of earth over it—a shallow scooped-out place on the exact top of the hill facing the Channel. It made an unsightly hump all down the middle of the garden. The lawn had, of course, ceased to exist; the rose garden at the end kept up an obstinate and unaided struggle; only the vegetable garden (minus its sweet peas and lavender and the rest) looked halfway normal. From the summer house at the top you could see the great sheet of flame on the other side of the Channel, and greater explosions were distinct against the minor thunder.

We went down to the Granville to spend the night. It was still open, although its good-humored proprietress told us she would have to close in a day or so. The clients consisted of ourselves and an elderly naval officer. We went into the hotel bar for a drink before dinner and found one strange new thing: the village boys, who in peacetime had left the Granville Bar, as if by instinct, to the uses of the gentry, now frequented it in some number and seemed quite at home there. In our walk through the village and out on the cliff we saw only boarded-up houses. That was Molly Eyre-Crabbe's house, where we used to go to laugh and tell stories at just this hour in the evening, and look out from time to time for a brief, venomous quarrel over what boat was passing in the Channel; here was Locksley, a big house where they had an auction once after the owner's death, and I bought a lot of books and Dinah her Crown Derby coffee set; here was a cottage belonging to a friend who loved to hear music and deified Toscanini.

At night there were strange noises. One explosion, which seemed to be just under our window, took place at just six in the morning. I suppose it must have been a mine in the Channel below us. I got up to look out of the window. The dawn was coming up very red. The sheet of flame seemed bigger than ever over there, at Calais.

We went back to London on a boat train the next morning. It was the last boat train I ever saw with Pullmans and all accommodations; for all I know it was the last one that ever ran. The evacuation of the British army from the continent had actually begun, although its great and difficult phase was still before us. In the Pullman going up, seated directly opposite us, was an army chaplain who had just arrived from the other side and was eager to talk. I dodged his eye successfully, but a rather prim-looking City man who sat down at the same table with him had no such luck. The chaplain was in a rage and wanted to be heard.

"I've just come in on the last boat there'll ever be," he said, and sounded as if he meant it. "The things I've seen would make your hair stand on end. There'll be a lot of things different when this war is over. What are they going to do with all the boys left over there, that's what I want to know? Bombed from morning to night, always on the run ... I've seen things I'll never forget. .... Rich and poor. Do you think there'll be any rich or poor when this is over?"

The exact line and weight of the chaplain's complaint escaped me throughout the journey. From time to time the City man would nod a terrified assent or would say: "Indeed, yes. Quite so." Other passengers looked frowningly over the edges of their papers and whispered together. The chaplain really was talking too much and too loudly. Then I still had no idea of how much and how loudly Englishmen could talk when they got thoroughly aroused. Or of how incoherent—how like the vague mutiny of this chaplain—their anger could be.

On the train that morning we had unlimited quantities of bread, butter and sugar, with plenty of good tea (Earl Grey's mixture, I think), along with orange juice, excellent ham and two eggs apiece. On the wine card were all the known varieties of French mineral water, wines and liqueurs. These things were to disappear with such speed thereafter that it seems hardly credible that they once existed on the Dover train. I took many trains to and from Dover in the months to come, and hardly ever did so without thinking at least once of the ample breakfast in the Pullman car that sunny morning, of the shocked City man and the angry chaplain.

4

Dinah got her ship and took her way across the disturbed Atlantic without mishap. I stayed on in London trying (for a few days at least) to find a way of returning to Paris for the inevitable retreat of the French army and government. I still thought, only half-heartedly because in truth I knew better, and knew by bitter experience—but still could not escape the habit of thinking—that what one wrote about such things could in some way affect or accelerate the course of events. I wanted to help to make my own countrymen realize the urgency of the danger to themselves, to their institutions and preferred structure, in this stupendous German victory. But the point of view no longer influenced the official French: they were, in London as in Paris, given over to full, un-relieved panic. The French Embassy in London, during those June days when I haunted it in hope of getting my visa, was a melancholy sight, with packing cases in the corridors and white-faced attendants who scarcely remem-bered which secretaries dealt with which questions. There was no hope of helpful action out of them, but I persisted until that day when we heard that Paris had fallen.

During this time I began to frequent the House of Commons, particularly on the days when the Prime Min-ister was to speak. Mr. Kennedy, our Ambassador, used to give me a ticket in the diplomatic gallery—I had no press status—and I would slip in at four in the afternoon, just in time to hear Winston speak. I heard all the great speeches, that of June 4th and that of June 18th among them, the almost incredible speeches which covered the great tragic situations of France's fall, the evacuation from Dunkirk and the resolve to defend the island inch by inch. Mr. Churchill at this time (June, 1940) occupied a posi-tion which it has been given to few men in human history to hold, and it has always seemed to me that he held it first of all because of those speeches. Decisions were made, and great ones; many deeds were done; his swift, unannounced and dangerous flights to France during the

final days of the Third Republic were among them; and
yet the quality of the man came out most of all in those
speeches in the House of Commons, and they aroused
an echo in the English people. He spoke to them in the
language of Shakespeare (modernized, it is true, but the
unmistakable language), and they, no less remarkable in
their resurrection, understood it. You could find this way
of thinking and feeling, expressed in just such high, clear
words, in all the historical plays of Shakespeare. It completely transcended any personal or class limitations of
the sort which have so often deadened the authoritative
voices of England, and the people knew this by instinct,
powerful and sure. Winston's speeches were simply English. It was difficult indeed to realize that only a month
before this same people had still been content to let itself be chloroformed by the small-minded and dreary
sophistry of Neville Chamberlain—and it was stranger still
to see that man sitting there, a cadaveric gray shadow,
observing from Winston's side (if he could observe) the
vast ruin he had helped to bring about.

The first time I ever entered the House of Commons
was on a day when Mr. Churchill did not speak. He was
in France. It was May 22nd, and I had just arrived in
London. I lunched with Lady Diana Cooper, who dropped
me off at St. Stephen's Portal afterward. As the taxi drew
up there she saw the workmen putting up barbed wire
around the Houses of Parliament and said, in that curi-
ously husky voice: "So it's come to this, has it?" The sand-
bags and machine-gun emplacements were being improvised all over Westminster, and miles of barbed wire—then
new and glistening—had just that morning appeared in
the heart of London. When I went into the diplomatic
gallery I found only a small attendance, as word had been
passed round that Mr. Churchill would not speak. Instead,

we were afforded the sight and sound of Major Attlee, the head of the Labour Party and second in command of the new government, presenting a law which sounded like social revolution.

It was and remains the most comprehensive assumption of powers ever made by a modern democratic government. It declared in the plainest language that for the duration of the present emergency all persons and all property were at the disposal of the State. Under this law —which consisted of a single sentence and was passed through its three readings at a single sitting—the State could do anything it chose, subject only to the formal censorship of the House of Commons. As it turned out, the law was used with caution, almost with reluctance, and the government showed an extreme sensitivity to a House of Commons opinion as well as to the opinion of the country as reflected in the press; but on paper, at any rate, on the day when it was proposed and passed, it looked like a general revolutionary revision of society.

Mr. Attlee read it out in a colorless voice—his voice— and I nearly toppled out of the gallery in astonishment. There were plenty of others in London who took it, as I did, on its plain profession. I lunched the next day with Mr. H. G. Wells, who opened the talk by saying, rather happily, "The revolution in England has now begun." He may indeed have been right—and probably was—but as the months passed and the fulminating sentence was never put into effect I began to see how slow beginnings may sometimes be. The virtual conscription of labor, the "Essential Works Orders" issued by the Ministry of Labour under this law to freeze certain classes of labor to its task, the seizure of certain houses and the progressive taxation of capital and earnings, all put together, did constitute an immense change in the England of 1940–1942, but a considerable part of this change could have been brought about under existing legislation. Perhaps the purpose of a law so drastic was to bring home to the entire population how desperate was their pass, how limitless their sacrifice might have to be; but the events themselves took care of that realization before the year was out.

The army came back from Dunkirk, having lost all its arms, ammunition and equipment. During the week of the evacuation it seemed hardly possible that so many men could be safely taken off the French beaches. It was true, as Mr. Churchill said in the House, that "wars are not won by evacuations," and yet the escape of the army from Dunkirk was so much a happier event than we had expected that it came near to producing the illusion of victory. Most of those who knew anything at all of the situation expected the British army, with that French army which accompanied it, to be annihilated or taken prisoner. The men's return, battered and disgruntled as many of them were, and often with no arms at all, was what Mr. Churchill called "a deliverance," an event outside the calculations of probability. Through the next weeks I met a good many of the men who had conducted the evacuation and pieced together, after the event, some notion of the wild enterprise, in which boats of all sizes made their way across the Channel, through treacherous weather and waters, to pick up all the soldiers they could carry. I knew one man who had made nine crossings and professed to be reading a novel by Anthony Trollope to his wardroom in the quiet moments; there was another, down at Dover, who did eight trips in a seventy-foot yacht and loaded his ship to the gunwales. I heard stories of collisions by night, misunderstandings and disaster. And yet the bulk of the army was brought back. I think it was a considerable comfort to many who thought of the Ger-

man invasion as certain; even though this army was unarmed and broken, it was an army, and could stand and
fight again if the arms came in time.

Those few weeks in London were keyed too high for
regular work or for exact recollection. Sometimes I wonder what I did through all that time. I had engagements
to write for American magazines, but did not do so; it
would have been impossible just then. I remember one
extraordinary cablegram I received just about then from
my agent, quoting an offer from an editor. He was prepared to pay a very large sum for "an eye-witness account
of the German entry into London, twenty-five thousand
words." I did not answer this, but puzzled a good bit then
and since over what he might have meant. Where did he
think I would be when Hitler rode into London? As a
writer whose total work, of whatever kind or date, was
forbidden by the Gestapo,* I had no claim on the kindness of Dr. Goebbels; and a recent decree of the conquer-
ing Germans in the West had made German law appli-
cable to all journalists of whatever nation who attacked
"the Third Reich or its leaders." Whatever else might happen, I did not think myself entitled to a ringside seat for
Hitler's entrance into London.

That entrance was strangely delayed. One night, at
dinner at Lady Maureen Stanley's, a cabinet minister of
the first consequence produced a slip of paper from his
pocket and showed me some figures written on it. They
were, as I remember, to a total of some 267,000. This was
the number of British and French soldiers who had been
safely brought home from Dunkirk up until eight o'clock
that night. It began to be clear that the salt water of the
English Channel, narrow though it was, would at least
delay the Nazi enterprise. One day in July I heard that

* Himmler's decree of January 11, 1940.

rifles had arrived from Canada; they were old rifles, but they were better than none. During that month rifles, machine guns and sub-machine guns arrived from Canada and the United States; the Home Guard—thus christened by Winston instead of an awkward earlier name—began to train for combat in every village street; the R.A.F., which had been husbanded in the French campaign as in Norway, began to show its mettle and its numbers. The situation was as bad as it could be, I suppose; the island was certainly without adequate defense against a determined invader; and yet, by the tautening nerve and heightened head of people—just the people you happened to know or to meet—I felt that the story was by no means over. Both the French and the Germans fully expected this people to sue for peace, but exactly the opposite response to disaster was, in fact, being evoked by tradition, character and circumstance. "We shall fight on the beaches, we shall fight on the hills"—by July, at any rate, I knew that they meant it.

Down in the country the Home Guard and other local authorities were rounding up all possible weapons. Vanessa Bell, in her cottage in Sussex, had an ancient blunderbuss hanging on the wall; it had been put there by some impulse years before and forgotten; the visiting Home Guard took it just the same. In the northeast counties I was told that even the butcher knives were being sharpened, and yet by a sort of tacit, combined but unorganized understanding, all English people tried to avoid emphasis upon the terrible crisis of their destiny. This made some of my American friends in London sure that the English did not "realize" what was happening. They would speak with great violence upon occasion, anxious to bring about this "realization"; but of course the thing was fully realized all along. Bill Stoneman ( *Chicago Daily*

*News)*, meeting Lady Diana Cooper at Beaverbrook's house, said: "Do you *realize* what's going on? The Germans are rolling like burning lava over the whole world. Burning lava." From that day to this she has referred to him as "Lava." Knick—H. R. Knickerbocker—turned up at the end of June from Bordeaux, and took it as his mission to break the bad news to his friends; with him too I believe it was a work of supererogation. In fact the English all knew that they stood upon the brink of death, but, being conditioned in their own style, preferred not to state it too often or too strongly. The great, solemn statements were, again by tacit consent, left to Mr. Churchill; and after listening to one of these statements the usual English response was to turn off the radio, sigh, and speak of something else—of how well Winston had spoken, of what the next day's task might be, but not, in my experience, of the actual imminence of conquest. The great underlying truth of England's near-helplessness before a formidable foe was there, always there, but it was too strong for ordinary speech.

The Germans, of course, deflected by the necessity of taking over France, could under no circumstances have come across the Channel as soon as we then thought. June and much of July were lost by them in the preoccupation with France. But even then, to our astonishment, we learned that they were not ready. First they had perhaps not expected such sweeping victory, but once it had been achieved, as we know from many indications, they thought the fall of France would induce England to make peace. When this was proved a gross miscalculation they began, from all the ports of Holland, Belgium and France, those great "invasion exercises" in which they spent a great part of the summer, and it was only then that it dawned on us how they were actually not ready.

Reflecting upon it afterward, it seemed to me fairly obvious that a huge German army of landlubbers would require special training before being sent across the sea in boats. Many of them had never seen the sea, and to cross the Channel in small boats is an undertaking of considerable difficulty. A completely air-borne invasion demands complete air supremacy; thus the barrier, geographically so slight, was enough to enforce delay. I still think it would have been possible for the Germans to invade England in late July or August if they had relentlessly used their air force without counting the cost, and if they had been willing to sacrifice large numbers of their land soldiers in the crossing. They did not so decide—not, I should think, for reasons of humanity, but because they feared to fail. They temporized by training their men in boats, by pouring out threats on the radio, by seeming to be forever on the verge of the great enterprise. Some of their "invasion exercises" were bombed by the R.A.F. and a good many were photographed; and when another spring had come these exercises were not resumed, for Hitler had turned elsewhere.

Between June and September of 1940 the invasion threat did, I think, incessantly press upon all minds in England. I cannot remember hearing anybody speak of Egypt or India then; world strategy and geopolitics meant little to people who stood under such a blackening cloud. Yet Mr. Churchill must have been thinking in terms of the world, or at least of the empire, for it was then—in the most ominous days—that he decided to send reinforcements to Egypt and the Near East. He did so out of the slender resources left to him by the disastrous continental campaign, and took a great risk in doing so; the daring course again proved the wisest. At the time we knew little or nothing about it, and might perhaps have thought the decision rash if we had known. Our nerves were keyed to the contest that involved all present lives on that island, and drew us most of all to the south coast, to the cliffs of Dover.

I started going back to Dover in July. It seemed to me that the classic, unchangeable routes were always the roads of conquest—that Hitler would come to England the shortest way, the way approved by history and geography. His invasion of the West had taken the route of all invasions since Caesar; there were sound reasons for it. The routes of conquest are indeed the routes of Caesar, Napoleon and Alexander; at one time or another Hitler has attempted all three, quite possibly because the exploits of his predecessors captivate his imagination; but those routes were in no case chosen by individual talent or whim. They were fixed by conditions over which Hitler had no more control than Napoleon. Dover-Folkestone was the point closest to the continent; the narrow seas were too narrow and too treacherously channeled for the big ships of the navy; the jump, if it were to be made, should in reason be made here, within easy operating range for the whole German air force including fighter planes.

There had been German raids over a great many places in England—all military objectives at least in theory—before the long air battle of the South began. These were raids made by a small number of airplanes which frequently lost their way and dropped their bombs harmlessly in open fields from five to fifteen miles off from their presumed targets. The Germans must have been somewhat at a loss, unused to the crowded English country with its close, confused network of communications; targets must be hard to find in such a country; the atmosphere even by day is not one of great clarity. I went down to Cardiff in late June to broadcast to America on a program of Ed Murrow's for the Columbia Broadcasting System. It was a round-up, and other men spoke from Belfast, Glasgow, Manchester and Birmingham. In Cardiff, at the Welsh ports and up in the lush valleys where the coal mines are, I found plenty of evidence of German bombing and very little evidence of real damage. Even in the Cardiff docks it was remarkable how many bombs had neatly missed doing harm. In a suburb across the water from the docks there were ruined houses but there had been almost no casualties. There I saw, for the first time in England, the kind of sight that had been so familiar in Spain—houses almost totally ruined, yet with a bowl of roses standing undisturbed on an intact table, or with a second floor sticking out, without walls or ceiling, over the rubbish of the rest. In that Cardiff suburb one bomb had landed in the garden behind a school for small children (what was once called a "dame's school"). The house was a ruin, but none of the children had been hurt. They had all huddled together in the closet underneath the stairs on the ground floor, and the stairs remained after the rest of the house had mostly fallen in. The teacher at this dame's school told me about one small boy of four who inquired, when the tempest was over: "Was that a bomb?" He was rather proud than otherwise when he learned that this was the case.

Up in Norfolk, where I went to stay at Venetia Montagu's house, there actually was a raid somewhere in the neighborhood one night and I slept through it, to hear the tale incredulously next morning. There was night and day raiding, on a small scale, all through June and July, and I suppose one reason why the country at large paid it so little heed was that everybody felt the approach of a far greater test to which this was only the tentative prel-

ude. There were strange errors of the German night bombers, as when the Luftwaffe announced that it had bombed
Bristol when in fact it had bombed Cardiff; there were
the first German planes crashing in the country, the first
rumors of fifth-column activity, of spy signals to the
raiders, of dire collusions and conspiracies. But all this
was as nothing to the fire that was set alight in August
and September, when the whole country went into battle
array, and—as is now clear—the Germans met their first
defeat.

## 5

Down at Dover the hostelry at which the press and considerable sections of the navy and garrison congregated
was the Grand Hotel. It was one of those hotels on the
Marine Parade, down at the end underneath the great cliff
of Dover Castle, and in the years of peacetime I had been
unaware of its existence. But since the army and navy
had taken most of the other hotels—including the old
Lord Warden, the most familiar—this was now the chief
one left to private enterprise. Its owner was doing the sort
of business hotel men must dream of, a sort of cross between Yukon gold-rush and Elks' convention. If or when
you got a room, you shared it with anybody who happened to be put in it; you slept in sitting rooms or writing
rooms if there was nothing else; and you made no exag-
gerated claims on the available service. There was still
plenty of food and drink then, and the water ran hot in
the bath when you could get into it. Under the circumstances it always seemed to me that the Grand Hotel
did a fairly good job, and when we compared it, as press
people will, with hotels similarly overrun by war, we
thought it came off well. At any rate it achieved dignity

in its finish, for one fine day, before the paint was dry
on the "redecoration" which its sanguine manager had
ordered, the inevitable bomb came along and wrecked
one half of the house. But before that happened, throughout July, August and most of September, the crowded and
(shall we say?) shabby hotel on Dover Beach went
through all the intense excitement, the high and hopeful
bewilderment, of the Battle of Britain.

We did not call it the Battle of Britain; indeed I never
knew that name for it until the following spring, when
an Air Ministry booklet came out under that title and
revealed all the secrets we had been forbidden to mention
in 1940. We knew it was a battle, but we did not know
it was *the* Battle of Britain. Neither did the hotel manager,
the barmaid or the waiters in the Grand Hotel. They all
had their businesses: the long, arduous effort at "redecoration," which meant painting some of the grimier halls,
was the chief of these. Our navy friends were also intent
upon other affairs, the patrol of shark-infested waters by
small fishing trawlers, the struggle of motor-torpedo boats
against superior speed and arms at night. The men of the
regiments in garrison had least of all to do and were perhaps the least spirited, waiting, as they did week after
week, for the shock of invasion.

And the press . . . Well, the press, as always, dedicated
itself to the daily event. Each battle in the air was described separately in words which varied from the sober
exactitude of the *Times* to the inexpensive rhetoric of
Hearst and the United Press. One reporter for the latter
organization, on a day when the Germans had flown fairly
low, described them as "rolling over the housetops of
Dover." Some of the correspondents had a range of vision
unique in the annals of physiological science. One of the
extremely well-known ones wrote a story in which he said

he could see "Hitler's armada" on the other side of the
Channel, gathered for the invasion. Others were able to
see and describe battles which had happened ten or
twelve miles away. Still others knew exactly what the
falling German aviators said and thought when they hit
the English ground. The whole event was, indeed, so unprecedented in human experience, so filled with sharp
drama and heroism in the boldest color and accent, that
it made an unprecedented appeal to every imagination,
called forth whatever there was to be called from every
mind. If there had been a poet at Dover he would have
written poetry; as it was, the press dipped into its paint-
pot and slashed out the red and purple and gold, poster-
like, all askew and elongated and fearsome with false
proportions, but despite its haste and inaccuracy it did
succeed in giving the whole world some idea of what that
struggle was like while it was still going on. In this respect, as in so many others, the battles over the south of
England were unlike any that had preceded them in history.

The first high cliff to the west of Dover (Folkestone
direction) is called Shakespeare Cliff. It gets its name
from the scene in *King Lear*, which, legend says, was written of this place. There is a walk up from the paved street
to near the brow of the hill, and beyond that you step
out on the great open cliff which continues, broken by
dips and bights, to the Valiant Sailor above Folkestone.
Only the first great cliff beyond Dover bears the name of
Shakespeare Cliff. In the hollow behind it was an inn, the
King Lear, and halfway to the Valiant Sailor was another
pub, the Maid of Honor. On these cliffs and on the cliff
road, at these pubs and between them, we passed a good
part of the weeks while the struggle went on in the air
above us. We had quickly constructed a sort of life of our

own there, the spectators of the epic; some of us lived on
the cliffs; one—Art Menken, the March of Time photog-
rapher—did some yeoman work digging potatoes when he
was not otherwise engaged. High in the wind and the
sun, in the most brilliant summer weather for many seasons, we watched that assault in awe, conscious that the
whole destiny of mankind was in all probability being
decided above our heads. When we saw the clash of silver
plane and black, or watched the slow descent of the
fleecy white parachute, we felt our earth-bound nature,
like moles, and burrowed in the hollows. There were
times when an episode brought us to our feet with the
constriction of the throat that might have been a cheer
if it had dared—if it had dared run the risk of turning into
a sob. For, as a matter of fact, the terrible beauty of air
battle lies chiefly in this, that it is an individual conflict:
the moment of combat is like the clash of knights in armor,
and no matter what colors the tournament wears, that
clash of the single life against life will never leave the
heart unstirred. You could read of casualties by the thousand in a battle on land and calculate their results, the
territory gained or lost, the consequences to the enemy;
you could not see a duel in the air without thinking of
two hawklike youths in armor, brief falcon lives launched
one against one in the briefest, purest combat ever known.

The Germans began their attacks on the south of
England in the week of July 4th–10th off Portland and
Dover and down the Channel. For the first weeks of the
struggle they concentrated on shipping and ports, attacking principally convoys which passed from the west
through the Channel and around to London. The official
version of these battles is that they cost the Germans
a great deal without commensurate success in their objec-

tive, and that interception by the R.A.F. fighter planes grew more formidable every week.

This may be so, judged from the point of view of figures and tabulations. To the observer, however—not merely to me, but to everybody who witnessed these attacks—they seemed very successful. Ships were sunk day after day by dive-bombers, and casualties on the ships that did not sink were severe. Convoys grew less frequent in the Channel; the navy was obliged to cease using the port of Dover altogether after August 3rd; for a while in August no convoys passed at all. Off Deal the masts of the sunken ships dotted the waters for a great area, and were still there a year later. The port of London, once the greatest in the world, became almost completely derelict. The Stuka—Junkers 87-B—was the chief instrument in this attack on shipping, and although it afterward proved vulnerable to attack when it ventured inland, its performance against the ships in convoy was, by my own observation and that of all to whom I spoke, deadly accurate. The Battle of the Channel—while names are being made up, let us make up this one—considered not as part of the Battle of Britain but as a preparation for it, was to the best of my knowledge and belief a German victory.

I first saw the Stuka in the actions of July 28th and 29th and August 3rd, at Dover. I had seen it in Spain, where it was used over the Republican trenches and retreating troops. In Spain it was, I believe, a somewhat less proficient machine in that it had to straighten out from its dive; the steep V-shaped dive and ascent were what distinguished Junkers 87-B from 87-A. Its maneuverability enabled it to deceive the predictor machinery of an antiaircraft battery in 1940, and by this means it could defy gunfire with—so far as I ever saw—impunity. I also had the impression that it could run away from the English fighter planes, because I never saw one attacked by a Spitfire or Hurricane. This was, as it turns out, an error in judgment; Spitfire and Hurricane are faster planes and are well able to shoot down the Stuka when they are thrown against it. The fact was that the R.A.F. was not being thrown away in the early part of the battle; it was being husbanded as carefully as possible against the great trial that was coming; and we may all be grateful for it. The battles of September strained the R.A.F. to its limits, and if precious fighters had been thrown out over the Channel in large numbers to begin with, they would not have survived to meet the greater challenge of the Luftwaffe in the following weeks.

In those first actions I saw over the port of Dover and in the Channel, R.A.F. interception was almost entirely over land and consisted in duels with the Messerschmitt 109. The Messerschmitts came over in large formations and often engaged all the available fighter planes on a certain part of the coast, so that the Stuka could actually dart across from France, dive over a convoy and dart back again, without ever being in danger of attack from the English fighter. The Messerschmitts came into action in large numbers and at varying levels. Very often since those days I have met people who expressed doubt at the story of five or six English fighters engaging twenty or thirty Germans; some such doubters have been experts in air warfare, or at least so estimated; to them all I can say is that I saw it happen not once but many times. All who were on the Dover cliffs during July and August of 1940 know that it is true. The battles happened within plain view; some were directly over our heads; the stupidity of the censors prevented our saying so at the time, or indeed saying any numbers; and yet it was one of the most

astounding sights any man could see, an irrefutable proof
of valor. The Spitfires rose like larks, glittering against
the sun, to maneuver for position and attack. The sickening zoom of one fighter diving over another, the blunt
rattle of machine-gun fire high in the air, the streak of
smoke of a plane plummeting to earth, and the long, see-
saw descent of the wounded fighter falling from the clouds
beneath his shining white parachute—these sights and
sounds were familiar to us after two or three weeks, as to
so many other people along the southern coast. In every
such battle that I saw, the English had the best of it, and
in every such battle they were greatly outnumbered.

From the first attack I saw the most vivid memory is,
even so, the deadly, vulture-like Stuka. I had gone down
to Dover alone to see what was happening; the day when
we hunted in packs had not yet come. When the sirens
sounded for the third or fourth time that day I went out
to the Marine Parade—the walk along the beach—like
everybody else. The air-raid wardens vainly urged us to
stand back or to take cover. At that time no bombs had
yet fallen on Dover, and the mere threat of falling shrapnel was not enough to discourage the curious. As I was
standing there, squinting at the sky, trying to distinguish
one plane from another in the glare of sun upon cloud, the
Stukas arrived.

There were only three, as I remember, and they came
into the attack one by one, very swiftly, and made off
again. The whole thing was over in two or three minutes
at the most. They were attacking the port and shipping
in it; even now it is probably unwise to tell exactly what
they accomplished, even if I knew exactly; it is enough to
say that they did considerable damage. But the awe-
inspiring thing to me was the precision of their dive, the
impression it gave of mechanical resistlessness. They were

near; it seemed to me, as I scurried for a doorway, that they were diving directly over this very point; and yet all the anti-aircraft around the port blazed away at them with no effect at all. They executed their missions, one by one, and vanished again into the dazzling sun-drenched mist over the Channel. Meanwhile in the glaring clouds over us the battle between the fighters was still going on, as we could hear when the roar of gunfire and falling bomb had died away. Sometimes the glitter of their wings cut through the mist and flashed as an assurance that the battle was not ended, would never be ended so long as there were brave youths and good machines on our side.

For it was at Dover, I think, that the side of England became "our side" in my eyes. I had distrusted and disliked British imperialism all my life, and the lamentable events of 1938, in which the Chamberlain government gave over the strategical predominance of Europe to Hitler, had strengthened these feelings to the point of bitterness. Soviet Russia, which had seemed for some years to steer a straight course in opposition to Fascism, had out-Muniched Chamberlain with the Nazi-Soviet Pact of August, 1939, directly preceding and perhaps producing —or at least encouraging—the German decision to go to war. Experience had shown that there was no health in the French Republic. Small wonder, then, that I came perilously near to the sour and sterile misconceptions of "isolationism" in 1939–1940, thinking that the free or freedom-looking peoples of Europe had deserved their impending conquest by the enemy of the human race. I never fell into the error of supposing that we in America could remain aloof from the planetary struggle (in this I was never even remotely "isolationist"), but I felt, with an immense sadness, that there was no single positive principle to which we could appeal for union against Fascist

oppression. In this motley crew, in this array of mutually
distrustful peoples, slothful and self-indulgent, none willing to give battle until it was forced upon them, none concerned with faith or truth or a reasoned hope for the
future, ignominiously standing by while the enemy obliterated one after another of their earlier champions, what
was the flag, the belief, the battle-cry? None could be
seen, none heard. Selfish, divided and uncertain, my own
country shared every fault of the British and French except, perhaps, their cleverness. The Russians had betrayed
us more cynically than any Westerner could have managed, flattering themselves that they were the cleverest
crooks of all; if you believed, as I did and do, in the common humanity of all nations, you came at times very near
to an anarchistic mistrust of all government and all state
organization, suspecting that in fact the fate of mankind
was everywhere entrusted to cliques and camarillas of
scoundrels, while the universal conscience, through some
cosmic accident (perhaps from sun-spots) slept and cried
out in dreams. This fatalism and sense of inevitable tragedy had grown heavy during the years when Spain,
Czechoslovakia and China were sacrificed to the comfort
of England, France and the United States. Events in their
relentless march seemed to prove, ever more conclusively,
that only Hitler had a plan, a program and the directed
force to carry it out; only he had the sense to think of the
world as a whole.

At Dover the first sharp thrust of hope penetrated this
gloom. The battles over the cliffs proved that the British
could and would fight for their own freedom, if for nothing else, and that they would do so against colossal odds.
Greed and stupidity had led them to this pass, in which
they fought alone; things might have been very different,
but this was, in fact, how they were. The flash of the

Spitfire's wing, then, through the misty glare of the summer sky, was the first flash of a sharpened sword; they *would* fight, they *would* hold out, and in the steady development of the laws of history the Russians and Americans, willy-nilly, whatever their imagined clevernesses or evasions, would eventually be obliged also to fight, each for himself but in the objective result each for all, so that a pattern of victory—now, on the cliffs of Dover, only faintly discernible—would at last appear and glow into life. This would happen, must happen; the tree must grow from the acorn, the flower from the seed, the vast common result from the first single effort. But along this development would lie uncounted graves; and if the imagination recoiled from so long a prospect of suffering, it had to draw strength again from the deepest of instincts, a faith in humanity, so as to be able to believe that at the end of the sacrifice there would come forth a voice heard, without benefit or barrier of language, in the heart's blood of the people, speaking in the pulses and the glands and brain, saying: *Man, man, upon what altar have you immolated your youth?* To this final question arising from the depths there would be no easy answer in the vocabularies of capitalism, imperialism or national pride. Something to which their striving has produced no key must dwell upon that altar, exacting tribute so bitter and profuse. I call it the dignity and freedom of mankind, all mankind of every strain and color and habitation: the direct antithesis of the tribal concept. For this, large, remote and not yet seen, the brave youths in the Spitfires— who thought they fought only for England—offered their lives. The long battle now beginning would in its course shatter or exhaust the economic and social power of older systems, war-engendering systems, so that even the enemy's victories would contribute to his defeat by obliging us, on our side, to make ever larger and larger our pledge to freedom. We could never regain the lost half of the world in any other way, and we could never regain it at all without the will to fight. This was now appearing, for the first time, on the side which I—like millions of my countrymen—now called "our side."

Such were the vast and shadowy outlines of a possible future which appeared in the sky over the cliffs of Dover, drawn in the mist by the Spitfire's wing.

6

The story of the Battle of Britain has been ably told over and over again. It is no part of my purpose to attempt to tell it here. We did not know the story at the time; we watched these conflicts and wondered. It now seems clear that the launching of the great fighter and bomber formations over England during August and September, 1940, were the first part of a plan for invasion. The Luftwaffe intended to knock the R.A.F. out of the sky and then proceed with the conquest. The Germans undoubtedly knew (as we of the press did not) how slender were the resources of the R.A.F. in machines and pilots of the first quality. On the great days (August 8th, August 15th, September 15th) the Germans sent over Junkers, Heinkel, Messerschmitt and Dornier planes in immense numbers, from nine to eleven hundred of them in a single day, attacking airdromes, factories and command posts, attempting most of all to annihilate the R.A.F. Battles were going on all over the South of England. Many of them we saw from the south cliffs, others in the Thames estuary and the neighborhood of London. The German losses grew greater all the time, until, with the approach of bad weather, the whole attempt had to be given up. That is the story.*

Our press contingent on Shakespeare Cliff during those weeks was made up of Helen Kirkpatrick (*Chicago Daily News*) and Virginia Cowles (Sunday *Times* of London), the only two women who regularly did such work, and of a collection of American and English correspondents who had been through most of the earlier phases of this war. They included Knickerbocker and Quentin Reynolds from time to time, Ben Robertson (*PM*) and Ed Murrow (Columbia Broadcasting System) more regularly. Later on Whitelaw Reid (*New York Herald Tribune*) moved on to the cliff; Ed Beattie (United Press) was sometimes there; Art Menken (The March of Time) lived on the cliff all through August. We had alarums and excursions, including one invasion alarm on August 31st which put the whole coast on the alert from midnight until two or three in the morning. It was of naval origin, and came from Portsmouth, I believe. Like one or two other such alerts in other parts of England, it was never fully explained. In general we lived in expectation of a full German attack any night, and the nerves of some of our friends grew so exacerbated by suspense that they actually said they would welcome it.

The daily spectacle was out of all ordinary experience or easy credibility. In color alone it defied description. Sometimes the Messerschmitts would attack our barrage balloons with green or yellow tracer bullets; the silver balloons would explode in flame and sink gracefully to the earth; our Bofors guns around the port would attack the Messerschmitts with balls of fire. The intrepidity, indeed foolhardiness, of the Messerschmitt pilots was fab-

* The Air Ministry's booklet, *The Battle of Britain*, gives a good account of it, with maps and figures; the story is also authoritatively told by David Garnett in *War in the Air*.

ulous. On their way home they attacked our barrage balloons—which cost little and were easily replaced—at the risk of their planes and their lives. I saw one such Messerschmitt dive over the port to get a balloon just at sundown one evening; he had to come down to not much more than a thousand feet; he missed his balloon and the Bofors guns got him, so that he plummeted into the water; from any point of view his was a useless death. Dr. Richardson, who had to attend to many of the German boys when they came down in parachutes (it was his doorway to which I most frequently resorted in bombing attacks) told me that most of them were shot through the seat, owing to Messerschmitt's unwise economy of armor in that place; the machine-gun bullets often lodged in the pelvis and required a difficult operation to extract. Dr. Richardson, like everybody else in Dover, worked hard and expected no thanks. His house stood four-square on the beach, in the line of fire, with a Bofors battery in front of it. That Bofors battery, which had been in Norway and stayed at Dover only two or three weeks, was commanded by a fellow who sticks in my memory because of his unconscious bravado. I saw him one day during a dive-bombing attack directing the fire of his guns. He was wearing the scarlet forage cap of the artilleryman—strictly forbidden in action; he should have had on a steel helmet—and he was twirling a swagger-stick in his right hand. He could twirl the stick rapidly in the air without ever dropping it, and he did so throughout the attack of the vulture-like Stuka. When I made some jocular remark about it afterward, he said: "Oh, was I doing that? I didn't notice."

In the early days I was accredited to an anti-aircraft post down at the end of the beach, underneath the Castle, and I spent many hours there. Unfortunately, whenever the Germans attacked, that stretch of beach was so dangerous that I could never get down to my post until the worst was over; the falling shrapnel alone was enough to make the walk (or run) impossible. When I made the run one day during a lull in the action and reported to the lieutenant in charge of the gun-site, he nodded absently and said: "What did you think of the fire?" I said I thought it seemed to come a little short of the planes. "That's it," he said sadly, "a little short and not high enough." This appeared to be Lieutenant Streatfield's only preoccupation, although his open gun-site was in the most dangerous corner of the beach.

Sometimes new weapons, to which we were never allowed to refer in press dispatches, made their appearance. There were two of these which were accredited by current report to Professor Lindeman, Mr. Churchill's physicist friend. At the time they were not successful, but as their principles may yet prove susceptible of development as a weapon against German planes, it is too early to describe them. They were spectacular in effect, adding their unexpected flash to the incredible color and glitter of the battle. On the day when Mr. Churchill visited Dover (August 16th, I believe) these weapons were set off as a demonstration for him and attracted a brief but intense visit from our Germans friends across the Channel.

Then, one day in August, the shelling began. I was in bed when it started, at an hour which shames me to confess: it was eleven o'clock in the morning. Peter Beatty and his huge Alsatian dog had arrived to haul me out of bed. The sound of the exploding shells drove the dog under my bed, which he nearly overturned with his agitated heaving. For some minutes Peter and I debated over these recurrent explosions. He thought they were ordinary bombs and I thought they were something different; then

I concluded they were bombs and he disagreed. Finally, with a mighty effort, I got out of bed and went to the bathroom to look out. There, directly under my window in the port, high trajectory shells were exploding in the water; they made the little patrol boats dance like corks. Out in the Channel a convoy was passing, the first in weeks, and the shells were exploding in and around it. Two destroyers rushed busily up and down on both sides of the convoy, setting up a smoke screen. Across the Channel—it was a bright day—the four flashes of the battery could be distinctly seen. Twenty seconds later (I timed it) the explosions occurred.

This first shelling of the port and the Channel convoy took one hour and twenty minutes. It was a complete failure; not one ship was hit. Peter and I drove to Margate that afternoon to watch the convoy steam around the end of the coast and head for London. All the ships—sixteen of them—were intact and the convoy was in good order. However, the existence of the German battery across the narrow sea was what eventually caused most of the civilian population to leave Dover. My friends, Mr. Gunn the goldsmith and Mr. Lukey the liquor dealer, along with a good many others I had known from the days when I lived in our village, closed up their shops and moved farther inland. Shells were falling in the town and the danger was, abruptly, too great to be treated lightly. Dover began to look like Deal—that is, like a deserted city, deserted by all but the military and naval forces.

Sometimes during August when I went up to London I lunched with Mr. and Mrs. Shaw. Mr. Shaw had been ill the preceding winter, but his astringent sanity was unimpaired. On one occasion I remember particularly an improvisation he made about the French. It went (roughly) like this:

"Of course it's perfectly obvious what the French will do. They'll say, here we've been trying for years to get rid of that wretched British Empire and those wretched English. Now's our chance. We'll simply join up with Hitler and put an end to it."

I was startled at what he said; it took me another year to see how nearly correct (perhaps wholly correct) he had been. Speaking of Hitler, he said:

"Now there's just one man who ought to be sent to deal with him, and that's myself. He and I are the only two people who have read Wagner's *Art and Revolution*."

There was little evidence of weariness, none of failing spirit. One day when I was there he tried on a new steel helmet. "Somebody sent me the thing," he said, "and I suppose I may as well learn how to wear it." The strap got entangled with his beard and he had a brief, hilarious engagement with it. He looked extraordinarily symbolic when he got it on and grinned from beneath its rakish shadow. Shaw in a steel helmet, H. G. Wells going back into the house to get his gas mask—these were strange sights.

Up at St. Margaret's, between Dover and Deal, our village was also deserted. One by one the people went away, some of them in the government's evacuation scheme and some to visit relatives farther inland. Our village was in the direct line both for shells and for bombs and received more than its allowance of both. Edward, who kept the garage on the top of the hill, stayed in the village and drove the ambulance. "I'm in a safe spot here," he said. "This place is too near for the far ones and too far for the near ones. They never hit just here."

They never did hit just there, but they hit everywhere else. The village churchyard was plowed up by a big bomb; the gravestones were thrown crazily about, the dead of generations disinterred. The mute forefathers of the hamlet were, indeed, among the first to suffer. Afterward the houses on the cliff and the positions all along to Dover were considerably damaged by weeks of shelling and bombing.

I used to go up to our village from time to time to see how it fared. Bloms had been evacuated by the hospital people and taken over by the soldiers. They had their mess in the New Room, where I used to work, and the rest of the house was their quarters. The grass had almost all been worn away; the center of the garden was still occupied by the big, useless dug-out; the roses were bedraggled but obstinate. I could nearly always get some onions and some roses from the garden. The coast of France was clearly visible from that place through most of August. When I stood there I remembered many things—the quiet garden that once was here, serene and safe, and how I used to visit it as a sort of refuge from the terrible struggle in Spain, and how the flowers in the sunlight never could altogether drive out of my mind the desperate brown hills above the Ebro. The vision mists over; past and present are one; is that the Channel flowing before me, or the Ebro itself, the first or the last line, the frontier?

It must be here, I thought, the line we shall hold forever: the line that must never be passed if we are to survive and make the world whole: here is the Ebro, the Yangtze, the Volga, here is the Channel: let us stand and fight, retreat no more. *Camaradas, no podremos perder mas territorio.* Those were the words of Dolores the Pasionaria at Madrid in 1938: we can lose no more territory. Such a point comes in every war. So far as Hitler's advance westward is concerned, I think it was reached at our village in 1940—there and in the sky above it.

# 4. The Haystack

ON SATURDAY, September 7, 1940, Ed Murrow, Ben Robertson and I drove down the Thames to Tilbury and crossed to Gravesend. There had been considerable bombing in the Thames estuary for some weeks. Tilbury in particular had been repeatedly hit, and we wanted to get some idea of the extent of the damage and how it was being repaired.

Edward Murrow, dark and taciturn and often beset by gloom, was at the same time capable of sustained hilarity and high spirits; the range of his moral orchestra was great. He was the European director for the Columbia Broadcasting System, and even before the war I had sometimes spoken to America over his air. He was now using that air himself to such purpose that he became—particularly in 1940 and 1941—one of the familiar voices of the nation; I discovered afterward that he was as well known to families throughout the country as their own members. The men and women who speak from that inexplicable instrument in the American living room have a place in the national mind unlike that of politicians, journalists or writers; they live in the house, so to speak. Ed was talking to millions of Americans at certain stated hours every day, and for many of them he was like part of the evening meal, as indispensable as a knife and fork. He used this new, strange potency with caution, as did most of his colleagues, restricting himself to an account of the latest news with little or no comment upon it, and yet (like Bill

Shirer, who did the same thing from Berlin) there was sometimes a world of significance in the turn of a phrase, the accent of the voice. He was fiercely in earnest about the war, fiercely impatient with sham, incompetence and muddle; he liked the English people well enough to be savagely critical of their government; and yet he was capable of putting forward a calm, uncolored version of all the vast drama of the day so that it passed both the British censors and the radio regulations at home. For a sustained effort, his daily broadcasts to America during 1940 and 1941 seem to me the finest thing the new instrument of communication has given us. The instrument is a thing of the moment, like the air over which it breathes; these broadcasts * are not the same thing in print. They depend upon the events of a single day, the quality of a voice which has been tempered by fury, fatigue or sorrow, the particular phrasing of an hour. I used to hear Ed, seated in a stuffy little room in the bowels of the earth underneath the B.B.C. building, and imagine the thousands upon thousands of American living rooms and dining rooms in which these words were being heard with all the possible combinations and gradations of attention or inattention. The radio has never ceased to fill me with awe, no matter what the trivial uses to which it may be and has been put; it was most awe-inspiring, I think, in that Studio BD, three or four floors down into the earth beneath the B.B.C. building. On some nights when I went there I was allowed to hear the conversations between London, New York, Rome and Paris—conversations "on the circuit," which meant that they went over the air without being broadcast. Then Paris was heard no more; then Rome vanished; soon only London and New York were left. One night I heard the American technician and the

* Collected and published in 1941 under the title *This Is London*.

English technician talking back and forth, keeping the circuit open as they waited for the broadcast. They asked each other questions about the weather, "How is it over there?" and the like. The American said he wanted to come to England some day. The Englishman remarked that he saw no reason for this: "You're better off where you are," he said. The American voice came back: "Oh, I want to come over and see some things. I want to see Darwin's resi*dence.*" The last syllable of this word was heavily accented, as it is in the Middle West. Often since then I have mused at this strange ambition and wondered by what accident it might some day be gratified.

As a correspondent—that is, going about the ways of the world, seeing things and talking to people—Ed Murrow seemed to me as remarkable as he was at his own microphone. His courage, endurance and obliviousness to fatigue made it possible for him to survive many months of a cruel schedule. He could go without sleep as long as might be necessary, broadcasting at all sorts of hours and working like a slave between times. His courage was of the kind I most respect: that is, it did not consist in lack of sensitivity to danger, but in a professional determination to ignore it in the interests of his job. I have been whirled around London in his open car while the bombs were thundering down and the searchlights made fantastic patterns in the sky; I am always prompt to proclaim my fear on such occasions. Ed would get a little grimmer, a little wrier and drier, and say little or nothing. In the first air raid over London (August 24, 1940), when areas far to the east were bombed and great fires started in the night sky, Ed and I were broadcasting in a sort of round-up with several other speakers stationed throughout London. Ed himself was on the steps of St. Martin-in-the-Fields, in Trafalgar Square; I was on a balcony of the Piccadilly

Hotel, overlooking Piccadilly; Eric Sevareid was at the Palais de Danse in Hammersmith; Mr. J. B. Priestley was, I think, at the Cenotaph. The sirens sounded just as Ed was beginning to speak. We did not hear each other broadcast; we began and ended on a light signal without having any idea of what the others had said; it was all improvised, and must have sounded extraordinarily unreal to the listeners across the sea. Your truly realistic air-raid broadcast could only be made, I should imagine, in a magnificent New York studio with an infinity of gadgets for sound effects and ample time for rehearsal. Our air-raid broadcast involved nothing more than the connivance of time and space (an intersection of time-space lines), so that as we described the behavior of the people in our line of vision, and spoke of the glow in the sky, we were all aware that it very probably would convince the listener less than any well-drilled studio performance.

Yet it was real, and none of us is likely to forget it. The bombs did not come near us—none fell in the center of London—and the guns, too, were mostly down the river; but it was the first raid. The Germans used screaming bombs that night (I heard two of them) and the long wail was indeed a dreadful sound. The fire down the river glowed all night. Ed and I drove down to London Bridge to look at it, and there, well after midnight, we looked down the darkling river to the conflagration and realized, I think, that we were at the beginning of a mighty ordeal —an ordeal not for us in particular but for this imperturbable people, the English, this once mighty and still valorous people in whose hands had lain the scepter of the world.

Ben Robertson was the correspondent for *PM* of New York, a militantly anti-Fascist newspaper founded earlier that year. It was too new for the British to have heard much about it, and Ben's first weeks in London had been plagued by the necessity of explaining to everybody he met that *PM* was a newspaper, that its name was indeed *PM*, that it had no other name, and that it was actually printed and circulated to a choice list of subscribers every day. Ben, round-faced and a youthful thirty-four or thirty-five years of age, sputtered like a college freshman when he had to deal with repeated incidents of this kind. The difficulty was solved by the London practice of reprinting dispatches which had appeared in New York; a few of Ben's were cabled back to London and appeared in the *Times* and *Telegraph*—"Mr. Ben Robertson says in today's *PM*"—and established his identity on a really firm basis. Before long he was as known in London as the oldest resident, and much better liked than most, since his amiable and gregarious nature found many friends. He had, and has, an unshakable South Carolina accent, which endeared him to Lady Astor's heart; she made him a familiar of her house, both at Cliveden and at Plymouth; by September, when he had been in England a few weeks, he knew as many people as most men who had worked in London for years in peacetime.

Indeed the zeal with which London people, particularly those in political and governmental circles, welcomed the American correspondents in 1940 was an index to their true sense of the situation. They might not talk about it frankly, but in their innermost consciousness they were sure that the war could not be won by England alone. America was tardy, reluctant; the American correspondents had the ear of America; therefore the American correspondents were to be flattered, courted, made much of. This was the pattern. I do not suggest that it was a course deliberately adopted, as upon a signal or order— English people do not operate in that way—but it is what

happened. Not to put too cynical an interpretation upon
it, I think the conversation of the American correspondents did provide some interest as being for the most part
related to the events of the day, the events overshadowing
all others; moreover, the separateness, the difference, was
in itself an element of interest. Knick, for example, although passionately against Hitler in all things and therefore most anxious for England to resist and win, did not
have in the least an English point of view; therefore, whatever he said tended to shed a little light among people
who had known nothing but their own point of view for
a long time. Virginia Cowles had been living in England
for two or three years, or rather returning to London as a
base of operations from Czechoslovakia, Spain, Finland
and France; she had many friends there, many of them
in the government; for a good deal of the time she was
living at Lady Maureen Stanley's house, when Mr. Stanley
was Secretary of State for War; in compound words like
"Anglo-American" or "socio-professional" she occupied
very nearly the position of the hyphen, and with a hyphen
of such charm many things were possible. My friends
Helen Kirkpatrick and Bill Stoneman (both of the *Chicago
Daily News*) also circulated pretty much everywhere in
London, and contributed no little to the storming of the
gates. When I first worked in London, in 1925, hardly
any of the American correspondents had friends outside
the profession itself, and few or perhaps none, to the best
of my knowledge, were on friendly lunch-and-dinner
terms with the great; by 1940 this had changed. In re-
ferring to such a change as "the storming of the gates" I
suggest a much more deliberate action on both sides than
had in reality taken place—there was no attack and no
necessity for one. The business of the foreign correspondent had come to engage the activities of a considerable

number of men in the years between the two wars, and by 1940 many of them were as seasoned and weatherwise in the developing processes of Fascism and war as anybody else on our side of the fence. Their minds were no longer made up for them by supercilious young men from the Foreign Office or the Quai d'Orsay, who in bygone days used to hand out "interpretations" with a fair assurance of having them passed on to the American public. Too often in recent years the Foreign Office and the Quai d'Orsay had been glaringly wrong, proved wrong by events; too often my colleagues, disagreeing with the constituted authority, had been proved right by events; it was therefore no longer possible to treat them with the haughtiness of superior knowledge. Neither was it possible to ignore the growing certainty that America paid more attention to them, by and large, than to the so-called "responsible" public men who made professional careers in politics. Such considerations fortified the natural disposition of hospitable London people to receive new opinions, impressions, ideas; the American correspondent thereupon came—in times of sore trial, it is true—into his heyday as a figure in London life. By the following summer, 1941, there were few people in London better known than Quentin Reynolds, for example, the jovial and warm-hearted Quent, whose face was to be seen everywhere, whose autograph was valued like that of a film star, and whose occasional broadcasts for the B.B.C.—delivered in a rumbling bass drawl which sounded ultra-American—were listened to by the entire nation. Dorothy Thompson, when she came over a year later, was treated like a visiting sovereign; Raymond Gram Swing and others were only a little less regal in their progress from cabinet minister to cabinet minister; to Clare Luce—who was there at Dunkirk time—no door was closed, no voice unkind. These were the brief, crowded visits of our most celebrated press writers. They flashed across the London sky and were gone, having in many cases unnerved even the most imperturbable dignitaries by the careless assurance of their passage. But among those who stayed month after month, year after year, going away only to return, Quent Reynolds was the one who most touched the British imagination, seemed most American and at the same time most solidly a friend. I think many English people saw in him (whom they had not known until 1940 or, even more, 1941), a sort of promise of American participation in the war. His tributes to English courage and perseverance, expressed without reserve, delighted a people which had some distaste for self-praise and yet knew that it had deserved well: he said what they did not quite like to say themselves. Small wonder that he came to be, beyond all the rest of us put together, a symbol of the friendly American press in English eyes, an earnest of great efforts to be made on their behalf in the time to come.

I have named only some of the better known among the American correspondents. There were many others. I think the total number on the official list in 1940 was about a hundred and fifty, more than half of them concentrated in the largest offices, the Associated Press, United Press, *New York Times* and the Hearst services. They were young and old, newcomers to England and old residents, often fiercely critical of the English and of their government, and yet, in the ordeal which began in September, 1940, I think they performed a service to the general cause merely by sticking to their jobs. They were the mirror which caught and passed on to America the reflection of England's stoical, good-humored endurance, the spirit of the London streets, the underlying toughness and tenacity of this people. A mirror does not always reflect truly, particularly at such an angle; but it does reflect. Without some such apparatus—and this drama was played out in consciousness of it, as a stage play runs its course in awareness of the audience—some things might have been different: London might conceivably have been less admirable, America even more tardy. The American press, reporting with great speed and a considerable admixture of emotion (you cannot avoid some emotion under repeated bombing), did, I think, fulfill its historical role from London as well as from Dover, even though the actual narratives transmitted were sometimes of little historical or evidential value.

Among these instruments of an inevitable development Ed Murrow, Ben Robertson, Bill Stoneman, Knickerbocker, Helen and Virginia, to name only those I knew best, were probably more conscious than most; but the youngest A.P. reporter, fresh off the boat, played the same part. You could not write of these things without producing an effect upon the mind and heart of America, whether such was your intention or not. The mere transmission of the recorded event (no matter what the emphasis, color or even distortion) was enough.

## 2

We drove through ruined areas in Tilbury's mean streets and saw how the people would creep back to the very edge of the ruins, into houses which had been condemned as unsafe. An old man in his shirt sleeves, smoking a pipe on the doorstep of a more or less intact house on the brink of a crater, was watching his grand-daughter play in the gutter. A woman hung out clothes on the line; the dust had hardly settled properly from the last night's bombing.

The children, like children of other races all over the earth, found toys in the wreckage and treasured bits of shrapnel. (Down at Dover a Messerschmitt cannon shell was worth three big chunks of shrapnel, in the barter of their kind.) The barrage balloons, which had become far more numerous of late, swung lazily in the clouded sunlight. We lunched at the riverside inn and crossed in the automobile ferry to Gravesend. The vast river, which used to be crowded with every kind of shipping at this point, was almost deserted. Launches and small craft belonging to the patrols were to be seen making their rounds; the ferry still ran; we saw one freighter making its way up to the docks. At Gravesend the inn beside the river was open and seemed to be doing good business; we had difficulty getting rooms for the night.

From Gravesend, busy with Saturday afternoon shoppers, we drove up the hill and off in the direction of Chatham. The road over the hill was dotted with signs of the air war. At one crossroads a crew stood guard over an air-raid siren installation. Ben told us about the siren near the Bank of England, which neither Ed nor I had noticed: it flowered in a big horn from the feet of the Duke of Wellington's statue. At one wayside inn the mistress of the house was cheerful. "We always go upstairs when the sirens sound," she said. "We get worried downstairs; we think it's safer up there." A week or so later this inn— which was a landmark for us after this day—had ceased to exist. There had been scattered bombs all over this area, and we saw a good many craters which represented little or no real damage. We spent some hours vainly chasing the ghost of a Dornier plane which was said to have crashed the day before somewhere in the neighborhood. Ed's car nosed its way through shaded lanes into forgotten villages where it was difficult to imagine that such an invention as the airplane was even known. The Dornier was elusive: everybody had heard of it, nobody had seen it, and, of course, we had new directions in each village. After some hours of this we turned back toward the Thames and were driving through flat fields when we noticed some aircraftsmen working on a wrecked plane. We got out to investigate and found a Hurricane which had crashed some days before. It was being stripped for everything of value or use that was left intact on it. We had bought some apples at a farmhouse where we stopped during the afternoon; now, on a sloping bank beside the road, we stretched out to eat apples and feel the warmth of the late afternoon sun.

At this point it began—the great air attack which was to last for weeks and end in a confession of failure (one of the very few) by the Germans.

The first thing we heard was a far-off hum of many motors. The familiar sound brought us to our feet at once, and before we had had time to get our bearings the first formation was directly over us. The roar of anti-aircraft and bombs had come swiftly nearer until it now seemed very close. The first formation was of thirty or more planes at a considerable altitude, fifteen thousand feet (perhaps) or above. Each plane was distinct and black in the clear afternoon sky, and they took their orderly, undisturbed course straight up the river. The thunder of the bombs grew heavier as we stood there in the road, peering up under our tin hats. To the left of us a flight of Hurricanes rushed into the sky like larks and pursued the black visitors farther up the river. The rat-tat-tat of the machine guns died away.

"This is a bad place to be," said I, ever mindful of security, "in case there are more of them. Let's get farther up from the river, where we can see without catching bombs."

We got into the car and drove toward the hilltop, where the main road ran from Chatham to Gravesend. Whilst we were driving another formation went over and the bombs thundered again. Without attempting to go farther we left the car at the side of the main road and took refuge in a sunken road—a small, old road that had seen many wars—cutting into it at right angles. Interception from the airdromes down-river was going on meanwhile, and the machine-gun chatter could be heard in intervals of bombing and cannonade.

Our sunken road had all the properties of a good ditch. I have ever been a partisan of the good ditch, and think every modern road should be built with one alongside. Here we could flatten ourselves against the tufted side bank when the planes were directly overhead, and when they had passed beyond us we could crawl up and look over the edge. Before we had been here long, a bus on the Chatham-Gravesend line stopped at our refuge and disgorged its few passengers, a conductor and a guard. During the next half hour, when all hell seemed to have broken loose in the air above and all around us, the conductor sat beside the sunken road and totted up his totals of passengers, fares and journeys. The guard was a little more communicative. He told us a story.

"There was a bloody monkey hanging by his bloody tail in the jungle," he narrated, "and along came a bloody air-raid warden. One monkey says to the other monkey, 'Look out, Jock, here's this bloody bastard comin' along to civilize us.'"

From time to time we crawled to the edge of our ditch— an ancient and honorable road, but a ditch to me—and looked over it. Dense clouds of smoke were rising along the banks of the river. Flames had broken out here and there, particularly in the part of the river opposite us. The roar of anti-aircraft was the principal and most persistent noise, but it was punctuated by the deep, reverberant thunder of the bombs, heard more penetratingly here because we were beneath and against the earth. During the battle, Hurricanes returned to their roost to refuel and re-arm; we saw two or three such returns; we saw them, or others like them, take off soon thereafter. The sun was setting when it was all over.

At last there was silence in our area, although an occasional far-off boom reminded us that the Germans were making their way home to France by another route. We got up from our refuge and shook off the dust. After a brief consultation we decided to return to Gravesend to see what had been hit in our part of the river.

As we drove along the highway we had many clear views of the Thames bank on the other side and a little lower down. Great blobs of flame, identifiable as the flame from oil fires, rose in the air, were swallowed by black smoke and rose again, monstrous signals of destruction over a wide area. This was Thameshaven, where there had been vast petroleum tanks. Farther up the river, where the docks were, dense black clouds had formed, but no flame was yet to be seen from this point. All the way up the river these clouds were in process of formation. A crazy rhyme from childhood ran in my head then and all through the night: London's burning, London's burning. It was hard to realize that this thing, so long expected, so certain of advent, had come to pass. The three of us looked, estimated, calculated. It seemed (and, as it turned out afterward, was) the most destructive foray the enemy had yet made upon us.

We went down to the inn by the waterside and had dinner. There was a crowd of navy and river patrol people there, discussing the raid. Nothing had been seriously damaged in Gravesend—although when we went to the police station to report our presence before dinner we found it propped up as the result of a previous raid—and all the speculation was upon places opposite, on the other side of the river. Tilbury had, as they said, taken "another packet." The docks were in flames farther up. Thameshaven was gone.

Ed and Ben and I were—for no clear reason—quite certain that the Germans would return that night. My feeling was that they would not have made such a tremendous attack in daylight, when it was bound to be costly, if they did not intend a continuation in the inexpensive hours of darkness. We voted to get through our dinner and return to our ditch, which had suited our purposes well, as soon as it got quite dark.

By the time we had done so we could already hear gunfire afar off on the coast beyond the estuary. We explored the field near our ditch and discovered a convenient haystack. "This will come in handy," Ed said, "if we get cold later on." We knew that there was at least one fighter station near us—more probably two—and an anti-aircraft battery somewhere in the neighborhood, since the shrapnel had fallen here in the afternoon. For purposes of observation we decided to divide our time between the haystack and the ditch, depending upon the amount of stuff that might be falling in the neighborhood.

We had been there no time at all—scarcely ten minutes —when the first German planes came over, heralded by very heavy anti-aircraft fire from the coast. We heard the anti-aircraft before we heard the German motors, and then, steady and relentless, the throb of the desynchronized engines. We had all grown so familiar with this intermittent purr—the tiger's purr—that we could distinguish it quite easily from any other, and no expert testimony to the contrary could make us think otherwise. The intermittent throb came closer, stronger, and, as we cowered beside the haystack, passed directly over our heads. By the sound we judged it to be two or at most three airplanes. There was a flash in the moonlight; we thought this might be wings; it was impossible to be sure. About three minutes later the same thing happened again: the roar of anti-aircraft on the coast heralded the approach of another pair or trio of German planes which throbbed over our heads and were gone up the river. This happened a third, fourth, fifth time: by now it seemed that all the anti-aircraft in England were active, filling all the air with sound. The bombs were falling now, too—falling on London, far up the Thames, far beyond the area reached by this afternoon's raids. The fires that had been started in the afternoon now lined the river with flame. Great solid blobs of flame rose from high up the river, were obliterated and rose again, like those at Thameshaven opposite us: more petroleum was afire. "They're following the line of the river," Ed said, "as easily as if it were a main street. They come in at Margate and curve round the water line and all the way up. Are you glad you're not in London tonight?" We wondered what was happening in London, what would be left, whether our own houses had been hit, what was to become of the homeless, whether there would be many casualties and whether the surface shelters—so trumpery looking in the middle of the street—would survive the shock.

So far as we could estimate there seemed to be about two German bombers at a time coming over at three-minute intervals. As we were afterward informed by those

who should know, this observation was correct. Except for
a very occasional flash of metal high up in the sky, caught
by the beam of a searchlight, we saw none of these machines, but we could hear them most distinctly, singly
and in pairs, as they made their way up the firelit river.
Hour after hour they came on, cruelly undisturbed, or so
it seemed to us, by the efforts of anti-aircraft gunnery.
Chatham was now letting loose a terrific fire, probably, as
we thought (and were again proved right by subsequent
information) from naval guns. The flames seemed to
spread far beyond the unseen horizon, into the farthest
reaches of the dark. The monstrous inferno before us was
like nothing I or anybody else in this century had ever
seen. The burning of Smyrna by the Turks in 1922 (I had
often heard of it) could only have been insignificant in
comparison. It was like a vision of the end of the world.

It grew cold; we crawled under the haystack and lit our
cigarettes with great care, lest a small fire be added to the
immensity of London burning. We were subdued, horror-
struck at the possibilities. No city could endure much of
this punishment and survive. There seemed no end to it;
hour upon hour passed and the bombers were still coming
on, two at a time at three-minute intervals, directly over
our heads.

What a place to be, I was thinking, what a strange survey of damnation! Here on a hilltop by the Thames we
watched the centuries hurl themselves into the flames:
Wat Tyler and John Lackland, Edward the Black Prince
and Will Shakespeare, Nelson and Fair Rosamond, all the
song and all the story, now to be burnt out in the place of
their echoes. Remember, man, thou art but dust, and unto
dust thou shalt return. But what dust? Only the powdery
dust of a fire set by maniacs, or the natural dust of the
road and the field that will flower again? If you loved the

world and the beasts that dwelt upon it, you could not believe that any part of it would truly perish. Let the Germans burn and destroy, unhappy barbarians: in the end they must kneel among the ruins. This power that they had, that they have had in recurrent frenzy since the day when their long-haired ancestor first leaned upon his spear in the conquered Forum Romanum, was of a kind not yet suited to civilized dominion, fit only for the uses to which it was now applied, this night, this very night as we watched in darkness by the haystack: the murdering flames were theirs, the slow building and the small fire by the hearth were ours. Who could convince them that the fire they set this night would consume them, too, before it was quenched? Flame would convince them, flame only: and of all the bleak certainties of the night, this was most certain, that we should be obliged to use all their weapons, one by one, before we might break this power. So the conflagration before us was not only London burning, but Nürnberg and Cologne, Munich and even Vienna, places we have loved and may never see again.

It was three in the morning before we ended our vigil. There had been no slackening in the German attack. They still came on in pairs at three-minute intervals: the fires burned high as far as we could see, from a point directly opposite our hilltop to the blackness beyond London. But we were exhausted by now, hardly able to keep awake in spite of the thunder all round us. Clearly this would go on all night. Our chances of being hit were no greater in the inn at Gravesend than here beneath our haystack; the shrapnel that fell along the road might equally well fall here; we decided to go back and go to bed. Ed drove along with some care for a while, ready to stop the car and take refuge beside the road if too much activity surrounded us. After a bit he decided that this was a hairsplitting business in the greater gamble; he stepped on the accelerator and we speeded on into Gravesend, listening to the bombs and dazed by the searchlights, incredulous and very weary. These were things that were hard to believe even when you saw them.

The inn was shaking and quaking with the explosions; nobody had gone to bed. We had a glass of beer each; the licensing hours made little difference under such conditions. The whole river was lighted by the intense glare of the flames opposite. When we went upstairs we had to draw the curtains tight in our rooms; the glare illuminated the whole room otherwise. Ed and Ben shared one room and I took the other; there were only two free in the inn. The floor shook, the walls quivered; it was a strange sort of rest to which we were relegated; but we were too tired to care much. If a bomb landed on this inn it would be sheer chance, and if it landed when we were asleep we might never know it. We went to bed and I, at any rate, slept very well in spite of the unceasing explosions. It seems that the inn shook and shivered all night long, the windows breaking and the noise interrupting all slumber but mine.

I did, however, have a vivid dream which must have been created by the glare and roar in which I slept. I dreamed that I was in New Orleans (a city which I had then never visited) while the Germans made an invasion there with aircraft and ships. The flames, flares, searchlights and reverberant thunder of the night were reproduced faithfully in this dream, although upon a scene so different. Then, with that instantaneous and unexplained transition to which we are accustomed only in dreams, I was in Kansas City, arguing with an air-line official about a passage to Chicago. The official told me I could not travel; St. Louis had fallen to the German force from New

Orleans and the line of the Mississippi was cut; no planes would go to Chicago again. This was, I suppose, some reflection of innumerable difficulties I had had in this and other years since 1938; it was a little like the Fascist thrust across Spain in 1938, a little like the sweep across Northern France; it was merely translated into the language of my own country, the Mississippi valley where I was born. For a moment I saw the great river flowing with a glitter of silver and yellow between flat banks, as it flows in the prairie country, and a white steamer was half sunk at one side; there were flames over a city beyond there, and the German planes were thick in the sky above. I do not know if this city was St. Louis or not; at the time I think I had that idea vaguely, but I could not remember when I came to tell Ben and Ed the next morning. That the Germans had pierced to the heart of our country was, however, absolutely distinct and indubitable. I awoke; all the thunder of the night had died away; when I went to the window and pulled the curtains I saw a clear morning on the Thames, clear but dark, for thick black clouds of smoke covered the sun and all the river while the flames continued to line the shore down below. It was Sunday, September 8, 1940.

The three of us drove round our side of the Thames for a while that morning, talked to people, collected some impressions of the night as it had seemed to others, derived some idea of what the damage had been in these parts. Later on we took the ferry (it was running again) to Tilbury and set out on our long and painful journey through the devastated East End.

Whole blocks of houses had been laid flat; whole areas were still burning; many were the detours we had to make around the ruins. Wherever we passed, there had been destruction, injury and suffering; there had frequently been death. These scenes have been often described and often photographed. I have no appetite for horrors and see little need to add my details to those already recorded by others. What I remember best are the living people, living and uninjured, waiting patiently in line for the busses with their bundles of clothing under their arms. These were the homeless or the frightened, going up to the West End or to the centers of the relief organizations; moving, ever moving, like the poor in all wars, taking to the road. They did it, however, in a patient and orderly way, their faces a little stunned, a little shocked. The deep shelters were crowded that night and many of the people went to them before the gray smoke-covered afternoon had ended. All along the way we were barred from the river, for there had been the docks, the factories, the mills and the petroleum stores which were now in the ruins or still burning. This was the first and most disastrous German attack upon London itself. There had been others in the outskirts; this was an attack upon the old gray city and those who lived in it, an attack executed with great force and order, eminently successful, never to be forgotten. Only in the following spring (April 16 and May 10, 1941) were greater raids possible—greater, that is, in the number of planes sent over—but even in those later holocausts there was no greater damage. The first night was by all odds the worst.


3


The whole world knows what followed. Every night for what seemed interminable weeks, the Germans sent bombing aircraft over London, beginning at eight o'clock and ending at six the next morning. They were punctual and systematic to a degree; we always knew when they would come and when they would go. During September these night attacks were supplemented by a good many day raids, the strongest of which were on the 11th, 15th and 27th. Up until September 15th it seemed likely that these furious attempts to beat down London were intended as a prelude to invasion; after that date the hope of invasion must have dwindled to nothing, and the air offensive was continued merely with a view to disrupting industrial production, office work and life itself in the densely populated Thames valley. In October the weather supervened; the raids died away, became weaker and less frequent; the winter was an obstacle not so much because of the overcast in England itself, but because of the fog-laden fields in Northern France which the Germans were using.

Never again, after the first night, did I obtain such an apocalyptic view of the unequal battle. After September 8th I was in it, under it, part of it; I never saw more than some part of the whole. I was at this time sending dispatches to America (to the North American Newspaper Alliance) and occasionally broadcasting for Ed Murrow; I kept fairly busy, like most of my colleagues, and in spite of everything we were cheerful, probably more cheerful than before. I think there can be little doubt that our spirits mounted, now that the worst (or nearly the worst) had come, and the reason was clear: it was that the English people were rising to this occasion in a manner worthy of their history.

I do not agree with those observers who hold that the English have a monopoly on endurance and tenacity; I cannot do so because I have been in Spain and China. But the English way of resisting terrible adversity is peculiar to the national character. It is neither more nor less courageous than that of other peoples; it is merely different. The difference consists chiefly in the most celebrated of insular mannerisms, that which understates and under-values. Psychologically this is no doubt a compensatory device at all times, but under the conditions of September and October, 1940, it became almost a mania. A man who had seen his house destroyed and his family's life endangered would have thought himself a sorry knave if he referred to it as anything but "a bit of trouble." The most desperate attack or alarm was referred to as "a flap"; the gravest incident was not thought to justify any undue departure from customary behavior. I remember one day at the height of the "blitz" (as we unfortunately called it) when I was sitting in Ed Murrow's drawing room drinking a placid whisky and soda. His office had been bombed for the second time and his secretaries were working in another room of his flat, whither they had removed what could be salvaged of the office furniture. Miss Campbell, the chief of the C.B.S. secretaries, came into the room. "I don't want to disturb you, sir," she said in her cool, trim voice, "but I think the house is on fire." We looked out the window and saw, indeed, a posse of firemen breaking in; the only error was that the fire was next door.

Those secretaries, for example—Ed's and everybody else's—who came to work every morning—did they ever know how large a part they played in the immense civilian victory known as the London bombing? They had to rise at all hours of the morning to get to work even approximately on time. Their busses had to make new and strange detours to avoid the ruins of the night; they never knew that the office would be there in the morning or their homes be intact when they returned at night; they never knew that the bus would even run; they were uncertain (if they thought at all) to survive the journey. Yet they kept to their hours, sleeping little or not at all, and even when their eyes were puffed almost shut with fatigue, they sustained their even-tempered routine. "Don't you worry about me, sir," they would say. "I shall be all right." Down in Fleet Street, where I used to go to see Mr. Sargint of the North American Newspaper Alliance (who was himself doing air-raid warden's duty every night in Maida Vale and correspondent's duty every day in Fleet Street), there were two or three cool-voiced girls who never seemed to think there was the slightest occasion for remark in their daily journey across London. Their journey, all these journeys taken through the ruins of the night before by all the millions of men and women going to their work, their offices or their factories, constituted the victory of London. For what had been mainly aimed at by the bombing attacks, once the hope of invasion had faded, was a disruption of the life and productivity in the London area: this they, the "little" people, the so-called "little" people, defeated.

It became almost a point of honor to stay in London, even over the weekend. We all knew, I think, that the objective was to sow panic and cause an abandonment of the daily work of the vast concentration called the London area. Ten million people lived and worked here. If they should ever begin to run away (as Paris ran away) there was no hope of continuing the war on terms offering a chance of survival. Consequently many people stayed in London when there was no strict necessity to do so, merely because by so doing they maintained the brave and tragic pretense that there really was no occasion for alarm.

I do not want to exaggerate the toughness of the Londoners or to sentimentalize over their epic endurance. Many among them broke and fled; I had friends who did so, who spent scarcely a night under the bombs from September 7th onward; I knew people who sat wretchedly over their whisky-sodas and deplored the whole war. One such man (who was never seen in London after the bombings began) told me he saw no purpose in continuing the war. "We'll get nothing out of it, win or lose," he said. "Everything will go to the Morrisons and Bevins, whatever happens." There were a good many who said, in strict privacy, that they saw no way in which England could win the war. To them I could only say what I have always said in public and in private, that the war would be won when America and Russia were also in it; it was cold comfort. In those days, with America hysterical but powerless, with Russia almost an enemy, the eventuality seemed too remote to do any good against the present fact of bombs, incendiaries and land-mines.

But those weaker ones of whom I speak were among the rich, idle and self-indulgent, those who could not cut down their requirements and risk their naked lives. I never saw much of this spirit among the poor. My own housekeeper was the only one I ever knew, and she, poor woman, was ill and unable to sleep at night because of the bombs. The poor of the London streets had little in the way of possessions to lose, and they preferred London, even if it meant death, to the unfamiliar tranquillity of the country. Then, too, most of them derived a fierce exhilaration from the struggle, for they knew, with the profound instinct of the people, that it was a struggle—that merely by being here, by continuing to exist, by doing their jobs whatever they were, the men and women of London were engaging in battle.

Among the people there was a great reluctance to change established habits. This is why only the very poor, at that period, had the habit of going to shelters. The very poor had been desperately badly hit on the first night and thousands among them had nowhere but the shelters to go to; they were, by the conditions of life, less hidebound than the middle classes, and they saw nothing particularly shocking about the promiscuity and acute discomfort of the crowded tube stations. But the huge middle and lower-middle classes disliked the shelters as they disliked any other disturbance of their routine. Their respectability and bone-deep conservatism rebelled at anything that threw them into unwanted familiarity with the poorest and dirtiest Cockney mass. Lady Diana Cooper had a charming young secretary who was obliged to make her daily journey from a remote part of London. Diana wanted to save her the dangers of the night, and arranged for her a place in the deep shelter of the Ministry of Information —one of the best in London. The girl's mother allowed her to pass one night there and then refused to permit it further. "It's not decent," she said, "with all those men."

Again it should be said, to counter-balance the somewhat prettified picture of London under the bombing that has been put abroad, that terror and ugliness were not unknown among the crowded mass in the deep shelters. It should also be said, risking diverse accusations, that in my opinion the poorest and dirtiest of the East End Cockneys are not (by the conditions of their life) permitted to develop the most admirable characteristics. They are not heroes; neither are they bulldogs. They sniveled and quaked under the bombs, huddled together in their filth like so many frightened animals. Could it be otherwise? I only went to these deep shelters once or twice to see what they were like, and came out again almost choked by the smells, physical and psychological, that filled such lower air. Among these people there was an astonishing number of foreigners. This may have been because Whitechapel and Blackfriars are the abode of poor foreigners by tradition, but also, perhaps, because the foreign parts of the

London population had less incentive to get jobs above ground and brave the bombs. Certainly in those fetid underground caves you heard practically every language, European or Asiatic, that exists in the world today, and I do not remember hearing such languages among those who worked above ground. Again, how could it be otherwise? The fact is only worth mentioning because a much too simplified version of London under the bombs has been given the widest circulation: we are told that it was a city of heroes, that cowardice was unknown there, and that no trial was too much for the spirit of the people. Such was not the case. It would be outside the limitations of human nature, in all its splendor and misery, to breed a whole race of heroes in the submerged and groveling lowest layer of capitalist society. What was not possible in peace was not possible in war.

Nevertheless, those who remained above ground and worked—and there were millions of them—made a brave show of it. The bus conductor, the shop assistant, the office worker, the policeman, the thousand and one varieties of economic man visible in the most cursory walk across London, demonstrated the fixed determination of the great majority to survive this ordeal so as to have no shame of it afterward. In a way, the common resolution was to ignore the bombs as much as possible. They all reminded me of Lady Ottoline Morrell, a friend now dead, a lady given to much eccentricity of manner and raiment, who once sat in a little restaurant in Rome under a grape-arbor and refused to go inside even though great splashing drops of rain were falling. "What will you do if it really does rain, and rain heavily?" another friend asked. "I shall ignore it," Ottoline said with deep tranquillity. She was a Cavendish-Bentinck by birth, and therefore inherited the iron of the aristocratic tradition, but there was a good deal of the same iron in all English people when it came to the test. They were determined not to make a fuss, to understate the matter as thoroughly as possible, to do their jobs and to survive. It was this all-powerful auxiliary, the resistant iron in the soul of the people, which made it possible for the R.A.F. to win the resounding victories of Dover and London.

For the R.A.F. was, of course, fighting all the time. Every daylight raid of the Germans was intercepted at various points coming and going, with a rising degree of success for the Spitfires and Hurricanes. By the end of September the Luftwaffe had lost so severely that the attempt to raid London by day was given up; only the nightly visit continued, in varying measures of strength and effectiveness, from eight in the evening until six the next morning, but the days were at least free for work, for binding up the wounds, for clearing away the débris.

## 4

It was not only the very poor in the deep shelters who huddled together for comfort during the bombings. Friends tended to congregate, to drink, dance, talk and pretend, for hours at a time, that the walls were secure, that the roof would not fall, that the concussion was not at this moment shaking the house. In the earlier days, before the Dorchester Hotel closed its outside terrace—the one we called "the cockle-shell," with nothing but a thin roof over it, separate from the towering hotel—I danced there at times when the whole place quivered like an aspen-leaf. Those who had no jobs to do outside in the night (air-raid warden, ambulance driver, volunteer fireman or the like) came together toward eight o'clock and stayed together as

long as possible. It was always late, and with much reluctance, that we separated to our various beds. I would walk
home to Charles Street, where I lived, hugging the walls
of the houses to escape the shrapnel, thankful for the tin
hat I had borrowed from David Bruce weeks before and
never returned, and wondering when I would get to sleep.
In the morning I would wake up, more often than not, to
find the pictures askew and china ornaments smashed on
the floor; sometimes there were cracks in the windows;
but the house itself was never hit. It blew up months later
(April 16, 1941) when I was on my way back to it from
America.

American visitors to England are always put on the defensive about their upper-class friends, as if only the poor
and unhappy were worth a thought. I know the point of
view that produces this attitude: we have seen too many
ambassadors, journalists and politicians go to England and
be smothered in the embraces of the governing and privileged groups. I think myself immune to such dangers because my interest and intent lie in such a different groove.
I have no patience with the feudal system, no tolerance
for organized privilege, no political wish that is not influenced by the desire to see poverty abolished and an honorable socialist equality insured to every man alive. This
does not, however, impede my swift and easy accommo-
dation to the forms of life produced by privilege. I can
go on for weeks in the company of the rich and the powerful without a qualm. I know that my brothers are toiling
and dying, that the whole earth is a hecatomb; swift
shadows of their misery sometimes pass across the lighted
feast; in my blood and brain and heart I am with them.
And yet, in actual fact, I may be drinking champagne with
a duke or exchanging dirty jokes with a packet of thought-
less young officers. I do not know whether this is a com-

mon experience or not; I think probably not. Few prole-
tarians have traversed the whole social system of an age
and come to speaking terms with it, polite and conversable
terms, without forswearing their own identity or their
innermost faith. The deep and unspoken sympathy I have
always felt with Mr. H. G. Wells is due, I think, to this
characteristic (or peculiarity) which we have in common.
He moves in the society of the rich, the great, the privileged, without for one moment forgetting either the
kitchen stairs at Bromley or the supreme purposes for
which he has lived. In my less effective or enduring way, I
think the same is true of me. And too, like Mr. Wells, I am
just as fond of my upper-class friends as of any others:
they are also people. This is perhaps why my fellow-
socialists who belong to organized political parties have
always mistrusted or upbraided me. They have what they
call "class enemies." I have none.

Certainly many of the friends whom I most often saw
during the London ordeal were far from proletarian. Bill
Stoneman, my fierce friend of the *Chicago Daily News*,
used to be shocked and disgusted at the way I spent my
leisure. Bill was—until he gave it up in despair—my hair
shirt. He used to rail at me for living at Claridge's in the
midst of all the surviving luxury of London. "You can't
stay in a place like that," he would say, frowning with the
intensity of his meaning. "You *can't*. It's wrong, it's absolutely wrong." Out of sheer weakness of character, early in
the summer I moved out to his house in Chelsea, but after
I became thoroughly aware of its situation, with power
stations to right and left of it, I moved back to Mayfair
again. There were bound to be bombs everywhere, but
more around the power stations than anywhere else. Bill
also used to discourage the practice of taking taxicabs.
"You're only using up the gasoline that these people

need," he would say. "God, how they're going to need it! You take a bus." It was no use telling him that I was in a hurry, that I did not know the bus lines, or that the taxi drivers had to make a living; he was as ferocious about this as about any other subject. But most of all he condemned what the French would call my *fréquentations*, the people to whom I resorted for my hours of gregarious pleasure. During the few days I had spent at his house he had been obliged to answer the telephone for me a number of times, and he would leave sarcastic little notes beside the instrument saying, "The Duchess of Westminster wants you to come to cocktails tomorrow. Will you please ring up the King tonight? And don't forget Lady Astor." Among such messages there would be one true one (from Loelia Westminster, for example) and two or three fabrications of his satirical roguery. I got so that I was unable to tell the true from the false, and one night when I came in late and Bill told me I was summoned to the Chief of the Imperial Staff I very nearly didn't go; I thought it was another of his japes. Ed Murrow was not far behind him in this vein of attack and little Hilde Marchant—of the *Daily Express*—spitfire Hilde, whom I used to hide behind on Shakespeare Cliff—was often merry at my expense for the same reason.

The Duff Coopers, the Halifaxes, the Weizmanns and what seemed a phalanx of other public characters lived at the Dorchester Hotel, seduced, I think, by the idea that it was the most modern of hotel structures and the one least likely to collapse under the bombs. I never shared the delusion that the Dorchester was safe; I thought it merely lucky. It is indeed extraordinary that no direct hit was ever made on this huge caravanserai during those nights when the bombs fell all around it. It used to sway in the air like a tree in a storm; you could feel the swing and resilient yielding of the steel structure; on the upper floors in particular you had an extraordinary sensation of clinging to the bent bough. The Duff Coopers lived in rooms on the uppermost floor, looking over the Park. Duff was Minister of Information and—because he had resigned from the cabinet two years before in protest against the Munich Agreement—had the honor of being named third in Hitler's trio of English enemies (Churchill, Eden and Cooper). Diana, so exquisite and remote at first glance, so full of an incongruously robust common sense upon acquaintance—half poem and half bread—kept a spirited assembly at her side in the evenings. I think her beauty and the poetic quality that clings to her were somehow contradicted and therefore made complete by that ready humor in all things, that fearless anti-bunk frankness of speech and manner, to which she owes (I have been told) a fair number of enemies. I was and have remained among her devotees, appreciating at all times the special quality of irresistible fragility, of strength clothed in weakness, which deceived not a few. At Dunkirk time she carried tea-trays and slops from morning to night at a canteen which served the returned warriors; then, "broken with fatigue" as she said, she would change into some frivolous regalia and dine with friends in the restaurant downstairs in the Dorchester, or go with me to the slightly raucous hideaway called the Players. Later on (1941) she was running a farm on the government's agricultural quota scheme, mixing the slops for the pigs, milking cow and goat, making cheeses, keeping bees, a "one-woman farm" which contributed its assigned share of food. During the bombings in September she remained in London not because she liked the bombs—she confessed herself terrified throughout, "bathed in sweat" as she said—but because she had the firm conviction that Duff would never get to his office on time, or receive proper meals, or find his clothing, if she were not there to see to it.

I used to dine with the Coopers often; in the worst bombing days I was there nearly every night. There were half a dozen regulars in Diana's court. She was fond of Lady Maureen Stanley (who has since died) and took me to that hospitable house upon occasion—a house where the whole government was in and out at some time or other. Lady Juliet Duff, Moura von Budberg, Virginia Cowles, Lady Pamela Berry—these were some of those who dined at the Coopers' table while the hotel rocked. The men were for the most part government people, some in and some out, since even the bitter disagreement over Munich had not eradicated the habit these people have of thinking of themselves as a special, coherent and related group. Political argument sometimes ran fairly high, especially if the past was (as it had to be) called into question; but I think what united these people was in reality stronger than what divided them. I seldom took part in their arguments because my own beliefs arose from such a different soil; when I did argue, unfortunately, I was likely to lose my temper and shout, which benefited nobody. There was one particularly lamentable occasion—the night of the Battle of Oran, July 3rd—when I shouted across the table at Brendan Bracken to such effect that I thought only a return to America would erase the memory. I actually went all the way to Galway, intending to take the *Washington* and sail home, and was only dissuaded at the last moment by the reflection that I was leaving the pattern of things far less than complete, that I had some kind of professional duty to see it through into some kind of conclusion.

The London bombings were, temporarily, conclusive. They proved the ability of the great city and its people to

stand severe punishment, the resolution of the Churchill
government to fight to the last, the inability of the German
Air Force alone to win the war. And even though I did
spend so many of my evenings in a rather silken circle, I
think I learned there what I could not have learned in the
crowded and pestiferous tube stations—that is, that England would not submit to the Nazi.

For the truth of the matter is that a people may be as
brave as you like, as tough and as tenacious as you like,
and it falls just the same if its government has no will.
What I learned among my friends of the Tory governing
class was that they were united around Churchill in the
determination to fight out this war to the end; that they
were willing to accept any collaboration they could get for
this purpose; that they would court Russia, accept an ever-
widening range of socialist modification, surrender many
or most of their privileges, admit past errors and accept
new colleagues, all perhaps with a hope of defending their
essential philosophy when the war was won, but at any
rate without present reserves. In this will to fight they differed totally from the panic-stricken clique which had
governed France in the fateful days of May. Nobody
could ever convince me that the French people are less
valorous than any other; indeed, the whole history of
France denies such an assumption. What happened in
France was due most of all to the lack of will and faith in
the governing regions and to the degree in which that
corrupt camarilla had lost the confidence of the masses.
You could say anything you pleased about the Tory governing class in England, but you had to see that they still
possessed conscience, will, determination and a genuine
patriotism (i.e., fierce and defensive love of the native
soil, to be clearly distinguished from such overgrowths as
imperialism). The difference between the Churchills,

Edens, Duff Coopers and their like on the one side, and the Reynauds, Daladiers and Gamelins on the other, was too obvious for argument, and again the instinct of the people asserted itself with its resistless power. For Paris ran away—ran away long before there was any necessity to do so—ran away literally by the million; and ran away because there was no possible faith in a government dominated by the Comtesse de Portes. London did not run away, and I think chiefly because London believed in Churchill and his government and took its stand with them.

In so saying I am not ignoring the objective military situation. Of course it is true that France lay like a carpet before the invader's foot, while England could gird for battle behind her immemorial moat. The Channel was mighty as of old. But what it did not and could not do was stave off the terrors of invasion through the air. These terrors came and London survived them without running away because London believed in its government. This may well be the crowning achievement of the class which has ruled England for so many centuries.

5

There were some gatherings in that time which I shall long remember. At least two of them were in Lady Colefax's house at 19 Lord North Street. Sibyl Colefax had long been one of the most celebrated of London hostesses, a *salonière* who liked music, books and characters. She may also have liked "celebrities"; it is an accusation always made against the habitually hospitable and there may be something in it; but, as Lynn Fontanne once remarked, "Sibyl is very kind to people who *aren't* famous." On the

two occasions I have in mind the company was a considerable part of the story. One was a musical evening: we
sat and listened to Mozart and Schubert exquisitely played
by violin, viola and piano while the bombs and the cannonade resounded from somewhere down the river. The
two small rooms were not crowded; we sat motionless, the
conflict of sounds like a conflict of ideas in the single mind;
both kinds of music were German. There is no need to
name the guests who were suspended in that hour between peace and war, between the time that is gone forever and the unknowable future. They were, as is usual
in Sibyl's house, men and women of all the known kinds,
born to breed and die, but distinguished for some special
quality along the way. I remember Mr. Somerset
Maugham (who had escaped from France some time
earlier in a coal boat) leaning his head wearily against his
hand as he listened; I remember Lady Diana Cooper's
lovely face in a dark corner glowing palely, as if frozen
there. Perhaps the two kinds of music made each inaudible
in turn to all, as they were to me; it was Schubert or the
bombs; human ears were not made for both at the same
time. Art, love and death (to choose boldly among the
plain big words that mean what they say) were all in the air
of the house for an hour, intermingled, beckoning, receding, dying out among the curtains, contained for once in
a small space like a lyric.

On another day later on, in the full bombing season,
there was a spirited and talkative lunch at Sibyl's. The
company included H. G. Wells, Somerset Maugham,
Bruce Lockhart, Moura von Budberg and Diana Cooper.
Mr. Wells was being particularly malicious about God,
one of his favorite themes (à propos of a prose poem by
François Mauriac which Mr. Maugham had produced).
As he held forth with his usual perky, cheerful insistence,

with many a "that sort of thing" and "don't you know," the bombs began to thunder down. Sibyl got a little nervous. "I don't like this a bit," she said. "What if a bomb should land here now? It's much too good a bag for the Germans," she said, nodding toward the literary gentlemen. "Why don't we go to the shelter? It's not much good, but it's better than just sitting here." There was a little flurry of discussion and she was voted down; a minute or two later, when the noise seemed to be coming very near, she brought it up again.

"I refuse to go to the shelter," said Mr. Wells with happy perversity, "until I have had my cheese. I'm enjoying a very good lunch. Why should I be disturbed by some wretched little barbarian adolescents in a machine? This thing has no surprises for me. I foresaw it long ago. Sibyl, I want my cheese."

Sibyl was obliged to give him his cheese and I suppose we all reflected the same thing, which was that, indeed, this very Mr. Wells had foreseen aerial warfare even before the invention of the airplane: somehow a startling fact as we sat there and listened to the explosions. Sibyl's invaluable factotum, Fleming (a severe and elderly woman who always gave Noel Coward an extra helping of everything, particularly puddings) came into the room and put up the wooden frames which hid the windows. "At least we may as well be spared the effort of dodging the broken glass," Sibyl said. She had lost the glass out of her windows three or four times in the past weeks and had some feeling on the subject. We sat there under the electric lights at midday, with the windows blocked off, while Mr. Wells resumed both his cheese and his discourse.

Sibyl's house had been crowded on Monday evenings all summer long; a duke or a cabinet minister, a violinist or a pretty actress, were without novelty in that assembly.

One night Noel Coward played and sang his ribald ditty
about "The Stately Homes of England." The Duke of
Devonshire wrinkled his nose and said: "I don't think it's
a bit funny, do you, Diana?" Sometimes I went there alone
and Sibyl showed me her scrapbooks, her mementos—
things of Kipling's, of Max Beerbohm's, the traces of a life
much given to appreciating talent. No character lends
itself more easily to satire than that of the hostess who
likes exceptional people, and I think (or have been told)
that Sibyl has had her share of lampooning. This seems to
me the peak of ingratitude, since in point of fact the very
quality attacked (the liking for exceptional people) is the
one which makes her house frequented and enjoyed. Her
birdlike alertness, awareness, her kindness of heart and
zest for character, and above all the singularly integrated
and continuous expression of her distinctive catalytic
function in society, set her off as a bold spirit in a horrid
time. *Libre je suis née et libre je veux mourir,* said that very
different lady, Bizet's Carmen. Sibyl was a hostess born
and a hostess would she die; let the bombs fall and the
roof collapse; will you come to dinner? The writers who
have written books, plays and stories about her all paid
tribute, unwittingly, to a positive entity in a negative field.

The Ronald Trees gave parties at their house in Queen
Anne's Gate until the bombing in the neighborhood grew
too severe; when you went anywhere to dinner after September 8th you were more than likely to have to spend
the night in the basement. The Duchess of Westminster
had a "day" (Thursday, I think) when many people came
together in her beautifully decorated modern house in
Little College Street; there were other centers of a spirited
refusal to admit the gravity of the hour. I think one of
the oddest assemblies, most original in intent and development, was an afternoon party given by David Bowes-Lyon

so that his sister, the Queen, might meet the American press.

David was chief of the press section at the Ministry of Economic Warfare and had a weekly conference to which, as a rule, the second- or third-ranking correspondent in each American newspaper office in London was sent. The chiefs of the American newspaper bureaus went occasionally, but not regularly, since economic warfare could seldom be counted upon to yield the main "story" of the day (and, as is well known, the chief correspondents are only interested in the main story). Consequently David's acquaintance in the American press was chiefly among the second- and third-string men. When he decided that the Queen and the American press ought to meet, it was only natural that he should choose the men known to him. As a result he left out some of the most notable of our colleagues—Knick and Quent Reynolds, for example—through sheer inadvertence, and included a large number of the youth of the profession. As it turned out, it was a happy choice: the boys liked the Queen and she liked them, and the whole affair was not at all a bad thing for England.

When David telephoned me at an unearthly hour one morning I found it hard to understand. "The press meet the Queen?" I echoed into the telephone. "But how can that be? Have you consulted all the authorities? Isn't it against all the rules?" He was brave about rules. "I suppose it's revolutionary," he said, "but why not? I think it might be good for her and I think it might be good for all of you, too." He appointed the hour and the place, the next day at 16 Charles Street, Berkeley Square (Mrs. Ronald Greville's house).

At the time named Bill Stoneman and I, having washed our faces and shined our shoes, made our way down the street. (I lived a few doors from Number 16.) A good

many of the press had already arrived and milled about
rather uncertainly. David was in charge of the operation
and took the boys one by one over to the corner by the
window, where the Queen sat. Each of the correspondents
had six or eight minutes' talk with her and then made way
for another. I watched them go through the process. Each
in turn approached with a rather worried look, not, certainly, as if the prospect was all delight. Each in turn
thawed under the influence of her simple, friendly charm;
and each one, when he got up, was smiling and conquered. It was no doubt rather an ordeal for the Queen,
too, but one for which nature and training had fitted her
surpassingly well. I thought her candid eyes and touch-
ingly pure voice (an almost childlike voice) did more to
disarm us all, if we needed disarming, than any amount
of splendor might have done.

Sometime in September (was it on the 15th?) the German day raiders made an attack on Buckingham Palace.
David Bowes-Lyon had just moved into the palace that
day, having been bombed out of his quarters elsewhere.
He told me that the King and Queen were not in the shelter at the moment of the attack, and raced for it just in
time. There can be little doubt that this attack, which
was made deliberately in broad daylight from a low altitude, popularized the monarchy among whole groups and
classes which had been apathetic or hostile to it before.
John Strachey told me about a bus conductor friend of
his, a "bit of a Red," whose comment on it was: "Well,
blimey if I ever thought the Jerries would go for Buckingham Palace. I thought all those people were in it together."
From the point of view of practical wartime politics it was
a cardinal error on the part of the Germans; there was the
beginning of a socially ominous situation in the earlier
days and nights of bombing when the East End suffered

so much more than any other part of London; a really
clever bombing policy on the part of the Germans might
have encouraged movements of popular revolt rather than
of popular unity. The bombing of the Palace was a dramatic signal to the whole nation that no English life was
safe, and springs of old loyalty were touched. I still doubt
if the monarchy signifies much to the broadest mass in
England, and of course I can only regard its historical use-
fulness as having been terminated some time ago, with the
single legalistic exception of the Statute of Westminster.
Even so, life in wartime is not a reasoned affair, nor do
people whose lives hang by a hair make much effort to
resist waves of emotion. Thus the monarchy reconquered
in a day a great deal of its symbolic value to the nation,
and even if the feelings set up in September were neither
permanent nor deep, they served a purpose (the essential
purpose of unity in resistance) for that necessary while.
To the fulfilment of this useful purpose I am sure that
Queen Elizabeth contributed a great deal. She went
among the most stricken people of the most ravaged dis-
tricts in the East End and no guards were necessary; the
people stretched out their hands to her and touched her,
unhindered; she walked among their ruins as a living
proof that the monarchy exists with the consent of the
governed. No dictator in Europe could dare trust his life
in this way to the unguarded hands of the disinherited.

It may seem that I give entirely too much space to the
ornaments and the survivals at a time when millions were
in peril and privation. I do so because these ornaments
and survivals still play a great part in the life of England.
The government of Great Britain is still essentially a Tory
government, although its policy is very often far to the
left of its true aims. The primary characteristic of Tory
government is social, not economic or even political; that

is, the retention of power in the hands of a single class is what distinguishes it from other governments. Some Tory governments in England were far to the "left" of any French Republican government of the day—to the left in foreign policy and in many elements (social insurance, for example) of domestic policy. So long as power remained within the governing class, as it did from the days of Queen Anne until 1924, political differences (as between Conservative and Liberal) could arouse great passions but little change upon the surface of parliamentary society. Electoral reform was brought about by the conscience of the Liberal part of the governing class, abetted by fear of popular agitation; but once the era of reform had come to an end the people governing England were still, with a few notable exceptions, the children and grandchildren of those who had fought the parliamentary battle over it. Ramsay MacDonald's first Labour government in 1924 and still more his second one in 1929 showed that the social influences of Tory control were more powerful than the public vote itself, and in no respect did the Socialist government prove itself more sensitive to popular necessity than those which preceded or followed it. How, indeed, could it be otherwise, when the House of Commons is itself a sort of club, when the great departments of state are all manned by the youth of the governing class and when the influence of social life in London is as powerful upon the legislator as any known beliefs in economics, sociology or religion? For a Socialist government in England to set about its proclaimed task (even admitting "the inevitability of gradualness," whatever that may mean) would involve abolishing the whole Civil Service in such all-important ministries as the Foreign Office, Home Office, Treasury, Colonial Office and India Office; it would compel ministers and legislators to be immune to all blandishments from the departing order; it would mean an attempt, throughout the whole social range, to obliterate barriers which have grown as innumerable as they are mighty in the most caste-conscious of modern European peoples. Small wonder that the timid Socialists of Mac-Donald's generation made no real effort at it, but subsided into the glue of the governing class and left the true socio-political problem, the transfer of power into other hands, still wholly unanswered.

I am by no means prepared to say that this was, as it turned out, a bad thing. Certainly no Socialist leader who has yet appeared in England possesses one-tenth of the qualifications for the task of 1940 that were concentrated in the single person of Churchill. I met workers of various kinds in England then, before and afterward who could think straighter than almost anybody except the best minds of the governing class; in a local miners' council in Warwickshire the following year I heard debate which was clearer and better in every respect than any ordinary debate in the House of Commons. But the transfer of power in England at any time before the present would have meant nothing more nor less than an immense social revolution, exhausting, dividing and embittering the human material of the nation. A country which had gone through such an experience in the recent past could not have withstood the shattering blows of 1940, any more than the nascent Bolshevik Russia of Lenin and Trotsky could have continued war with Imperial Germany. When we remember the attitude of Transport House (the areopagitica of British labor) during the years 1933–1939, and how Mr. Ernest Bevin made no secret of his belief that sixpence more on the daily wage of the British dock worker was more important than the loss of Spain, Czechoslovakia and half the world besides, then we must discern, in the operation of the historical forces, a needed and salutary delay (due to the parliamentary system, to insularity and conservatism among the workers, and to the principles of self-renewal and miscegenation in the governing class) which saved us from the terrible possibility of a Brest-Litovsk in the West. If it is true, as I believe, that the preservation and continuance of the great line of Western democratic development toward the emergence of ever larger masses to the surface of life depends in this era upon the defeat of the essentially tribal and retrogressive forces commanded by Hitler, then a Tory government with broad national support was necessary in 1940 because no other would have dared (or, politically speaking, been able) to continue the war.

6

I had some acquaintance with intellectuals of the Left at that time, as before and since; they were in rather a sorry state. Those directly immersed in the affairs of the Parliamentary Labour Party (like Professor Harold Laski) had become, for the time being, simply politicians, concerned with the electoral truce and with what, under that arrangement with Churchill, they could obtain for their party leadership. Among those who had passed the years 1936–1939 in happy alliance with the Communists there was an even sorer confusion: they either adopted the "Communist Party line" (in a few cases) and were miserably unhappy and self-contradictory with it, or they wasted an immense amount of time and newsprint making attacks upon it. Mr. Victor Gollancz was in this latter state; so was my friend John Strachey at first. The exigencies of 1940 brought John out of the sectarian mire; by

July he was an air-raid warden half the week in London
and a Home Guard the other half in the country; by September he was in the Air Force. Other Left intellectuals
(I am speaking now of non-Communists) spent their efforts on an attempt to keep their ideas alive, in print and
before the public, without lagging in support for the war:
this was true of Aneurin Bevan and Russell Strauss, the
main supports of the *People's Tribune*. Their colleague,
Sir Stafford Cripps, had been sent off by Churchill at Dunkirk time on his mission to Russia—that mission which Hitler was to turn from total failure into the semblance of a
dazzling success.

I was somewhat ill at ease with Left intellectuals just
then because I saw little sense in any of their activity—
except, of course, John Strachey's. My Communist friend
Claude Cockburn, with whom I had argued and laughed
through many an hour in the preceding years, was almost
beyond conversation in 1940. At the time of the Nazi-
Soviet Pacts (August 21st and, more significant, the
Friendship Pact of September 29, 1939) I had seen in
America the incapacity of any Communist intellectual to
think for himself or to adhere to what he had for years
thought he had thought. I hardly supposed the English
Communists would be the same: after all, they were in the
firing line. But I found out—and not only with Claude—
that they were no different from Communists anywhere
else. The papal bull had gone out from Moscow, and there
was no questioning it. Claude actually argued with me
until about three in the morning, one night, on the general
proposition that Hitler's victory made no essential difference: "He's the merest incident, without significance," he
kept saying, "without significance." At another point:
"How many lines do you suppose Genghis Khan occupies
in the *Encyclopædia Britannica*? How many lines? Half

a column. No more." It seemed to me a very strange argument from a man who had once passionately believed that Fascism was the enemy of humanity and should be fought on every field. The truth about Claude and all Communists was that their essential loyalty was to the Soviet Union; the Soviet Union's supreme authorities had decided that for self-preservation a pact with Germany was necessary; therefore they thought it was necessary, too. But the American and British Communists would never say this plainly—they talked nonsense about Hitler being in reality no enemy; that Churchill was a worse enemy, and so on and so on, round and round. I was perfectly well aware, and told them not once but many times, that they would have to change their tune when Hitler attacked Russia, as he some day inevitably would (I had also written this in magazines during 1940 and 1941); but that line of talk produced nothing but ribald laughter. Hitler would never dare attack Russia; Stalin was playing the most astute of games; this was an "imperialist war" and he was going to stay out of it. If you said (as I said and still say) that the Nazi-Soviet Pact was not astute at all; that it gave the signal for the war and guaranteed that it would be fought on Hitler's terms, one front at a time; that it would in the end come back upon the Soviet Union with terrific force; then I was a scoundrelly capitalist scrivener, an apologist for the empire-builders or a dupe of Churchillian persuasions.

John Strachey took me out to the country one Sunday to lunch and spend the afternoon with Victor Gollancz and his family. Mr. and Mrs. Maisky were there; I had never met them before. So was dear Jennie Lee, the Scotch lass grown up, who seems to me to have more sense of reality in her little finger than most of the "Left intellectuals" in their collective assembly of intellect. So was Quo Tai-chi, the Chinese Ambassador, whom I had met years before in the bad days in Shanghai (1027) and was to meet again in Chungking. The Soviet Ambassador, Maisky, whom I was to know much better later on and appreciate very highly indeed, was going through a period as difficult as any he had traversed through his long and difficult mission to England. He had labored patiently for seven years without making any great impression upon the Chamberlains, Halifaxes and Baldwins among whom his lot had been cast. Tenaciously, day after day, he had struggled through the murky tergiversations of the Non-Intervention Committee, trying to extract from the moral deaf-mutes who ran it some faint recognition of the Spanish Republic's right to live. The whole catastrophic development of the year 1938—the strangling of Spain, the betrayal of Czechoslovakia and the frank acknowledgment at Munich of Hitler's mastery—had taken place against his protest or without his knowledge. Chamberlain, it seems (and Halifax, too) never dreamed of consulting the Soviet Ambassador in the airy chatter with which they disposed of the Eastern front against Germany. Then on March 15, 1939, when Hitler marched into Prague, all this changed overnight: Chamberlain saw the impossibility of his policy, in the face of the rising anger of the English people, and came—so fantastically late—to the realization that the fortunes of an inevitable war against Germany depended considerably upon an understanding with Russia. Mr. Maisky became a popular figure in England for a few months (March to August, 1939) while the ill-managed and half-hearted efforts at an alliance were being made in Moscow. Then, after the Nazi-Soviet Pact—a vast historical error, I am convinced, but one which in retrospect is not difficult to understand—Maisky went back under a cloud, with whole classes of the population in England

regarding him with a suspicious eye and others sure that
he represented not only his own country, but the German
enemy.

With all this, the Maiskys had systematically worked for
an understanding with England and had grown—a little
unwillingly, perhaps—to like the country. Most of all, at
the present moment they shared all the hazards of English
life; bombs had fallen all around them in London; on this
very afternoon there was an air-raid warning, and, as we
walked in Gollancz's placid country garden, we scanned
the sky for alien planes. There is something more powerful
than ideas in the peril shared, and I believe the Maiskys
came closer to England during the bombings than they
would have been willing to admit. They did not talk politics, of course, but indulged in a good-humored Sunday
afternoon discussion of all the events and ideas of the day,
based upon wide reading in the periodicals. In the following year, when I knew Maisky better and spent many
week-ends with him, I found out that he read the whole
British press, practically without exception, daily and
weekly. It may be remarked, incidentally, that I never
knew any English public figure whose knowledge in this
field was as complete as Maisky's. Your English cabinet
minister was susceptible to the tradition of literary politics
(he could quote Latin to his purpose) and liked to let it
be known that he relaxed upon John Donne, Milton and
the *Religio Medici;* but he seldom read more than two or
three newspapers in a day and took a sort of pride in not
knowing current details. I have heard figures of the first
consequence in English politics say, "Oh, yes, who *is* our
ambassador in Tokyo now?" or "What exactly *did* we do
about the Ethiopian question?" Lord Balfour once said to
a friend of mine: "What exactly *is* the Balfour Note? Did
I write it, and if not why is it called by my name?"

This exalted literary and philosophic turn of mind was perfect for the parliamentary life of 1880; it produced all those remarkable characters on both sides of the fence, Gladstone and Salisbury, John Morley, Augustine Birrell, Lord Rosebery, Arthur Balfour and George Curzon; it gave a tone to the House of Commons which may never be recaptured in a political assembly. But it consorted ill with the turbulence and terror of 1940, a period in which the utmost violence of feeling stirred in the depths of the people and was echoed in the desperate events of the time. Maisky, with his practical grasp of day-by-day changes in thought and emotion, his genial but unruffled contemplation of the whole war in all its details, seemed to me one of the most thoroughly competent observers I had the fortune to meet in England.

Walking up and down there in Gollancz's sunlit garden, waiting for the bombs which never came, watching Madame Maisky pick a sunflower to pieces for its seeds, hearing Quo Tai-chi's placid voice in amiable discourse upon distasteful things (the Burma Road had just been closed by Lord Halifax)—there and then, as in so many places during this period, I thought with a sort of aching anxiety that this was the true alliance against Hitler: Russia, China, England and my own country. Until it came there was no chance of victory; and would it come too late? The consolidation of Germany's interests with those of Japan was coming on apace, but our greater and most necessary consolidation was as far off as ever. My own country was completely given over to the hysteria and confusion of an unnecessary election—a circumstance upon which the Germans had clearly counted, and counted all too successfully. China was nearly crushed; Russia was still playing the game of the ultra-clever, the supremely astute, the double-double-double cross, the most disastrous of all games; and England alone, with its manifold weaknesses abroad and abiding inner strength on the actual home island, was warding off the conqueror.

No bombs fell that day in the country. The Chinese Ambassador drove me back to London in his car and half-way there I grew drowsy. "Go to sleep," he said in his benevolent way, "I have some papers to read." I slept until we were somewhere in the West End. I was awakened by the signals of the hour (a siren, or anti-aircraft or a bomb falling, I cannot now remember which); we were back in London.

## 7

Goering was going to "sweep the R.A.F. from the skies." He did not do so. Day after day the German losses grew greater although the forces opposed to them were smaller in number. This was due not only to the superb quality of the Spitfire and of the fighter pilots but to the flexibility and intelligence of their control. I visited the control center of Number Eleven Group, outside London, and saw the heart of the network, the calm men, not young, who operated it, and the ease with which they outguessed the German or combat tactics in the air. The German here, as always, tended to follow a formula; if you knew he had a habit of running diversionary attacks in advance of his main one, you dodged his diversions (sent no fighters up after it) and released your young eagles when the main attack came. You had occasionally to take a chance (every five or six times) on the preliminary diversion being a main attack, judging by the number of bombers involved; you had to have every inch of the map thoroughly in mind, so that a main thrust at a vital point should not go through unchallenged; you had in every way to make the most of a force which was the finest in the world and the deadliest, but outnumbered. All this was done with the machinery at hand before the immense development of radiolocation devices—a development which is one of the strange miracles of this war and came in a few months between 1940 and 1941.

I saw the fighter pilots in their hours of waiting, their hours on the alert, their young eyes haunted; not many survived this year. I went with other colleagues out to a bomber station in Cambridgeshire for a night and watched the green-eyed bombers lumber up from all directions in the darkness for their flight to Germany. From these visits, from the known figures of the German losses in day raids, from the decreasing incidence of those raids, I acquired— as we all did—a profound respect for the R.A.F. as it is in England. What it was in Norway and France, what it was afterward in the Orient, are other stories; but here in England it was a weapon like the finest steel, sharp and well directed, invincible in its hour. "Never," said Winston, "have so many owed so much to so few," and the phrase made the rounds of the world, for it was the truth.

There was still no answer to night bombing at that time. Every night at eight the Germans came and stayed until six in the morning. When the party could not be strung out any longer and I went home alone to Charles Street I used to sit there and listen to the bombs whistling down while the shrapnel clattered on the window sill and in the courtyard outside. When the bombs fell in Berkeley Square our house almost collapsed from concussion; I have always been surprised that it did not.

I was in the House of Commons in one of the day bombings (September 17th, I believe). The House had reassembled rather defiantly, well aware that a raid was almost certain to take place. Mr. Churchill was announced to speak. Our Ambassador, Mr. Kennedy, had the amiable habit of giving me a ticket to the diplomatic gallery, since I was not on the press lists and consequently could not get a ticket otherwise. Hardly had I entered St. Stephen's Portal on that day when I was whisked off to a shelter marked "For Peers and Other Persons." The raid had begun. It was, I think, the oddest shelter I had ever seen, a sort of cellar underneath the Palace of Westminster, filled at the moment with gentlemen in white wigs and gowns. When we were released from this confinement and I gained my place in the diplomatic gallery I saw that Mr. Maisky and the Duke of Alba, Franco's ambassador, were the only foreign representatives of high rank there. They sat on the same bench with a space between them. The session was short, for Mr. Churchill had decided upon a secret meeting. When he delivered the time-honored formula for the exclusion of visitors he looked up at the diplomatic gallery and delivered it plain: "I espy strangers." As we walked out, I said to Maisky: "Which is the stranger in this place, you or Alba?" He smiled his inscrutable smile, famous in London (we used to call him Il Giocondo) and said: "Who can tell?" And in 1940, indeed, it was not easy to be sure.

One night I went out with the London Fire Brigade. Douglas Williams had just taken over the American section at the Ministry of Information and was introducing some of the ideas of a practical correspondent into that hitherto bewildered body. He wanted to make it possible for us to see the elements of the struggle at first hand, and by luck I came into the first group organized to go out with the fire-fighters. Robert Lowe (*Liberty Magazine*), William McGaffney (Associated Press) and I were the three. It proved a little difficult to get to the Fire Brigade headquarters across Lambeth Bridge at the hour ap-

pointed: the raid was on in the greatest intensity (indeed
it was as strong that night as ever before or afterward)
and an unprecedented barrage had been sent up against
it. I was dining with Bertram Cruger in Hays Mews and
had a breakneck journey across London through the falling shrapnel to get to the Fire Brigade. The driver who
took me through it (an old faithful of Bert's) must have
been almost unique in his kind, because between Hays
Mews and the Fire Brigade headquarters we never encountered another car—nothing but the blaze and roar of
the embattled night. Bob Lowe was already there, waiting, and had grown a little impatient; several alarms of
fire had already come in and we had our choice of areas
to visit. When McGaffney arrived Bob made off in one
Brigade car, the two of us in another. We were headed for
the huge food markets at Smithfield, which had been fired
half an hour before by innumerable incendiaries.

That scene of busy and even cheerful effort against a
background of sheer hell is one that will long remain in
my memory. The firemen, a very large proportion of them
auxiliaries (volunteers), were working with pump, hose
and ladder upon an area which seemed too far gone in
flames to be brought under control. The gravest danger
lay in a certain building, separated by about twenty feet
from the flames, in which explosive chemicals were known
to be stored. The ceaseless effort of some five hundred
men working with a hundred pumps warded off this danger and circumscribed the fire while we watched. The
watchmen and wardens had extinguished a great many
incendiary bombs (they lay all about us) but some had
caught in inflammable materials just beneath the roofs and
set the mighty blaze. (Next to the fire in Oxford Street it
was the greatest that month.) One fireman who was working from the top of a swivel ladder caught my eye; he sig-

naled with his left hand when he wanted the ground workers to shift his ladder or lean it forward; geysers of sparks and balls of fire were going up all around his black figure against the glare. He had a telephone with him but was often too busy to use it. During the whole time—and we were there more than two hours—the bombs were thundering down all over London, the guns were blazing away, and we were hardly aware of them. In our circle of flame and water the fire was the thing, the fire and the desperate effort to quell it; the whole war had receded for that lurid moment into outer obscurity.

It was impossible to get home to Berkeley Square that night; I went with McGaffney to the Associated Press, off Fleet Street down toward the river. There I saw how my colleagues of that organization worked, crowded together in the basement room. When they could not get home they slept on the benches. With the easy fellowship of wartime they gave me a typewriter so that I could write my dispatch and a telephone so that I could pass it through the censorship. After some hours I grew too tired to care much about the bombs any more and started to walk home. The sky was all aglow with the terrible light of many fires, and the bombs as they came down all seemed aimed at this street. When I reached the Strand I found a lone taxicab stationed there, complete with driver. I asked him (rather tentatively) if he could drive me home to Berkeley Square.

"I'll take you anywhere you want to go on land, Guv'-nor," he said in the broadest Cockney, "but I tell you I won't go anywhere out to sea in this here taxi-cab."

The nights and the days receded into a past that can never be forgotten; the day raids ceased; the night raids grew a little less fierce; it was October. With the coming of bad weather there was some hope that the Luftwaffe would confess itself defeated for this year, at least. The great civilian victory had taken place and London would not run away. It was time for me to go home. I had lecture engagements from one end of the United States to the other. I felt a certain reluctance at going away, as if I were deserting the ship, the valiant and battered ship, but I had no choice. As it turned out I need have felt no such reluctance, for the nightly raids ceased soon after my departure and never resumed again with the same regularity. The battle of the burning haystack was won.

Mazzini said to the brief and imperishable Roman Republic of 1839, "We must act like men who have the enemy at their gates, and at the same time like men who are working for eternity." The London of a hundred years later had amply carried out the first part of this injunction and even gave suggestions—I thought more than a suggestion at times—of the second part as well. In the slow unfolding of this planetary struggle the second would come, must come.

Ed Murrow and Ben Robertson saw me through the hasty packing and departure from Paddington. The Air Ministry had given me no more than two or three hours to catch a train; there was unexpectedly a place free on the plane the next morning to Lisbon. In the murky, blacked-out station, where passengers sought distractedly for their trains in the dark, Ed and Ben and I had a farewell beer. Just as we were finishing it the sirens wailed again, punctually as always; the night's raid was beginning. I thought of the winter's ordeal to which I was leaving them and all my friends in London, of the bombs, the cold, the discouragement; I thought also, with the firmest assurance, that they would be there when I returned. So the dark train pulled out for Bristol as the first bombs of the night were falling, and I set my face to the lighted West.

# 5. Land of the Free

THE LIGHTED WEST was always a bit strange at first, after the blackout and the bombs. This return to relatively carefree cultures was nothing new to me. I had made exactly the same kind of journey every time I went from Barcelona to Paris during the Spanish war. What you felt first of all (not only I felt, but all who have made such journeys felt) was this: how can people be so foolish as to suppose themselves safe? Why do they not realize that the time is short, that the sinister conspiracy cannot be brought to success without also engulfing them, and why do they not prepare swiftly, with open eyes, for an absolutely inevitable war?

As a matter of fact, when I reached home again in October, 1940, some preparation was being made. Many, perhaps most, of the men competent to judge such matters were aware that America's participation in the war was eventually certain and that nothing we might do or try to do would stave it off now. The time for stopping Hitler's comprehensive scheme for reorganization of the world was 1936 or, at the latest, 1938. From the moment the Munich Agreement was signed, September 29, 1938, an immense and all-inclusive war became inevitable; the second and super-Munich Agreement one year later—I mean the Friendship Pact between Russia and Germany—guaranteed that this war would be fought, in all its earlier stages, precisely on Hitler's terms, which is to say, upon one front at a time. The Russians have paid for that error with their blood, as we all must pay in our turn; but in 1940 they were still operating under the remarkable delusion that they had outwitted the whole world. I dreaded for my own country the contagion of such error, and read the public speeches of public men with deep foreboding. My personal knowledge of both the President and Mr. Wendell Willkie made me believe that these men fully understood the all-inclusive and uncompromising nature of the world struggle, and yet both of them told the American people that "our boys" would never be sent to fight abroad again. Clearly this meant, if it meant anything at all, that we were going to wait until the Germans and Japanese had conquered all the rest of the world and could crush us with an invincible weight, killing our boys not on foreign lands but in the prairies and mountain passes of our own country.

Mr. Willkie and the President had been conducting a spirited election campaign against each other all summer long. From my point of view it was a wholly unnecessary election, not because I thought the President indispensable—no human being is indispensable—but because our danger was so great, the lost time to be made up so immense, the work to be done so urgent, that we had no right to waste our energies in the sheer hysteria of a general election. And this election seemed, more than any other I remembered for many years, to arouse violent passions. Each side accused the other of responsibility for an astonishing list of social and economic phenomena, hardly any of which could legitimately be traced to a political origin. It was scarcely Mr. Roosevelt's fault that the capitalist system in the United States was shaken to its depths on the very day when he first took office; he had, it seemed to me, patched it together again rather competently, so that it still gave the illusion of validity to those who did not examine too closely. Neither could Mr. Willkie be blamed for weaknesses of the profit system in which both sides believed. It was perfectly clear to me that no Republican administration would dare repeal the social legislation passed during the Roosevelt regime; and since this was what the Republicans chiefly objected to, what was the sense of the argument? It seemed to me an aching pity that our form of political democracy, so clumsy and so impenetrably professionalized that the ordinary citizen had no true voice in it, could not have been sharpened and refined in the years of peace so that now, when the Republic itself was in danger, we might dispense with elections and get on with our job. To my way of thinking—and I believe in democracy far more than most of our politicians do—there was not much power in a vote when the persons for whom we were asked to vote were chosen by irresponsible party machines over which we, the people, had no sort of control. I might, as an ordinary citizen, have preferred to vote for somebody who was neither Mr. Roosevelt nor Mr. Willkie; I might have wanted to vote for Professor Einstein or Mayor LaGuardia of New York; the law permitted me to do so, but such votes were "crank" votes and in no way affected the result. Every four years, under this arrangement, the whole country was dazed and stultified by an orgy of verbigeration, the point of which was that one man or the other (X or Y—no third or fourth choice) was the only man in the whole nation who was fit to conduct its public affairs. These candidates were chosen for us by a complicated undercover machine which had no place in our Constitution; mediocrity was usually preferred to merit; no man, however able, could reach the arcana of the party machines and compel their acquiescence in his candidacy unless he had spent many years in the profession of political merchandising. This was true even of Lincoln. Usually our good presidents were accidents and our bad ones were strictly normal products of party politics. There had been incomprehensible choices, such as the weary accolade of the hotel bedroom which made a president out of Senator Harding of Ohio.

Mr. Roosevelt and Mr. Willkie escaped all these generalizations, as it happened; but in this case there was even less reason for heat and fury. They did not really disagree on anything important. Both were able men, both amply qualified for the presidency. It mattered extraordinarily little which was elected. Mr. Roosevelt was in some ways a more "regular" politician; that is, he had unquestionably made his way by means of the party machine; Mr. Willkie, who had never held or sought a public office, was the result of sheer panic on the part of the Republican convention when they saw the petty ineptitude of his rivals. So, for once, two good men were offered to the choice of the electors: but why? If you already have a good cook why disrupt your household by a furious competitive tourney with another, especially when the house is on fire?

Mr. Willkie was traveling through the whole country on a special train, speaking many times every day, exhausting himself in an effort to win the unnecessary battle. His partisans were ferocious; I found them (those known to me) almost out of their minds on this question. They saw in Mr. Willkie every quality of greatness, and in Mr. Roosevelt every wicked and unworthy trait known to analysis. The President's partisans were almost as bad, but were saved from the same fever temperature by their confidence of victory. The only person I met during those days who did not talk about this election as if the fate of humanity depended upon it was the President himself. I went to Washington to see him and he talked, with great directness and simplicity, about the war—the only subject that seemed to me worth the attention of any serious mind at the time. I did not see Mr. Willkie during that period, but if I had done so I have no doubt he would have been no different.

If I had voted in that election I think I should have voted for Mr. Roosevelt, merely because the change of administration is a grave and vexatious thing. When one President goes out and another goes in, thousands upon thousands of other offices change hands; totally new men go into the most critical positions and take valuable months learning what they have to do; a sort of menopause occurs in the life of the national government. We had no time for that. Moreover, Willkie was supported by a strange collection of forces, among which that of the isolationists was most to be deplored. I knew very well that he did not share their views (I had known Mr. Willkie for some time), but the danger was that he might not be able to shake them off if they helped elect him. They could never have permanently affected any issue, first because all the logic of history was against them and second because they were a minority in the country; the inevitable result would come whatever they did; but they might, if given office, be able to commit some very nearly irreparable mistakes. A person like Mr. Hamilton Fish of New York, confused and semi-Fascist in mind, might have to be made Secretary of War, for example—it was not impossible; stranger things have happened in American politics. What then? Could any limit be assigned to the errors possible in a department administered by Mr. Hamilton Fish?

For these reasons—very moderate ones on the whole—I found myself more on the side of the President's partisans than on that of Mr. Willkie's. As the actual election

day approached I even caught a little of the general fever
and began to think that the world would be lost if the
President did not win. When the fever had died down I
thought, and think now, that these periodical convulsions
are a bad thing not only for the body politic, but for the
persons who make it up; they cease to think; they are engulfed by unreason. Some day we may achieve some
simpler, quicker and more rational way of electing our
Presidents, and some way of omitting even that simplified
election when the gravest crisis is upon us. Until the sim-
plification is made we are doomed to a quadrennial seizure
and must, I suppose, put up with it.

I found it very difficult to put first things first because
I began my lecture tour almost as soon as I got off the
Clipper. I talked of the war, only of the war, its origins,
nature and course up to now; but it proved impossible to
impress upon any audience the supreme and almost exclu-
sive importance of this subject. In the first place nobody
in my audiences anywhere seemed to realize how great
the danger was; it was inconceivably remote to most of
them, barely apparent to others. There was a certain
amount of sentimental pro-English feeling, particularly in
the South and in New England, and there was a general
dislike of the Nazis; but of realization that we were the
ultimate enemy of both Germany and Japan, that we must
fight, that we had no choice in the matter—of this there
was not a trace. I never had the slightest patience with
sentimental twaddle about fighting "for England" or "for
China," and the people who talked in such terms (there
were a few in every audience) were those with whom I
found it most difficult to deal. Women who spoke to me
with tears in their eyes about the necessity for "aiding
England" were undoubtedly sincere, and I tried to avoid
offending their sensibilities, but the fact was that "aid to

England" seemed to me, both as a phrase and as an idea, to be utterly false. We had given no aid to England and were under no obligation to do so; our responsibility was first to ourselves and then to the whole world. In the state of unreadiness in which we found ourselves after the collapse of France there was extremely little, except food, that we could contribute to England's defense. Certain factories and mills were producing war materials for the British, but upon a cash basis—we were not even affording our so-called friends the ordinary commercial credits extended to any business house in peacetime. There was no regulation of the profits in war goods, no urgency in their production or delivery, no sense of shame about our lavish deliveries of essential materials to the Germans before 1939 and to the Japanese at the present time. I was astounded to discover that the alliance between Germany and Japan, which had been announced while I was on the flight from England to America, seemed to have disturbed nobody in the general public. The kind of people who came to my lectures (prosperous for the most part, and thus secure against the ordinary perils) had only the most comfortable ideas about the Japanese and could not credit any interpretation which made the Tripartite Alliance of September, 1940, seem more than an ingenious piece of blackmail. It was by now well understood that the Germans were dangerous, although of course less powerful than ourselves; it was beyond the wildest imaginings of most Americans that the Japanese could do us any harm. The very published terms of the Tripartite Alliance constituted a threat against us, but if it had ever been intended as hollow blackmail (which I do not believe and did not believe then) it would have failed of its effect against the armor of American self-satisfaction.

And then, of course, in every audience, in every city

and town, I ran against the ruling preoccupation with this wretched election. Questions about the election or its results, although irrelevant to my subject, had to be answered at length. How did the English feel about the election? What did I think the Germans felt? What would be our course if Mr. Willkie were elected? How was I going to vote? Did I think the President had done enough to aid Britain? Did I think the President had done enough to ensure, simultaneously, our own neutrality and the defeat of Germany?

People who want to eat their cake and have it too are thus finicky about the ingredients of the icing. In replying to all such questions I attempted to be as objective as possible, but to make it quite clear that I, at least (for what my opinion might be worth), considered this election deplorable and unnecessary and felt certain that the Germans had counted upon it to paralyze us during a summer of immense historic movement.

## 2

During the first three winters of the war (1939–1940, 1940–1941 and 1941–1942) I made long lecture tours from one end of the United States to the other. There was hardly any area I did not visit at some time during those three winters. I did this for two reasons: first, to make a living; second, to deliver by hand, so to speak, direct to the consumer, some part of what I thought true and necessary to be said. Most of my lectures—about three-quarters of them at any rate—were open to the public, that is to anybody who had the price of a ticket. As a result, during these three tours I did reach a very considerable number of people in all parts of the country and was able to judge by their questions, both in the lecture hall and from smaller gatherings afterward, how they thought and felt about the war. This opportunity to get at the pulse and temperature of large numbers of people was valuable, more valuable than the money I made from the tours (I could have made that more easily in other ways). It afforded a sort of information you could never get from the press. If you had studied all the leading newspapers of the United States, daily and Sunday, over these same successive years, making all due allowances for editorial language and the enthusiasm of headline writers, you would have come to the conclusion that the country was in deadly earnest about the war. You would have found certain well-known and fairly consistent isolationist papers, others which believed in "intervention" as it was called; you would have found none which did not seem to consider the war to be a matter which deeply concerned us.

And this would have misrepresented the temper of the country completely, because the country did not feel that the war deeply concerned it. During my first winter on tour (1939–1940) there was some excuse for perplexity. The campaign between Finland and Russia had obscured all the essential questions under a mass of new and distracting detail. I bitterly disliked the Russian attack upon Finland and could not believe it had not been possible in some way, by bribes or threats, to obtain from the Mannerheim regime the positions the Soviet Union required for the defense of Leningrad. At the same time I was sickened by the outburst of sentimentality in the United States over "poor little Finland"—this after years of aggression, during which one "poor little" country after another had disappeared unwept. The people most prominent in collecting money for Finland (Mr. Herbert Hoover, Colonel Charles Augustus Lindbergh) were not of a type calcu-

lated to arouse much enthusiasm for their cause, at least
in me. None of these people had come forward for Spain,
Czechoslovakia or China: they reserved their efforts for
"poor little Finland," a country which, by the misfortune
of its geographic position, could only serve the military
ends of either Russia or Germany. What the most active
of the "poor little Finland" people meant, it seemed to me,
was that they preferred Germany to have the control of
that country. This may not have been in their consciousness; but at any rate it was clear that they had done nothing for Germany's victims and were prepared to do great
things for Russia's. They filled the newspapers with their
appeals, held meetings, took up collections and carried on
a resounding moralistico-humanitarian campaign.

I was never willing to take part in any of this because
I distrusted its motive and leadership. I did not know
enough about those obscure negotiations in Moscow in the
autumn to be sure whether the Mannerheim régime had
brought this misfortune upon itself with open eyes or not;
I was not sure where the Germans stood with respect to
the whole affair; I did not possess any information in
which I had confidence on the Russian intentions. Under
the circumstances it seemed to me better to leave the Fin-
nish war to the Hoovers and Lindberghs and stick to what
I knew with reasonable assurance to be true. This subjected me to some vilification from letter-writers in various
places, and it was sometimes very difficult on public platforms to maintain against hecklers and questioners, as I
did, that in my opinion Finland was a side-issue to the
main war and should not be made to obscure the fundamental conflict.

At one moment during the winter my friend, Leland
Stowe, then in Helsinki and overwrought—as most of our
foreign correspondents were—by sympathy for the Finns,

cabled me that two hundred American aviators with their machines (presumably fighter planes) could turn the tide there; would I take steps?

I did not possess two hundred aviators and their machines just then; I sent the telegram on to Colonel Lindbergh, a more competent authority in this matter. I heard no more of it.

3

The depth of American unconcern in the first winter of the war was immeasurable. This came from numerous, unconnected and often contradictory circumstances. The Communists in the United States, recovering with discomfort from their astonishment at the Nazi-Soviet Pact, were now telling their constituents that the war (which they had advocated for years) was an "imperialist capitalist war," that those who supported the Anglo-French side were tools of the imperialists, that nothing good could come of it, and that Hitler was in no way better or worse than his opponents. Their party membership was negligible and their influence had sharply declined after the Stalin-Hitler agreements, but they could still be heard in certain Left intellectual and labor circles. The big business people were for the most part doing well, after some lean years, and saw no reason to agitate themselves unduly over a conflict which had not yet really come to a head. Their general feelings were (for business reasons) rather more inclined toward the British and French than toward the Germans, but among them were many men who told me, in so-called "reasonable" arguments after dinner at night, that a German-dominated Europe would be just as easy to trade with as any other. Among them were some sharply anti-British minds which inherited the American distrust of perfidious Albion; I think these were not in the majority, but they had influence. Among intellectuals there remained, along with great dislike for Hitler, a pronounced pacifist tinge left over from the last war. And among the youth, above all—and I had many opportunities to talk to them in the universities and colleges—there was the resentful consciousness that if we ever did participate in the struggle they would have to do the fighting; this made them distrustful of any statement, however moderate, which seemed to prefer one side against the other in the so-called "European" war. You could quote *Mein Kampf* to them by the yard, give them the texts of German songs and Nazi party doctrines: they refused, for reasons of their own convenience, to believe that the Hitler scheme for a new world order was quite simply that, neither more nor less, and that no part of the world could be left out of it.

As a result of all these and many other states of mind, the general attitude toward the gathering storm was one of almost inconceivable apathy. People forget these things. They will tell you now that they were aware from the beginning that this struggle would involve us. They did not say so (most of them) in the winter of 1939–1940.

Nor did they have any notion of the military might of Germany. Anybody who could count divisions should have been able to see that two hundred is more than one hundred—not to speak of the tank and airplane weapons—but the delusion still persisted that "the French army is the best in the world." Military experts all over the world were vociferously telling the public that Germany's economic plight, the British blockade and the Maginot Line would between them make a *Blitzkrieg* in the West impossible. Such optimistic experts, during the first winter of the war, encouraged the belief that Germany's collapse would come of itself; that "time was on the side of the allies"; that all we had to do was wait, and the Nazi structure would come crumbling down. Here again (like Knickerbocker, Dorothy Thompson and a considerable number of my colleagues who were not "experts" but had lived through the rise of Fascism in Europe) I disagreed with the predominant opinion. I thought Germany had an excellent chance to win the war against any combination the Allies might contrive against her; I said so every night from the platform. One night in Albany a lady rose from her seat at question time and said to me: "From what you have said I gather that you think Germany can win this war. Have I understood you correctly?" I replied: "You certainly have." The lady laughed aloud as she sat down, and a refined titter spread from her to other parts of the assembly.

We know, of course, that there was (as Senator Borah had said) "something phony about this war." In other words, the hope of a *paix blanche,* a negotiated arrangement consecrating Hitler's acquisitions of territory without further annexations and without bloodshed in the West, had not yet died out among French and British politicians. The French political class was in the habit of using the word *l'irréparable* to describe any possible attack on Germany from the Western front. They hoped *l'irréparable* would not be done; they were afraid of Reynaud because they thought him likely to commit it. The R.A.F. made long and hazardous forays over Germany merely to drop leaflets. With Russia standing off, cynical and at times on the verge of full alliance with Germany, with America remote and indifferent, with the military unreadiness of both France and Britain glaringly apparent to those who knew, excuses may indeed be found for the governing groups both in London and Paris. They knew that the war had to be either "phony," in this present sense, or a German victory. It could be nothing else. But American indifference was fed, encouraged and in some areas and groups made adamant by this very "phoniness" which the situation inevitably created.

In the second winter (1940–1941) a very different frame of mind existed. By and large, America was frightened. The catastrophic suddenness of the French collapse had awakened the whole country to the reality of German might and German intentions. I have been told that hardly anybody expected England to survive the months of June and July. The battles over Dover and the bombing of London had served to instill some hope—not much but some—into American minds. It was the era of passionate admiration for British courage and endurance (you may not remember, but this is so; it was followed a year and a half later by an equally sheeplike aversion to the British, after they had become our allies, and a general inclination to deny them every warrior quality). The country was as a whole still determined to stay out of the war, but it was to the same degree determined to revictual and supply the British Isles and sustain their resistance. Meanwhile a conscription law had been passed and an army was in process of creation. In private conversation with thoughtful men you realized that the nature of the struggle was understood, that not many hoped to keep us out of it forever, and that not many liked the anomaly we represented in the present stage—that of a nation engaging its wealth and its machines to buy the blood of others.

With all this, the people in general were reluctant to go too far lest it involve us in real hostilities. In the Middle West, in particular, a bitterness was rising against any commitment, either in the Atlantic or the Pacific, which would involve us in war. Colonel Lindbergh had warned the public that we had made enemies of "the first military powers of Europe and Asia": a very true statement except that it put the cart before the horse; the first military powers of Europe and Asia had made enemies of us. This certainty appalled the Middle West, which had no patience with the causes of the situation but feared its results. Powerful organizations came into being with the purpose of obstructing the administration's policy of support for Great Britain and (to a lesser degree) for China. The best known of these was the America First Committee. Nowhere, as I have said before, did the Tripartite Pact of September, 1940, between Germany, Japan and Italy, make a deep impression, and nowhere was it thought that our enemies had already agreed upon a policy and a plan. It was on the contrary thought—and I consider this one of the strangest manias that ever afflicted a great nation—that we could never be attacked, that the decision of what we were to do lay solely in our own hands. Alone of all nations that ever existed in the world's history, we were immune; that was the doctrine of the America First Committee. It was publicly stated by Colonel Lindbergh, speaking as an expert in these matters, that no part of our country or possessions could ever be subjected to attack. Again and again I was questioned on this point after I had finished my nightly lecture. "You seem to think we are in danger ourselves. Where can anybody attack us?" I used to give a number of alternatives, east and west— Brazil to Florida, the northeastern approaches, Pearl Harbor, the Philippines. There was blank incredulity at every one of them. When I said, as I often did, that the attack might come first from Japan, most of my hearers gaped in astonishment. Lively though our apprehension had been after the fall of France, vigorously though we wished for

Germany's defeat, there appeared to be no concern at all about the Japanese except in California, Oregon and Washington.

Opposed to the America First Committee, and antedating it by about a year, was the William Allen White Committee to Defend America by Aiding the Allies. Its purpose was to support the administration's policy and urge it on still further. Later on Mr. White resigned as chairman of this body and it turned into the Fight for Freedom Committee (with Herbert Agar as its presiding spirit). These two organizations, the parent and child, both wished to force the pace by arousing public opinion; and although I was in general sympathy with the animating ideas of Mr. Agar and his associates, I was in total disagreement over the method. To me these societies for encouraging this, that and the other opinion on vast questions of war and peace were operating upon a false basis. They seemed to consider that in these apocalyptic days all you had to do to achieve a certain result was to convince or persuade enough people that it was desirable. This is not the case and has not, I think, ever been the case. Nations (as distinct from their political leaders) are not really open to argument. They are convinced by events, persuaded by passions, swayed by great currents of feeling not always open to analysis. The sinking of the *Maine* in Havana harbor in 1898 produced such a great current of feeling, upon which we went to war with Spain; the moment for that sudden spurt of youthful energy had come. The sinking of the *Panay* in the Yangtze River in 1937—a very deliberate act by the Japanese, intended to enrage us—left the country as a whole quite cold and not, indeed, much interested. What was the difference between the two cases? Aside from the financial interests which urged us into war with Spain—interests unknown to the public at the time—why was American feeling so aroused in 1898 and so apathetic in 1937?

You may say that this is a matter of propaganda; I should disagree. All the evidence is that the sinking of the *Maine* produced a nation-wide outburst of anger as soon as it was known, without any aid from propaganda or any encouragement by government. It happened. When the *Panay* sank it did not happen.

I do not want to go much further into this doctrine of persuasion by events, because it would lead me into a series of hypotheses which can never be proved. In brief, what I mean is that no form of propaganda is wholly effective upon the *decision* for peace or war. The most astute propaganda, that of the Nazis for example, is that which represents the nation as aggrieved, suffering, put upon, conspired against, maligned and misunderstood. Upon that basis the government can always decide for itself what it wishes to do and can represent this decision as being forced upon it by the wickedness of the foreigner. But the other sort of propaganda, the American kind, speaks only to those who are already convinced and merely sets up a series of rival and competitive organizations clamoring for the attention of a weary public. Professional publicity agents and advertising men are engaged, at fat salaries, to put out advertisements, arrange mass meetings, get "publicity stories" of various sorts into the newspapers, contrive radio programs and send out reams of mimeographed opinions to chosen lists of people. I was on many of these lists for years: the committees with long names urged me to think this way or that, vote for this or that candidate, sign petitions, make speeches, and above all, to give money. I was never persuaded of anything by such means, nor do I think anybody else has been. In my experience of such matters, which has been considerable, no mass meeting draws more than a negligible number of the unconvinced, few people read mimeographed sheets sent in the mail, and nobody makes up his mind upon the evidence of a radio program.

During the Spanish war I was willing to do practically anything I was asked to do for Spanish Relief; the same is true for China Relief; it was true for British and later for Russian War Relief. This was, in my mind, a different matter. In asking Americans to contribute money for the alleviation of suffering in countries which for so long have been fighting our battles, I always felt that some tangible result might ensue. Even if such organizations are absurdly topheavy with salaried employees, this was the fault of the American system, not of the purposes in view; and if even one Chinese soldier had his wounds healed by such means, no matter how uneconomic the administration of relief might be, it was worth the effort. I did not so highly regard the almighty dollar that I considered the loss of some money in transit as being very serious. Before we were through these woods, as I knew very well and have known for a good many years now, the billions of dollars that would flow out would make whatever was wasted in the effort to get a trickle of relief to Spain or China seem insignificant. Consequently I spoke for these purposes many times, and begged for them without a qualm, even when I knew (as was periodically "exposed" in some xenophobe publication) that only a part of the proceeds actually bound up the wounds of the sufferers.

Similarly I would beg for the Negroes, or for all Jews who were not Zionists, or for refugees from any country invaded by military oppressors. I have often done so. But, according to my theory of what is useful and what is useless, I could not take part in these organized and semi-professional efforts to persuade the American people that they should decide the great question of war and peace by an exercise of the reasoned will. It seemed to me rather like trying to argue with the weather.

For by the end of my tour in the winter of 1940–1941 I had been greatly fortified in the opinion that only events would have any real effect upon the American mind in its relationship to the rest of the world. I had come to the belief, in fact, that we would not make a decision and were incapable of doing so. My conclusion from about the first month of the tour was growing firmer every day. It was that we would never declare war; that it would be declared upon us; that war would come only when we were attacked. This might be soon or late, but until it came we as a people were bound to nourish our illusions and ourselves with them, confused but comfortable, well fed and well housed on the whole, tabulating our "opinions" every few weeks by means of a professional poll-taker, and happy to think that we could disagree so politely on so many things at once. Through the second half of that second winter, whenever I was asked when we might be involved in the war, I always made the same reply: "When we are attacked."

The third winter's tour (1941–1942) was very different. We were at war. Not to confuse the story of our changing mind as it seemed to me, I leave that to the end.

4

If you did not believe in the possibility of persuading or convincing a great nation upon the most important decision it can ever be asked to make, then what of democracy? Could you believe in democracy at all if you thought it incapable of such decisions?

This was a question that rose instantly to the surface once you had reached this point in the argument. The conception of government by the popular will came to us by way of the Greek city-states, organizations so small that a general meeting of the citizens was always possible and a common conviction could be reached by the deliberation of all free men. To translate such concepts into larger and more complicated forms was a task that much engaged the minds of those who founded the American Republic, as we know from the papers in *The Federalist*. The invention of representative rather than direct democracy was Hamilton's solution, defended with skill and all the power of a first-class mind, but in his arguments drawn from Greek and English examples he allowed too little for the ever widening space that must come, in a large and growing country, between the people themselves and their representatives, as well as the innumerable evils that might arise in the unspecified processes by which candidates were to be chosen. Hamilton's (and Madison's) answer to such part of this inquiry as they had foreseen was, of course, the strengthening of the executive power by endowing it with control of foreign policy, the armed forces and the great question of peace and war. No writing of Hamilton's is abler than that in which he argues that the safety of the Republic depends upon such control by the executive; and I find it, on the face of things, irrefutable.

Yet nobody in Hamilton's time could have foreseen the radio or even the telephone; in spite of Leonardo da Vinci and a few other dreamers, none anticipated the airplane; not many had any idea of steam locomotive or automobile. The immense development of the modern American press was something that would have amazed or horrified all of them. It was quite obvious that the technical enrichment of ordinary life, with its vulgarization of ideas and dissemination of information, was something for which none of those who framed the American Constitution could possibly have made provision. They expected the Senate to be made up of wiser and older men, chosen by indirection; they centered the legislative authority partly there and partly in the popular House of Representatives; they expected the executive and judiciary to be independent of legislative controls, and created hopeful and provident safeguards for the serenity and independence of the executive decision on the greatest of national problems. Never could they have foreseen the day when every citizen would know every great event practically as soon as it had happened; they had no notion that a time would come when the Chief Executive could speak simultaneously to every inhabitant of a vastly increased territory; they did not even dream of the Aeolian harp that history was one day to make of the mind and heart of a people. Naturally the institutions they created must come in time to seem cramped, inadequate, without room for manifold reality; and however jealously guarded and revered such institutions might be as the primary structure of our freedom, they must in practice devolve (at least in part) upon the merely vestigial or formal, while the vitality of the democratic process passed to a very considerable degree into those communications of intention, opinion, information and feeling which had not existed when our state was built.

This was, it seemed to me, exactly what had happened, without any widespread consciousness of the gradual transformation among those whose lives were governed by it. There had been transfers and exchanges of authority among the originally distinct branches of government; the Senate had usurped far more importance in foreign policy

than the Constitution intended; the highest judiciary almost from the beginning (from the time of Marshall) had
seized upon a political power, through its right to inter-
pret the Constitution, the consequences of which appear
nowhere to have been anticipated by the founders of the
Republic. To counterbalance these encroachments from
one side and the other the executive branch of the government had acquired more power and prestige in every generation through its control of appointments, its supremacy
in matters of war or peace, and the attrition of rival claims
from the separate state governments. From Lincoln's day
onward there was a centralization which, however strongly
opposed upon single questions, displayed an irresistibly
progressive or intensifying tendency, a sort of centrifugal
acceleration which brought us to a point, in this respect,
very far indeed from the intentions of those who created
our written Constitution.

All these changes had taken place gradually, by the
interaction of all the known forces, in a process in which
geography and climate had played their part no less than
political friction and compromise, economic stresses and
social adjustment. The modern balance of political powers
was not at all what it had been in 1789. But far more remarkable than these practical accommodations—which
were after all only a sort of muscular co-ordination of the
governmental body—was the direct connection which
modern techniques had established between the public
mind and the public event. In the midst of such communicative profusion, such a maze of integuments between all
the citizenry, it was no longer possible for the Federal
government in any of its branches to come to its decisions
like a separate organism, and then separately present its
record for the arbitrage of a public vote a year or two or
four years later. The connections were all much too close;

the nervous system of the country tingled with awareness at the moment of action; the deed could not be judged afterward, or perhaps at all; it took place at the will of all, in a sense determined by the naked popular sensibilities at any given stage. This laying bare of the public's nerve centers rendered executive, legislature and judiciary all alike more immediately responsible not to the electorate (which, as I have said, had only a choice between candidates selected in occult and irresponsible ways) but to the nation itself—in a word, to the democracy. Again and again the surge and thrust of public feeling on any given question, showing itself not in the least by electoral or any other constitutional means, but by public talk and discussion, by songs and jokes, by folklore and the spontaneous choice of spokesmen among the professional oracles of radio and press, directly defeated the intentions of the elected government. Mr. Roosevelt himself, with his power and prestige unimpaired and with a legislative majority strong enough to put through any law he desired, was forced to give in to public feeling on the question of reorganization of the Supreme Court. The popular instinct chose for its spokesmen in this matter all those who opposed Mr. Roosevelt's intention; there was nothing for him to do but yield. Made even wiser by this defeat, he never again attempted to enforce a decision against the evident inclination, will or instinct of the people.

One instrument created in this new process of democratic control was the professional oracles (known as "commentators") to whom I have referred above. They were men and women who wrote for the press or talked on the radio about public affairs, and did so as a means of livelihood (in short, my colleagues). Some had a greater sense of political responsibility than others; some had none; some seemed to me devoid of any qualification in intelligence, education or experience for their new and immeasurable function in society. The public chose among them for capricious reasons—this one had "a nice voice," the other one "talked like people down our way," the accent of one or the phraseology of another would catch the popular ear and win favor for a season. The popular suffrage thus exercised showed itself in various ways, all carefully tabulated by the systems in use among radio and advertising companies. If the greatest part of the American public wanted to listen to Mr. John Smith at eight o'clock every evening, there were ways of finding this out; and if Mr. John Smith was paid for his eloquence by a certain toothpaste or soup manufacturer, the consumption of that toothpaste or soup would go up on the wave of Mr. Smith's popularity. The public did not choose its radio or press favorites for their opinions, but because of "personality" and other more commercially negotiable assets. Nevertheless, if opinion ran strongly enough in any channel, the most popular favorite could be discarded and forgotten when he tried to stem the tide. This perfectly free and natural process was, as I have said, tabulated by commercial enterprises for commercial purposes, but they could not control it. No power on earth could force the American people to listen to any one professional oracle in preference to another; in this matter they chose for themselves, not always for any explicable reason, but at least freely.

Songs and folklore (in which I include the jokes which sweep the country with every change and development, some of them obscene and some merely funny but all significant) played their part in this new function of democratic control. Jokes traveled as if by telepathy or black magic; you heard one in New York one week and San Francisco the next; they knew no limits of circulation even though the best of them were too rude for print. The choice among films was another way in which the popular instinct showed itself: out of hundreds of stories registered on film every year at Hollywood, the public chose certain ones for its chiefest favor, and no wise man of the film industry could be sure which these would be. I know of no clearer indication that the American public was averse to taking a stand on the world conflict in 1939 and 1940 than the fact that the films which attempted to deal in some way with such questions were popular failures.

All this was extra-constitutional control, produced by techniques in use for no more than a few decades. It was the way democracy exerted its truest influence upon the course of events. The electorate was neither superseded nor overshadowed by such diversified instruments of choice; the relation was rather that between conscious and subconscious. Elections were still the conscious exercise of choice, but politicians studied the currents of public feeling and strove to placate or obey the public will before an election should take place. This was why the whole process of representative democracy had changed its character, had become much tighter and swifter, although the institutions themselves remained static, traditional and professionalized in the hands of a political priesthood.

What did Plato, Montesquieu, Hamilton, Tocqueville or any of the rest of them know of this kind of democracy? It did not work according to any of the laws or principles discerned by philosophic thought on the subject. In its actual operation it came much nearer to the half-articulated "dynamism" of the Nazi leaders than to parliamentary or representative democracy as established in England, France and (originally) the United States. But from my point of view it was a truer and surer system of democratic control, at least on great questions, because the popular will did not depend upon indirect and irresponsibly manipulated representation. The "men without faces," as Miss Clare Boothe has called them—the numerous members of Congress who are unknown to any public outside their own constituencies—do not dare affront the public will in great matters, and they know the public will by means completely outside the constitutional system. Thus the Hamiltonian and Jeffersonian concepts are alike valid, so far as forms go, and alike obsolete, so far as the machinery of expression of popular will is concerned in a nation which governs itself by electricity.

Hitler's dynamism was thus in a sense more adjusted to contemporary reality than were the political traditions of representative democracy, in that he acknowledged an almost telepathic national or tribal consciousness and strove to increase and control it by an appeal to every passion. His system was false because it reposed upon trickery, the "big lie" and the notion that emotional stimulation or evocation, skillfully done, can permanently direct the course of a nation's effort and destiny; it was evil because it aimed at the political and economic enslavement of all persons not born German, and at the extermination of opposing thought even among Germans; it was ultimately doomed, whatever its successes, because it ran counter to the deepest desires of most human beings. But in spite of all this it had immense delusive power among Germans because, discarding all pretense at persuading or convincing, it proclaimed; it merely, but powerfully, asserted; it was like a voice from the tribal subconscious, and institutions crumbled before it.

No such voice could speak in the Western democracies because the popular will was too tenacious of its freedom both in England and in America. There could be, under the conditions obtaining, no such concentration upon a single leader, no such obedience to a self-consecrated prophet. Yet skillful and intelligent men had come to great authority in these democratic nations by augmenting their legal or constitutional powers through direct communication with the whole nation—again not the electorate alone, but all men, women and children. Mr. Roosevelt had done this with great effectiveness in the United States, employing the press and radio, personality and legend, to captivate the public consciousness and lead it along new paths, sometimes in direct disagreement with other organs of the government, often against the supposed mandate of the preceding elective act. Mr. Churchill made a less complete adjustment to the new systems of democratic procedure (he was much slower to adapt himself to the microphone and remained for a long time inaccessible to the press), but his own gifts broke down all the barriers between a Prime Minister and the general public: he spoke with such eloquence, and was in appearance and manner so akin to what the instinct of England in 1940 demanded, that he, too, acquired an extra-constitutional power based upon all these psychological forces which modern techniques have released into the consciousness of nations. The symbols and mysticism of the German-Italian Fascist system were repugnant to the taste of England and America, but in their very different way the leaders of these democracies, leading and following, advancing and receding in accordance with their sensitiveness to the popular will, employed an equally new method of government.

The glaring defect of such a system was that no grave decision could be taken until the whole people had displayed its readiness for it. This made national policy vacillating in the extreme from 1918 to 1940 in the United States. All Presidents, all secretaries of state felt the need of either staving off a world war or preparing for it, but none could do so until the people were ready. And in this matter no people ever is ready: the people would never choose war if they could have peace. I have known too many Germans, even Nazis, who thought war would never come ("the Führer will never allow it"), to believe for one moment that Germany as a whole chose war. They were systematically deluded into the belief that their Führer, by a combination of genius and obviously superior force, could achieve his ends without fighting. The Americans were no different from other peoples; they did not want war. The difference in the two systems is that under Fascist rule all these techniques of communication, this development of such a co-consciousness that it amounts almost to telepathy, is systematically directed toward the single end, union, war and conquest; it originates from above. Under the American and the much slower but similar English systems the co-consciousness develops from below, from the immense complication and thoughtlessness and wisdom and folly of the people, swaying toward a dance craze or a film mania today, a solemn resolution tomorrow, in accordance with the incidence of events or the economic imperatives of the time. This was, in fact, the contemporary form of democracy, and like all other natural growths it was quite independent of written law or established institutions.

The conclusion is obvious that if all states were democracies, that is to say organized to obey the popular will, there could be no wars. This is the broadest and firmest reason for believing in a democratic system; but when you have said this you have at the same time acknowledged the fearful handicap of a democracy in conflict with an astute autocracy which knows how to use the contemporary means of directing a people's will. You are driven to the conclusion (no different from Hitler's in effect) that one system or the other must prevail. There are innumerable possible varieties of democracy, at least in form, but in their essence they all acknowledge the origin of power in the will of the people; and the twentieth century—at least in America—had called into being a whole new world of possibilities for the expression of this will. How, then, could Mr. Roosevelt do other than lead and follow, advance and recede, in accordance with this new and intimate relationship between the government and the governed, this semi-telepathic and half-conscious interfluence of currents unknown to law?

I thought the democracy incapable of deciding to go to war, but I thought no less of it for that. It would clearly have been desirable to avert the terrible extremity of world conflict by suppressing Hitlerism some years before, but it had proved impossible to achieve any community of purpose among the British, French, Russians and Americans, the nations in gravest danger. Since this was impossible, the Americans were no more to be blamed than any other people for the refusal, which lies deep in nature, to acknowledge facts until they are thrust upon the consciousness by incontrovertible events. Consequently I believed fully in the validity of the democracy and still felt that it would arm itself and fight only when it was directly, physically attacked—which meant that the initiative lay, as always, with the autocratic and tribal conspiracy of Germany, Italy and Japan. This put us to a fearful military disadvantage and exposed our true allies to years of an unequal struggle in which some of them must succumb. I stated these views in print and from public platforms; it was not a popular opinion; consequently I never joined the ranks of my more fortunate colleagues who became chosen oracles of public opinion. But I did feel, to the depths, how mighty was the latent

power of a people like this, how resistless even in the
frivolity of its temporary crazes, how united in consciousness, how blest by geography, climate, geology and the
tradition of freedom, how unlikely it was to covet the
physical possessions of other peoples and how greatly it
would exert its electronic and magnetic force when the
event called forth all its energy upon fields of battle. It
was exposed to none of the suspicion which surrounded
the intentions of the British; it was encumbered by no
formulated economic doctrine, like the Russians; its consciousness might be an Aeolian harp in the remaining
hours of peace, but its arm and its anvil were strong.
Among the elements composing the pattern, this one had
been most consistently misjudged by the Fascist conspira-
tors. The margin of their error was perhaps small, for we
were not quick to exert our power and might have been
too late; but the error was nevertheless fundamental. This
was, with all its contradictions (among which the existence of a sub-citizen class of Negroes was the most startling), still the most democratic of nations in spirit and
intent, the one in which a popular will could most acutely
be felt; it had the possibility of almost limitless growth
and change in its susceptibility to technical advance; it
could hear voices and wield the sword in its own way, no
less than the Germans; and, since it was protected by
nature from the necessities or desires which lead to
aggression, it contained no threat to the freedom of mankind but a hope—I thought and think the highest hope—
for its preservation.

Thus by the end of the second year of the war I had
come, not fatalistically but upon what seemed to me the
clear evidence, to think that there was little use attempting to persuade or convince this people, which was, as I
have said, governed by electricity; when the hour struck
it would arise.

# 6. The "Grand Climacteric"

On Wednesday, April 16, 1941, my wife and I took the Clipper for Bermuda and Lisbon. We had to spend the night in Bermuda because of Atlantic weather; on the next morning we read that the night in London had been terrible, the worst bombing since the beginning of the war. Subsequent information has confirmed the extent of the raid, which, with the great fire of the preceding December and the heavy, high-explosive bombing of the following May 10th, were London's worst nights.

I was going over on a contract with the *Saturday Evening Post;* Dinah was to write a book on ordinary life in war-time London, with photographs by Robert Capa.* The *Post* contract was a matter of particular jubilation to me because it indicated a change of heart, or at least a change of policy, on the part of that important publication. I was known to be unshakably anti-Fascist, and also what the *Post* would have called "interventionist" in the slang of the period. I was not "interventionist" at all; I had never advocated anything; I had merely said consistently, and for some years past, that this was a world struggle which must inevitably involve us sooner or later; but it was enough, in the vocabulary of the day, to make you "interventionist." The *Post* had been what was called "isolationist." For such a publication to come forward of its own free will and offer me a contract on very liberal terms was not only astonishing; it was a significant indi-

* Published as *The Battle of Waterloo Road.*

294

cation of changing points of view. So, at least, I took it to be.

The scented isle of Bermuda, the swift Clipper to Lisbon, a wait there briefer than usual, and a journey by the Dutch (K.L.M.) plane up the western edge of Europe: we were in half-ruined Bristol. The wreckage in the center of the town was much worse than last year, it seemed to me, but activity seemed no less and the train left on time. On the way to London we made almost normal speed. There was none of the agonized shunting and shifting, stopping in blacked-out country, waiting for bombs, that had characterized a train journey in the preceding autumn; there was a restaurant car and the crowd was not unmanageable. At Paddington we even found a taxi without much trouble. In those small things which make up a first impression, things seemed better—more under control, more "normal"—than they had been on my departure six months before.

We went to Claridge's and remained there a great part of the summer. It was a favorite haunt of the Americans from our Embassy, and although economy might have dictated a less elegant repair, it served our turn very well. Except for some cracked windows and a shattered glass on the shower bath, it survived the whole period of bombing (up to and including May 10th) without scar.

It was when I began to go about my business on the following day that I found London somewhat changed. There was a good deal more wreckage, some of it quite recent. The severe bombing of April 16th had been followed by one on April 19th which was only a little less severe. Work was progressing steadily among the ruins, but few streets were clear for all of their length. A vast land-mine (one of the unmentionable items under censorship rules then) had landed in Piccadilly and devastated an area near Burlington House. Detours innumerable had to be made in any journey across London. Down in the city the winter's occasional raids had wreaked particular havoc, and there were some whole blocks laid level.

But more than the physical ruin was the psychological decline. I believe this exact period (from April 16 to June 22, 1941) marked the lowest ebb in British spirit, if I can judge by London alone. Good weather was coming and there was nothing to look forward to but more and more bombing. America was as far away from war as ever, and everybody had given up hope of anything from Russia. There seemed nothing for it but for England—which meant, probably, first of all London—to take the grueling punishment again this year as last, and hang on like grim death hoping for some event to change the state of the world. Hoping, that is, without much hope; for the arrangement of forces did not suggest a likely deliverance.

My friends told me something of the kind as soon as I arrived. Ed Murrow, Ben Robertson and Bill Stoneman all came to Claridge's that first night; all agreed.

"You won't find any of the high-spirited we-can-take-it stuff of last year," they said. "There are a lot fewer parties. We none of us run around the streets during bombings as we used to do. People stay at home; they go to the shelters; they are getting a little grim. All the novelty of this is gone. The epic period is over. Food has something to do with it, too—everybody is probably a little undernourished. Whatever it is, there's a big difference."

My first task was to arrange with the Admiralty for a journey out on the Atlantic to see the convoy system. In the course of those conversations I had to go to the Admiralty a number of times and found it, too, a little disheveled. There had been a number of direct hits on April 16th (three, I believe) and the débris had not all been cleared away. The halls were dirty; plaster fell now and then; the courtyards were in confusion. At the Ministry of Information I found the American section working without windows; the glass had been blown out and none had been put in yet to take its place; Douglas Williams and his assistants worked in overcoats.

The back of Number 7 Charles Street, Berkeley Square, where I had lived the year before and had hoped to live again this year, was blown out on April 16th. I knew everybody in the house and none had been injured. Most of them had been away; only Victor Gordon-Lennox was at home (in the bedroom where I had lived the year before) and slept contentedly through the bombing, with plaster all over his bed and the next room in ruins. This house or that was gone; this person or that was in the country, or in a hotel, or sleeping at an office, because his quarters were no more. Ed Murrow's office had been moved something like four times; the B.B.C. had been hit again and again and all that district showed the consequences. Down the river, north and south, the dwellings of the London poor had again collapsed under the onslaught, although nothing in that regard equaled what we had seen after the first bombings of September, 1940.

The Admiralty gave me my orders after a few days: I was to go to Liverpool and report to the Commander-in-Chief of the Western Approaches.

2

The destroyer to which I was assigned was called the *Walker*, and belonged to the V-and-W class built during the last war. It was thus roughly contemporary with the fifty over-age American destroyers which had been transferred to Britain under the agreement of the preceding summer, with naval and air bases for the Americans in the Western hemisphere as payment. We had some of those old American destroyers, rechristened and somewhat modernized, among the escort vessels led by the *Walker*. They had some advantages over their British contemporaries, particularly in the matter of comfort (sleeping quarters, ice-boxes, etc.), but they rolled mightily in even a moderate sea and were, by the standards of the British Navy, hopelessly top-heavy. We had in addition three of the hastily built corvettes of this war, belonging to the Flower class (*Hyacinth, Honeysuckle* and the like); they also rolled a good deal and were not much flattered in naval conversation. My destroyer, the *Walker*, was a remarkably seaworthy ship by all accounts and had weathered the terrible storms of the preceding winter (the worst storms for years) without much damage. I had no opportunity for judging the foul-weather qualities of the ship, since we made our journey under exquisite skies over a calm and summery sea.

The ship's captain (Commander McIntyre) was so much like a favorite storybook hero of mine that I called him Captain Horatio Hornblower. The youngest subaltern, whose real name was Bray, became Mr. Midshipman Easy in my mind; there were others who fitted naturally into the pattern of all the sea stories landlubbers usually read. I was given the Captain's after cabin to occupy in solitary splendor, since he never left his lair under the bridge when the ship was at sea. Before we were ready to leave Liverpool a petty officer went about the decks bellowing, "Everybody got their Mae Wests? Who hasn't got a Mae West?" I was given a Mae West, a pneumatic tire to wear around the chest at all times and inflate in case the ship went down. I felt that I was much too poor a swimmer to be aided by such means in any case, so I put it on the locker beside my bed, where it stayed for the voyage. The officers started out in sea-kit and sea-boots, which they never removed until the journey was over. I slept in a proper bed and regularly dressed and undressed, as if on shore; one day I even had a bath; I had no regular hours or discipline and could do as I pleased. As it turned out, I formed the habit of standing all the night watches on the bridge and sleeping in the morning, which is (I think) what most naval officers would do if they had their own way. To stand watch hour after hour in the cold and moonlit night, speaking seldom, alert and yet abstracted, eyes never turned from the far shining water, the water infested by death but ever beautiful—this must be the high and characteristic moment of the sea for those who live on the sea.

The approach to Liverpool through the Mersey is very long and had been much visited by the German airplanes dropping magnetic mines. A clear channel must be kept swept by eternal vigilance, and only through this could the convoy or escort vessels pass. As it happened, we set off a mine before we were well out into the Irish Sea; it made a heavy clanking noise against the side of the ship and for a moment I thought we had dropped a depth charge; it exploded with no damage to anybody.

We scudded along the gray Irish Sea at some twenty knots an hour. We were bound for the river near Londonderry, where we were to refuel and get provisions. In the late afternoon the Irish coast looked rich, wet and sunny, a lush and opulent coast in that light; small boats put out with quantities of milk, eggs and butter to sell, products which had already begun to be scarce in England.

"Sometimes an old lady comes out on the Free State side, over there, and waves a Union Jack at us," Captain

Hornblower said, musing. "I often wonder about her. Funny old girl. She's not here today. Wonder what's the matter with her. She seldom misses. I suppose if she were on the Ulster side she'd be waving the Free State flag."

When we had refueled and were making our way around the north coast to the ocean the Captain took particular care to show me his house.

"That's what we call my house," he said, handing me his field glasses. "It's a peaceful-looking place. That's the sort of place I'd like to settle down in when this is over. Or anyhow that's what I like to think."

It was a white cottage set in a fold of the green cliff, with a road and a barn and flowers visible. On the voyage in and the voyage out, all through the past two years, Captain Horatio Hornblower had been looking up at this spot in rain or shine and thinking that it would be nice to live there when peace came, and go fishing at times or walk a dog on the cliff.

"It's probably a very dirty house inside," I told him. "There may be no floor to it, and a fireplace where they burn peat and the smoke chokes you. You wouldn't like that."

"Maybe so, maybe so," he said. "But it does no harm to think about it, does it?"

When we had seen the last of Ireland we were at large on the trackless ocean. It was all very well to remind yourself that this was the main-traveled road of the sea, and that the bulk of the tonnage came and went this way; even so, we saw no ships at all, day or night. The days were mostly bright, even when there was a little mist rising from the water; the nights were clear and the moon was growing full. I was fascinated above all by the devices for radio-location, the anti-submarine gadgets, which were duly explained to me and duly forgotten. Technical se-

THE "GRAND CLIMACTERIC"      301

crets of this kind are safe enough with an observer as dense in such matters as myself. It was my first acquaintance with the great radio secrets of this war, which I later learned to be a chapter of the utmost importance both in the air and on the sea. When the war is over these things may be revealed in whole or in part by those competent to speak in the matter. For my part it is all black magic, as it always will be, beyond explanation.

Between tea and dinner we used to play bridge. Nobody but the engineer (known as "Chief," of course) could really play the game, but we made up in enthusiasm for what we lacked in skill. The officers told me they had played bridge with their German captives the preceding winter when they had picked up the survivors of two submarines. This was a tale often told: how the *Walker* had rammed one submarine and destroyed another by depth charges, with the *Vannock*, a sister ship, accounting for one more. (The *Vannock* probably also claimed two; between them they were sure they had accounted for three, but an unfeeling Admiralty would only allow the two between them.) This great engagement was the high point of the *Walker's* long service. The German survivors, including a celebrated submarine captain, had been fished out of the sea and brought home to Liverpool as prisoners. They had displayed considerable spirit until their actual arrival in England, which had produced for the first time a look of gloom on their faces. Some of them played good bridge and joined in the ward-room game, along with some survivors from a Canadian freighter they had torpedoed. The Germans had been surprised at the food on the *Walker*, above all at the butter. As they ate it they inquired: "Is it real?" The submarine captain spoke good English and seemed to know a great deal about things in England.

"I thought he was quite a good fellah," Captain Horatio Hornblower said, "until I read up on some of the things he had done as a sub captain."

All the way out to a mid-Atlantic latitude we were on the lookout for the victims of submarine warfare. Once we passed a corpse: Chinese. Twice we changed our course to investigate rafts or bits of wreckage in the hope of saving a life. This was, it seemed to me, the chief difference between one side and the other in this war: on our side human life was valued, was saved whenever possible; on the other side human life was only relatively valuable, that is, if it happened to be German or in some way helpful to German plans. By all testimony the German submarines never picked up survivors in the water; often they fired upon the strugglers.

The Captain was an expert on marine birds and could pick out varieties among them when no variation was apparent to the landsman's eye. Month after month he had scoured this ocean, hunting down submarines, escorting cargo vessels, getting out to meet a convoy or being detached to a new chase. If there can be said to be paths over the sea he knew them. He took bearings by the stars. As his Number One, Mr. Langton, said with great finality one day: "The sun's no good. You can have the sun. The only thing that's any good at all, for a bearing, is the stars."

Messages poured in, telling us the number and position of the German and Italian submarines. There were Italians also in the Western ocean, but according to the Captain they never attacked armed vessels—only unarmed stragglers or tramps. The Germans seemed to be numerous and disposed well along the route we had to follow. The Admiralty messages (carefully written out in the radio room and brought up in envelopes like an invitation to dinner) rained down thickly as we approached our destination:

the convoy we had gone to meet was being shadowed. On the night before we met the convoy there was particular anxiety, for in these waters over which we passed a particularly notable little pack had been detected. Nothing happened. I stood all the night watches, sharing gratefully in the hot chocolate that was occasionally brought up for the officer on duty. We had occasional alarms from the anti-submarine machinery and once or twice we saw sights which aroused speculation. Once Bray, who was standing the middle watch, grew rather excited over a strange light upon the horizon. He called to the yeoman, who stared through glasses and was equally mystified.

"Captain, sir," Bray shouted into the mouthpiece on the bridge, "Captain, sir! Strange light on the port beam! Can't make it out, sir!"

The Captain, who at wide intervals took an hour or two's sleep in his forward cabin directly beneath the bridge, got up and climbed the ladder, swearing gently to himself. He took the glasses from Bray and stared at the distant light. Here I made my one and only contribution as observer on the voyage.

"I don't know what it is," said I, "but it looks to me like a rainbow."

"Well, I'm damned," said the Captain slowly, glasses fixed to his eyes. "That's exactly what it is. I'm damned. A moon rainbow. In all the years I've been to sea I never saw one before. A moon rainbow."

It was a faint shimmering light that began to show tinges of color. Slowly it grew stronger; we stood there silent and watched the marvel. The moon was turning an arc of the sea-mist into prismatic display, exquisitely faint but growing more distinct as we watched, its arc extending, extending far into the night sky, fading there and growing stronger again as it descended, a rainbow that at last touched the sea on both ends and kept its continuity even in the palest summit of the arc. Captain Horatio Hornblower and Mr. Midshipman Easy were dumb before the beauty of it. The Captain stood there until it was gone, until not a trace remained. When he turned to go down again he made his usual remark: "Well, as the fellah says, when you've seen one wave you've seen 'em all."

One day (I think it was the next day after the moon rainbow) we met our convoy. We were due at the rendezvous at twelve o'clock noon, and we arrived exactly at that hour, exactly in the middle of the long line of ships drawn up for review. The Captain was justifiably pleased at such precision. He had been on the look-out for over an hour—so had we all—and it was he who saw the first wisps of smoke, some minutes before any of the rest could. He gave his directions and brought us up to the center of the line at the moment appointed.

There followed the stately maneuver of taking over the convoy. The signals fluttered out, were read and answered. The leading escort ship from Iceland said to us: "Well met." We took over from that ship and talked by signal to the flagship of the convoy, a converted merchant vessel. The destroyers and corvettes from Iceland retired and we —who had been alone up to an hour before—signaled our orders to the destroyers and corvettes of our own escort. Then the *Walker* passed the convoy in review.

The whole proceeding was as grandly serious as the tourney on the Field of the Cloth of Gold. Here we were in mid-Atlantic, surrounded by deadly foes beneath the water, perhaps beneath us; the components of the convoy were no great shakes to look at, singly, most of them being tankers and Norwegian and Dutch freighters and shabby, hard-bitten sea-tramps of that ilk; none of our escort vessels was either elegant or even particularly clean; and yet the whole effect was one that brought a lump to the throat. In the sparkling sea the convoy vessels rode a perfect line, a mile or two (I could not tell) in breadth; when we passed them they dipped their flags and we dipped ours; the sailors in dungarees on the decks, Norwegians, British, Dutch and Greek, cheered as we passed and waved their hats; a Sunderland flying boat appeared from nowhere and circled above us in the cold bright air. We were "well met."

I could tell that it was not only I, the landsman, who felt the exaltation of this meeting and review in mid-Atlantic. All the officers were on deck, all were relatively silent and intent on the spectacle. Those whose duty it was to check off the ships of the convoy did so; the others merely looked, as I did. There were not many large ships; most of them were grimy little tubs; but they brought food and aircraft and munitions and had come thus far through great peril without injury; they were now the responsibility of our escort. When we finished the review and took our place to lead them home, I think a change had come over everybody on the ship.

And, of course, with good reason: the next two nights were the most dangerous ones. The submarines were signaled on all sides of us, and once we dropped some depth charges, but no attack took place. Our officers had been vigilant before, in a rather light-hearted way; now they did not relax at all. I believe the Captain had no sleep whatever on either of those two nights. I watched until dawn and then, when the streaks of light showed up our valiant tramps still in line, their flags flying and their dirty hulls forging still ahead, I clambered down the ladder and went aft to the quarter-deck to look at them. I never saw a braver sight and never hope to see one—the dirty little tramps that saved the world. Without them England could never have survived, and if England had not survived there could have been no hope in the West.

One day was Sunday and Mr. Langton, the Number One, read out prayers on the quarter-deck. The language was that of the Book of Common Prayer, for sailors at sea, for those in peril perhaps; I have lost the notes I made of this and many other things, the language of the ship's orders, the oddities of the cruise; all I remember is that it was suitable language, read out very loudly in an extremely non-ecclesiastical voice. The sailors sang hymns, also very loudly and off key, but had a very good time doing so. The whole thing was extremely short and without any effort at solemnity, on the tiny quarter-deck with the smell of cooking out from the galley. I liked it better than I do most prayers.

One afternoon the Captain said to me: "Have you ever gone through the Western Isles of Scotland?" I said I had not. "I think we'll go that way," he said. "We can go any way we like. The convoy has to break up now anyhow— some are for Belfast and some for Glasgow and some for Liverpool. I think you should see the Western Isles. We'll take that way."

We anchored once in a nameless loch (nameless here, anyhow) in the wild hills, and then headed south through the isles. All one night we passed between the mainland and the islands. The loveliest were at dawn—Skye, I think, and its neighbors—and I asked the yeoman if he did not think so.

"How do you like this, yeoman?" I asked him as he stood on his eternal watch.

"I don't like it much, sir," he said. "It reminds me too much of Norway."

The *Walker* had been much engaged in Norway, and

those who were aboard ship then had never forgotten it.

When the isles were past and we came again to the Irish Sea I went to sleep. I was on the bridge again for our entrance to Liverpool. As we came up to the Admiralty Dock all the officers were looking anxiously through glasses; the radio had announced heavy raids on Liverpool for all the past week, and nobody knew quite what might be awaiting us. The Captain was particularly concerned over his car, which he had left on the Admiralty Dock just opposite the *Walker's* berth. As we drew near he was able to see the car through his powerful glasses and sighed with content.

"She's still there," he said happily. "She's not much of a car but I depend on her. I shouldn't like Jerry to smash her up." Then, with a brusque change of tone: "Hell and damnation!" he said. "What is that bloody thing over there? Look there, Bray, do you see what I see? Oh, Lord, what we'll get tonight!"

Bray looked and made similar exclamations. At first I did not understand what it was that agitated them. "It's the *Furious*," they said. "It must be the *Furious*."

"What's the matter with the *Furious*?" I wanted to know.

"Nothing at all," the Captain said dryly, "except that Jerry will come over and drop every damned thing he possesses tonight. They always make straight for those things. If I'd known the *Furious* was here I might have delayed coming in until tomorrow. They can't keep her here. It's too dangerous for everybody else."

The aircraft carrier was indeed comfortably situated well to the inside of the Admiralty Dock, her vast expanse visible to any scouting plane, with what seemed dozens of destroyers near enough to share all her dangers.

"I've never been anywhere near an aircraft carrier yet,"

the Captain said, "without getting a hell of a lot of bombs. I'd rather be anywhere else."

He forgot his agitation as soon as we got in, for there was no less a dignitary than Captain D himself (the commander of destroyers) representing the Commander-in-Chief of the Western Approaches, come to decorate the captain and two officers of the *Walker* for the remarkable feat of the preceding February when they sank two submarines according to themselves and one according to the Admiralty. The whole of that night battle, illuminated by flaming tankers and made memorable by a head-on ramming of one submarine, was almost as lively in my mind by now as it was in theirs. The ward-room decided to celebrate the occasion, and Captain Horatio Hornblower ruled that I could not possibly go ashore until the celebration had taken place.

"We've got that champagne," Bray said, "the armistice champagne."

"Bring it out," Number One said. "Even the armistice won't be any better occasion than a D.S.C."

Captain Hornblower had never dined in the ward-room while we were at sea and had only come aft once or twice in the entire journey. For him to eat a special dinner there, with the champagne that had been set aside for the armistice, made the evening notable. We drank toasts to victory and peace, to the *Walker* ("the old tin can," Captain Hornblower usually called it), to us all.

Then the raid began. I think it started around ten o'clock at night, as nearly as I can remember. It was not an all-night affair like a London raid, but it seemed far more concentrated upon an area, far more intense and effective. At first, with the sirens and the crashing of the anti-aircraft, we were slow to take alarm. But then the Captain remembered the *Furious*.

"Oh, Lord," he groaned, "there's that bloody carrier out there. They're bound to come for it. Oh, Lord, oh, Lord!"

It took me some time to realize that what chiefly caused his fear was the small Austin car he had parked across on the other side of the dock. When we all came on deck he made his way, in spite of the rain of shrapnel, off to verify the safety of the car; it was still there but the journey took him some time. While he was away I repaired to the quarter-deck with Number One and some of the subs. The air was filled with the flashes of anti-aircraft explosion, the thunder of bombs, the clatter of shrapnel on our own and other ships. We were packed into the Admiralty Dock like sardines, I no longer remember how many destroyers. The bombers were at times visible, black shapes against a clouded sky, and at times only the broken roar of their motors indicated their presence. When a bomb rustled down with its swishing, hissing whine in our immediate neighborhood we all flung ourselves to the deck with great eagerness, putting the galley plates between us and the outer world. Part of the time I was crouched behind these galley plates, which had holes blown in them as we sheltered there. One of the holes could not have been more than a couple of inches from my head. It was in no way a safe place; the destroyer next us was hit, the dock on the other side was hit, one ship was on fire and another was said to be sinking. Our own plates and superstructure were pierced again and again by fragments.

As is the way of raids, this one had moments of relative lull followed by new intensities. I do not know how long it lasted. It was the great raid of May 8, 1941, the last and greatest of the series on Liverpool. When it came to an end the city and port were temporarily paralyzed. Nothing worked, neither telephone nor telegraph nor railroad nor tram-lines. There were no taxis, no busses, no cars. It was impossible for me to leave the ship that night, as my orders had read; I must stay over and see what the morning afforded.

I walked out, across the damaged destroyer next to us and onto the dock. There we found Captain Horatio Hornblower mourning over his Austin car. It had been smashed to bits as part of a larger hit. He was in no mood for talk; we went on to the stricken ships and struggling men along the dock.

The sinking destroyer did not sink; the burning ship was saved; the *Furious*, swept with shrapnel and bomb fragments throughout the raid, had no real damage; but this we did not know that night. In the darkness and confusion it seemed that the marauders had devastated the harbor. I went back to the *Walker* and, eventually, to sleep.

In the morning it was a long time before I could get any form of conveyance into Liverpool. Everything had come to a stop. The electricity, even, was gone; the locks could not be worked; the ships in the dock had to wait for the tide to get out. All were anxious to get out on the tide, for another such raid the next night would (as always) much more than merely double the damage.

At last a W.V.S. driver appeared to take some officers up to Captain D at headquarters and I was ordered into that car. I knew a good deal about the W.V.S. (Women's Voluntary Services) because the founder of the organization, Lady Reading, had taken my wife in tow in London and had already done a great deal toward helping her study of war work. I had seen the W.V.S. at work after air raids and had acquired a respect for its efforts; but on that morning in Liverpool, when nothing but the W.V.S. did seem to function, my esteem went up to new heights.

Liverpool was a sorry sight. It was ever a dreary place,

dull and sad-eyed under gloomy skies, but on that morning of misery it wore the wretched look of ruin. No matter what devastation was made in London, it never had
this oppressive effect; there was a great difference in London; the London spirit and the London laughter made it
different. I am quite ready to admit that London was
playing a stirring part on the stage of the world, was
conscious of it, and played it with a certain amount of
bravado; everybody felt an obligation to behave well in
London and to be as cheerful as possible—even gay—about
it. No such obligation rested upon the smokes and smells
of Liverpool. The wrecked houses, the melancholy migration of families with carts, baby carriages, wagons; the
dreary streets laid low; the fine dust in the air, that
choked you when you breathed deep; the pall of smoke
over the normal smoke or mixed with it; all this was oppressive, lay heavy upon you; you felt the tragedy of the
night but wanted—since you could do nothing much anyhow—to leave it behind.

So ended my brief glimpse of the Royal Navy. If I was
not misled by my own observations, it must indeed be one
of the finest services the world has seen. I was not on a
show ship at all; I was on "an old tin can," one of the
oldest and least valuable ships of the whole navy; but it
was a thoroughly serviceable ship in which every man did
his duty twenty-four hours a day with good nature and
practiced ability. I felt an immense confidence in these
men. I would have entrusted Captain Horatio Hornblower
with anything I possessed, including my life, with the
certainty that it would be in the best possible hands. On
duty night and day, week in and week out, in every kind
of weather, these men had only the very briefest of leaves
—usually a few days every four or five months when the
ship had to have her bottom scraped. The strain on the

navy had been terrific since the summer of 1940. In point of fact no merchant shipping of any nation anywhere on earth was safe unless it was protected or convoyed by ships of this navy. The lines of communication sustained by it were longer than any hitherto known to warfare. To get supplies or troops to Egypt it was necessary to go all around Africa; German submarines had operated everywhere, even in the Indian Ocean; there were German raiders in the South Pacific; wherever there was salt water this navy had to guard its main channels against the marauder. And with all this there was no haste, no scanting of the job; I have remarked before how we paused in the sea to investigate every bit of wreckage in the hope of saving a life.

When I wrote a magazine piece about the convoy system and this brief experience of it, I ended the account with the words: "When our hour strikes, I hope our own navy will do as well." The *Saturday Evening Post* omitted that line.

3

The great air raid of May 10, 1941, the last and worst, took place a night or so after my return to London. Anybody who lived through it will remember it forever. The Germans had actually sent a slightly larger number of bombers across on April 16th, but for some reason they did less damage, made less impression on London's mind and body, than the raiders of May 10th. The fires of May 10th also destroyed so many of the places Londoners had known and loved, wiped out such familiar friends, that they seemed to strike home more than any other since the first ones.

That was the night St. Clement Dane's went; the

Queen's Hall too, and Dunhill's shop in Jermyn Street, and a great chunk of Bond Street; many kinds of London were incinerated at the same time. The fires set alight seemed to blaze from every corner of the metropolis. From the roof of Claridge's Hotel one had the feeling of being on a gigantic funeral pyre around which the flames arose in inevitable and deadly circles. It was the first heavy raid Dinah had seen and she wanted to spend hours on the roof. We did go up there two or three times with General Lee, then our military attaché, and Ben Cohen, who represented the President in some capacity; they were fellow-Claridgers and we found them in the lobby of the hotel. I was very nervous about Dinah, and with reason; she was obliged to spend the next two or three weeks in the London Clinic as a result of this night. The night had a certain terrible beauty, it is true; no holocaust of the war had a more hellish splendor than this, because the night was clear and the fires burned bright over a vast area. In the morning there was dust over everything in London, dust in the lower air and more thickly in the overcast made by smoke and cloud. On that darkened day we saw the firemen still struggling against flames in many areas, struggling with every difficulty since some of the water mains had burst.

We did not know then that this was to be the last raid. We expected the Germans to return, if they could do so, on the following night. All experience had shown that the raid repeated becomes much more effective than arithmetical progression would suggest. A second such night would have been more deadly than the first, striking when many essential services were either broken down or strained to the limit; a third would have been more deadly than the second. But there were no more: May 10th was the end, the end of a great epic. There is still time for the Germans to strike at London, of course, but when or if they do all the conditions will have altered and the results cannot be the same. Even on May 10, 1941, the results achieved by British night fighters were remarkable, amounting to about ten percent of the attacking force shot down and many more damaged. With the progress made then and since then in the radio devices involved, it is more than likely that any future air attack on London by night would cost more than it might be worth to the Germans.

On Monday night, May 12th, I left Dinah at the Clinic and went over to Athenaeum Court to have dinner with Helen Kirkpatrick, Bill Stoneman and Ed Beattie. Bill and Ed had drawn lots to go over Berlin in a bomber. This expedition, for which the American press had long clamored, was now approved by the R.A.F. but only a small number of correspondents could be taken. When the lots were drawn, Ed and Bill were among the chosen. I did not envy them, although I suppose if I had been in the lottery (as I could not be, since it was restricted to regular correspondents for the daily press) I might have worked up a similar desire to win the dangerous privilege. In any case their departure, which was set for the next day, called for a farewell dinner, and no formality was neglected. (Actually the American Embassy intervened with strong disapproval and caused the project to be abandoned; this we were not to know for two or three days.)

After dinner I left my colleagues to go to the Clinic, and returned to the Athenaeum late that night (eleven o'clock or so) further to solemnize the occasion. I had stopped a moment at Claridge's on the way, to be greeted by the hall porter with the immense and mystifying news that Rudolf Hess had landed in Scotland two nights before, while the May 10th raids were going on.

On my return to the Athenaeum I found all thought of the forthcoming bomber trip to Berlin had been lost in the fascination of this news, the strangest and least predictable event of the whole war. Ed and Bill were telephoning in all directions—to their offices; to Duff Cooper; to Brendan Bracken; to Number 10 Downing Street. They wanted to go to Scotland at once, to interview Hess, to help the interrogation, to spread the glad tidings. Ed Beattie spoke good German and had known the man in Berlin. Everywhere they met with the same mystification, uncertainty and unwillingness to open up this most luscious of stories. Ed and Bill blamed it on the chronic inability of British governing minds to understand the necessity for speed, the importance of propaganda and the desirability of making a sensation in the American press. At the moment I was inclined to think as they did, by sheer professional habit, although from the beginning I had some faint suspicion that there was more in this than could be told. Later on, as I pieced the story together, a bit from this source and a bit from that, I came to the conclusion that for once the journalistic criticism was hopelessly wrong—that in the immensity of the issues presented to Mr. Churchill's mind by this event, by far the least important was the impression made on the American press or public. Judging by what I know (or think I know) now, the course adopted was eminently correct and could not have been more astutely chosen and pursued. To tell as little as possible about Hess, his mission or his whereabouts was bound to annoy the House of Commons, to mystify the Americans, to give rise to all sorts of fantastic rumors and speculations. These were undesirable results.

But to have told the whole story (as our press wanted) would have been far, far worse, because at a moment of the most delicate historic balance, a moment pregnant with consequences for generations to come, it was above all things desirable to obtain and retain the confidence—as much as possible—of the Russians.

On the face of it the story was incredible. I have met intelligent and well-informed persons who believed, even a year later, that it was simply untrue—that Hess never came to Scotland at all, that it was a British trick. I am certain that if Mr. Churchill had made the whole affair public, allowing a five days' journalistic sensation to become more important than the whole conduct of the war, this impression ("a British trick") would have been more widespread, particularly in German-dominated Europe; and, gravest of all, he would have infuriated the Russians at the very moment when it was most important to have them see that Hitler was our common enemy.

I do not know whether the Russians believed the story or not, at the beginning. I have a sort of idea that they did not. If it had been turned into a journalistic holiday they certainly would have disbelieved it altogether.

Some day there will probably be an official document, a Blue Book or White Paper, which gives a full account of the Hess affair. It should be one of the most fascinating documents of the war. Until it is at hand we can only speculate. My speculation is perhaps as good as anybody's outside of the official world because I heard fragments of the truth from persons who undoubtedly knew all of it. By long experience I have become rather practiced at making a mosaic out of such fragments. For what it is worth, here is my mosaic of the Hess affair:

The *Führer's Stellvertreter* (the Leader's Place-Taker, that is to say, the substitute or representative of Hitler,

appointed officially for that purpose) made the flight to
Scotland to propose terms of agreement with the British.
His general argument was along the lines of the Nazi-
Nordic mania. England and Germany were the great Nordic powers; it was nonsense for them to destroy each other
to the ultimate benefit of nobody but the sub-human Slavs
and the mongrel, half-breed Americans. Nazi Germany
was about to undertake the culminating and supreme part
of its historic mission, the destruction of the Bolshevik,
Jewish, Slavic and sub-human menace of the Soviet Union.
Upon undertaking this splendid *Welthistorisches* task it
did not wish to have the kindred race of the English in
opposition. Why should not Nordic Germany and Nordic
England come to terms of agreement? England could keep
her Empire, with some minor rectifications of frontiers in
Africa for the benefit of Mussolini, who had to be fed
something. The British fleet was to be untouched. There
was to be a pact of *twenty-five years' non-aggression* between Nordic England and Nordic Germany. (As distinguished, I suppose, from the ten years' non-aggression
with France or the fifteen years' pact with Poland.) These
extremely generous and noble terms were to be discussed
with any "reasonable" government of England, but not
with Mr. Churchill. As soon as Mr. Churchill had been
dismissed and a "reasonable" government set up, Hess
was willing to go into the whole affair and arrange for a
"reasonable" state of affairs in Europe in preparation for
the attack on the Soviet Union.

This is a telescoped and simplified version of what I
believe came out of the interrogations of Hess. I omit all
the minor mysteries that arose during those weeks: the
reasons why Hess tried to do all this through the Duke of
Hamilton, the journeys of Mr. Ivone Kirkpatrick to Scotland, and all the rest of it. In the main, through the inci-

dental complications of a half-crazy exploit, the fact that emerges is that Hess had a serious purpose in his flight to Scotland, a purpose which the British government did well to study seriously and to keep a secret. It is my understanding that they communicated all this information fully and loyally to the Soviet Government, without delay, feeling that the matter was of more import to that government than to any other. I believe the same information was made available to the American government and served to prepare them psychologically for what was coming. Meanwhile the Nazi authorities in Berlin lost themselves in contradictory explanations of the episode, broadcasting one night that Hess was a maniac, the next that he was a self-sacrificing martyr, the next that he was a traitor. It seemed quite obvious that the German government as a whole knew nothing of his mission—certainly that the Propaganda-ministerium, Dr. Goebbels' organization, had been caught unawares by the extraordinary event and had no story ready to explain it.

There remained, and still remains, only one question of genuine interest with regard to Hess' mission. That is, how full was his authority, to what extent was it Hitler's plan and order, and what did Hitler gamble on this mad idea?

It is my conviction, based upon a dozen small facts that have to be stuck together to mean anything, that the plan was Hitler's. At the same time I believe he told it to nobody but Hess himself (there are many indications that it was a secret to other German leaders). I understand that Hess maintained throughout his interrogation that he was acting entirely on his own initiative, attempting to make a peace agreement because he felt that anything else would be ruinous, and that he at no point engaged the responsibility of either the Nazi party or of Hitler himself.

This was a correct Nazi party attitude: he was a prisoner and had to take full responsibility himself for everything he did and said. And yet how could he have undertaken such a mission without the authority of his Führer, whom he, more than any other Nazi chief, had blindly worshipped?

Upon the face of it, Hitler must have been a party to this plan. Hess was his closest friend, part author of his sacred book, *Mein Kampf;* the racial ideas of the Nazi movement were at least as much Hess' as Hitler's; the notion of Germany-allied-with-England, which runs through *Mein Kampf,* had been a governing notion of Rudolf Hess for years. It does not seem possible that Hess—in spite of his great authority as the *Führer's Stellvertreter* and third-ranking personage of the Reich—could have seized a Messerschmitt 110 on the airdrome at Augsburg and taken off for Scotland *with extra gasoline tanks and on a radio beam* unless the extraordinary order had been given from on high. We know that he went to exactly where he meant to go, and that he came down (having exhausted his gasoline) within a mile or two of the Duke of Hamilton, whom he wished to see as an intermediary in his plans. Could any of this have taken place by the mere whim of a maniac? I think not.

The choice of the Duke of Hamilton as go-between was one of the craziest parts of the plan. The Nazi leaders have never known much about foreign countries, however erudite their professorial instructors have been; the learning of General Haushofer has never really made up for the bone-deep provincialism of Hitler himself, or of Hess or Himmler. These people unquestionably thought that a duke was by nature their ally, that dukes exercised a dominating power in the government of England, that Mr. Churchill could be dismissed easily if the governing classes felt they had to do it to make peace, and that the Hess mission had a very good chance of success. Above all they were impressed by the sheer generosity of their own terms—twenty-five full years of non-aggression, during which the British Empire was to be untouched. Hitler had never met any Englishmen except Mr. Chamberlain, Lord Halifax and Sir Neville Henderson. It was hardly to be expected that he would form a correct estimate of the spirit or intentions of the British government from the examples he had seen. He did realize that Mr. Churchill was an implacable enemy, and one of the facts that first emerged (indeed, immediately) from the Hess affair was that Hess' mission was not to Churchill at all, but to some optimum "reasonable" government which he expected to be formed at his desire.

So far as I understand it, the poor Duke of Hamilton was horrified by the whole business and felt himself dishonored for all time by being associated with it. After his first interview with Hess he flew down to London in a panic; he arrived on that Sunday (May 11th) and had to go to Dytchley to see the Prime Minister; he was sent back to London to talk to Mr. Eden; it was only on Monday that Mr. Ivone Kirkpatrick (who had known Hess and spoke good German) took over the responsibility of going to Scotland for further talks with the strange visitor. I have heard that the Duke of Hamilton, a straightforward and rather non-political young man, was so overcome by shame at being chosen by Hess that he tried to resign all his Court positions and honors and was only dissuaded from such a course by Mr. Churchill. However that may be, it is incontestable that every step of the Hess business exhibited, more than anything else, the astounding ignorance of the Nazi leaders. They appear never to have heard of the British constitution or of the fact that, with all its oligarchical administrative machinery, its "old school tie" and the rest of it, the government of England is democratic in form.

The mistake was grave. As I have already indicated, the British government kept its own counsel so far as the public was concerned, declaring only that Hess was a prisoner of war like any other German aviator and would be treated accordingly. In private, I have heard and believe, the information derived from the interrogations of Hess was fully imparted to the most concerned party, the Soviet Government, and the whole fantastic story was relayed across the Atlantic by safe means to Mr. Roosevelt. There was a strong tendency to disbelief on all sides at first, as was only natural. It hardly seemed possible that the Germans could have made such an error. Yet, as the month wore on, and May turned into June, and there were no more raids over England, and every scrap of information from the continent indicated that the German divisions were massing in the East, incredulity had to give way to a sort of dazed belief that this was, in simple fact, the Nazi plan. They were going to attack Russia, and Hess had been sent to arrange for a comfortable quiet on the Western front. Now, as at all times, Hitler stuck to his central military article of faith, which was that Germany could always win so long as she had to fight on only one front at a time.

In giving this mosaic, this reconstruction of the Hess story from scores of bits and pieces, I do not pretend that I have not, here and there, guessed or jumped a bridge. It is, even so, what I believe. I came to believe it only after weeks or months of considering the scraps of the truth that came my way. If it proves in the end to be grossly wrong at any essential point, I should be greatly surprised.

At the time, of course, it was hard to realize that the British government was handling this affair in the right way. The American press as a whole was convinced that so much silence was nugatory, that the public had a right to know what was going on, and that the British were "missing a bet" in not working the whole Hess imbroglio for every ounce of "publicity" that could be got out of it. The *Saturday Evening Post* once sent me a cablegram declaring that they would pay a larger sum than anybody else (the sum not named—merely larger than any other offer) for "Hess' life story." I passed the telegram on to Number 10 Downing Street without comment, and received the reply I expected from Brendan Bracken. "I scarcely think," said Brendan, "that the Prime Minister wishes to go into the business of literary agent at this time."

4

During this spring and summer I saw a great deal of Don Juan Negrin. At the time of the fall of France he had succeeded in chartering a boat from a port near Bordeaux and had taken off a considerable number of Spanish Republican officials as well as documents of the Spanish Republican Government. He had expected to be rather ill received in England, but was on the contrary treated with great courtesy, although none of his party had passports other than those issued by their own defeated and exiled government. Don Juan had found a cottage at Bovingdon in Hertfordshire, about an hour's drive from London, and here, with such books as he had managed to save, with friends who were for the most part also exiles, he maintained his old robust spirits as he watched the evolution of a process he had, for the most part, clearly foreseen earlier than anybody else known to me. Casares Quiroga, also a former Prime Minister of Spain, lived in the house, as did Madame Isabelle Blum, a Socialist member of the Belgian parliament; others—including Azcarate, the Spanish Ambassador to England in Republican days, who lived not far away—came and went. It grew to be a practice with me to spend the week-end in this cottage of Don Juan's, for he had declared early in May that the house was open to me at all times, and I knew that he (unlike most people) meant what he said. It was a rambling and unpretentious house of no particular style, with a garden big enough to roam in, and the lanes in the neighborhood—seldom visited by strange motor cars—were very pleasant for walking in the late afternoon or early morning. Nobody in the house kept track of your movements; you came or went as you pleased, so long as you gave decent notice of your intentions with respect to meals; you could read or write or walk or sleep in perfect freedom. Don Juan used to give Dinah and me his own room for the week-end, while he moved into the study next door. Our diversions were not many: the cat, the dog, the birds that nested in the vines, and above all, the engrossing occupation of riding the bicycle. From a London which seemed more than ever tense just then—which seemed, in fact, to be holding its breath—this was a refuge of thoughtful and friendly peace.

The other regular week-end visitors, besides ourselves, were the Soviet Ambassador, Ivan Maisky and his wife. They had links with Don Juan over the Spanish war, during which Maisky had been the one battler for the Spanish Republic in the lamentable Non-Intervention Committee. Negrin had met him only lately, in exile, but they found that they had a good deal to say to each

other. I think each appreciated in the other the sound
and weight of genuine ability undisturbed by ambition.
They had in common the quality of being able to look
at events objectively, examining each from every point
of view; Don Juan was loquacious and Maisky was not,
but they were alike capable of many hours on the same
subject; and, in spite of tempestuous lives, neither of
them had lost the willingness to laugh. Above all, I think,
they shared a certain imperturbability, the result of long
experience and much consideration of possibilities: that
is, neither was much surprised at anything that happened. This gave them not only a special competence
in discussion, but a basis of understanding that made
true discussion (as distinguished from the airing of opinions or prejudices) productive of some result.

Madame Maisky had all the charm and spirit, the swift
alternation from grave to gay, which we are accustomed
to think of as particularly Slavic. Her English was not as
fluent as her husband's and perhaps for this reason, perhaps for another, she took little or no part in political
talk. She knitted, walked, rode the bicycle, smiled; I
think she particularly enjoyed any conversation about
music or the theatre, and had once had ambitions toward
the theatre herself. Don Juan had a good many records
and we used to play them on Sunday evenings. The
Spanish ones, particularly those from the civil war, and
a few Mexican records were her favorites. On great occasions we always played *Riego's Hymn,* the song that
had become (nobody knows quite how) the battle song
of the Spanish Republic. It brought back all the hopes
and resolutions of pre-Munich days, the scenes themselves, the crackle of machine-gun fire in Madrid, the
brown hills above the Ebro; all this of only three years
before—but three such years! Sometimes Madame Maisky

sang to herself, very softly, while she untangled her yarn, weaving it from chair to chair. She liked old Russian songs, which she would break off and explain as she went along. She was fond of the cat, the dogs, the birds; for two or three weeks she fed a whole family of birds in a nest in the vines, and was distressed when one day they were no longer there. Both she and the Ambassador were novices at the bicycle, and in the early summer both fell off a good deal. These were the small dramas of the garden, and the contrast with what actually was preoccupying us all did not make them less important on the surface of life in Bovingdon.

On Sunday mornings we spent many hours reading the newspapers and the weeklies. Maisky was indefatigable in this respect; he missed nothing. We also listened to all the important broadcasts of the B.B.C., of the Vichy French and sometimes (when we could get them) of the Germans. During the time when the German divisions were massing in the East, the tension of feeling, of suspicion, of uncertainty and of blank incredulity was great among people who knew; it was difficult to talk of anything important; it was a relief to ride the bicycle. Don Juan sometimes talked to me, on long walks up and down the lanes, of what he felt about it all. He had never for one moment relaxed his antagonism to the Fascists; he was not a Communist—was about as non-political as a politician could be—and the Nazi-Soviet Pact had in no way affected his attitude toward the essential questions. For this very reason he could not discuss the Pact or its results with Maisky, and did not. He liked to talk it all out to me—what was likely to happen, and how and when. He felt the urgency of some kind of conversation between the British and the Russians, some settlement of their smaller differences in view of their larger reasons for agreement. Sir Stafford Cripps had been a year in Moscow and had failed to make any headway; he was now coming home. It seemed doubtful if he would go back, or if, indeed, any ambassador to Moscow would be appointed; at least so the newspapers said. Negrin thought this highly unfortunate at such a moment, and was fertile in ideas of how the coldness and distrust between Hitler's two opponents might be overcome. At one time he thought Lord Beaverbrook was the man who could do the necessary work; I even went so far as to pass on this opinion to Lord Beaverbrook when I saw him, only to be told that now, at this moment, nobody dared say or do anything lest it provoke the attack. It was a moment of suspended animation, a moment of painful waiting for an almost certain but still incredible climax. In the garden at Bovingdon I think everybody felt that the war was about to begin in grimmest earnest, and that all we had seen before would be as nothing to the struggle that now impended.

Maisky took little part in such talk. One evening, when he walked in the garden with me and I speculated very tentatively on the possibility of an understanding between England and Russia, he did say a word or two. "They must have something to offer," he said, "and they must mean what they say. One thing I am sure of. Nobody is going to get the Red Army for sixpence." On another occasion he said very earnestly: "There are only two armies in the world today. One is the German Army and the other is the Red Army. This is the simplest statement of the military situation. Whoever decides a course, in Berlin or London or elsewhere, must do so in view of that dominating fact. Neither of these armies can be had for sixpence."

5

The actual day of June 22, 1941, found us in strange surroundings. We had been asked to Dytchley that weekend and were far from the atmosphere of the cottage at Bovingdon. Dytchley was a beautiful house of Queen Anne's day, built by the Dillon family; it had been bought and restored some years before by Nancy and Ronald Tree. (Ronny was Parliamentary Undersecretary to the Ministry of Information in 1941.) Few of the great houses in England kept open now; Dytchley was one, and week-ends there were graced by many members of the government, including the Prime Minister, Eden and the Duff Coopers. I suppose that for the anti-Munich, anti-Fascist wing of the Conservative party it probably played much the same part that was assigned to Cliveden, Lady Astor's house, in Chamberlain's time. At any rate it did play a part and I acknowledged a lively curiosity about it, snapping up the invitation before Nancy and Ronny had time to make it explicit.

There was a large party but, to my surprise, no politicians and no journalists were included in it. One phalanx consisted of young people, friends and contemporaries of the Trees' son. Lord Hartington, one of the Manners boys, the Archduke Robert of Austria—such was the tenor of the gathering. The phalanx of elders was made up on similar principles, and the whole thing would have glittered considerably in the columns of any newspaper. Saturday night after dinner I had a fairly sharp tilt with the Archduke Robert of Austria on the subject of the Red Army, on which he claimed special information. I had none and claimed none, but Maisky (and also

Benes) had given me considerable confidence in it. I was therefore surprised to hear the Archduke state that it was without modern equipment, devoid of discipline or spirit, and certain to collapse in any real test against the Germans. The Archduke was young, but like many other royalties he had superb confidence in the validity of his own prejudices.

On Sunday morning Dinah and I slept late and dawdled over our dressing. This house invited ease by its combination of beauty and comfort, so that you were very likely to pause, half-dressed, and gaze for an hour down the sunny terraces upon which your windows opened, wondering at the dead generations. It was noon when we came downstairs and started to walk in the garden, vaguely on the search for Nancy or Ronny, but most of all bemused by the spectacle of an exquisite garden on a really perfect day. Down toward the end of a walk through high box hedges we came suddenly upon Ronny and the Duchess of Rutland. "What do you think of the news?" said he. "What news?" said I. "The Germans attacked Russia all along the frontier at dawn this morning," he said.

The rest of the day passed in a kind of double trance, in which what you were thinking about had nothing to do with what you said or did. We went for a long walk in the woods in the afternoon; Dinah and the other women guests made a tour of the house; no doubt various things took place and conversations occurred, but the subject of what had now happened to the war was not much mentioned. The Prime Minister was to speak at nine o'clock that evening over a general broadcast to the world, and until he had done so I doubt if anybody in this gathering wished to hazard much of an opinion. A radio was brought into the dining room that night and the whole company fell into silence when nine o'clock came.

That speech was one of Mr. Churchill's most remarkable efforts. By his own will and intuition he achieved the resolution to proclaim Russia an ally and to pledge all possible help to Russia in the common struggle—this although there had been no conversations and no shadow of encouragement from Moscow. At that very week-end at Chequers, where Mr. Churchill heard the news, one of the guests was Sir Stafford Cripps, who had come home to acknowledge the failure of his mission to Moscow and to resign. A declaration as wholehearted as Mr. Churchill's that night not only gave the British public its keynote but enabled the American government also to acknowledge Russia, the unspeakable Bolshevik, as a friend. I learned afterward that this declaration, so prompt and so resolute, had been Mr. Churchill's own work; that there was no cabinet meeting that day; that such consultation as had taken place was by telephone; and that some members of the government were astounded to find Russia now a full-fledged ally. Certainly in the room where I heard it, although one or two voices were raised to praise the speech, the general feeling was one of consternation at the turn of events.

We returned to London when the speech was over. The Archduke Robert came out on the steps to say good-bye and to have the last word in our argument.

"Come to me in two weeks' time and tell me what you think then about the Red Army," he said. "That will be just about the time when Stalin and the Free Russian Government arrive in London to take up headquarters."

I saw the Archduke some weeks later, passing by at Claridge's, and I must say he had the grace to acknowledge that his judgment had been a little hasty.

6

Opinions more weighted with authority than those of the young Archduke were on his side. "Experts" of various sorts considered that the Red Army would collapse in a few weeks. This was the prevailing opinion among journalists and politicians, although Mr. Churchill's declaration made it practically impossible for them to say so publicly. When Ed Murrow asked me to broadcast to America on this subject he found the text I prepared altogether too optimistic.

"You are under no censorship so far as I am concerned," he said. "You can say anything you want to say. But I think, for your own sake, you oughtn't to stick your neck out so far. Tone it down. Qualify it a little. It's too strong."

I did qualify it a little—a very little. In the final version what I said, substantially, was this: that the Red Army would no doubt be obliged to retreat, but that it would not collapse and would still be fighting, on whatever line, when the war ended, "even though it should retreat to Irkutsk," I remember saying in one passage of this effort. I had fortified my general information about the Red Army by some talks with Maisky and Benes, and thought I had some right to say what I did as an antidote to the "expert" opinions that abounded in the opposing sense. I ended by quoting a phrase of Maisky's, an old Russian peasant proverb: "Nothing is worse," says the proverb, "than when the scythe hits a stone." I gave it as my conclusion that the German scythe had hit a stone.

A year later, these things seemed obvious. In late June and early July of 1941, such had been our experience of incessant German victory that very few people known to me were willing to concede the possibility that, even with great advances and triumphs, the German Army could *not* truly conquer Russia or annihilate the Red Army. It was August before it began to dawn on all of our friends that when Winston called this event (the German attack on Russia) the "grand climacteric" of the war, he might just conceivably have been stating the plain truth.

I went to see President Benes soon after June 22nd. He had maintained a military mission in Russia for years and knew more about the Red Army than almost any other leader on the allied side. I found him confident that by this decision Hitler had lost the war. At the same time Benes felt that Hitler had taken the only possible decision; that to go on indefinitely warring against England and exhausting himself while the Red Army grew stronger at his back would have been madness; that the destruction of the Red Army was necessary to the fulfilment of any plan for German hegemony not only in the world, but even on the continent of Europe. Benes thought that Hitler could not have chosen otherwise, but that, at the same time, this decision was fatal to his plans because it would hurl the best of his armies to death against an innumerable, disciplined and relentless foe with every advantage of space and climate. The Czechoslovak information services had been remarkably good on this subject, as usual, and Benes had known of Hitler's intention since late February, of his actual dispositions and plans since April. He had not found much belief in this information at the time; it was May before it began to be accepted as probably true. It seems to have been Benes' historical role to warn his Western democratic allies of coming events in vain, and then to see his analysis justified by the acts of the adversary.

In August my wife, having finished her work in Lambeth, went back to America. I stayed on a few weeks more in London, partly because I felt the necessity of going somewhere else—Russia or the Far East—to complete the picture I was trying to make of the war, and partly because there still was work for me to do in England. I had spent some time on the questions of labor and man-power, visited factories and mines, investigated war legislation under the Emergency Powers Act, "dilution" in factories (the use of women or unskilled workers to eke out the supply of the skilled) and similar subjects; I had done one long magazine article on economic warfare; I wanted now to get some idea of the international brigades that were in training in England, the nucleus of an international army. By arrangement with the competent ministries I was able to visit the French, the Norwegians, Belgians, Czechoslovaks and Poles at their camps in England and Scotland, and to form some notion of the bitter and resolute will that had brought them here. In every one of these armies I met with extraordinary stories of escape from the Nazis, fresh evidence of the refusal of free men to be quiescent under tyranny. Some of the French boys had come from just across the Channel—half an hour away by airplane—but it had taken them up to a year to make the journey across France and Spain. There were Czechs who had come from peaceful jobs in South America or South Africa, Poles who had traveled half round the world to get here; there were stories of swimming the icy Loire at night, crossing the Pyrenees in the snow, fierce wounds and strange deliverances. One's imagination saw them coming by all the roads of Europe, hiding by day and walking by night, appealing to the priest or the mayor or the peasant women by the roadside, an army of the future, an assurance for the present that the free peoples of Europe had not accepted slavery. Some of these nuclear armies were more important in size and equipment than others; the French and Poles were most numerous, the Norwegians possibly the most relentlessly trained for the task they had in mind. I visited the Norwegians in the far north of Scotland, on a hillside from which, they said, it was easy to imagine the Norse coast opposite; they showed me wrestling and strangling exercises of the most savage order (the so-called "commando techniques") and put almost too much vigor into it.

At Bovingdon every week-end we examined the information in the papers, listened to the radio, followed with anxiety the changing line of the military positions in Russia. Madame Maisky had not welcomed the war. "I do not like this," she said that first week. "War is never a good thing. War is a bad thing always, under all conditions. But now it is decided. Now we shall fight." Maisky, coming to a luncheon of the American Press Association at the Savoy—a luncheon in his honor, for which Bill Stoneman had dug up the largest Soviet flag in England—gave us his analysis of the situation and when asked what would happen then, said with finality, "Then comes the winter."

At Bovingdon on Sunday evenings we always drank a toast to the Red Army. Mr. Maisky, who did not otherwise drink wine, would swallow half a glassful for this toast; we drank it standing and without comment. Sometimes Madame Maisky seemed close to tears; she could never forget the essential thing, the death and suffering of so many of her own people. The terrible struggle in the East, surging back and forth over a front of a thousand miles, was more real to her imagination than it was to most in London. Some bland and satisfied exteriors in London just then were almost more than I could bear; you could almost hear the rumble of digestive bliss as their owners reflected that this night there would be no bombs, that the bombs were all falling in Russia. The extreme safety of England at this time was proved by a large number of visits from distinguished Americans who had not had time to come over before. The common people of England, knowing full well to what they owed this respite from German attack, clamored for all possible help to Russia; the British and American governments both acted with reasonable promptness; the Beaverbrook and Harriman missions went to Moscow. At the same time the full brunt of the German attack fell upon the Red Army alone; Hitler was again fighting on only one front at a time; the Western front was all water from Norway to Spain.

I wanted to return home by way of Russia and the Far East, but the difficulties seemed almost insurmountable just then. Maisky was quite willing to apply for my visa but had no idea whether I would get it or whether there would be room for me in any available form of transport. Under the circumstances it seemed better to do what I had to do from America. Averill Harriman was going back to Moscow; he might take me along; if not I could go to the Far East and survey the probable area of the coming Japanese attack. Certainly the war had assumed such dimensions now that you could not see it clearly at all if you saw it only from England. The day when England had held the bridge was now over.

I made some brief farewells one day: Mr. Eden, Mr. Winant, the Maiskys. Eden's popularity was again in

the ascendant, since he had been right on so many matters; I think he felt it and, with all his simplicity and
good sense, he could not help showing some slight grati-
fication at the results. Mr. Winant was more deeply concerned about the ordinary values of life and death than
are most men who wander or climb into high positions;
his burning sincerity came from some such inner fire and
made it a little strange that he should ever have become
an ambassador. The Maiskys had put a bottle of whisky
on the study table in their Embassy. To my astonishment
Maisky drank a little of it and so did Madame Maisky,
although they both disliked the stuff. It was for our toast
that they had ordered the drink: our toast to the Red
Army.

# 7. A Moment in Chungking

The seventh of November, 1941, began in Chungking as a day of impenetrable mist, with cold, white veils concealing the two rivers and the high hills. Out of the milky morning twilight arose the cries of the boatmen and coolies of burden, louder than usual, as the work of the great, sprawling town went on unseen. Every drop of water had to be carried up these towering hills on human shoulders; every object we used had been borne painfully at some time or other up from the life-giving river.

Owen Lattimore had asked me to breakfast with him. Toward 8:30 that morning I walked the little way from Chialing House, where I lived, down the hill to him. He was political adviser to Chiang Kai-shek, and few foreigners ever spoke Chinese as well (or in as many varieties) as he did. He lived in a well-built modern house with a roof garden, belonging (like so many other houses in various parts of China) to T. V. Soong. The government had taken it over now as a hostel for distinguished strangers. The day was to come when it was to house an American general on active duty. Its gray stone squareness was a landmark on the hillside; when there was no fog it could be seen from miles away, up and down the Chialing River.

I enjoyed my breakfast with Lattimore but observed that even at this intimate hour he was not alone. At all or most moments he seemed to be accompanied by a representative of the Generalissimo, a highly intelligent and conversable Chinese who tended to dominate the conversation. When the talk veered toward any delicate subject, such as the relations between the Chungking Government and the Communists of the Northwest, this authority intervened with large, general and no doubt incontrovertible statements which did not quite apply to the specific question. Owen seemed a little anxious that I should not too narrowly observe the tactics of this mentor, lest it be thought that his freedom as political adviser was not perfect. I asked if he believed he had been useful in that role during the past three months and he said yes: in a number of matters he had been able to further the general interests of China and the anti-Fascist world by particular detail. I had enough faith in Lattimore to think that if intelligence and devotion to China could achieve such purposes, he was right in so believing.

After breakfast, as I was going back up the hill to Chialing House, the sun came out. With the sudden irrefutable authority it can exercise even in a Chungking November, it dispelled the mist in a few minutes. The river came into sight, immense and very dirty, with the battered junks of the boatmen toiling along its channels. On either side the great hills covered with houses and ruins became visible again as the fog rolled back, lifted and vanished. On the highest hills were the Russian Embassy and the house (not the offices) of the British Ambassador. There were enough rich Chinese and foreigners in Chungking in peacetime to have built numerous large houses, so that the task of finding places for all the people and machinery of the central government was at least not impossible. Much had been bombed and rebuilt in two years, sometimes more than once. Sir Archibald Clark-Kerr, the British Ambassador, pointing to the holes in his hospitable roof, would say: "But you see I don't really mind. I consider myself fair game for the Japanese."

With the fog gone you could see it all—the coolies chanting in cadence as they toiled up the hill, pulling intolerable loads, smiling as you passed them; the military base hospital on the other bank, where the wounded boys also smiled at you from their beds when you went through; the bomb craters where water has gathered and women wash their clothing without soap; the dark-eyed children playing among the ruins. Patient and cheerful they all were, performing work beyond computation— 250,000 of them building the Burma Road with no tools; millions going through the process of slow starvation; other millions who fought with no other weapon than the rifle and the machine-gun. Here they were, the Chinese, smiling at the sun now, glad to see the last of the fog. How could you contemplate them? Why should one people have to endure so much? These were the things you said to yourself as the sun picked out the details of their misery. There could be no words for a sorrow so immense.

After a while Lattimore came up the hill and took me on to the Russian Embassy in his car. Without a car it would have seemed to me practically impossible to get there, the highest point on the highest hill; and yet the road was dotted with people of all nations climbing to sign their names in the Soviet book.

The house was a large one in late Victorian style. It reminded me of the old Potter Palmer house on Lake Shore Drive in Chicago. The Soviet Ambassador, Paniushkin, received his guests in the hall. For conversational purposes he relied upon a tall, affable secretary by the name of Federenko, who spoke excellent Chinese and English—both learned, I believe, in the Soviet Union. Federenko took Lattimore and me into a room on the right. I had not been there more than ten seconds before I realized that I had stumbled into the wrong place. It was full of cabinet ministers, generals and the like, all of the highest rank. Wang Hsueh-chieh, the Minister of Information, took pity on me and remarked kindly: "Do not be alarmed. There is no protocol on these occasions." I sat at the end of the table beside a sensible-looking Chinese lady who turned out to be Mme Feng Yü-hsiang, wife of the Christian General. Her vast, good-humored husband, when reminded of the fact that I had visited him at Loyang in 1927, professed to remember it, which was very Christian of him. The ranking Russian general proposed a toast, drunk in Caucasian wine, to Mme Feng; there were Russian *zakuski* on the table, and I nibbled at some ham, feeling that I had no right to it. As soon as there was any movement at all in the room I slipped out to the hall and found my way to the other rooms, where the lesser fry, my colleagues and such, stood about with glasses in their hands, speaking of the news from Moscow and occasionally toasting the Red Army.

There were some Chinese Communists at the party; I met one. Although their organization was illegal as a party, it was tolerated in some respects. For example, they published a newspaper, although it was not allowed to call itself a Communist party organ and was submitted to the heaviest censorship. The Eighth Route Army, disowned and unpaid since January 1st, nevertheless had a representative at Chungking who was more or less official; he was Chou En-lai, member of the Central Committee of the Chinese Communist party. But at the same time nobody was allowed to travel out to the Eighth Route Army and nobody from Yenan was allowed to come to Chungking. The ambiguity of the position, the hostility that never died but was covered over by bland assurances, the combination of internecine war and official courtesy, were baffling to the observer, no matter how deeply rooted in the traditions of Chinese politics.

The Communists seemed to be chiefly in a room which was reserved for the Sino-Russian cultural relations society. I saw no Americans there. The embassies had attended this celebration in force, naturally, and our American military and naval attachés wore their full-dress uniform for the first time in many months. The whole scene was curious in the extreme; one thought of the guns at Kalinin and Tula, of what it must be like today on the road to Samara. The Tass correspondent told me I should never say Samara any more: I should say Kuibyshev.

Lattimore took me, with Edgar Mowrer and R. A. Gunnison, down to the city to our next appointment, which was lunch with the Minister of War, Ho Yin-ching. By leaving the crowded Russian Embassy rather early, we missed, I believe, the ceremonial visit of Chiang Kai-shek. Lunch with the Minister of War proved to be a feast—not altogether in honor of the twenty-fourth anniversary of the Soviet revolution, if I judged this gentleman's politics correctly, but a feast just the same. General Ho, imperturbable and uncommunicative, was said to be the only person in China, save one, who exercised any great power. His other guests included the Roman Catholic bishop of Nanking (Chinese) who had spent ten years in Rome and spoke fluent Italian. We had Kweichow food, including a fish which, His Excellency and His Grace said, was often to be found climbing trees in that province. This aroused Edgar's journalistic curiosity and he obtained an authoritative account of the creature, with a detailed drawing by the Minister himself. It looked more like a lizard than a fish to me. I created a rather awkward silence at one moment by saying that the chopsticks at the Soviet Embassy had the Principles of Dr. Sun Yat-sen on them (the four characters, San Min Chu I). There were no characters on the chopsticks at this hospitable table, and my innocent remark therefore seemed, as I noticed with embarrassment, to contain a criticism.

At three we went to the Press Hostel in Edgar's car and collected some other visiting journalists for our interview with the chairman of the Military Affairs Committee, Chiang Kai-shek. It had been arranged that the visitors would see him separately for ten minutes each and that the entire resident foreign press would come in afterward for tea and a prepared statement. This was apparently very unusual; the Generalissimo had seldom received the press all together in this manner.

The house, comfortable but not one of the largest in Chungking, was halfway up another hill. The five visitors waited in an anteroom on one side of the hall while Hollington Tong, head of the press bureau, rather nervously marshaled his forces. He took in Edgar first, me next, Leland Stowe and the other two "in the order of their arrival in Chungking."

The room in which we were successively received used to be, it seemed, the Generalissimo's study. It was now a living room, not of exceptional size, but quite big enough and comfortably furnished. Mme Chiang Kai-shek (Soong Mei-ling) sat in an armchair beside the fire, the Generalissimo in another beside her. Hollington Tong, sitting opposite the Generalissimo, acted as interpreter, with occasional help from Mme Chiang when a word was in question.

My questions were few. I realized that it would serve no useful purpose to examine Chiang himself upon the information of the day; that was available from hundreds of subsidiary sources; the barrier of language ruled out ordinary conversation, in which, whatever the subject, innumerable lights and shades reveal so much more than is said; there remained questions of bare principle. I asked the Generalissimo how he considered that the principles of Sun Yat-sen, upon which the whole Chinese national revolution was based, were being applied in 1941. He replied that the effectiveness of the principles was fifty percent upon the first (nationalism), thirty percent, upon the second (the people's rights) and twenty percent, upon the third (the people's welfare). I remarked that in my ignorance, so long away from China across the far seas, I had supposed the emphasis to be otherwise: that the second principle, for example (the rights of the people), had been much overlooked owing to the exigencies of the war. Chiang replied that my misapprehension was due to distance; that in fact the people were enjoying a wide measure of democratic right, and that district autonomy was being developed, in matters appropriate to it, as never before in China's history. I asked him if he still considered his to be a revolutionary government and he replied that he did.

This was, in substance, the gist of the conversation—a brief exchange, indeed, and one which gave little light. Chiang Kai-shek displayed no sign of discomfort at being reminded of the principles of the Chinese revolution; indeed his expression suggested a certain amusement at the spectacle of a foreigner reviving such forgotten things. His wife, whose acquaintance with the West was considerable, grew a little nervous and interrupted once or twice with vivacity; I had the impression that she did not like the questions or the answers. When my time was up I went out and was succeeded by another (Lee Stowe, I think).

After the separate interviews were over, the resident colleagues arrived for tea and we were summoned back into the big room. Tea was present in a most welcome amplitude. There was a small chocolate cake which I shall long remember (*mille feuille*, it was—I have no idea how the ingredients could have been obtained in Chungking except, perhaps, by air from Burma or Hongkong). Mme Chiang, slender and beautiful in an embroidered Chinese dress, talked with her accustomed animation to a number of my colleagues in succession. Then we all subsided into chairs while the Generalissimo read out a prepared statement on China's war and China's relation to the Russian, British and American efforts.

Late at night, after dinner, Edgar and I succeeded in talking to Chou En-lai, representative in Chungking of the Chinese Communists (officially, of the Eighth Route Army). He had been difficult to find for some days. He told us that it had been over six months since he had been able to see Chiang Kai-shek, that all communication with his headquarters at Yenan had ceased, except for the government radio, and that he was under the closest and strongest surveillance at all times. His house was, in fact, next door to the headquarters of Tai-li, the chief of the Chinese Gestapo. Chou gave evidence of intelligence and humor, a far more sensitive and living organism than Chiang Kai-shek—but, I think, less strong.

There was moonlight on the hills and the two rivers when we walked back to the Chialing Hostel. This had been a crowded day, exceptional even for the most hurried visitor. From these scenes and people, what would abide in the memory tomorrow or next year, what would vanish? Some faces: the immobility of Chiang Kai-shek's head, the contrasting mobility of Chou En-lai; Soong Mei-ling's grace of movement; the mélange at the Russian Embassy; American officers in full-dress uniform. But I thought what would remain longest would be that moment in the morning when the fog lifted, as I was coming up the hill from Lattimore's house and the whole life of the rivers and the hills came out of the mist, the whole life of China maybe, the bowed head, the humble heart, the supreme splendor.

2

What was in reality the position of the Chinese revolution, of the military effort, of the government, of the people? I thought it was, by all the evidence available to me, very different from the beribboned daguerreotype presented in official statements. All of this was neither so clear nor so elevated as democratic opinion in Western countries liked to think. The dictatorship of the generals had paralyzed all democratic processes, even within the fossilized remnants of the Kuomintang; there were pro-Japanese and pro-Nazi sentiments in high government places; repression of the opposition was more cruel (in the sense of physical torture) than anything yet developed in Europe; the currency was slipping into ruin and the people were starving because they could not afford to buy the food that was displayed in every street. It seemed to me that the liberal and democratizing influences upon the Chungking government had a constant, uphill struggle to maintain even the phraseology of progressive rule —and for the reality there was a slender, distant hope.

We had been too ready, in the West, to forget the strong German and Japanese influences that had existed in Kuomintang government circles from 1928 to 1936. These had gone under a cloud when Japan started the war of invasion in 1937; the united front of all Chinese parties was organized, its honeymoon the 1938–1939 period at Hankow; Soviet Russia again became the friend of China, sending supplies and advisers to Chiang Kai-shek's government. But the men who inclined toward the German way of doing things, and had more than an inclination toward making terms with Japan, never vanished from the government; they were still there in very important positions, and it seemed to me that if Germany were to win a real victory over Russia they would probably exert more influence than ever before. Meanwhile the united front had ceased to exist, and although the Communist and semi-Communist armies continued to fight the Japanese, they were blockaded by the central Chinese government in a way which could only indicate the ever-present possibility of civil war.

I had no wish to overstress these dire possibilities. I had, on the contrary, every hope that the democratizing forces might predominate, that the indispensable combination of Russia-China-England-America might be created and that together we might win the war. This has never ceased to be my ruling preoccupation during the years which supplied the material for this book; the book is itself an effort in that direction. But I saw no possible good result from spreading butter and sugar over the truth. It had come to be an established tradition that no American journalist wishing well to China could possibly visit Chungking without going into ecstasies over the beauty of Mme Chiang, the heroic determination of the Generalissimo, the prowess of the Chinese armies and the general nobility of all hands. I thought much of what had been written in this vein was not only nonsense, but harmful nonsense—harmful to those elements in Chinese life which struggled for improvement; harmful to the war effort in its tendency to encourage giving China anything a few generals might ask, without controls or accounting; harm-

ful to the American people in the great task that now falls
upon it, that of achieving a clear-eyed view of the world
in full realization of its immense responsibility.

The main figure in the Chungking government, Chiang
Kai-shek, had certainly displayed a consistent desire to
resist the Japanese and to continue the war under all circumstances. So far the "peace-and-civil war" party (that
which would prefer to make some sort of peace with
Japan and turn its attention to civil war against the Communists) had not dared to oppose him openly on this
ground. But it showed its force in its stranglehold on the
military and political organization, its Gestapo methods
of repression, its control of revenue and disbursement.
Tai-li, head of the Gestapo, was more powerful now than
ever before, and new concentration camps were being
formed all the time. Open admiration of German methods
had been expressed to me by cabinet ministers trained in
Germany, and they—or at the very least two of them—had
no faith in any real help from the democracies or in any
ultimate victory over Germany.

It was salutary to remember that General von Falkenhausen, now Hitler's governor in the Low Countries and
much busied, at just this time, with the execution of hos-
tages, had been one of the most popular and valued members of the Chiang Kai-shek coterie for some years. A whole
school of Chinese generals made it their pleasure to imitate Falkenhausen's methods and manners, shooting people
with the same relish they obtained by breaking a violin
over the violinist's head after a feast. Falkenhausen is said
to have told his friends at the end of his term as military
adviser, when he was recalled to Germany, that he would
see them again "by way of Chinese Turkestan." And it was
my impression that some of them fully believed him—that
is, believed that Germany would conquer Russia and move

east. In that case they would have a surer friend than the democracies, one more congenial to their tastes.

Wonderful as the Chinese people had shown themselves to be in their resistance, and above all in their patient endurance of ills without number, they had never been fortunate in their governments in modern times. The most stable and unifying element in the present Chungking government was undoubtedly the Generalissimo, Chiang Kai-shek, but he had maintained his power these past fourteen years mainly by playing off one section against another, dividing to rule. His course had been governed by no known principle except that of survival. He could torture the Communists one day and call on their help the next without the slightest compunction. He did not seem to care who profiteered on the public funds or who trafficked with the enemy. There were people in his government who maintained communication with Wang Ching-wei at Nanking and through Wang with the Japanese; members of the Chiang and Wang governments even met sometimes, with Japanese blessing, at Hongkong; the Generalissimo ignored whatever he wished to ignore. The structure of the Kuomintang itself, the Chinese National party, had been fossilized, had lost its vitality, its capacity for change, its base in the masses of the people; the same professional clique that took control in 1927 was here today, richer and older and fatter, but essentially the same.

The people were, in fact, without rights, legal, political or social; they were at the mercy of the military in every concern of life. As for their welfare, it had never been worse; they were dying of starvation. The currency had been so frittered away that prices were now completely out of hand. Prices everywhere followed the foreign exchange rate, which in turn had been pushed up by inflation and extravagance. A pair of leather shoes cost 375 Chinese dollars in Chungking, and the monthly wage of a qualified doctor in the National Health Administration was $400. A doctor in the Army Medical Corps was paid $200 a month, which would buy him one shoe and leave a little money over for dissipation. It cost a dollar for a coolie to buy a bowl of noodles. The malnutrition among the people was extreme; the doctors said it was going up every month among the school children. Nevertheless you could buy practically anything you wanted in Chungking if you had the price.

The inflation had reached such heights that it was the merest commonplace to observe that the government's one real resource was the printing-press. Such an inflation was neither directed nor controlled, so far as I could find out; it was not even planned. It simply happened. The government borrowed from one of the four banks which were empowered to issue banknotes; they issued notes to cover, and the price of rice, noodles and tea went sky-high.

With all this desperate misery among the people, great fortunes were being made by the political and military groups. It mattered little about the names of those who grew rich; they were too well known in China and too little known outside. But the "cornering" of certain products, wholesale profiteering on others by means of government contracts, were characteristic of this whole period while the people of China were being subjected to martyrdom. Such things could be found in many countries but not on such a scale or for so long a time; not, above all, in the midst of such national disaster.

The Lend-Lease Act, passed in Washington the preceding spring, now proposed to pour in a great supply of the necessary instruments for the prosecution of the war. It remained to be seen whether this wealth would go the way of China's national wealth or would be discreetly supervised in a way that might guarantee its use, mainly, for the purposes intended. If it were so supervised, it might greatly strengthen the hands of those who genuinely wished to win the war against Japan and make the beginnings of a democratic regime in China; if it were poured into the hands of the generals it would only perpetuate their power.

Among the liberalizing influences around Chiang Kai-shek I counted, first of all, his wife. On some occasions known to me, some of them decisive, she had out-argued the clique who held other views. The Foreign Minister, Quo Tai-chi, was firmly committed to alliance with the democratic powers. On taking office in the summer, after his return from London, he had broken off relations with Germany and Italy. The Minister of War, Ho Yin-ching, was accounted chief of the reactionary group and bore an evil repute among the people. But their opinion counted little, for in this regime there was no machinery for consultation of the people, no elections of any kind and even no meetings of the fossilized Kuomintang for months or years at a time. In fact Chiang Kai-shek told me that even after the war the franchise could not be given to the people, since the "period of tutelage" (Sun Yat-sen's phrase, turned to a use so different) was still in existence.

For the misery of the people the present regime did not even offer the solace of political agitation. Meetings, posters, parades—all that machinery for the excitement of mass feeling—had once formed the spearhead of the Kuomintang's advance over China in the far-off days of 1927. All this was gone. Opponents of the regime said Chiang no longer dared to permit a mass meeting for fear of what the people might do. Whether for this reason or for another, agitation of this kind did not exist. It might seem that a mass meeting would be a poor substitute for a square meal, and yet political experience has shown that it sometimes works very well in just that capacity, given certain conditions. Chungking did not even try it.

All this might suggest that the great revolution of 1911–1927, based upon the principles of Sun Yat-sen, had ended in a regime which amalgamated all the evils it set out to destroy. This was not true, either: the social change had been immense, ideas had been put into the air which would never die. The government at Chungking was far better in its purposes and even in most of its methods than the old war-lord rule. Above all, it was national—that is, it spoke in the name of China and not for one section or group. It contained men and women who would never cease struggling to leave things a little better than they found them. But it seemed to me worth while to point out that they struggled against powerful forces, of which the forces within their own gates were not the least inimical to the true China. The true China, made up of the millions who struggled, suffered and died with smaller recompense than most who pass through life, had not yet found its way. It was doing no service to these suffering millions to flatter their military and political rulers, I concluded, and although it was in America's interest to support them in the struggle against Japan, we ought certainly to do so with our eyes open. If we did so, I thought, we should not only help an incomparable nation to survive but we might even strengthen the best elements in its governing organism as against the worst.

The military situation of the Chungking government was also much misunderstood by the West. Japan's inability to conquer the whole of China had been evident for some time, but this was by no means due to the efforts of the Chungking government's army. At this moment the

Japanese had abandoned Changsha and Chengchow, the two important railway junctions without which their lines, even in long-held territory, were jagged and incomplete. They had narrowly escaped losing Ichang a month earlier; the rice and grain they plundered at Chengchow and Changsha were compensations indeed, but not for their military prestige. After four and a half years of the struggle, Japan was still far from anything like a stabilized position. The Chungking government's authority south of the Yellow and Yangtze Rivers extended through the Japanese lines, behind them and between them; people, goods and even mail circulated right through the Japanese as if they did not exist. The Japanese would occupy a city —Ichang, for instance—and hedge themselves in with strong points and big guns; there they would sit. The Chinese, having no big guns, could not attack them, but the Chinese people could surround them like a hostile sea.

Even so, determined effort on a very great scale could "liquidate the China incident," as General Tojo had promised on taking power in Japan a month earlier. This seemed to be clearly admitted by the competent authorities when they were talking straight (*i.e.*, not for the newsreels). As a rule, Chinese armies had melted away before any Japanese advance. What made many of these advances partial and impermanent was the size of China, which demanded a far larger occupying force than Japan could well spare from the necessities (real or imagined) of a Pacific imperial position. The positive Chinese attack upon Japanese occupying troops took place chiefly by means of guerrilla fighting, the attack upon communications, the "scorched-earth" policy and other methods more closely associated with the Communist armies or with the peasant bands than with the regular forces of the Chungking government.

In Chungking's war—the Resistance War in its official form—the vital point was the Burma Road. If that highway could be cut it was difficult to see how the central government could continue to arm its men and continue the fight. I thought the Japanese were bound to attack the Burma Road soon; I thought they would do so across the province of Yunnan from French Indo-China, where they had lately been concentrating large forces. It did not seem to me possible that the Japanese could fail to cut the Burma Road if they made a determined effort to do so; and once the Burma Road was gone, what could Chungking do?

Up and down, from Rangoon to Kunming to Chungking, I had tried to get some idea of the problems of the Burma Road. It seemed to me that this line of supply governed the whole course of the war. (Now that Japan has long since cut the road I still think so; victory for China must come by the lost lifeline, the lifeline that must be regained.)

The construction of the Burma Road without modern machinery was one of those Chinese miracles worked by patience, stubbornness and vast man-power. Its operation by the time I knew anything of it was a different sort of Chinese phenomenon, less admirable but no less persistent in the history of China: it was inefficient and corrupt. I do not intend to go into detail at this late date upon the methods of tax-collecting, profiteering and extravagance which took such a heavy toll of the goods brought up the road; there is not much use recalling the poor maintenance, confusion of authority and lack of control which made the Road business—which was of course the liveliest business in China—formidably uneconomic. It may be enough to say that in the month of October, out of 18,000 tons of material leaving Rangoon on this route, only 1200 got to

Chungking. Of course this was not as bad as it sounded —much of the material was probably intended for other places, and a good twenty-five percent of it was the gasoline normally consumed in the long journey. But even so it gave an idea of the difficulty. This twisting, turning, insecure highway over mountain and plain was within bombing distance for the Japanese in Indo-China and was also, at certain seasons, almost expunged by rain. How could it be strengthened, protected, maintained, its administration corrected, its true purposes guaranteed? This seemed to me one of the main problems of the Lend-Lease policy so far as China was concerned.

I had been delighted to find Americans everywhere— experts in this and that, engineers, builders, doctors, men who would make the supply system work if they were allowed to do so. The Lend-Lease policy was not going to be a blind outpouring of the fruits of American effort; there was every evidence that it would be applied with intelligence. Plans were in the making for a railroad to connect the British-Burmese railhead at Lashio with Kunming, so that the highway need not take the bulk of the traffic—it was to be finished at the end of 1942, an optimum date very remarkable under the circumstances. I feared that this, like so many other plans made under the arrangements obtaining in the summer of 1941, might come to nothing through the almost forgotten possibility that Japan would strike first.

3

I had come to Chungking by a long and devious route. On leaving London in September I had still some hope of going there by way of Russia. At home I found this impossible; I turned quickly to the other course and made my way, after a week in New York and Washington, to San Francisco. The flight from New York to New York was over immense territories, and yet I was able to buy the entire ticket from the Pan-American office opposite the Grand Central Station, over the counter, cash down and no questions asked, just as if it were a ticket to the nearest suburb.

My way led by Honolulu, Canton Island, New Caledonia, New Zealand (Auckland), Australia (Sydney) and then up by Townsville and Darwin to Surabaya, Batavia, Singapore, Bangkok, Rangoon, Kunming and Chungking. It was Pan-American Clipper to New Zealand, British Imperial Airways (a Sunderland flying boat) from there to Australia, British again to Surabaya, Dutch to Batavia and to Singapore, British again to Bangkok and Rangoon, where (with C.N.A.C.) I rejoined the American system. Such a journey has only been possible in the past two years, and the route I took was still new. I think mine was only the third or fourth regular flight to New Zealand. The way led over the enormous, empty South Pacific to the tiny coral atoll, lost in the blue sea, which bears the name of Canton Island. I thought the startling comfort of the Pan-American Hotel in this remote isle was a triumph of organization, just as the Clipper flights themselves were. At Nouméa in New Caledonia we were lodged in a yacht that had once belonged to an American millionaire; on the little island we had our first glimpses of Melanesian types, black men with hair fuzzed out and sometimes dyed. There was a French boy on the Clipper who was going out to Nouméa to take some post under De Gaulle's administration there. *"Je n'ai pas besoin de passeport ici,"* he said with tears in his eyes. *"Je suis en France."* The French flag was flying over the customs shed and the familiar blue uniform was in control here. New Caledonia, I learned, was rich in nickel and chrome; the product went chiefly to the United States; yet it was Australian soldiers who had made possible the transfer of administration to De Gaulle's men.

In New Zealand, just then entering upon its spring season, I made some attempt to see elements of the war effort —the training schemes, naval base, R.N.Z.A.F.—but what I remember best of my brief visit is the blossoming of peach, nectarine and plum trees, the look of the countryside, like England in a somewhat more spacious way, and the transplanted English flowers in cottage gardens along the road. I thought there was an air of Englishness over everything here, the voices, the food, the newspapers and the houses. Swift and fleeting impressions, these are worth little; and yet the contrast between New Zealand and Australia is so striking that it must suggest the complexity of developments which differentiated, in a time so short, people of identical or similar stock.

In Australia I was flown about to R.A.A.F. stations and army camps, had—like the lady in the song—a bird's-eye view of Sydney, and proceeded northward by way of Townsville and Darwin. Townsville with its row of palms against the silver sea was probably more distinctively Australian than anything else I saw. We stayed there a day and a night because of engine trouble, and I recall its somewhat dingy shopping street and its gorgeous moonlit palms better than most things along the way.

Darwin, on the other side of the aboriginal forests and deserts of Western Australia, was hotly tropical again; the seasons were not only reversed in these latitudes, but were closely telescoped together by the speed of our journey. The Australian government was spending great efforts on the construction of a base at Darwin, greatly to the distaste of the troops stationed there; they used to break the shop windows in the little town with great regularity, rioting punctually at ten o'clock when the beer-halls closed, and the sound of their discontent went on far into the night.

In Java, both at Surabaya and Batavia, I tried not only to get an idea of the extent of the Dutch defenses but also of their position with respect to the inhabitants of the islands. I knew perfectly well that the five thousand islands of the Netherlands Indies were of many races and spoke many languages; I was aware that notions of self-government in such a congeries were always a little illusory; and yet I felt uneasy at the Dutch refusal to take Indonesian Nationalism seriously. Even if it were true that the Indonesian Nationalists were "a tiny minority" (as nationalists are in most countries), this did not make them negligible. And the Dutch had indeed proved that they were not negligible by taking repressive measures against them. The rights of free speech and free assembly had been abolished in the Netherlands Indies, and some hundreds of Nationalist leaders had been "isolated"—that is, sent into exile to the remote outer islands. These things revealed, clearly enough, the seriousness with which the Dutch government itself regarded the Nationalist movement. And yet the officials in Surabaya and Batavia affected to take that movement lightly. It was the same old story: "a handful of agitators," as in Ireland, India, Egypt, were held responsible for the unquestioned revival of national feeling. No imperialist power has ever yet been able to see that the "handful of agitators" only obtain their influence by virtue of the fact that they express emotions (not to put it any higher) which are none the less general because most of those who feel them are ignorant and poor. A country may be disunited on every other subject, may be indeed quite incapable of orderly self-government, and yet may achieve a passionate and singleminded unity on the single subject of national independence.

My Dutch friends in Batavia did introduce me to some Indonesian nationalists of the more conservative faction, who introduced me to others; after a few days I began to perceive that there was plenty of material here for trouble even in the rollicking times of peace. Now that Japan openly threatened the peace of South Asia, was there any real sense in ignoring the existence of a national problem? Would not the frustrated nationalism, even of a "handful of agitators," be a powerful aid to the invader?

I should like to reprint, without change or comment, the article I sent to the New York *Herald Tribune* on October 15, 1941, about the general situation in the Indies:

BATAVIA, October 15th—No part of the Pacific defense system is of more vital concern to the United States than the Netherlands East Indies, both politically and economically. An unfriendly power in control of this immense empire would be able to crowd us out of East Asia, cut us off from the essential supplies of rubber and tin, strangle the Philippines and annihilate our eastern trade. Since the conquest of Holland in May, 1940, these five thousand islands have been cut adrift from their mother country and have been—ostensibly—easy prey for a powerful neighbor.

But there was a hitch in that scheme. The Indies are neither Indo-China nor Siam; they are, fortunately, a good deal farther away from any important Japanese base than those countries, and they are governed by some hard-headed Dutchmen who have no wish or will to enter Japan's "co-prosperity sphere." Indeed the phrase "co-prosperity sphere" becomes the weirdest sort of joke when applied to Japan and the Indies. The Indies are rich beyond the dreams of avarice; except good coal and iron, they produce practically everything important to their existence and for a huge export trade; they have so much rice that they feed the densest population on the globe (on the island of Java). The Japanese "prosperity" which this realm of plenty is supposed to share consists of famine, war and pestilence; the proposal is rather as if a pauper should say to Croesus, "let me share my wealth with you."

The Dutch Indies Government went through two protracted series of negotiations with the Japanese—first with Mr. Kobayashi, who tried the high hand and the conqueror's manners; then with the skillful and experienced diplomatist Kenkichi Yoshizawa. Both sets of conversations came to nothing. Japan was asking concessions and pledges which would, in effect, have mortgaged the wealth of the Indies to her enterprises. The Indies Government said its last word on June 6th of this year, in a note which amounted to plain refusal. Since then there have been some talks about the application of the "freezing" orders, but objectively speaking the trade between the two countries has come to an end. Yet we may be sure that this lull is temporary, created by the situation in Russia and China. Prince Konoye has said that the Indies are a question of "life or death" for the Japanese nation, and there can be no doubt that when opportunity offers Japan will try again, either by threats or (if possible) by force.

These islands, with a population of seventy millions, produce vast quantities of petroleum, rubber, tin, sugar, coffee, tea, cotton, kapok, quinine and tobacco, with profitable smaller exports of sisal, vegetable oils (copra and palm-oil chiefly), nutmeg, pepper and cassava. The spices and indigo which once made the Indies desirable to the navigators of Portugal and Spain have been succeeded by all this range of agricultural and mineral production, partly because nature so ordered it, and partly because the Dutch colonial administration, after many false starts and periods of stagnation, has for the past fifty years been one of the most enlightened and competent in the world. It may almost be said that the Indies are the only real colony in Asia, since only here do the Europeans come and live and work and stay. The 250,000 Dutchmen in the archipelago are few in comparison to the seventy million total population, but they are distinguished from other European colonists in that they are (for the most part) here to stay; a very considerable number of them were born here; they belong to the coun-

try. In the unguessable future, if the Indies survive the storms
that are at hand, it seems that the autonomy to which all races
look forward can only be made feasible by the ability and
energy of the Dutch, working in collaboration with the Indonesian majority.

Java, the "pearl of the Indies," is still, of course, the heart
and soul of this empire. It has forty million people in an area
of little more than fifty thousand square miles, and although
many of these millions are what the West would call desperately poor, their standard of living is appreciably higher than
that in other tropical countries of Asia. The island can feed
them all, and does; it even exports rice to the Outer Isles. Some
of the Outer Isles were only brought under effective Dutch
rule during the present century, although they have been
Dutch on the map for three hundred years. From upper
Sumatra, on the Straits of Malacca, to upper Celebes, near the
Philippine Islands, the whole three thousand miles of archipelago are now fully administered by the Dutch under constitutional arrangements which have undergone a whole series
of reforms in the past thirty years. The system differs considerably from that of the British or French; it reposes in general upon local authorities and native custom; it has seldom
taken a military character for more than a few weeks at a
time, and it has not been much harassed by native national-
isms. At present there is no freedom of speech or assembly,
the censorship is severe and the police are powerful; but even
before these emergency rules came into being the Nationalist
movement (active in 1921–1927) had gone into a decline. In
spite of their historic tradition of exploitation, the Dutch in the
present century have distinguished themselves by an eagerness to hear the native's complaint and to satisfy it. Their
record in education and hygiene, although they got off to a
late start, has been admirable for some decades past, and they
have lately been clearing off a good many of the relics of their
age-old dualism, the system under which there was one law
for the native and another for the European. In the result, at
the present crucial moment, they govern in comparative internal peace.

Their defense problem is, of course, of primary interest to

any American visitor. From what I have seen I should say that they are determined to resist any attempt at conquest, that they have been working hard since May, 1940, to build up their defensive power, and that—with any luck at all—they could inflict severe damage upon any invading force. I am not, however, sure that they could resist attack on a large scale. It seems to me that Japan's intentions here are restrained not so much by the defensive power of the Indies themselves as by the question of what the Americans and British—particularly the Americans—would do. Here, as elsewhere in the Pacific, the power that immobilizes Japan for the moment is centered at Pearl Harbor, in Hawaii.

By this I do not mean that the defense forces of the Indies are negligible. They are good and they are growing. The naval base at Surabaya is a scene of great activity; ships of almost all sizes are repaired there, motor torpedo boats are built, bombs and torpedoes manufactured. The Indies motor torpedo boat (smaller than the English or German varieties) is an example of Dutch ingenuity: its engines come from old airplanes and its torpedo tubes from old destroyers. American instructors are helping to build up a force of good pilots, Dutch, Indonesian and Chinese-Indonesian. There is a munitions industry up at Bandoeng in the hills, the military headquarters. The beaches have the familiar burden of barbed wire and pill-boxes, not everywhere of course, but in areas where invasion may be expected.

But it would be very dangerous to assume that these measures guarantee any form or degree of safety. I have read in print, and have heard from responsible American officials, statements to the effect that the Indies are receiving "the very latest type" of American airplanes and war supplies under the Lend-Lease Act. This is not true. The American material delivered to the Indies is of obsolete or obsolescent type and it is all paid for in cash. The only difference the Lend-Lease Act has made so far is that instead of paying seventy per cent of the purchase price in advance, the Indies Government now pays only fifteen per cent. The American airplanes I have seen here would not be considered fit for operational duty in any theatre of war where they would have to encounter first-class aviation. They consist of Martin bombers, Brewster fighters ("Buffaloes"), some Curtiss P-40's, and the like. It may be true that they are equal to known Japanese types in performance, but they have not the speed, height, armor or armament to go against good contemporary airplanes of the German or English standard. I have yet to see any reason why we should assume that the Japanese have not now, or cannot obtain, good modern airplanes from Germany. If they have Junkers and Messerschmitts, either from Germany or made in Japan under German direction, they certainly can outclass the machines we are sending out here.

The best plane we have sent here is, without a doubt, the ever-beautiful Catalina (Consolidated's PBY-2). Its powerful line and superb soaring flight make the old Dorniers and Fokkers of the sea patrol look a little shabby. But even the Catalina, wonderful though it is, is not a combat plane. It can patrol these seas with the utmost efficiency and report any approaching fleet, but it cannot stop it. For that essential operation the Dutch are relying principally upon American products which are not up to the contemporary standard. I realize how these things get into a hopeless tangle of priorities and preferences, but if the Indies are (as I believe) a region of vital importance to us, we should certainly make an effort to sell its government our best airplanes rather than our second or third best. No fleet and no army could effectively defend all of these islands; the defense must be mainly in the air; the fact is realized on all sides. It is therefore supremely important to strengthen the air force here before next spring; if it is not done, we run a staggering risk.

The Indies air force now has about fifty fields throughout the islands, and the planes would be well used. Even with the present material—which is, of course, good, although not equal to German or English machines—the defense would be vigorous. But the calculations I have heard seem to be based upon the notion that Japan has nothing up her sleeve, no really good planes, for instance; and such an assumption seems to me unreasonable. Why, if this is so, are there so many hundreds of German engineers in Japan? Have they gone there to admire the landscape?

Singapore was scarcely more reassuring than Java. A superb confidence reigned, but even the most cursory look during the first day or two showed that the great naval base was not secure. I know that it was in Singapore that I first became convinced that the Japanese would strike soon, that there was no other course left to them, and that their plans were already made. The resignation of Prince Konoye and the accession of General Tojo had not signified much to me, although the language of the new Premier was strong enough. But when I began to hear, on the best possible authority, of the movement of large Japanese forces to Indo-China and Hainan; when I related this to the warlike language of those who governed Japan; when I considered how difficult it was for the Japanese, more even than for other empire-dreamers, to retrace their steps; then, putting all together, I came to the conclusion that they would attack before long. At this time (mid-October), I remember, my guess was that they would attack in force across the province of Yunnan with a view to cutting the Burma Road; I expected them to occupy Siam and perhaps make a thrust across Burma, even though this meant war with Great Britain and presented great risk of war with the United States. I had not yet reached the conclusion (which I did a few weeks later) that it would be more logical for them to take on the whole job at the same time and gain the advantages of surprise and superior preparation.

Singapore was a mass of contradictions. It had a vast naval base, one of the largest in the world, and it had no navy. The naval fortress was defended chiefly by land and air arms of no great strength. Sir Geoffrey Layton, the Admiral, made occasional broadcasts in which he promised that ships would come in case of need; but in the meantime any child could see that the naval base was

almost idle. Australians, New Zealanders, British and
Indian troops had lately come to defend Malaya, but they
were new to the country and were only now (in October)
beginning to dig themselves into positions to resist attack.
Attack would not be easy—I thought it would be impossible—across the dense jungle, but it could be made down
the main roads unless these were thoroughly protected by
air. Most of the problem of defense seemed to come back
to air power.

I thought (assuming that adequate air power could be
gathered in Singapore swiftly) that it was unlikely the
Japanese would attack here until they had gathered up
the easier and riper plums. And I was disturbed by what
seemed to me the main contradiction in the whole business: that is, that Singapore was a naval base, and therefore by definition a base for offensive and not defensive
action. To build so great a base and then treat it purely
defensively was a sort of military nonsense. I concluded
that the defensive frame of mind was the result of circumstances the world over—the loss of all continental
Europe, the terrible strain on the British navy everywhere,
the legacy of 1940. Nobody spoke of Singapore as a base
for attack; the whole talk was of how it could be defended.

The city was over two-thirds Chinese in population, and
as was usual in the Pacific, these parsimonious and indefatigable people had obtained control of many undertakings and gained great wealth. The jealousy of less enterprising peoples showed itself in anti-Chinese sentiment,
as in the Indies and Philippines. But this would be of
small use to the Japanese, for anti-Japanese sentiment was
even stronger.

One day at a jungle river north of Singapore I watched
some Australians loading goods on a motor launch. It was
a steaming hot, dark green, broad-leaved Douanier Rous-

seau sort of jungle, in which many monkeys were to be seen a little way up the road. The Australians were loading their launch to take it downstream to their post near Mersing. I saw green beans and California oranges and many other good things—exotic here—loaded on the boat. The brown, lean, half-naked Australians set off in the tropical afternoon while a handful of natives, some Malay and some Chinese, looked on from the muddy bank. The Australians were singing very loudly, and somewhat off-key, "Sweet Adeline." Their raucous dissent with their surroundings was, I think, the pure essence of Singapore— jazz dancing on the edge of the jungle, unthinking but offensive racial pride, a general clash of unrelated forces and a great unawareness of destiny.

I enjoyed life in the city itself. Diana Cooper and I used to wander in the shopping streets in the mornings and buy trinkets, carrying on conversation by sign-manual with the amiable, fat and money-wise Singapore Chinese. I discovered that many of them—perhaps most—had never seen China, but they contributed large sums to Chinese war collections and relief funds, and sometimes their children returned to China. One of the finest Chinese I knew in Chungking, Dr. Robert Lim of the Army Medical service, was born a Singapore man and returned in adult life to China because he felt, in this hodge-podge of the Orient, like a man without a country.

There were streets in the city that looked like Venice (and smelled like it, too); there were others that suggested a provincial town in France; there was a pompous seafront street like the Bund at Shanghai. The wealth of the foreign inhabitants (by which I mean those who were neither Chinese, Malay nor Hindu) was great, and I entered some houses which startled me by their opulence and bad taste. Nowhere was there any sign of wartime

rationing. It irritated me exceedingly to see English goods
in profusion, cigarettes and clothing and whisky and gin,
things which were either severely rationed or next to impossible to get in England. The Empire, as usual, had to
maintain its prestige, and did so by exporting to such
mushroom excrescences as Singapore and Hongkong all
the English-made goods that English people had to do
without.

Edgar Mowrer had traveled with me from Java, and
from Singapore on we operated as a team. In Bangkok
we both received very strongly the impression that Japan's
arrangements had already been made; certain members
of the government to whom we talked made no secret of
it. Prince Varnvaidya, a member of the royal family who
was adviser to the Foreign Office and of great power in
the government, told us there would be resistance to a
Japanese occupation "for the sake of our posterity—merely
to prove that Thailand was once a nation." In Rangoon
we were given an even dourer account of the state of
affairs: Burma was more defenseless than any other country we had been through, and moreover the population
was so venomously anti-British that it would welcome a
Japanese occupation. Winston Churchill's photograph in
the newsreel theatres was hissed; Hitler's was applauded.
The intelligence officer who told me this also said he was
far more worried about the Burmese population than he
was about the Japanese. He was at least half right, which
was more than could be said for a number of officials in
those regions.

From Rangoon we went up the Mandalay railroad as
far as Taungoo, where Colonel Claire Chennault's volunteer force of fighter pilots had been collected. The existence of this force—the American Volunteer Group—was
at the time a great secret and Chennault exacted from us

a promise not to speak of it publicly or in print. This promise may be considered liquidated by now in a spate of newspaper and magazine stories about the A.V.G., the "Flying Tigers" as they were soon to be called. When I visited them they were still in training, since their men and matériel were far from complete. Joe Alsop, who was acting as Chennault's assistant, took us in and made us guests of the outfit at their quarters on the R.A.F. airdrome. We had a pleasant enough night and day there, but I was moved by certain incidents to observe that the volunteers had no feelings of friendliness toward the R.A.F., the British in general, or, indeed, toward any but Americans. I thought they were in this stage rather undisciplined and much given to complaint; they disliked and distrusted their airplane (the P-40, one of its earlier vintages), and had received full information on the performance of the new Japanese fighter plane called Model Zero. Colonel Chennault was the first person who ever gave me any account of this airplane; he had reconstructed one that fell in the province of Szechuan and knew its quality. He was in process of developing and teaching to his group of young men just those hit-and-run tactics which were afterward, and not very long afterward, to make them famous.

The creation of a first-class fighting force out of this material was a triumph of the personality, will and talent of Claire Chennault. I do not mean to suggest that the human material was not good; far from it; they were good boys, all of them; but they came from all over the United States, had never been together before, had little or no reason for coming here except for adventure or money, and—being totally inexperienced—were apparently always being surprised, unfavorably surprised, by the geography, climate, customs and institutions existing outside of the

United States. To take a new and raw force like this and weld it together, to make of it a first-class air weapon, to give it the spirit and dash and fire of a proud fighting unit, were great achievements. Chennault did it by his talent for command, his imposing personality and his iron will. He knew the P-40 was no match for the Zero, and taught his tactics on that basis. That is, the P-40 could not "fight" the Zero, in the sense that the Spitfire and Messerschmitt had fought over the cliffs of Dover. What it could do, with its limitations in ceiling and rate of climb, was to make one run at a Zero and then disappear with a certain advantage in speed. Chennault created the A.V.G. system there, on the airdrome at Taungoo, basing himself upon the known characteristics of the enemy plane and the known performance of his own. These were unorthodox tactics, but they afterward provided the most brilliant series of victories in air combat which the war in the East was to see.

By some magic which I never fully understood, Edgar or Joe or both of them prevailed upon the C.N.A.C. plane from Rangoon to stop at Taungoo and pick us up for the journey to Kunming. It was satisfactory, somehow—since we all have our vestiges of nationalism—to find that this Douglas plane was run almost exactly like a Douglas passenger plane at home, with the same trim stewardess in uniform and the same neat, aseptic lunch; the only difference was that the stewardess was Chinese. C.N.A.C. (Chinese National Aviation Corporation) was one of the wonders of the war in China, flying over Japanese lines and in Japanese-controlled air, performing miracles of maintenance, coming down on airdromes which would have seemed impossible for a DC-3 at home, and doing the whole thing with almost no losses. (I think one airplane was shot down, no more.)

We saw little of the Burma Road on this journey because C.N.A.C. tactics consisted in seeking cloud cover whenever possible. That journey and the succeeding one to Chungking took place almost entirely in clouds and at considerable altitudes. At Kunming, where Edgar and I spent a day or two, we were lodged in a house of T. V. Soong's just where the Burma Road comes to an end outside the city. Even there, at the end of the Road with the city in sight, there were broken-down trucks all along the way, as—I believe—there were at frequent intervals in the long highway to Lashio.

The arrival of the plane at Chungking was irresistibly exciting. One moment we were in the clouds and the next moment we were swooping down over the unique city between its two rivers. I had never seen Chungking before—in my day in China, years before, anybody who had been up the Yangtze as far as Ichang was accounted an explorer—and I suppose the representative or symbolic quality of its name, a name like a battle-flag, had something to do with the excitement that first view of the city produced in me. I have had some critical things to say of Chinese generals and cliques, but never at any time have I failed in faith or hope in China. Much of that faith and hope had been associated with Chungking, not because the individual leaders at Chungking evoked it, but because China and the Chinese people, greater by far than these transitory shadows, took their last stand in this remote fastness above the Yangtze gorges. There is a pulse in the conscience of the world that throbs into life at the very name of Chungking. Four years of a heart-breaking struggle had washed the national government up upon this hillside; and whatever one thought of the national government, the fact that it *was* national, that it spoke for China and defended the dignity and freedom of Chinese people against the barbarian invader, at times made everything else unimportant. The ten or fifteen minutes necessary to make a landing at Chungking were such a time as this.

But the city would always be remarkable, I think, because it perches on precipitous hills between great rivers, the Yangtze and the Chialing. In my first glimpse of it, it was drenched in rain—a very characteristic downpour. Our plane landed on the extremely short concrete strip built on an island in the Yangtze; I think it is not much more than 2,000 feet in length, which would not be considered safe for landing a Douglas in America. Our pilot brought us to a stop just when I thought we were going to slide on into the river; we got out into the torrent of rain. From this island across to the city in a boat, and from the landing place up the thousand steps to the top, we absorbed enough rain-water for any ordinary season. Edgar, the most cheerful of traveling companions, kept up a fire of comment on the weather, our fellow-travelers, our destination and our plans. Jimmy Wei from Hollington Tong's office had come to meet us and tried to get me into a sedan chair for the journey up the hillside; I knew my own weight much too well to yield, and proceeded up the steps at a spirited and very ill-advised clip, arriving at the top, exhausted, long before our luggage did. With the aid of Lattimore, who had been on the plane from Kunming and had a car waiting, we arrived at last, soaked to the skin and chattering with cold, at the Chialing Hostel.

The discomfort of the life of my press colleagues in Chungking was considerable. The Press Hostel, a collection of mud huts, had been bombed and rebuilt more than once, I believe; this was where most of the regular Chungking correspondents lived. There were young people of great quality among them—Betty Graham, who had made a tremendous journey through Honan and Shansi during the preceding few months and had seen some of the fighting at Ichang, a girl with flaxen hair and innocent eyes whom you would never expect to wander so far from home; Mack Fisher, the U.P. correspondent, who saw all and knew all and did a regular day-in-and-day-out job of considerable difficulty; Jack Belden, most remarkable of all in some ways, who spoke floods of highly convincing Chinese and had friends in most quarters. These and others were in Chungking not for the job, which was not worth it, but because they felt, beyond all criticism, the thing I have already associated with Chungking: the faith and hope in China. In the effort which many people in all parts of the world have been making to relate things which should be related, to achieve associations of the like-minded, of the threatened and of the attacked, in an effort to prevent the enslavement of our common humanity to the Fascist conspiracy, these young newspaper people who stuck to China played no small part. They were among those who sometimes make me proud of my profession. In the battered town on the rainy hills above the muddy water, in the bombs and the summer's heat and the winter's cold, they were—just these few young people—a significant token. Their existence was a homage paid to China.

4

In Hongkong, purse-proud and contented Hongkong, I saw Mme Sun Yat-sen again after many years. She was living in a very modest retirement outside the city on the Kowloon side; she had never been willing to share in the great wealth of her brothers and sisters and was in possession of a motor car at this moment only because her brother T. V. had left it to her. (Once when some patriotic Chinese bought a car by subscription and presented it to her, Soong Ching-ling sold it and gave the money to the hospital funds.) Her grace and beauty were changeless, and again—as in 1927—I marveled at the iron will that could be housed in such fragility. She had made no compromises. In the years since 1927 all of her relatives had governed China—a circumstance they owed primarily to her—but she had never been a part of their scheme of things since she could not adopt their views. She was without influence upon either the Kuomintang or her own relatives. She made but one attempt to speak to a high Kuomintang gathering, on her one visit to Chungking, and urged upon them a return to the principles of Sun Yat-sen. When she had finished speaking, Wu Te-chen told the assembled delegates that Lady Sun was ill, and that this must be much regretted. Her sisters, Mme Kung and Mme Chiang, her brother T.V., her brothers-in-law and her nephews and nieces all together formed the most formidable political family in China, but Soong Ching-ling, upon whom their fortunes had been built, played no part in it.

She did not like living in Hongkong, a British Crown Colony, but she had no place in Chungking territory and no possibility of carrying on her work there. She was indefatigable in relief work, particularly for the guerrillas and others who received no official help from Chungking or elsewhere. Her dislike for luxury, ostentation, self-advertisement and vulgar personal ambitions came in part from natural good taste, but all of her ideas had been vitalized by her brief marriage to Sun Yat-sen. At the end of his life, at the beginning of hers, she had been married to the Founder of the Republic, and the social democracy (to give it Western terminology) of his point of view became her rule of life and politics. She had wanted to see the Kuomintang a national and social revolutionary party with roots in the broad masses of the people; its degeneration into a sort of Chinese Tammany Hall was the tragedy of her life. These things were known, and much more; no figure in China received the spontaneous respect of all men as did Soong Ching-ling.

What I valued most in the privilege of her friendship, speaking purely selfishly, was the justification of wider and more general faiths. She was an ever-fixed star that looked on tempests and was never shaken. Time, peril and confusion had no powers over her. Like a star, like a flower, she obeyed the laws of her nature and achieved all unconsciously the natural perfection of star or flower, things existing, things true for ever. I shall know in 1960, if we both live so long, what Mme Sun is thinking about the difficulties of that time in her own country; her purposes, like her austerities, will never break down. Thus it has been to me, at wide intervals of time and space, a sort of reassurance about humanity itself to have known her, to have heard her soft voice speak words simple, sincere and true, to know that such dedication is possible.

Hongkong itself, the great, rich city, overflowing with unrationed goods from England—all those cigarettes, all that whisky for the Japanese!—made no great appeal to me aside from the beauty of its situation. The authorities did not seem to think it could be defended against Japanese attack; its water supply problems were enough to make defense impracticable. Yet they were making preparations for defense, hastily and rather badly—enrolling the Chinese, for example: a thing which should have been done a year or two before, if at all. I thought it a doomed city, and marveled at the composure with which men of good sense made plans for next spring or next year. It was with considerable relief that I succeeded in getting onto the Sikorsky Clipper on November 12th and flew to Manila. Of this brief revisiting, much would evaporate from my mind before I had gone far: all this was too much like a photograph taken from the air. Yet I knew that one moment would remain in my memory as long as I should live. That was the moment when I stood on the hillside at Chungking on the seventh of November and watched the sun lift the mist from the river. What is illusion none can say, and the claim I am about to make is great: but in that fragment of time, as the coolies bore their intolerable burdens, as the chant came up the hillside, as river and hill emerged to life, it seemed to me that I could feel the beating of the heart of China.

# 8. Our War

THE PROBLEMS OF THE PHILIPPINES seemed to me downright trivial when they were set against the great passion and pain of China. My feeling, as I wrote to the New York *Herald Tribune* on November 19th, was that the Filipinos' contribution to the solving of Asia's problems would be small. "The new day in Asia will not rise here. Whatever the fortunes of the war to which (I believe) we are all inexorably committed, the words of Kipling's barracks-room song are truer than he thought: the dawn comes up like thunder, in fact, out of China 'cross the bay."

It was with genuine relief that I took the Clipper from Manila to go home. I was filled with apprehensions and had seen nothing (outside of China) to allay them. By now I was quite certain that Japan intended to make war soon. I said so at every stop across the Pacific and at San Francisco and New York on my return. I thought the attack would be formidable and would have great successes. The long days of the Clipper journey, with an enforced stay on Wake Island in the blue and summery sea, gave some respite from these somber anticipations and remain vivid in my memory. To start with, the passengers were not at all forthcoming. Some spoke not a word from Manila to Guam; others spoke to one or two acquaintances and to nobody else; the ferry pilots—there were parts of four bomber crews aboard—chiefly slept. They had been too gay and noisy the night before to feel talkative today. We had had a false start from Manila. The Clipper had

absorbed all its passengers and luggage at the Cavite
seaplane base and started its run at about half past three
in the morning. It made a longish run, tugging to get off,
and then the second starboard engine emitted a decisive
noise and ceased to function.

"Plug," the ferry pilots said to each other; this was on
the night of the false start, when they were feeling gay
and talkative.

It was all repeated the next morning, except that this
time the excitement of departure was lacking. The Clipper
took off with something like a maximum load, waddled
into the air like an elephant and set its course for Guam.
After the dense and humid heat of Manila it was pleasant
to climb into the upper air and feel more or less cool again.
I had lived in a refrigerator in Manila—what they call an
air-conditioned room, but it seems much icier there than
elsewhere—and my days had been spent in an agitating
alternance between that and the city's heat. On a really
breathless evening it was my custom (like so many others
in Manila) to pass rapidly from my refrigerator to the
equally refrigerated cathedral of Jai Alai, there to eat and
drink and watch the Basque pelota players under the
highly modern dome. The passage across the city always
seemed like a warm bath.

Well, that was over. I thought of Manila, and of Don
Manuel Quezon in his palace, and of various friends there.
I remembered the delegation of schoolboys who came to
ask me what they ought to do in air raids. I had told them
to go to their local office of civilian defense and they said
there was none. Quezon in emphatic, clipped accent, his
violet silk necktie and his fresh violet boutonnière quiver-
ing in sympathy, leaned across the luncheon table. "Either
we shall have war immediately, very soon, or it will never
come at all." The great sleepy city, with no anti-aircraft

guns and no air-raid shelters, spoke of war day and night, in the shop as in the palace, in the club and on the street. An army wife, a very amusing woman, had said at a cocktail party only two nights before: "Evacuate? Catch me doing it. It's sheer heaven here for an ageing female. Two or three hundred men to every woman. I'm staying." The Basque pelota players at the Jai Alai, when I was introduced to them one night, all inquired eagerly after Ernest Hemingway, of whom they knew only that he was their principal American friend. Douglas MacArthur, striding up and down in his shaded office within the walls of the old city, emphasized his every statement with gesture and ornate imagery: he harkened and heard, coming nearer every hour, the trumpets of immortality. Mr. Sayre, the High Commissioner, in gentle, thoughtful words, deprecated it all: it was all so unnecessary and at the same time improbable. He did not really believe it. "You journalists," he had the air of saying, without ever putting it so rudely into words, "are always alarmists."

We had our usual Clipper meals at the usual frequent intervals. Time is so fluid on these journeys that I have long since given up the attempt to change my watch more than once a day. You eat when you are fed, and let the stewards decide whether to call it breakfast, lunch or dinner. The passengers never failed to do justice to the meals no matter how often they occurred. The ferry pilots displayed a rare talent for finding places to sleep. When I went back into the tail of the ship to get some cigarettes out of my overcoat I found three or four of them there, rolled up in blankets on the naked metal floor.

It was in the middle of the afternoon, as it seemed to us, when the stewards went the rounds of the windows, blacking them out. This blackout consisted of pulling down the curtains and fixing them at the bottom. They remained loose at the sides, and many passengers shame-lessly gawked through the crack thus provided. We swooped down through the clouds and alighted on the smooth blue water of the seaplane base at Guam; the amateur blackout was lifted, and we looked out upon the scurrying launch of the Pan-American company.

The passengers were taken ashore by boat and released into a customs and immigration shed. It was warm on shore, but not as hot as in Manila. Officers in khaki sat behind two desks in the shed, checking our names off a list, marking our nationalities. Except for a mysterious Swiss, a Chinese general and a Siamese jeweler (at least he said he was a jeweler), we were, I believe, all Americans. In the rather awkward group of officers and passengers, standing in wait, I became aware of a smart figure, all white and gold. At first I was too dazzled by the starchy, spotless white and the gleaming gold to see the face above it, or to realize that I was being addressed.

"I am Captain Todd," the apparition said. "I am A.D.C. to the Governor. He sent me to meet you and ask if you would dine with him tonight."

This honor befell me through the kind offices of a major in Manila, friend of Quezon and head of the telephone company, who had cabled ahead. I accepted it promptly, and, having checked in at both official desks, walked up the hill from the customs shed with Captain Todd. I was ashamed of my dirty khaki shirt and shorts, as of my two days' beard.

"I'll have time to shave and change my clothes, won't I?" I asked the dazzling officer. "I don't know how much time we've lost or gained, and maybe it's tomorrow so far as my watch can tell."

"The luggage will be coming up to the Pan-American Hotel and you'll have some time," Captain Todd said.

"Maybe you'd like a drink while we wait for it. The palace is on the other side of the island, at Agaña."

We went into the Pan-American Hotel, a long, low structure built in two wings out from a central lounge. In the room to which I was assigned I sat down on one bed and Captain Todd sat on the other. When he took off his white cap I saw that he had a pleasant grin and a twinkle in his eye. The drinks arrived and I felt better.

"That *fourragère* around your shoulder is pretty impressive," I said. "How do you rate that? I have to put on my dark glasses to look at it."

"It's pretty hot stuff, don't you think?" he said. "I get fifteen dollars a month extra for it. The A.D.C. to a governor can wear a gold *fourragère*. Properly speaking these are called *aiguillettes*."

Then he went off into an explanation of who could wear what *fourragère*, but it was a little technical for me; I thought perhaps he had mistaken me for George Fielding Eliot.

"It's all I can do to tell a general from a sergeant," I said. "Shall we have another drink and do you think the baggage is coming?"

The bag was delivered in due course, but we had had time for three drinks while we waited. By this time I was feeling less dirty, and with any encouragement I might have presented myself at the Palace unwashed. Captain Todd's reverence for his Governor dispelled any such notions. According to him, the Governor was the kindest and best of men, exercising regal powers in equal, moderate justice. In Guam the executive, legislative and judicial powers were vested in one person, the representative of the United States, Captain McMillin, U.S.N. I shaved and changed into my whitest Manila sharkskin suit.

When we emerged into the lounge of the Pan-American

Hotel most of the bomber crews had already washed and changed. Many of them wore violent Hawaiian shirts, green and orange and blue and red, with shorts or slacks of almost any color. All this riot of habiliment gave the hotel lounge a look of the musical comedy stage. Captain Todd saluted some of them and we went out to get into his car. As we drove across the island in the brief and opulent sunset he told me about Guam, his Governor and his job. It was a paradisiacal island, with an equable climate, agreeable inhabitants and no income tax. The Chamorros, natives of the island, were the best-looking and probably the cleverest of the Pacific island peoples, a mixture of Polynesian and Filipino and Spanish, with some touch of American navy added in the past few generations. The inhabitants had no political rights or functions, all power being lodged in the Governor. Captain Todd, as A.D.C. to the Governor, was also chief of police for the island and head of the insular intelligence.

"It's a wonderful job, really," he said, his whole face crinkling with laughter. "I get reports on what everybody's doing, all over the island. And then maybe I'll see them the next day at the club and I have to pretend I don't know what they've been up to. It's pretty funny, sometimes. Now that the women have all been moved back to the States it isn't so funny any more, but it used to be. And then I try cases, too, in the police court."

He told me the story of the Spanish Governor, who, when the American warships approached and fired a broadside, in 1898, sent out his A.D.C. in a launch with a white flag and the message: "The Governor presents his compliments and regrets that he is unable to return the American commander's salute, owing to the lack of gunpowder."

The road led through woods and over hills, through two

or three villages and past the marine officers' quarters, where we stopped for a few minutes to talk to the commander. The villages looked Spanish or Filipino. In Agaña, the capital of the island, the single street was lined with bars entitled "Dirty Dick's" and other humorous names. It seemed that there were about forty thousand Chamorros living on the island, a population very large for this limited area. Captain Todd, leaving the district of bars behind, turned smartly into the Plaza and drew up before the Palace.

It was a Plaza like that of any small provincial town in a Spanish country. One whole side was occupied by the jail; facing this was the Palace; on the third side was the Cathedral and the palace of the bishop; on the fourth side was the barracks and the museum. In the swift tropical dusk the white buildings looked remote and shadowy; we might have been in Andalusia. Captain Todd left the car at the Palace gate; a marine saluted; we went up the broad staircase of Filipino hardwood to a colonnaded terrace above the patio. This terrace apparently connected the two parts of the Palace, and was open to such breeze as stirred on the outer side. The Governor, Captain McMillin, was seated on the terrace playing with a Chow dog. His movements were deliberate, his speech slow, and he seemed a little sad.

As we sat there talking, the Governor told me about a delegation of the islanders who had come to see him a few days before about a routine matter, drains or roads or something of the kind. When they had finished their business the spokesman of the delegation cleared his throat and made a little speech extending his sympathy. Captain McMillin was surprised.

"I am very grateful, but I do not know why I stand in need of sympathy," he said.

"Pardon, sir, but we think you are in the same position that the Spanish Governor was in 1898," the spokesman replied.

Captain McMillin was in the navy, and Captain Todd was in the marines; the difference of rank is great. So was the difference in ages: Todd (addressed as "Charlie" by the Governor) was perhaps twenty-seven or twenty-eight. They talked of some cases he had recently tried in the police court. A Chamorro had illicitly invaded the mined part of the beach and had caused an explosion in which two people were injured. This was typical, and all the cases sounded more like accidents or misunderstandings than crimes.

"It's an innocent island, sort of," Todd said with his cheerful grin. "I've never had a serious case to try since I came here."

We went in to a completely American dinner, in which even the vegetables and fruits were the sea-borne and ice-preserved product of the homeland. Governor McMillin talked a little about the visitors who had passed his way this past summer and autumn, the Duff Coopers, the Luces and others. It was becoming apparent to me that this grave, dignified officer was lonely. His position made it impossible for him to circulate as younger men might; the club and the hotel, the houses of the islanders, were not for him. His daughter had gone home; indeed all American women had been peremptorily ordered out of the smaller islands over a month before, on October 18th. He liked to listen to the radio at night, preferably to San Francisco, although he did not disdain the excellent broadcasts in English which came from Tokyo and Shanghai. It was his custom to drive out alone, for a little air, just before going to bed.

The brass band of the Insular Navy was playing outside

in the Plaza. The only music I recognized was "La Golon-drina," which made me think of similar plazas in Mexico. Just as we finished dinner the concert came to an end and we stood on the balcony to watch the white-clad musi-cians return to barracks. The Governor went in after a bit and tried to get some news on the radio, without success.

"In the event of a Japanese attack, Governor," I asked, "what would happen?"

"A serious attack," he said slowly, "could have only one result. I think you knew that before you asked the question."

After a while I made a move to go home. The Governor, grave and courteous as any of the hidalgos who had pre-ceded him in this palace, walked down the great stairs to the portal with me. The sentries presented arms smartly. Captain Todd, who had always intended to drive me back across the island, made his bid at this point.

"Antonio can take him back," the Governor objected. Captain Todd made a point of it; the Governor yielded, although I think he did not particularly want to be left alone. Todd and I got into the car and drove off without the chauffeur.

"Poor man," I said.

"Why?" Todd asked, steering deftly through the shad-ows on to the village road at the end of the Plaza.

"He wants to go home; he wants a ship to command. He's tired of Guam. Didn't you notice the way he spoke of various people who had been graduated from the Acad-emy with him—most of them admirals now?"

"Yes, but he'll get home in January, if the Japs don't come first, and he'll get a ship. He'll be all right. Nobody ever had a better superior to work for. He's tops."

He took another road and the car began to climb a hill. "I think you ought to see the Officers' Club," he said.

"It's the main thing on the island, especially now that the women have gone home."

We went into a large room which seemed empty, even though there were two tables occupied by about a dozen men. In the introductions I perceived that they were chiefly navy and marine officers, except for two of our ferry-bomber men from the Clipper. I sat down next to the doctor from the mine-sweeper *Penguin* and had a drink. They were getting up a poker game which, by the talk that went on, was intended to last all night.

"What's the use of going home?" one of the construction men inquired. "There's nothing to go home to."

This was a reference to something they mentioned fairly often, the departure of their families some weeks before.

"I think we'd better go along pretty soon," Charlie Todd said. "The Governor would probably like the car. He likes to drive around a little by himself in the evening before he goes to bed."

We left the handful of officers there in the room that seemed so vast and unfurnished. The last discussion I heard among them was about their Thanksgiving Day dinner, which was the next day.

Charlie drove me back swiftly enough, talking the while. He was going home on December 19th, to San Francisco, where his wife was already waiting for him. In all likelihood he would get a turn of duty on a ship, unless the navy pronounced him unfit for service. He had had some complicated and serious trouble with his kidneys; the navy was going to make a "survey" (apparently a thorough examination) and rule upon his case. He had some leave coming; he was going to spend it in San Francisco. I told him him I would be there in February and we fixed upon a day and place to meet.

"All this," he said, laughing, "providing the Japs aren't too quick for us."

In the Pan-American Hotel there were two or three passengers still playing cards or having drinks. I impressed upon Charlie the fact that it was too early to go to bed. It was, in fact, not much past ten o'clock. He conceded the point and sat down at a table on which, providentially, were to be found some poker dice in a leather cup. Before an hour or at most two had elapsed, we had become old friends, and there are few persons now living who could tell you more about Charlie Todd's kidneys or his career in the Marine Corps than I can. He was from Ohio State University and had gone straight to the Marine School at Philadelphia from there. One of the navigators from the PBY's (it was Cunningham) came and joined us for a while and we talked about airplanes.

"It's a funny thing they've never built a landing field here," Cunningham said.

"Not much level ground," Charlie remarked.

"There's enough level ground for two golf courses," I said. "You've been telling me about those two golf courses all evening. Why isn't there a landing field?"

"I dunno," Charlie confessed cheerfully. "But there's a lot of things we ought to have and don't."

"The nearest Japanese islands, Rodo and Saipan, have landing fields," Cunningham said.

"Damn tootin' they have," said Charlie.

He had the kind of hair that tousles itself, without wind or any other tactile agency. It was tousled now, and his spotless whites were a little wrinkled, but the gleaming ropes of the golden *fourragère* still gave him a look of high ceremony. In due course, after we had been for some time the only survivors in the lounge, he announced that he could stay no more. Once his white cap was firmly set and

he had straightened his tunic, he looked as spruce as he
had that afternoon when the Clipper came in. I went out
and saw him take the wheel of the Governor's car, and
we reiterated the date and meeting place, February 18th
in San Francisco.

"Banzai!" he said as he drove away.

Down at the seaplane base the Clipper was a swinging
white shadow in the last of the night. We left for Wake
Island at dawn.

2

Between Guam and Wake the passengers on the Clipper came to life for one another. There was an army wife
returning home with her small son, age four, who had
obviously been entrusted to the care of native nurses up
to now. The child talked a language with which no trans-
lator could have dealt. It seemed to be English, Spanish,
Tagalog and Chinese all at once. On taking off and on
alighting, he would suddenly become aware of the big
wings of the Boeing plane and would start an instant up-
roar, roughly like this: "Mummy, look at the big airplane!
Look at the big airplane! Mummy, you said we were going
on the big airplane! When are we going on the big airplane?" He was so impressed by these wings, which he
never seemed to notice while we were in flight, that he
refused to believe he was actually in the big airplane all
the time. This delusion continued until we disembarked
at Honolulu. His name was Johnny.

A couple from Hongkong had been—as I was informed
by most of the other passengers in turn—married only a
short time; they were perhaps in their sixties. Mr. Wes-
selius of the American Red Cross had been in China, the
Siamese jeweler had come from Bangkok to Singapore to

Manila by air, the Chinese general was on his way to Washington to discuss requirements under the Lease-Lend Act. There was one American woman whose husband, a British officer, was on active service in Libya. There was a Swiss gentleman who carried a large roll of American banknotes of all denominations and was always willing to make change for a poker game. Aside from these, myself and the crews of the Consolidated flying boats (PBY's), who were being ferried back to San Diego, there were no other passengers to Guam. At Guam we collected a few more. "Army," an officer and a gentleman, of the United States Marines named Armknecht; two high officials of the Pacific Naval Bases Companies, the associated concerns which were doing all the contracted work on the islands for the navy; and a pale, sweet-faced young girl who wept ceaselessly and spoke not at all. From "Army," who had been stationed at Guam and knew her, I learned that this young lady was on her way to visit an aunt in Baltimore, and her unhappiness was due to the fact that she had never before left the isle of her birth. The gentle Chamorro ways, the lovely Chamorro faces and the golden beaches of Guam were all she had ever known. By a sort of chivalrous respect never put into words, the male passengers on the Clipper made no attempt to break down the barrier a vast young grief had built around her. Even the rowdiest poker game, in the days that were coming, calmed to silence when she passed by. The plain sorrow of going away from home held her all week loug, until we lost sight of her at Honolulu.

For we stayed nearly a week at Wake. A storm had arisen in the Pacific—not a typhoon, but an ordinary storm of great violence. Its center was around Midway somewhere, and the Pan-American installations there suffered considerably; one seaman was killed. All the Clippers on

the ocean, the ones at Honolulu and Manila as well as ours
at Wake, were immobilized by the storm. Afterward I
heard that Midway had never seen a worse storm since
the seaplane base was created. While it was going on, we
at Wake were going through days of exquisite weather, in
a heat that was never stifling or unpleasant, on the white
coral sand and over the clear blue sea.

That afternoon when we alighted in the lagoon and
came up to be moored to the pier we had no idea of it.
To the best of our knowledge we were going on to Midway at dawn. It was Thanksgiving Day. We had had tur-
key aboard the Clipper, for lunch; we expected a large
Thanksgiving dinner that night, and, by the vagaries of
the calendar, we expected another Thanksgiving Day at
Midway. It so happens that the day you gain—the extra
day—tacks itself onto your existence between Wake and
Midway islands. I had lost twenty-four hours in the
South Seas, going out, and still felt a little puzzled over
the events that had apparently taken place during that
non-existent day. It was all explained to me, but in the
learned language which does, in the words of Bacon,
"wonderfullie obstruct the Understanding." This lost day
was now given back again, and with a certificate of the
Pan-American company to make it legal.

The Pan-American Hotel on Wake was like all the
others, two long, low wings and a central lounge and dining room. The wife of the station manager had not yet
gone home; she and the wife of the manager at Midway
were the only American women left in the Pacific Ocean.
Mrs. Wake had an autograph book which she asked me
to sign. The signature before mine, occupying a whole
page in English and Japanese, was that of Saburo Kurusu.
He had come through on his way to Washington just
two or three weeks before. Mrs. Wake was looking for-

ward to the next Clipper because it was bringing Litvinov. "But I don't know," she said reflectively, "if I'll have the nerve to ask him to sign. He's Russian."

Thanksgiving dinner was a lively affair. By this time we were beginning to know each other. The PBY crews, which had been a unit before, crystallized out into individuals. Their tacitly acknowledged leader was Dick Mitchell, addressed as Mitch, who looked like a hero and no doubt was one. He was very big, strong and handsome, so that it seemed downright unfair that he should also be a first-class pilot and a born leader. Most of the others deferred to his judgment and tended to imitate him (unconsciously, of course). There were three other captains, one of whom was Rodney Jackson, a thoughtful youth who did a lot of reading and writing. Among the navigators, radio operators and engineers were my friend Cunningham from Boston, red-haired, freckled and intelligent, young Kerry Coughlin from Mitch's crew, and a demon poker player from Texas, named Aycock. Soon after dinner some of the PBY men settled down to the poker game they had started on the Clipper. That night I was tired and went to bed.

We had our customary early start in the morning and flew out two and half hours toward Midway before we were ordered back to Wake. The storm had begun. For the next five days, although we saw nothing but fair weather, we listened to radio reports and waited.

There were many diversions once we got used to the fact that we could not move on at once. I was suffering from the traveler's curse, a lack of clean clothing; the laundry machine at Wake had broken down. I fell into the pleasant habit of walking over to the other island to buy shirts or handkerchiefs every morning. All the construction workers for the Naval Bases Company were housed on the other island, across a small bridge, and in the midst of their camp they had a well-equipped general store and commissary. There were two islands at Wake, by nature, and the new work undertaken for the navy had pierced one of them so as to create a third. Collectively they were known to the Pan-American company as "Wake Islands," and the plural was used on official stationery, but I have never heard anybody say it. Islands so small and so close together could not seem plural.

The sun was hot all day and the workers on the island wore as few clothes as possible. For many of them the day's costume consisted of very small shorts and a pair of sandals. There was a landing field on Wake, a stepping-stone for bombers on their way to the East; this was its chief present importance. The construction work for the naval base was proceeding day and night, and there were about 1,200 workers in the camp. This was about half an hour's walk from the Pan-American station. You went down a road of fine, dusty sand to the main highway which ran the length of the islands. This was a hard road and the trucks were roaring up and down it all day long. I walked over at least once every day, sometimes oftener, and never failed to be offered a lift several times on the way. Life on a desert island seems to conduce to friendliness. The naked workers, sometimes burned darker than any Chamorro, were always delighted when a Clipper came in so that they could get mail, hear news and ask questions. They were not supposed to come over to Pan-American's station and we were not supposed to go near their camp without a pass, but we all did so and were never stopped. As you came to the bridge between the islands you passed a watchman's hut with a sign on it saying: "Show Your Pass Before Crossing Bridge." But as there was never anybody in the watchman's hut we could not have done this, even if we had possessed passes.

The white coral sand reflected the blazing sun and held the heat until well after dark. Around the huge compound in the construction camp were ranged the houses of the workers, with a shower bath for every four men and a number of other accommodations unusual in such places. It was necessary to treat the men exceedingly well, pay them two or three times what they would have received at home, and humor even their unreasonable vagaries to some extent. Otherwise workers could not be recruited for islands so far out at sea, in such a dangerous position and so remote from the delights of Main Street. The commissary was the center of the camp. You could buy almost anything within reason there—no hard liquor, of course, but anything else. I acquired quite a wardrobe of Hawaiian shirts and underclothing, since the Pan-American laundry remained broken down. At the cigar counter they had chocolate bars kept on ice. This was necessary, the attendant explained, not only because they might otherwise melt, but also because the ants did not like ice. Ants were the most prolific fauna of the island, and the most difficult to discourage.

In the soda fountain on the other side of the general store a lean, brown-burned youth with no clothing visible above the counter dished out ice-cream sodas and Coca-Cola. He liked to talk (they all did) and kept up a cheerful chatter while you drank your coke. He also kept an autograph book and had the names of bomber captains in it. At noon, when the shift changed, a torrent of workers seethed across the broad compound and broke into the store, setting up half an hour's intense activity. Outside, in the blazing white compound, was an open-air movie theatre. I think a film called "The Flame of New Orleans," with Miss Marlene Dietrich, was one of those advertised during the week I was there. There was also a big poster calling upon anybody who had theatrical ability or experience to volunteer for the Wake Island Show. It was to be a musical entertainment of sorts, something like a college show, all men; it was to go on in December, sometime before Christmas.

Over on the Pan-American side of the island there was also an open-air movie theatre which most of the Clipper passengers and crew and a good many marines attended every night. After the first night I settled down as a regular customer in the poker game run by the PBY crews and had no time for film going. To start with, I was God's gift to the game, which had been going on for so long—seven or eight ferry trips across the ocean—that it stood in need of fresh money. However, after my second night I began to win and kept it up so relentlessly that some of the more suspicious aircraftsmen began to look upon me with disfavor. The game went on for as many hours as anybody wanted to play, and then afterward we raided the kitchen for food. To the astonishment of all, the Pan-American company never catechized or reprimanded, even when we had practically cleaned out the ice-box.

The principal sporting event on Wake Island was rat-shooting. Mitch had an air pistol and at night when everybody but the PBY crews and I had gone to bed the shooting began. Mitch was exceedingly good at it. A vast brown figure in a violent Honolulu shirt, shorts and sandals, he would creep about the place stealthily, killing rats as much by his cleverness as by bullets. He had by far the highest record in this respect. The rats were innumerable and most bold. They roamed over our feet as we played poker, ran at liberty through kitchens, dining room and lounge, and swarmed over the island outside. Any rumor that they have been, or could be, exterminated, is hereby denied. As a matter of fact, I thought them rather harmless little animals after a while. As they sat back and considered us with twinkling eyes, they reminded me much more of squirrels than of rats. Mitch was in earnest about his duty to destroy as many of them as possible. "What do you suppose would happen here if one infected rat got ashore?" he asked.

One night we were practicing with the air pistol and Kerry Coughlin, who was tired of rats, tried to hit the dinner gong on the other side of the lounge. This was a challenge to all present, and we accepted it. Alarmed Clipper passengers could be heard slamming and locking their doors. Nobody hit the gong.

Fishing was good at Wake, as around all these islands. I only went out one day. It was a day of soft, gleaming heat over the pure blue sea. Cunningham and some others, including our indefatigable Clipper captain, set to work as soon as the Pan-American launch had taken us out beyond the rocks at the end of the new channel. I lay on top of the launch and sun-bathed or read *The Federalist*. This, and *The G-String Murders*, had been my only literary purchases at the Philippine Education Company in Manila. I had given *The G-String Murders* to a colleague on the A.P. before leaving Manila and thus had nothing but *The Federalist* to read. Thinking that I might as well do it properly, so that I could find the quotable bits of incontrovertible authority when I needed them, I was annotating the book. Thus I would underline Madison's dictum, "If we are to be one nation in any respect, it clearly ought to be in respect to other nations," and mark a page reference to it in the fly-leaf, and immediately thereafter dodge to avoid getting smacked in the face by a struggling fish. The take was immense, and we had it for lunch the next day.

The bird life of the island was a source of great annoyance. There were, it seemed, millions of terns, which is about as noisy a bird as I have ever heard. They laid their eggs all over the island with complete disregard for human convenience. All the beaches were infested with them and they were protected by law. I never knew why. They are unpleasant to eye and ear, philoprogenitive beyond the bounds of decency, and a positive danger to a descending airplane. They fly in such thick clouds that they might quite easily damage a propeller. Until I saw the goonies on Midway I thought these among the most arrogant birds I had ever seen, least conscious of human rights on our common planet.

We had cocktails before dinner and sometimes highballs afterward, although neither in great number; it was not a very liquorous expedition. There was almost incessant talk about approaching war. Just then General Tojo had made his very solemn speech to the special session of the Japanese Diet, warning them of great events to come. It impressed me deeply; it was surrounded by all the ceremony of a supreme decision, the pilgrimage to the shrine at Kyoto included. The Wake *Wigwag* had duly reported all this. We sometimes had visitors from the navy or marines. One thin officer was called Devereux. The pilots and bomber crews were all fixed in one idea: they did not want to be on Wake when it was taken by the Japanese.

The sheer theatricality of the Pan-American Hotel there, with all the bright-clad and half-naked people talking about war, made me think of a play. Meeting Rodney Jackson one morning on my way over to the construction camp, I said: "I want to write a play about Wake Island. It's made for that purpose." Rodney answered: "That's funny. I've started a story about it. What's your play?"

My play, of course, was going to be about some Clipper
passengers stranded on Wake Island. There was a Chinese
lady and a Japanese diplomatist—a sort of Madame Sun
Yat-sen and Mr. Kurusu, although neither would have
been a portrait—and there were PBY pilots and crews and
a sad-eyed girl from Guam. Oddly enough, Rodney's short
story was going to be about roughly the same people,
although he had also added a tramp newspaper man to
his cast of characters. We thought it out separately and
compared notes, inviting the comment of our PBY friends
on the result. They made some quite constructive suggestions, I remember, including one to the effect that the
dauntless aviator and the sad-eyed girl from Guam might
get together in an argument over shooting rats. I incor-
porated this into my play at once. Rodney wrote a full
outline of his story and was about to begin writing the
thing itself when we left. I had only achieved a cast of
characters, setting, and general idea—which is about as far
as I am likely to get with any play. The climax of both
play and story was the same: the Clipper was disabled by
a Japanese attack and the passengers were saved by the
PBY pilots flying them to Honolulu. We argued for a long
time about whether there ought to be one PBY or several.
Neither the play nor the story survived our departure.

For we did, at last, get out. The storm died down on
Midway, and one morning—long after Thanksgiving, alas,
so that we were cheated of our double feast—we assembled again at dawn in the Clipper and rose from the silver
water. I thought I would remember Wake Island for a
long time. It was novel, tremulous and momentary, like
a dream. A splotch of white coral in the soundless sea,
a point of intersection in time-space. I wished I could
have written that play. One night we heard voices from
London there, coming crazily through the radio with in-

describable interruptions. In the general wrack of sound I had distinguished the voices of two friends, one very antique, John Gunther, and one of more recent date, Leslie Howard. They were answering questions on "Information, Please!" by a miraculous hook-up with New York. Nothing seemed more remote than London from Wake Island, and yet there it was, coming at us out of a box. The more places you go to the more it is the same place, I suppose. It is always where you are.

"Look at the big airplane, Mummy," Johnny shrieked, as we left the water. He was looking at our own wings, as usual. "When am I going to get into the big airplane, Mummy?"

3

Along the pier at Midway Island a line of curious onlookers watched us come down to the sea, transfer to a launch and file out on shore. These were mainly construction workers off duty, with a few marines. They shouted at us and grinned. The coming of a Clipper was, I suppose, the constantly renewed proof that they were not marooned in the ocean, and it made them feel cheerful. Midway was white sand, like Wake, only it looked bigger and all the installations visible from the seaplane base were on a bigger scale. Marine sentries, fully armed, stood along the pier and the road that led to the Pan-American Hotel. Mitch and Kerry and I elected to walk to the hotel; there were cars for those who wanted to ride.

"This walk along here," Mitch said, "is about all you'll see of Midway. The marines are tough. They don't let anybody wander around. You'll see; they've got a ring of sentries around the hotel."

We had gone only a few steps when we saw our first

goonies. These ridiculous birds inhabited the land, sea and air, but it was quite apparent that each of the elements had in some way modified their adaptability to the other, so that they looked clumsy and incompetent wherever they were. At certain times of the year they vanished from the land completely, and when they returned, after some months, they had quite lost the ability to come down and take off properly. Great, heavy, waddling creatures with ludicrous beaks, they wandered at will in the areas which suited their pleasure, paying no attention to the riparian rights or traffic conventions of that more absurd beast, man. They had been known to attack big trucks belonging to the U.S. Marines, and they scorned the movements of automobiles. The goony was protected by law, like the tern on Wake, and although the presence of such heavy, stupid birds in such vast numbers was a grave danger to aviation, you were not supposed to do anything about it. As a matter of fact the marines had been shooting them by the thousand, but the more you shot the more there seemed to be.

Along the sandy road and in the piled up dunes the goonies were coming and going, rubbing beaks, dancing, picking for food, landing and taking off. They had to make a long run for a take-off and did it with the utmost awkwardness. Apparently the very young birds could only take off from a height, like a glider. Most of them made very bad landings, and before I had been ten minutes on the island I saw one goony land with his toes in the sand, toppling him tail over head. The courtship dancing was also very peculiar. Instead of being performed by a proud male before an indifferent or coquettish female, as is the rule with all birds I had seen, both these creatures danced, with an indistinguishable clumsiness, so that you could not possibly tell which was the cock and which the hen.

The dance was heavy, ludicrous and without aesthetic value as display: the webbed feet were lifted awkwardly and set down again with a kind of lurch, while the head looked round for admiration. Male and female performed these gyrations and then rubbed beaks. We saw many love scenes in the hollows of the dunes. The marine sentries, very crisp and solid in khaki, with revolvers and rifles, looked upon the whole spectacle with indifference. The passion of Clipper passengers for the goony must have seemed to them, after a week or so on Midway, extremely provincial.

From an aerodynamic point of view the goony was one of the oddest birds in existence. That was why our PBY crews, who had seen them many times in ferry trips across the ocean, were ceaselessly fascinated by them. A goony takes off rather like a Boeing Clipper, and it sometimes seems that there is a pilot inside the bird: for the mistakes made by the goony are those made by human pilots. For example, the bird will fail to gain elevation fast enough and will run smack into a sand-dune or a bit of scrub. It will land at an excessive speed and roll head over heels, sometimes injuring itself. It will make a long run for the take-off and then fail to make it, owing to lack of acceleration proportioned to its load. The strange beast has to learn to fly, rather like a human being. Those who have watched the young birds in the proper season say the first flying lessons of the goony are extraordinarily like human instruction. Their falls and injuries during the period of training are very noticeable, as in their loss of land-adaptation during their mysterious long absences at sea.

Exhausted by contemplation of the goonies, I went to sleep, and was awakened toward dinner time by a telephone call from Mr. Shiek, the head of the Pacific Naval Bases enterprises on Midway. ("Spelled Shiek in the day-

time, Sheik at night," he explained.) He asked me to dinner over at the camp with some of the marine and naval
officers and his colleagues, the building engineers. "I'll
bring you down a pass," he said. "Otherwise you're not
supposed to go outside the immediate neighborhood of
the Pan-American Hotel." He brought the pass, but I was
never asked for it. As a matter of fact, although I saw
plenty of marine sentries in the afternoon when we landed,
I never saw one again through the long night.

We dined over at the camp, which was about twice the
size of the one at Wake Island. The marine and naval officers were a pleasant crowd and the food was excellent.
The chef, who came out and talked to us afterward, formerly worked at the Waldorf, he said. When dinner was
over Mr. Shiek took me on a tour of inspection of the
kitchens, the canteen and the whole camp. The vast, shining luxury of the kitchens impressed me most. I saw there
a doughnut machine (there was also one at Wake, I
heard) which was wonderful to behold. The doughnut
fell into a sizzling concoction of grease and sloshed around
in it with a circular motion until it emerged at the other
end of the affair completely cooked and smelling as it
should. The systems of refrigeration and baking were the
best obtainable and the whole thing was on a scale beyond
my comprehension. Mr. Shiek kept telling me how many
things each of these objects could produce in every minute. I was also fully informed on the cost.

The canteen was colossal. On a night like this, with two
Clippers in (the one from Honolulu had come in shortly
after ours) every worker in camp turned up to see about
mail from home, or from somewhere. The line at the U.S.
Post Office window was still long, although this had been
going on for some hours. There were billiard tables in operation, radios and juke-boxes squawking in various parts

of the vast room. The soda fountain was crowded and there was a lively poker and blackjack cubbyhole off at one end of the place. I stepped into the blackjack game and regretted it. The types around the table, however, were fascinating—almost too much like types in a Hollywood film of the Far West. There were ferocious bearded pirates and rum blokes with bleary eyes and kids trying to look tough. I felt that the presence of Mr. Shiek—who is to Midway Island what Hitler is to Berlin—somewhat cramped everybody's style, so I abandoned the canteen pretty soon, with, I must say, regret. I should have enjoyed an hour or two of exploration.

Mr. Shiek had produced, after dinner, a young colleague of mine called Edward Rocke, the editor of the *Goony Gazette*. This was the first mimeographed news sheet to be put out on the islands, and the Wake *Wigwag* ("published nearly every day") was, Rocke told me, only an imitation. Rocke had come to interview me for his paper. I told him (as I was to tell my colleagues in Honolulu and San Francisco in the next few days, with similar results) that war was inevitable very soon and that the visit of Mr. Kurusu was a smoke-screen pure and simple. Mr. Rocke wrote it down and smiled tolerantly. Then I began to interview Mr. Rocke and found out a good deal about the *Goony Gazette*. Rocke had come out to Midway as a restaurant helper, signing up at the recruiting office in Los Angeles. After he had been on the island a few weeks he started getting out a mimeographed news sheet, prepared on the basis of radio broadcasts he heard at the canteen. Although these broadcasts were available to anybody who wished to listen, the summary of them prepared by young Rocke was snapped up as soon as it appeared; it was a great success. Rocke and one Chinese helper from the restaurant, who was also interested in newspapers, did the whole thing themselves for no extra pay, listening to the radio and putting their summary onto a borrowed mimeograph. In a few weeks the *Goony Gazette* had become such an important part of camp life that the company was obliged to recognize its existence and give it some support. Young Rocke was permitted to give it half his time, then all his time; it appeared more and more frequently, until now it was a daily. I know of no more striking victory of the printed word over the radio—for, as I have said before, every word of news in the *Goony Gazette* was available to everybody in camp on the radio.

"Now," Rocke told me, "the company has sent out a linotype machine and we're going to have a regular daily printed paper. That is, as soon as we learn how to run the linotype machine. It's a little difficult right at first. I have a full-time assistant now, just for the writing of the paper, as well as my Chinese friend for the printing."

We wandered through the camp in the moonlight and looked in at the windows of some of the rooms. There were men studying, reading, sewing, sleeping. Midway, since it is in the temperate zone, had cool days and chilly evenings: we were on the very brink of December, and for the first time I could feel it in the air. The quarters of the workers looked like college dormitories. There were about twice as many workers here as on Wake, and everything was on a big scale, like the doughnut machine. Midway also possessed a landing field for airplanes as well as the seaplane base; most of these men were working at the new naval and air installations. I saw no air-raid shelters—indeed, had seen but one air-raid shelter in any territory under the American flag: that for the navy at Sangley Point, beyond Cavite.

When Rocke drove us home, some time when the hours were getting less small, he made a detour through the camp to the office of the *Goony Gazette*. We had to see the new linotype machine, he said. We clambered out into the sand and followed him dutifully. The machine was there; so was a small, properly littered office upstairs. There were great heaps of new copy paper which had been sent out from the mainland at the same time as the linotype machine.

"It's going to be a wonderful day when we set our first edition on the machine," young Rocke said. "I never thought that day would come."

Mitch and Rod were less interested in the *Goony Gazette* than I was; they turned on the big radio which was the chief part of the office equipment. The voice coming out of the box said that more Japanese troops had moved into Indo-China.

"You'd better learn how to print the *Goony Gazette* in Jap-talk," Mitch said.

It was very late when we went home to the Pan-American. The white sand island was ghostly in the darkest part of the night. We did not have to take off quite so early here, since the day's hop was the shortest of the trip. Only a few hours more, and we should be far from this atmosphere of premonition and half-hearted boasts, coming down with elephantine grace upon the water, the safe, friendly water of Pearl Harbor.

4

I got home on December 1st and had to start my lecture tour (my last) almost at once. The first engagement was in Baltimore on December 4th, the second before the National Association of Manufacturers in New York on December 5th. To both of these audiences I said, as seriously as I knew how, that we were on the verge of war, that we were going to be attacked, and that the world conflict was now about to enter on its final phase in which all the powers would be simultaneously involved. I do not think much impression was made by such warnings. Indeed, the *New York Times* of December 6, 1941, at the end of a long article on the other speeches at the Manufacturers' Association, remarked with visible restraint that Mr. Vincent Sheean "predicted" war within ten days—all they had seen fit to print of my somber and quite accurate account of the position. I had predicted nothing; I had merely made an intelligence report upon the intentions and capabilities of the enemy. And, as a matter of fact, war did come on the following day.

On that day, Sunday, December 7th, I was at Harry Luce's house in Connecticut, where my wife and I had gone for the week-end. There was a collection of foreign correspondents and writers, Virginia Cowles, John Whittaker, Lin Yu-tang, Mark Sullivan and others, not to speak of Harry and Clare Luce themselves. To most of us this event was instantly filled out with a thousand consequences. Some of us had expected attack (I had); some had expected war (Clare had); but I doubt very much if any of us thought, until that day, that the Japanese could successfully raid and damage the naval shipping in Pearl Harbor. It had always seemed to me just a little out of their reach, in spite of all their new bases in the Pacific islands. Looking over such files as I possess, I find that the only time I ever printed a reference to such a possibility was in an article in *Look* magazine, written March 25, 1941. I had mentioned Pearl Harbor as a possible point of attack sometimes on lecture tour, usually in answer to questions; but I doubt if it had ever seemed to me a very likely contingency. Certainly on that day, when the news came, I was stunned with astonishment; so, I think, were all the others in that gathering—men and women who, by profession, should have been able to estimate the general probabilities and possibilities better than most. We scattered from that hospitable house as if the plague had broken out, rushing each to his own place not because we had anything specific to do about the event, but because the first journalistic property of an event is to instigate motion.

I broadcast that night, choosing to speak about Wake Island, which I assumed to be attacked and knew (or thought I knew) must be lost; on December 10th I broadcast again, on the general plan of Japanese strategy, which I interpreted as an encirclement of China by the conquest of all neighboring territories to the south and southeast. From that time onward I was never asked to speak again on the radio. My lectures, which had been made the subject of contracts long in advance, were not subject to cancellation, whatever I said; but I had my difficulties with them, too. The trouble was that I could not get out of my head the two golf courses and no landing field on Guam, the naval planes packed in like sardines at Cavite, the raw and brash Australians swaggering across Malaya, the guns that would not shoot at Surabaya. I believe I knew from December 7th onward almost exactly what the course of the Japanese conquests would be up to and including New Guinea, and my chief trouble was that I insisted on saying these things in public before the public was ready to accept them. I was moved to exaggerate the enemy's capabilities sometimes through sheer nervous exasperation at the "victorious" nonsense our newspapers were printing every day. Once in Chicago I was goaded (by the row of smug faces at a table) into saying that the Japanese might occupy the whole of our Pacific coast; there were days

when the news was so appallingly bad, and was so totally
misunderstood by press and public, that I could hardly
speak at all. During this winter of Bataan and the Ma-
layan campaign, the loss of the Indies and the invasion of
Burma, when people like Charlie Todd were being hauled
off to prison camps in Japan and women like Soong Ching-
ling were fleeing for their lives, it was difficult to be patient with official half-truths and journalistic fiction. The
war was not real to our people, but it seemed to me it
would never become real unless they were told hard, brutal truth. As the disastrous winter wore on, the people
themselves became aware of our enemy's capacity and our
own lack of ready resources; and, as always, it was the
people who exacted, and finally obtained, a more sober
version of things from those whose duty it was to speak to
them. By the spring, the bleak spring of 1942, realization
had progressed so far that our people as a whole knew, at
last, that this was our war, that we had so far lost it, and
that a mighty effort and a mighty sacrifice were demanded
for our salvation.

The only elements of encouragement in the pattern of
events were provided by the Russians. And it was high
irony indeed to see how the bloody and determined battle
of the Red Army was seized upon and extolled by those
who had never once, in the preceding twenty years, had
a good word to say for Soviet Russia. By the spring of
1942 it was generally seen that Germany was so heavily
engaged in Russia that its power might never again be
what it had been in 1940. This realization made Russian
War Relief almost as fashionable as British War Relief had
been two years earlier, and bankers, politicians, society
ladies and bishops laid their names eagerly upon the letter-
head. Averell Harriman said in a public speech that the
Nazi-Soviet Pact had "saved Western civilization." I was

convinced that it had, on the contrary, brought Western civilization to the brink of destruction, and yet I wished the Red Army far more truly well than did most of these laudatory gentlemen. What they really meant (and never said) was that they were grateful for the respite bought by Russian blood; that, with any luck, Russia would break Germany's military strength so that the rest would be easy; that we might even find ourselves relatively unshaken in our power at a discernible point when Russia and Germany might have bled each other white.

I wanted to know something more about our own war and went down to Washington to find out. This was in May; the whole Eastern campaign had ended in Japanese victory and the time had come to recapitulate a little, to survey, to examine. By an arrangement I owed (I think) to the Writers' War Board, I was able to see some reports of our combat pilots from the Philippines and Java. It was these reports that convinced me that we, of ourselves, possessed the capacity to make war and take our true place in the world afterward.

## 5

I think no part of our defeat in the Far East, perhaps no episode in the history of this people, may touch the imagination of our descendants more than the story of our Army Air Force in the Pacific campaign between December 7th and the last days of April, 1942. It had not been told as one complete story because the primary necessities of warfare demanded that the operations be shrouded in obscurity. Bare and succinct, the communiqués from the War Department in Washington had announced from time to time that our aircraft had bombed at Legaspe, Lingayen or Davao, with estimates of the losses inflicted upon the Japanese. The press, floundering in a morass of unfamiliar geography and serious strategical misapprehensions, announced each of these actions as a resounding victory, but was unable, under the conditions, to give any real idea of what was taking place in the Philippine Islands or (later) in Java. The public accepted the local victories at face value, rejoiced for an hour, and then was disillusioned and uneasy to discover that these operations did not in fact prevent the Japanese occupation of the whole archipelago, the Philippines, Malaya, and the Indies, accompanied and followed by the conquest of Burma and the encirclement of China.

Against the dark shadows of those four or five months certain bold facts had stood out in the public imagination —our men on Bataan and Corregidor, the desperate naval struggle in the Java Sea, and, most of all, the dramatic personality of General Douglas MacArthur. Little was—or could be—said of the Army Air Force, because the essence of its activity was the surprise appearance from the clouds, its points of departure and its destinations alike unknown, its range of performance a mystery over the vast blue sea. Now that the Japanese enjoyed temporary possession of our air fields and those of our allies in the Indies and the Philippines, there was no further need or purpose in concealing the story: as I read it in Washington it sang out loud and clear, the absolute assurance of victory. When we had enough of them, such men and such machines could successfully confront any forces or combination of forces in the world.

On the sultry morning of Monday, December 8th (which was Sunday, December 7th in the United States), on the tropical islands of Luzon and Mindanao, between seven and eight o'clock, the first news of the Japanese attack on Pearl Harbor came over the radio to the listening airmen. They knew their combined force; they knew the nearness of the enemy and his immensely superior power of concentration; there was scarcely a man among them with combat experience; and yet they were ready to go at once. So far as I have been able to determine, they fueled and bomb-loaded then and there, without superior order. Meanwhile the signal fires were burning; the telephone and telegraph lines were being cut; the fifth column was active; everything was being made ready by the enemy within.

The air force in the islands was tiny. We had very few pursuit planes to begin with; after the first day's disastrous attacks we had less. MacArthur was actually left on Bataan with twelve P-40's which were to perish in the defense, one by one. That was his whole air force after the retirement to Bataan. Our principal strength in bombers consisted of thirty-four B-17 D's and E's (known as Flying Fortresses), sixteen at Clark Field near Manila, and eighteen on Mindanao. They had been flown there during the summer and autumn, hopping from island to island in the Pacific.

It seems clear that the B-17's were lined up on Clark Field; apparently they were being bombed-up again; it was at about 12.40 and the men were having lunch. Since eight in the morning some patrol and reconnaissance flights had taken place, but at this moment all sixteen of the B-17's at that field were on the ground. The Japanese bombers came in, no doubt from Formosa, and did a very thorough job. Apparently there was no interception. At any rate, the Japanese bombing was thorough and almost all the B-17's were wrecked. That is, thirteen of them were either destroyed or so badly damaged that they could not be flown. After the events of December 8th Captain Lee

B. Coats examined the planes and found that the other three were operable, but of these two were destroyed by accidents that day and the next morning, leaving only one B-17, out of that magnificent array, capable of being flown out to Mindanao. What became of the P-40's I did not discover, but they must have been destroyed in one way or another, on the ground or in combat against overwhelmingly superior Japanese forces, since only twelve of them survived even for the retirement to Bataan.

All the destruction was not done by the Japanese bombers; it was completed by Japanese fighter planes, no doubt Navy Zeros from an aircraft carrier. The timing was good and the operation, conducted from such different points in space and with such different elements, was unfortunately very successful; it made Clark Field almost useless and crippled the Army Air Force by suddenly reducing it almost one-half. One officer says the naval planes came in about three minutes after the land bombers had gone away; another gives a different time; but it is clear that there was no great interval. It would seem simple enough, that, if one did not realize the infinite number of possibilities of error and accident in carrying out the plan. Somebody in Tokyo ordered that the bombers should leave Formosa at a given hour, traverse the sea, find Clark Field and bomb it, getting the job done and returning to their base in time to permit the descent of a cloud of Zero fighters from another direction to strafe whatever was left on the ground. But between the order written in Tokyo and the actual disastrous attack on Clark Field there were all the usual difficulties of putting a plan into action; the point is that it seems to have been carried out exactly, or so exactly as to indicate what is, in fact, the chief military advantage of the Japanese, their unity and discipline. Many of our officers in the Far East underestimated the

Japanese until December 7th; perhaps many still do; those who were on Clark Field do not.

What followed was a demonstration of the capacities of our Army Air Force. The men from other fields took their planes where they were told to take them, and did what they were told to do. They accomplished astonishing missions without, apparently, realizing that there was anything remarkable about them. They appear to have operated in an almost total absence of the necessary ground support and communications. They flew from point to point as if in a vacuum, dropped their bombs according to instructions plus natural intelligence, and repaired to bases which—sometimes—they had never seen before, and had to find simply by instruments. Over such an area, with land and sea inextricably mixed, the navigation alone was something that almost defied belief. But they had many more difficulties to contend with than mere navigation. Their ground personnel was mostly lost from the first day, and they had to repair, refuel and rebomb their own planes after many hours of flight over the unknown sea. They had no field protection whatsoever in most of the places from which they had to operate; they were without refueling trucks, and in many places had to pour the gasoline into the airplanes from tin cans; their time was always limited, their orders peremptory, their information in a military sense practically non-existent. They did not even know where the Japanese were most of the time. They went from Point X to Point Y and bombed the Japanese ships, in spite of fantastic weather conditions (that is, weather conditions upon which they were uninformed) and fought off the Japanese Zero planes coming and going. In all of these B-17 operations we lost only five airplanes in the air; our other losses were all upon the ground. Our B-17's took such a toll of the Japanese interceptor planes that toward the end the Zero did not even attempt to fight except with greatly superior force, at certain angles and with every precaution possible to combat. Some of their experiences, as for example when Captain Wheless and his crew shot down seven out of eighteen Zero planes attacking him, exhausting the ammunition of all the others without losing his plane or abandoning his mission, gave them a salutary respect for the B-17, so that in later days they tried hard to improve the safety of their Zero plane.

With all this, it did not seem to me that the pilots, navigators, bombardiers, gunners and radio operators of a B-17 were any different from other young Americans. So far as I could see, they were characteristic products of our civilization. That is, they thought and talked in terms which took the mechanical achievement (the principal one) for granted, and, without a trace of false modesty or self-congratulation, they knew that they were good at their jobs. They returned from this disastrous Philippine and Indonesian campaign with, as an officer in their service said, "the bearing of victors." And rightly, because in the truest sense they were victors. Nineteen ships they operated, and that was all: and yet they constituted a whole air force.

They did considerable damage to the Japanese. The earliest and most widely known of their missions was that on which Captain Colin Kelly sank the battleship *Haruna,* according to our observation (denied by the Japanese) and afterward lost his own life by an attack of Zero planes as he was returning to Clark Field. Kelly does not seem to have been a "hero." There were, so far as I was able to ascertain, no "heroes" in the Army Air Force. He was a young American of pleasing character, appreciated by his associates in life and regretted by them in death. He had two remarkable strokes of luck, one good and one bad.

The good stroke was that when he made his run over the *Haruna* two or possibly three bombs hit their target where it would do the most effective work. The bad stroke was that as he was coming into the wreck of Clark Field his radio apparently did not operate and he therefore did not know that the Japanese were raiding the field. He flew into the midst of that raid and they poured bullets into him. I talked to Wheless about Kelly in May and, after some conversation on the subject, he summed up the whole thing in the terse idiom of their clan: "Kelly was a good guy," he said.

Not only the B-17's but also the B-24's employed by the Ferry Command in all the remarkable evacuations from the islands, used a field in the Philippines at night after the Japanese had taken command of sea, air and land areas for hundreds of miles in all directions. Flying from Darwin, in Australia, or Malang in Java, or any other point upon which they chanced to be based for the moment, the B-17's would refuel and attack, bombing the Japanese transports at Lingayen and Legaspe, making the roadstead at Davao an extremely unhealthy place, and going off to their brief but astonishing operations in Borneo, Celebes and the Macassar Strait. It seems quite clear that half a dozen of these remarkable machines barred the Macassar Strait to the Japanese main fleet for several days.

I was struck, like everybody else, with the story of Captain Hewitt Wheless, which had been partly told in the President's speech of April 28, 1942. Wheless said in his own account:

Our mission was to bomb transport and war vessels in the harbor of Legaspe. We took off at 9 A.M. December 14th in a B-17 and proceeded in formation until halfway to Legaspe, when we ran into a thick overcast. After going into the overcast we became separated. At 15,000 feet we lost our Number Two

engine and left the formation. That was due to lack of maintenance over a week's flying. So we came back down to 10,000
feet, restarted Number Two and continued on into the target
alone, with the intention of getting to the target first and trying
to catch it by surprise as we were alone. However, due to bad
weather we arrived at the target at approximately 2:20 P.M. By
this time the other planes had passed over the target, dropped
their bombs and pretty well stirred up the Japanese. As we
approached the target we were attacked by 18 pursuit planes.
Because we had already committed ourselves and were on our
bomb run at the time of the attack, we continued on in and
the Bombardier dropped our bombs in train, probably destroying one transport. We had 600-pound bombs and dropped all
of them. There were six transports lined up at the docks at
Legaspe. We had a thirty minute running fight with Navy
Zero fighters at 9,500 feet. The first four pursuits attacked
simultaneously at each side, right and left, and we shot both
down with side guns. The third came straight in on our tail;
a gunner shot him off. The second ship to attack killed our
radio operator, shot the engineer's right hand off and crippled
a gunner, leaving only one gunner to operate both side guns.
For the remainder of the flight only two side guns could be
operated. We continued a running fight for the next twenty-
five minutes, losing altitude slowly until we ended at 3,000
feet. During the fight we shot down three more Zeros and
possibly a seventh. However, the Jap pursuits had it pretty
much their own way owing to the fact that the side guns
jammed in all but ten minutes of the running fight. Our ship
was badly shot up. The first enemy pursuit shot out our Number
One engine. Sometimes during the attack the Number Four gas
tank was hit and literally blown out of place, allowing all the
gas in Number Four to run out. The radio was shot off the
cockpit by an explosive bullet from a 20-mm. cannon. The
oxygen system was entirely shot out. The tail wheel was shot
loose and the two front wheels shot flat. The remaining gas
tanks had absorbed plenty of lead. They did not leak because
they were sealproof. The fight continued for 75 miles. After
the Jap pursuits had shot out their ammunition they flew in
close, peered into our ship and returned to their base.

After the fight was over I flew back towards my base. I flew four hundred miles to Mindanao with two engines still going. Since it was just at dark I did not have time to reach my base, so I landed in the barricade near the beach on two flat tires and with no tail wheel at all. The plane, on hitting the ground, rolled fairly straight two hundred yards and then the brakes backed, causing the plane to stand straight up on its nose. However it settled back on its tail and all aboard managed to get out unhurt. We had eight men including myself. The wounded men were taken immediately to the hospital. Of the eight men, one was killed, the radio operator, one gunner was shot in the leg by an explosive bullet, a bad wound, the engineer was shot through the right hand. Our other gunner was shot through the wrist. However, this latter man continued to work the guns. The remainder of the crew were hit with small pieces of shrapnel from shells. As a matter of fact I combed it out of my hair for a week.

Aside from the quality of the men who would not turn back from their target but executed the mission and fought their way through, this story exhibited the quality of the B-17, once judged (two or three years before) so vulnerable to attack. Undoubtedly the reason why the Japanese Zeros, having exhausted their ammunition, came up close to peer inside the ship, was because they could not imagine why it still stayed up in the air. To suffer so much damage in an attack by eighteen swift fighter planes armed with machine guns and cannon and still to survive was not only a triumph for Wheless and all on this plane, but for every engineer, designer, workman and adviser who contributed to the creation of the contemporary B-17.

Captain William J. Bohnaker's story, less startling than Wheless' because he never had to take quite such punishment, confirmed and supported the general conclusion. He was on duty from Clark Field in the early days of the campaign, often under conditions which made "evasive action" the only possible course. (That is, when large numbers of Japanese planes were operating, thus obliging our few bombers to avoid them.)

On December 14th, on the orders of Major General Lewis H. Brereton, then Chief of Air to General Mac-Arthur, the remaining Flying Fortresses were withdrawn to Darwin, Australia. This wise decision retained the striking power of the ships without exposing them to the terrible risk of being wiped out helplessly on the ground. They continued, however, whether based at Darwin or in the Indies, to use their own field in Mindanao, under cover of night. They would set out from Darwin and make a rendezvous at Iloilo, say, for a bombing mission over (perhaps) Davao. No other machine could have done such things. Captain Bohnaker participated in the bombings at Davao and Lingayen. On December 31st he was ordered to a new base at Malang, in Java, with nine B-17's and 108 men. From here they flew to an operational base at Samarinda, about 60 miles northwest of Balikpapan on the Strait of Macassar. In the bombing of Davao roadstead from that base (December 31st) he believed the B-17's severely damaged one heavy cruiser, two light cruisers and two destroyers, with possibly also two submarines. Three days later they were able to observe the repair tugs working on the five damaged ships, and on that occasion they also hit an anti-aircraft battery.

During these January days the Japanese were—while continuing their pressure, somewhat less violently, on Corregidor and Bataan—preparing the great invasion of the Indies. They were moving on the extreme flank, at the Strait of Macassar, awaiting the fall of Singapore before performing the head-on attack. Our B-17's attacked them at Tarakan (where a frontal condition separated the ships and Major, now Colonel, Combs went in alone over the target) and

Balikpapan. These operations, carried out by a tiny number of planes (once by a single ship; once by six; when reinforcements arrived from Australia, by eight) were so successful that they held up the Japanese operation in the Macassar Strait and for a time denied that whole sea to the Japanese navy and transports. It was Captain Bohnaker's opinion that thirty-five Flying Fortresses could have stopped the invasion of the Indies on the Macassar side.

The conditions of the work were bad. After a seven-hour mission at very high altitudes, men had to come down and work for six or eight hours on the ground, taking the places of ground workers left in the Philippines. Weather information was extremely faulty; the Dutch airfields were practically without protection; the Japanese were flowing down south in—as one of the pilots remarked —"an apparently inexhaustible flood."

When the Japanese reached Bali the fate of the Indies was decided, but the Army Air Force continued its strong attacks with small numbers. At Bali, between the B-17's and the nine A-24's sent from Australia, the Air Force sank six transports and one cruiser, and it was noticed that the next day the two remaining Japanese cruisers had left. The Japanese then brought down twelve more transports and six warships to make their landing. When they took the Dutch airfield at Denpasar (Bali) they were in a favorable position. Their field was only fifty miles from ours and the most strenuous efforts at camouflage and concealment had to be made. Even so, we lost fifteen planes in two days by ground-strafing.

On January 20th seven P-40's arrived from Australia to protect the Surabaya naval base. There were a few Hurricanes sent from Malaya, and the Dutch Air Force, or what was left of it, participated in these last actions, but the total available force was woefully small.

When Captain Bohnaker left Java for Broome (Australia) on February 27th, he had chalked up two hundred and thirty hours of combat flight. He considered that against the five B-17's actually lost in the air during all these operations he could count on having shot down from fifty to sixty Japanese fighter planes. Some of his comments should be quoted. "On all the flights in which I participated," he says, "my navigator never became lost." When you considered the area flown over and the conditions of flight this was an astounding fact.

Bohnaker says:

"It is hard to say whose bombs hit in any mission, but I am sure that our bombardier sank at least four or five transports, hit two cruisers and one anti-aircraft shore battery and did much damage to hangars and field installations. Our gunners shot down two fighters for sure and damaged two more. We had a very fine crew and I was very proud of the work they did and I know every other pilot felt the same way."

Lieutenant Elliott Vandevanter, who was on practically all these same operations, had the last tactical airplane in commission in the campaign and ran a night mission alone over a Japanese convoy just before leaving Java. The next morning he took his B-17—the last remaining in Java—to Australia, and in it the commander of the bombardment group to which these ships belonged.

He had been in all the operations over Davao and Lingayen based on Darwin with a night-stop; he took part later in the operations from Malang and Samarinda; still later in those of the Macassar Strait and Bali. He thinks he hit a Japanese battleship in the big Davao bombing of December 31st, with two direct hits. He made three runs over the target, and on the last one "heavy anti-aircraft fire became accurate," but his ship and men were undamaged. In one of the missions over Japanese transport and naval craft at Bali, Vandevanter relates that he only had 150 miles to gain the indicated altitude (a very high one) which put the B-17 to another severe test; the plane could do it, and did.

This young pilot's last mission—when he was the "last tactical airplane in the Indies"—was over the Java Sea, as the great Japanese force was coming in. Of this, he says: "I could not see the convoy at all until anti-aircraft started. Then I picked them up clearly enough in brilliant moonlight. However, as we approached the target, clouds obscured them. We lined up on the anti-aircraft flashes and dropped our bombs. The results are unknown. We returned to Djodjakarta."

This again is one of those details which start the imagination on a journey. Out from Djodjakarta, where the beautiful ancient temples are, the lone B-17, a triumph of modern American manufacture, started on its mission over the equatorial ocean; between clouds and moonlight it sought its target, the vast and predatory Japanese force; lining up on the anti-aircraft flashes it bombed and went back to its airfield beside the temples, where gods older than those of the West were worshipped before America was discovered.

Such stories led my mind into paths new to me. The individual was less than nothing here; in a sense it was our civilization as a whole, its nature as determined by the land itself and the people who have lived on it in historical times, which found its fittest weapon in the fighting machine of the air.

From what I had read of Admiral Mahan's great work on *The Influence of Sea Power on History,* I retained most vividly the passages in which he traced the development of the leading naval and military establishments from their civil characters and geographical position. Thus England, a cold island with no imperative inducements to its excess population to stay at home, living (at least in modern times) chiefly by overseas trade, and dependent more than any other nation upon actual materials brought by sea routes, found its inevitable expression as a naval and colonial power. France, with a larger seacoast and a no less active population, had nevertheless been chiefly a military power throughout her history, because of her land neighbors and because the country of France itself, rich and agreeable to its sons, gave them no desire to seek their fortunes in far-off enterprises. According to Mahan's reasoning, France's failure as a colonial power (and it could be seen that France did fail in that respect) was essentially because colonies were not necessary to or even much valued by the French people.

Applying Mahan's reasoning to our own case in the present era led to the conclusion that our people's weapon was the airplane. Our children dreamed of airplanes; the schoolboys could build them of scrap wood; something of the kind had happened in all countries, but what so kindled the imagination of our youth was indeed something native to this culture more than to any other. The airplane, for all real purposes excepting only combat, was born here. It stood to our air power as a nation in precisely the same relationship as the British merchant marine to the British navy. Mahan's insistence upon the indispensable connection between those two elements, merchant marine and navy, which, taken together with geographically dispersed bases constitutes what is called sea-power, could be recalled with profit under the conditions of May, 1942. We were hastily improvising that merchant marine which should have been, in peacetime, the basis for naval development, and we were discovering that Mahan was

right; just as he was also right when he said that our enormous coast lines on two oceans—one element of sea-power
if the others were also present—would mean weakness
rather than strength if we ever had to carry important
supplies along them under enemy attack.

If we followed the reasoning of this eminently sensible
officer I thought we should be led to the belief that our
national genius, as he calls the nexus of all these conditions, made the airplane our principal natural weapon.
The argument I constructed went thus: If conditions
make it possible for us to produce large numbers of the
best airplanes in existence, which they do; and if the mechanical predilection of our people makes our youth more
inclined toward the air than toward the sea, which it does;
and if the wealth and material comfort of American life
disinclines any enormous number of our citizens toward
prolonged residence abroad, which they do; and if we have
in consequence shown a national disposition toward only
occasional and mainly peaceful excursions overseas, then
(following Mahan, who seems to me sensible but not neces-
sarily infallible) we are not an imperial or a colonial nation by nature, any more than France was, and sea-power
in the fullest sense will always evade us—that is to say,
naval control of all sea-routes such as England had in the
nineteenth century—and what our case calls for is, under
present conditions, a vast development of the air-power to
which we are historically called.

Further, we must see that in general our people have
no use for colonies or conquests, being sufficiently provided both with material resources and with thorny problems inside our own natural borders. Therefore we are
extremely unlikely to take, at any time we can now fore-
see, those prolonged and systematic measures of development which create the great naval or great military power.

As Mahan rather sorrowfully observed, it is alien to our national genius to spend all our time and resources in peacetime on such preparations. We should be glad of that. Like the Dutch in the period Mahan was considering we are stingy of our money for such purposes in peacetime, and sea-power depends almost wholly upon conditions existing in peacetime. Like the French, our undertakings in foreign countries are all for the purpose of making money with which to come back and enjoy life at home; our political principles—anti-imperialism, for example—are thus to a considerable extent the result of the material conditions of our life, plus whatever part of the experience of other peoples, the so-called wisdom of the ages, has established itself in the form of fixed or preferred principle among us. Thus, in principle, at least, we are humanitarian; this consideration reinforces our naturally anti-imperialist feeling in world politics, and gives us our vague and general sympathy for the oppressed peoples of other lands. All these things put together indicate that if we are historically permitted to create and exert the tremendous air-power of which we are capable, we shall not use it to conquer, oppress or exploit any other nation, but merely to see that insofar as human intention and organization can provide the machinery for its preservation, the peace of the world shall not again be broken. We know that we have this power in our country and people if we are resolved to use it, and although it would be contrary to common sense to argue that any system we might establish could preserve peace for ever, at least the material conditions of our history have made it somewhat more likely that a peace drawn up under our influence, achieved in part at least by our power, and owing its continuing organization to our support, would be a more humane and durable peace than one regulated entirely by the preoccupations of Europe, however important they may be to each separate nation or tribe. History and geography have provided us with a different kind of perspective, and in addition we belong to all races. We are therefore unlikely to make the same mistakes as the European peace-makers, and although we shall make plenty of our own, they may be less disastrous.

It seemed to me that the material conditions of the American people provided that they could be invincible if they had the weapons appropriate to those conditions, both for defense and for attack. Of the weapons our civilization provided, the most characteristic of this culture, the most suited to our people and to our necessities, was the airplane, and it was one which need not lead us into a career of conquest, colonialization or imperialism after the chastisement of the enemy.

So thinking, I found my own next step inevitable and took it at once by going into the Air Corps on May 28, 1942. The small individual act indicated a conclusion to which I was led by all the processes described in this book and by those which went before, establishing the necessity of survival not alone, but in association with those who prefer light to darkness, freedom to slavery. With our wide variations in purpose, our disagreements as between nations or groups within nations, the unifying principle of those who fight with us is this preference, which with some becomes a necessity so imperative that life itself is not conceivable on other terms. The pattern so slowly sketched in the events followed by this book, the pattern of associated effort by Russia, England, China and the United States, was now complete, was becoming more real every day. The task of each man who believed in its validity was to contribute to it, each in a different way, each with a chosen instrument in the same general direction.

So to the harness, surrendering for a while everything incompatible with the long, hard pull: this was what millions of men said to themselves as they enrolled in the factory or the field, the mine or the armed and uniformed services. The end is certain, and those who see it will know better than our fathers did how to arrange and think out the life of man so that its pain and sorrow will be lessened rather than made heavier by his own acts, so that if human intention and provision can ensure it, the peace of the world shall not again be broken.

# Name Index